MANAGING
IN ACADEMICS
A Health Center Model

MANAGING IN ACADEMICS
A Health Center Model

Jill Ridky, PhD

Director of Administration, Department of Surgery
Adjunct Assistant Professor in Social Medicine
University of North Carolina–Chapel Hill
Chapel Hill, North Carolina

George F. Sheldon, MD, FACS

Chairman, Department of Surgery
Zack D. Owens Distinguished Professor of Surgery
University of North Carolina–Chapel Hill
Chapel Hill, North Carolina

QUALITY MEDICAL PUBLISHING, INC

ST. LOUIS, MISSOURI
1993

COVER ART: *"Fencers" by Milton Avery (1944). Oil on canvas, 48¼" × 32¼". Reproduced by permission of the Santa Barbara Museum of Art, Santa Barbara, California. Given in memory of Maximilian von Romberg by Emily Hall, Baroness von Romberg.*

PUBLISHER   Karen Berger

PROJECT MANAGER   Suzanne Seeley Wakefield

PRODUCTION   Susan Trail

EDITING ASSISTANT   Kathleen J. Jenkins

BOOK DESIGN   Susan Trail

COVER DESIGN   Diane M. Beasley

Quality Medical Publishing, Inc.
11970 Borman Drive, Suite 222
St. Louis, Missouri 63146

LIBRARY OF CONGRESS CATALOGING-IN-PUBLICATION DATA

Managing in academics : a health center model / [edited by] Jill
   Ridky, George F. Sheldon.
        p.   cm.
   Includes bibliographical references and index.
   ISBN 0-942219-11-2
   1. Academic medical centers—United States—Administration.
   I. Ridky, Jill. II. Sheldon, George F.
   [DNLM: 1. Academic Medical Centers—organization & administration—
United States. WX 27 AA1 M26 1993]
RA971.M3464 1993
362.1—dc20
DNLM/DLC
for Library of Congress   93-23854
                                                                          CIP

TH/PC/PC
5   4   3   2   1

The major test of a modern
American university is how wisely and
quickly it adjusts to important
new possibilities.

CLARK KERR

About the Authors

— ❧ —

Jill Ridky, PhD, is Director of Administration in the Department of Surgery and Adjunct Assistant Professor in Social Medicine at the University of North Carolina–Chapel Hill. She received her masters and doctorate in Administration from the University of North Carolina–Chapel Hill. Her professional interests include financial management, administration, and organizational and human resource development in the academic and nonprofit sector. She has served as the Vice-President and President of the Association of Academic Surgical Administrators. In addition, she has written many articles and conducted presentations on management issues related to academic, health, and nonprofit organizations.

George F. Sheldon, MD, took his surgical residency at the University of California's San Francisco Medical Center after obtaining his BA and MD degrees from the University of Kansas. He completed fellowships at the Mayo Clinic under a National Heart Institute Fellowship and Harvard University's Peter Bent Brigham Hospital.

From 1971 to 1984 Dr. Sheldon evolved through the University of California, San Francisco system, becoming Professor in 1980, a period of time during which he was Chief of Trauma and Hyperalimentation Services at San Francisco General Hospital. In 1984 Dr. Sheldon was appointed Professor and Chairman of the University of North Carolina–Chapel Hill Department of Surgery and was named the Zack D. Owens Distinguished Professor of Surgery.

He is currently a Regent of the American College of Surgeons and Secretary of the American Surgical Association, is a past Chairman of the American Board of Surgery, and was President of the American Association for the Surgery of Trauma in 1984. Dr. Sheldon serves on ten editorial boards and on two committees of the Institute of Medicine. He has testified before Congress on issues of health manpower. He was a charter member of the Council on Graduate Medical Education (COGME).

Mary A. Belskis, MBA, is an Associate Director of the Office of Research Services at the University of North Carolina–Chapel Hill. She has more than 13 years' experience in research administration and was previously Director of Sponsored Programs at the University of Cincinnati Medical Center.

Richard S. Blackburn, MBA, PhD, is an Associate Professor of Organizational Behavior at the Kenan-Flagler Business School at the University of North Carolina–Chapel Hill. Professor Blackburn has consulted with a number of organizations, including Cummins Engine, Gillette, Burroughs Wellcome, Eli Lilly, the U.S. Army Research Institute, and several nonprofit organizations on such issues as leadership, motivation, and creative thinking.

His research interests include creativity and innovation, causes and consequences of quality in organizations, and the impact of corporate design and identity on corporate performance. His research work has been published in both professional and academic journals, and he has served on several editorial review boards. He is coauthor of *Managing Organizational Behavior,* a business textbook, published by the Richard D. Irwin Company.

Professor Blackburn earned his MBA and PhD in Organizational Behavior from the University of Wisconsin–Madison. He teaches in the undergraduate, MBA, doctoral, and executive programs at UNC and has received the AMF Excellence in Undergraduate Teaching Award and the Outstanding Young Executive Institute Teaching Award. He is a member of the American Psychological Association and the Academy of Management.

Carole J. Bland, PhD, is a Professor of Family Practice and Community Health at the University of Minnesota, where she has been a faculty member since 1974. She received an MA in Experimental Psychology and a Specialist Degree in Behavior Modification from Drake University in 1970. She received her doctorate from the University of Minnesota in 1974 in Educational Psychology with an emphasis in measurement, evaluation, and adult learning. During 1989 and 1990, she was a Fellow of the American Council on Education Leadership. She has served as a consultant on evaluation, curriculum development, faculty development, administrator development, and institutional vitality to departments, universities, foundations, professional associations, and the federal government. She has published more than 60 articles, chapters, and books, primarily on faculty and institutional development.

Edwin A. Capel, Jr. is currently the Director of Internal Audit at the University of North Carolina–Chapel Hill. He has more than 20 years' experience in government auditing, including financial compliance and operational audits. He is a member of the Institute of Internal Auditors, the Association of College and University Auditors, and the National Association of Certified Fraud Examiners. He has developed and leads workshops on fraud awareness for university and government managers. He is also a member of the American Academy of Certified Public Managers and the North Carolina Society of Certified Public Managers, for which he is currently serving as president.

Shelley N. Chou, MD, PhD, is Professor Emeritus, Department of Neurosurgery, and Associate to the Dean Emeritus, University of Minnesota Medical School in Minneapolis. He was chair of the department for 20 years until 1989. He received his MD from the University of Utah in 1949 and his MS and PhD in Neurosurgery in 1954 and 1964, respectively. He was a Visiting Scientist at NINDBS, NIH, in 1959. He served as a member of the American Board of Neurological Surgery and a member and chair of the Residency Review Committee for Neurosurgery, ACGME. He was visiting professor to more than 40 institutions worldwide. His major academic interest has been in cerebrovascular and spinal disorders. His publication in 1971 on pathological studies and recommendation of clinical criteria of brain death was instrumental in the later adoption of the brainstem death criterion in the United Kingdom. He has published 183 manuscripts to date.

D. Kay Clawson, MD, has a distinguished international reputation in medicine and medical education. After graduating from Harvard Medical School in 1952, he completed residencies at Stanford and studied with preeminent orthopaedic specialists in England and Europe. Dr. Clawson soon joined their ranks and has been in demand here and abroad as a visiting professor. He has been named an honorary member of the prestigious Royal Academy of Medicine in Valencia and Barcelona, Spain, and served as President of the Association of Orthopaedic Chairmen and the Association of Bone and Joint Surgeons.

In 1958, at the age of 31, he was named Head of the Division of Orthopaedic Surgery at the University of Washington, and in 1965 he was named Chairman of the newly created Department of Orthopaedics. He became Dean of the College of Medicine at the University of Kentucky in 1975 and was named Executive Vice-Chancellor of the University of Kansas Medical Center in 1983.

Dr. Clawson has held key positions in national organizations critical to medical education, including Chairman of the Council of Deans and Chairman of the Association of American Medical Colleges, which shares responsibility with the American Medical Association for accrediting medical schools. He has also served as Chairman of the Residency Review Committee for Orthopaedics and on the Executive Committee of the Accrediting Council for Graduate Medical Education.

Mary Sue Coleman, PhD, is Provost at the University of New Mexico, Albuquerque. Her research program has been funded for almost 20 years by the National Institutes of Health and she is the author or coauthor of more than 90 articles and book chapters on biochemistry of hematopoietic cells. She is a frequent member of editorial boards and member or chair of national scientific review panels for investigator-initiated and institutional grant proposals.

James L. Copeland, MBA, is Executive Vice-President of the Medical Foundation of North Carolina, Inc. Jim earned his MBA from Indiana University in 1963. He has completed 25 years in the field of advancement in higher education holding positions at Hanover College, Indiana, Baylor College of Medicine, Texas, and the University of North Carolina–Chapel Hill School of Medicine. He has participated in fund-raising efforts that have created more than $500 million in gifts. He is active with the Council for Advancement and Support of Education (CASE) and the National Society of Fund-Raising Executives (NSFRE) and has served on the national board of both associations.

Don E. Detmer, MD, received his medical degree from the University of Kansas in 1965 and completed his surgical internship and residency at Johns Hopkins University Hospital, the National Institutes of Health, and Duke University between 1965 and 1972. He then took a Health Policy Fellowship at the Institute of Medicine, National Academy of Sciences, and the Harvard Business School Program in Health Systems Management. From 1973 to 1984 he was on the faculty of the University of Wisconsin–Madison, becoming a full professor in 1980. While at the University of Wisconsin he founded that institution's Administrative Medicine Program, which trains clinicians for executive roles in health care. In 1984 Dr. Detmer became Vice-President for Health Sciences, Professor of Surgery, and Professor of Medical Informatics at the University of Utah. He assumed the vice-presidency for Health Sciences at the University of Virginia in 1988.

Dr. Detmer is a member of the Institute of Medicine. He directed the Institute of Medicine's medical record study and is a member of the Institute's board on health care studies. Formerly chair of the board of regents of the National Library of Medicine and the Pew Charitable Trust's health professions advisory group for medicine, he is a member of the board of directors of the Association for Health Services Research and is a trustee of the China Medical Board. He is the author of numerous articles and book chapters on surgery, health policy, and academic health center leadership.

Fusun Erkel, MD, MPH, is presently the Director of Continuous Quality Improvement at University of North Carolina Hospitals, a 665-bed teaching hospital. Dr. Erkel received her undergraduate degree and medical degree from Hacettepe University in Ankara, Turkey, where she also completed residency training in ophthalmology. After practicing ophthalmology in Ankara, Dr. Erkel came to Duke University to do corneal research in 1985.

Dr. Erkel received her master's in Public Health from the UNC School of Public Health and studied the practice variations for cataract surgery in

North Carolina. She has a special interest in the application of systems and continuous improvement theory in health care settings to improve patient outcomes and in national health policy to improve the health status of the society.

Marcia Day Finney, MA, received a BA in English Literature from Michigan State University in 1970 and took an MA in English literature in 1976 from the University of Virginia, where she was a Danforth Teaching Career Fellow. She is presently a candidate for a doctorate in English Literature at the University of Virginia. Ms. Finney taught English literature and women's studies at Northwestern University in 1974 and 1975. She became editor and assistant to the chair of the Department of Medicine at the University of Virginia in 1975. In 1989 she was named Special Assistant to the Vice-President for Health Sciences at the University of Virginia.

As a member of the faculty of the School of Medicine, Ms. Finney teaches bioethics, medical humanities, and patient-physician communication and sits on the institutional ethics committee and the health sciences arts committee. She is a member of the Society for Health and Human Values. Ms. Finney is a coadvisory editor of the *International Dictionary of Medicine and Biology* and author or coauthor of papers and book chapters on death and dying, physicians' ethical responsibilities, and the patient-physician relationship.

Laura N. Gasaway, MLS, JD (Lolly), is Director of the Law Library and Professor of Law at the University of North Carolina–Chapel Hill. As director, she manages the overall library functions and has a staff of 20. She teaches half-time in the law school; her courses are intellectual property and gender-based discrimination. She also teaches law librarianship and legal resources in the School of Information and Library Science. Before coming to Chapel Hill she served as the Director of the Law Library at the University of Houston and the University of Oklahoma. She received both BA and MLS degrees from the Texas Woman's University in 1967 and 1968 and her JD from the University of Houston in 1973.

Lolly has served on several committees at the University of North Carolina, such as the Chancellor's Advisory Committee, Committee on the Status of Women, Executive Committee, and Dean's Advisory Committee. She is a member of the American Bar Association Committee on Accreditation and is Chair of the Special Libraries Association Copyright Committee. She is active in the American Association of Law Libraries and was president in 1986-1987.

Jules I. Levine, PhD, graduated in 1960 from the University of Virginia with a BS in Electrical Engineering. Following 3 years of destroyer duty in the United States Navy, where he served as an electronics and combat information center officer, he joined the Westinghouse Electric Corporation, Aerospace

Division, as an engineer. During his 5 years with Westinghouse, he pursued graduate work at Johns Hopkins University, receiving a Master of Science degree in Management Science in 1968.

Dr. Levine returned to the University of Virginia to pursue a PhD in Biomedical Engineering, which he completed in 1972. At that time he was appointed an Assistant Professor in the University of Virginia School of Medicine and was responsible for research in the Center for Delivery of Health Care. As his research responsibilities grew, he developed the Division of Health Services Research and served as its director. In 1974 he assumed additional responsibilities as Assistant Dean in the School of Medicine and was promoted to Associate Dean in 1976 and Associate Professor in 1977.

In 1978 Dr. Levine was appointed Assistant Vice-President for Health Sciences, with broad responsibilities in the University of Virginia Health Sciences Center, including planning and facilities development. He recently served as Project Director for the $230 million Replacement Hospital Project at the University of Virginia and is now overseeing the planning and development of research, ambulatory care, inpatient, and infrastructure projects, with budgets in excess of $165 million. Dr. Levine was promoted to Professor of Health Sciences in 1986 and to Associate Vice-President for Health Sciences in 1989.

Robert P. Lowman, PhD, is director of the Office of Research Services at the University of North Carolina–Chapel Hill and Adjunct Associate Professor of Psychology. He has 16 years' experience in research administration, federal relations, and science policy studies and has written, lectured, and consulted throughout the country on those topics. He was senior editor of the first edition of the *American Psychological Association's Guide to Research Support.*

Robert Rutledge, MD, is an Associate Professor of Surgery in the School of Medicine at the University of North Carolina–Chapel Hill. Dr. Rutledge received his MD at the University of Florida–Gainesville and completed his residency at the University of North Carolina–Chapel Hill. He served as a Clinical Associate at the National Heart, Lung, and Blood Institutes of Health in Bethesda. In addition to Dr. Rutledge's specialized training in trauma, critical care and transplantation, he has added the specialty of medical informatics. Dr. Rutledge has written numerous articles and conducted numerous presentations to aid research, education, and clinical activities. He is a leading developer of medical informatic systems.

Thomas L. Schwenk, MD, is an Associate Professor of Family Practice at the University of Michigan Medical School in Ann Arbor, where he has served as Department Chairman since 1988. He received his MD from the University of Michigan in 1975, followed by family practice residency training and fellowship training (the Robert Wood Johnson Family Practice Faculty Development Fellowship) at the University of Utah Affiliated Hospitals, completed in 1978 and 1982, respectively. He has served as a visiting professor or department reviewer to more than 25 universities and as a faculty development consultant to several national programs.

Dr. Schwenk's research interests include depression and anxiety disorders in community-based family practices, difficult physician-patient relationships, and methods to promote exercise in clinical practice, resulting in more than 40 peer-reviewed and clinical publications. He is also the coauthor of a series of handbooks addressing various teaching skills and faculty development. His clinical practice emphasizes primary care, psychiatric illness, and sports medicine.

Frank T. Stritter, PhD, has been a staff member in the Office of Educational Development and a Professor in the Schools of Medicine and Education at the University of North Carolina–Chapel Hill since 1971. He earned a PhD in Education in 1968 from Syracuse University, Syracuse, New York, specializing in higher education. He has a long-standing interest in curriculum, instruction and clinical teaching, all in higher and professional education, as indicated by several studies on teaching that have appeared in such journals as the *Journal of Medical Education, Teaching and Learning in Medicine, Medical Education,* and *Medical Teacher.* He has authored a monograph for the National Library of Medicine entitled *Effective Clinical Teaching,* a chapter of the American Educational Research Association (AERA) *Third Handbook of Research on Teaching* entitled "Professional Education," and several other chapters in various books on aspects of teaching. He has organized and taught in several different programs for medical, dental, pharmacy, and allied health faculty development over the years. He is active in the American Educational Research Association, the Association for the Study of Higher Education, and the Association of American Medical Colleges.

Foreword

Colleges and universities have been caught up in the economic recession and are faced with decisions affecting those who will attend college, the allocation of resources for teaching and research, and the range and scope of public service to be rendered.

These circumstances signal the wise administrator to reexamine the management processes by which his or her institution or department now functions and to assess what future demands will really require. Long-range planning has become a necessary and essential management practice.

Dr. Jill Ridky, Dr. George Sheldon, and their colleagues have presented on the pages that follow ideas and documentation relating to academic management that will prove helpful and stimulating to a responsible academic administrator. This volume, then, is worthy of reading and study by those entrusted with the management of the academic enterprise.

William Friday

President, William R. Kenan, Jr. Fund
President Emeritus, University of North Carolina

A Personal Note to the Reader

The magnificent academic health centers across America strive daily to achieve their broad-based goals during a disturbing and tumultuous time. At present many institutions are constrained fiscally; many find it difficult to fund existing programs, let alone initiate funding for any new programs. Managers in academic health centers are our heroes. They are faced with enormous challenges and the daily rigors of administering and providing leadership in three distinct mission areas—patient care, education, and research—within the framework of a diverse organizational structure that encompasses medical schools, teaching hospitals, and practice plans.

Managing in Academics: A Health Center Model is intended for the managers of these complex organizations. *Managing in Academics* offers practical insights into each of the essentials of a successfully managed department, including such components as department and human resource development, recruitment and the selection process, delegating, leading a committee, financial management and fiscal responsibility, facility planning and management, quality management models, creativity among department members, research and educational development, legal issues, information systems, internal controls, and future trends in academic management.

We have divided the book into four sections: Environment, Development, Process, and Future. Each chapter is autonomous in construction, yet each builds on previous chapters to form a superstructure for management. The components discussed in each chapter are equally important and critical to effective management. The lessons and insights derived from academic health centers have direct application to other academic departments and programs. Throughout, concepts are highlighted with the use of Case Examples based on real situations encountered frequently in management.

The cover depicts the art of fencing, and there are many parallels to be drawn to management in academics. Both are an art, requiring skill, finesse, strategy, and balance. Also like fencing, academic management requires agility and other mental and physical qualities. Both also involve a seemingly endless number of variables, frequently requiring one to be an adroit tactician.

Successful management of an academic health center requires a blend of many disciplines, integrated to ultimately promote management and leadership. Skill and balance must be achieved and maintained among all these disciplines to create an effective and efficient organization. In a desire to achieve this effectiveness and efficiency and to provide leadership, the management must be careful not to destroy the essential nature of the organization. Managing in academics should not lead the organization to more constraints and obstacles but to become an improved and better functioning structure. Better management requires that certain guidelines be followed, including the careful allocation and utilization of resources, self-imposed limits on consumption, long-term goals, short-term choices, and a general attitude of and preference for trusteeship toward future generations.

Drawing on each of these essential ingredients, managers are invited through this book to develop the requisite skills and balance to effect the successful development of their own department's full potential, resulting ultimately in benefits for the larger society. Managers have been entrusted with substantial resources, put at their disposal through some institutional mechanism, and these managers are responsible for making those resources as productive as possible.

John Gardner once observed that a nation is never finished but must be built and rebuilt or recreated in each generation. The challenge for each manager in academic health centers is to develop and refine the components and adapt them to their specific organization's operation system. In addition to the daily operational responsibility, managers must constantly adjust to changing environments, always questioning needs, suggesting new approaches and methods, facilitating improvements, and moving the organization to the cutting edge of new services and accomplishments. Theodore Hesburgh, president of Notre Dame for 30 years, once said, "Higher education and every other enterprise moves forward when there is good leadership; otherwise, it stagnates. We need people with vision, people who have standards and toughness. . . . Of course, you need money, but money and no vision, you just squander it."

Thus we need managers to develop skills that will form organizational components into a consolidated, effective, and efficient entity. The best organizations artfully develop and consciously and practically move forward incrementally. They establish good formal and informal networks to obtain accurate information and keep pressing for quality growth, new approaches, and greater efficiency.

Acknowledgments

Our interest and experience with management issues in academic health centers led us to the development and fruition of *Managing in Academics*. We applaud our superb contributing authors for willingly sharing their expertise and wisdom. We are appreciative of the excellent assistance from Jill Dunn, who provided such excellent project management, and Robin Robinson for her graphics expertise. We would also like to recognize our family members for their love and support during our periods of long days and late nights—to Ruth, Ann, Betsy, and Julie, and to Richard, Jennifer, and Lillian, many thanks.

As in all areas of academic health care, the role of the manager is continuously evolving. In this book we have striven to provide a broad consideration of a range of topics relevant to managing in the health care setting. We are extremely grateful to the department chairs and academic managers who served as reviewers and helped us to shape this edition. We welcome suggestions from our readers to guide us in shaping our second edition.

Jill Ridky
George F. Sheldon

Contents

Part Three ❧ PROCESSES

Part Four ❧ FUTURE

MANAGING IN ACADEMICS
A Health Center Model

❧ Part One ❧

ENVIRONMENT

*The breath had been so pumped from my lungs as I went up that at the top
I could go no farther, and sat down at once. 'Now you must free yourself from sloth,'
my mother said, 'for, sitting on down or lying under covers, no one comes to Fame. . . .
Therefore get up, overcome your panting with the spirit which wins every battle if
it does not sink with its heavy body. A longer stairs must be climbed;
it is not enough to have left this one.'*

DANTE, *The Divine Comedy*

CHAPTER 1

The Academic Health Center: Issues and Leadership

Don E. Detmer • Marcia Day Finney

We cannot revive old factions
We cannot restore old policies
Or follow an antique drum.

T.S. ELIOT, *Four Quartets*

As new discoveries are made, new truths disclosed, and manners and opinions change with the change of circumstances, institutions must advance also, and keep pace with the times.

THOMAS JEFFERSON, 1816

Academic health centers (AHCs), also known as academic medical centers or health sciences centers, consist at minimum of a teaching hospital, a school of medicine, and one or more other schools teaching the healing arts and sciences, such as schools of nursing, public health, allied health, or dentistry. An AHC may or may not include a library devoted to the health sciences. Virtually all AHCs are integral components of major research universities. There are more than 100 such academic health centers within the United States today. Together they represent our nation's— indeed, the world's—principal investment in health care knowledge and expertise.

The AHC is as complex an organization as exists in our society today. Its walls enclose an enterprise that traditionally has tended to the sick and injured, educated both aspiring and mature health professionals, and created much, if not most, of medicine's new knowledge and technology.[1] Recently, for a variety of reasons, the agenda of the AHC has broadened significantly, even as constraints on resources have tightened, thus adding considerably to the challenge facing the AHC and its leaders.

Leadership of the academic health center is the focus of this chapter. We will examine the challenges facing the person who seeks to *lead* rather than simply to *manage* an AHC. In no way are leadership and management synonymous. While good management is needed to guide the organization through a given week or month, it is good leadership that is essential to shaping its direction over a period of years and to securing for it a brighter future.

To understand what is involved in leading an AHC, one must first understand the context or environment in which AHCs operate and the forces, external and internal, to which these institutions are now subject. We will explore some of those environmental issues, then discuss some additional issues that relate specifically to AHC leadership. We will close with some thoughts on educating the future leaders of the academic health center.

THE AHC AND THE EXTERNAL ENVIRONMENT

There is growing frustration among the American people—individual citizens, small-business owners, corporate executives, public servants, and health care professionals—with the state of American health care.[2] We do not have a true "system" of care, and the failings of our current pluralistic ad hoc "nonsystem" are beginning to outweigh its perceived benefits, including the patient's free choice of provider.[3] While health expenditures in the United States continue to climb despite the nation's general economic slowdown, as many as 40 million Americans are now medically indigent, and a number of state Medicaid programs are perceived to be inadequate.[3] Because AHCs deliver a significant amount of the indigent care in this country, indigent care financing is essential to the economic well-being of these organizations.[4]

Public expectations for care and for good outcomes of care remain very high. Utilization of health services continues to escalate, along with the costs of care, including the costs of pharmaceuticals.[5] Insurance companies are raising health care premiums, limiting coverage, and/or devising managed care programs to effect cost control, all of which troubles both the public and employers who provide health care benefits. So long as financial resources have been forthcoming from some quarter, the health care industry until very recently has been decidedly disinterested in serious reform.[6] So, too, the approach of the legal system toward medical malpractice/liability issues is limited. Although there was some movement toward tort reform, prospects for further substantive reform appear slim at present, and even where proposals are being tentatively advanced, there is no consensus on what steps should be taken next.[7] Faced with these growing problems of health care access, cost, and quality, the public has a message for political leaders and health professionals and the health care industry in general, for AHCs in particular: "America needs a health care system that is affordable, accessible, efficient, and effective. We don't know how to accomplish this. You're the experts—you tell us how to do it."

The AHC is thus in the spotlight in the national health care debate. Demands on AHCs, especially public AHCs, are considerable and escalating. Public AHCs are asked today to give renewed attention to the maldistribution of physicians and medical specialty services in their geographic regions. They are asked to help meet growing needs in critical public health areas, including mental health, substance abuse, acquired immunodeficiency syndrome (AIDS), and maternal/child health. They are asked not only to sustain the environment within which the latest biomedical research breakthroughs will be made, the newest clinical interventions tested, and the next generation of scientists and specialist physicians trained, but also to provide primary care for their immediate communities and to prepare a new cadre of generalist physicians. One of the chief challenges facing public AHCs today is that the funds available to them are insufficient to allow these institutions to address every one of these critical needs adequately.

Additionally, AHCs situated in larger cities are asked to cure all manner of urban social ills, including the consequences of homelessness, poverty, illiteracy, drug and alcohol abuse, and violence in the home and in the street. Most of these problems are multifactorial in cause, character, and consequence and extend well beyond the bounds of medicine and the other health sciences; the simple application of traditional medical interventions in these circumstances will likely prove inadequate, even wasteful. This is not to say that AHCs should not concern themselves with the health-related problems of their immediate communities, because such involvement is certainly appropriate; it also may improve the overall health of the community and at the same time foster better relations between the AHC and its neighbors.

Traditionally, the AHC has not marketed its services to prospective patients—it has not had to do so. Rather, it has been sought out by patients with complex, serious, rare, or high-risk conditions who need the AHC's diagnostic, therapeutic, or rehabilitative expertise; these patients identify the AHC as the sole regional source of cutting-edge specialty or subspecialty medical expertise. Of course, the AHC also serves the medically indigent patients from its region who knock at its door, because most other health care providers' doors are closed to them. Accustomed to serving these two dissimilar populations in fairly high volume, the AHC has amassed little experience as an effective marketer or efficient provider of ordinary, comprehensive health services to paying patients who could choose to go elsewhere.

Similarly, the AHC has had little experience with or expectations for delivering care on a continuing basis to defined populations residing within its service region. The institution has customarily provided discontinuous, episodic care based either on patient self-referral or on physician referrals from outlying communities. Many AHCs are now under pressure to develop their own general medical practices to serve the local community and/or managed care programs to contract for care with specific populations in the region (e.g., local government or corporate employees). A number have already created such programs.

In recent years, as American health care has shifted its focus from predominantly inpatient care to a balance of inpatient and outpatient care, most AHCs have found themselves in need of both major new ambulatory care facilities and expensive, up-to-date hospital facilities, especially very costly intensive care beds, and all the sophisticated diagnostic and therapeutic technology that supports these. Additionally, pressures mandating the timely and cost-effective delivery of ambulatory care have made it more necessary than ever for AHCs to put in place sophisticated, well-integrated computer systems to improve patient and physician scheduling, upgrade management of patient records, track outcomes of care, and ensure prompt, accurate billing. These challenges are magnified by the fact that AHC intensive care units, ambulatory surgery facilities, radiotherapy units, and clinics double as classrooms. In the AHC, inpatient and outpatient facilities and all systems for the organization and delivery of care must be designed to accommodate and operate efficiently not only for patients and their clinicians but also for health professional students and their teachers.

Both regulation *and* competition are features of contemporary American health care. These realities affect academic health centers variously. Many AHCs, especially public AHCs, are subject to extensive state and federal regulation, including regulations that run at cross-purposes with one another. Regulation at the state level varies considerably, but the states in the Northeast subject their health care institutions to the most rigorous regulation. Competition of an AHC with the other health care institutions in its immediate vicinity for patients is complicated by service cost–competitiveness. The expenses of caring for indigent persons and providing patient care while simultaneously educating young health professionals raise the AHC's patient care costs across the board and put such an institution at a competitive disadvantage with its neighbor providers, both private nonprofit and commercial. Insurers and businesses, shopping for the least costly health services available, are often not inclined to shoulder their fair community share of indigent-care and educational costs by paying the higher charges assessed by the AHC.

Similarly, the enormous cost of constructing and maintaining state-of-the-art facilities and equipment poses a tremendous challenge for every AHC. Yet while sharing facilities or high-technology equipment with neighboring health care institutions might offer AHCs some fiscal relief, such ventures remain today more risky in terms of antitrust threats than the fiscal jeopardy an AHC and its neighbor providers face when they duplicate expensive facilities, technologies, and programs.

THE AHC AND ITS PARENT UNIVERSITY

The relationship between an AHC and the research university of which it is a part is complex and sometimes uneasy, much like any parent/growing child relationship. There are both tensions and opportunities for cooperation between an AHC and its parent university. The sheer size of the AHC's physical plant and operating budget relative to those of the rest of the university may be disquieting, even threatening, to some university administrators and non-AHC faculty. This may be the case equally for the AHC whose physical plant is on the parent university's campus and the AHC that is located at a distance—even in another city—from the parent institution. (Although we will not discuss them here, there are advantages and disadvantages for the AHC to be geographically distant from the parent university.) Second, the strong service orientation of the AHC may be neither understood nor appreciated fully by faculty throughout the rest of the university. There may also be jealousy and resentment on the part of some non-AHC faculty over the higher incomes of AHC faculty-clinicians and over seeming discrepancies in teaching loads and research standards for university faculty when compared with their AHC counterparts.

These tensions are not new, nor are they any more pronounced today than they were a generation ago. Indeed, it is likely that future developments both in society and within our universities could, if anything, work to bring AHCs and their parent universities closer together. America's research universities are in a state of flux today as new forces, internal as well as external, begin to press them in compelling ways.[8,9] These forces deserve mention here.

First, the demographics of America's student population are changing. There are more women, more minorities, and more students over age 25 enrolled in our universities today than ever before. These learners are interested in a different mix of courses and academic experiences than was the highly homogenous, predominantly young white male student population of the past. This wave of change will have significant ripple effects within AHCs in terms of both student enrollments and faculty composition in health professional schools and the academic/clinical/research interests of students and faculty alike.

Second, an era of fiscal constraint challenges all of higher education to do more with less. Public funding for higher education is not expected to return any time soon to the generous levels that prevailed from the 1960s into the early 1980s, a period of unprecedented prosperity and expansionism for the nation's colleges, universities, and professional schools. Coincidental with new budget limitations—and a number of public research universities in the last 2 years have contended with budget reductions of as much as 15%—has come new public interest in institutional accountability and in the productivity of university faculties and programs. AHCs are by no means immune from this scrutiny. In fact, AHCs may be especially likely to come under review, given their large operating budgets, high faculty salaries, and the sometimes lengthy period between scientific breakthroughs in the laboratory and marketplace availability of research applications.

Third, public expectations related to AHCs are only a part of society's sweeping expectations for research universities.[10] States increasingly regard their research universities as essential components of the regional economic infrastructure. Research grants and contracts secured by university faculty are as much key sources of economic benefit to the state as they are intellectual goods. At the same time, the character of research is changing and its findings, implications, and *value* are not always easily grasped by the public or public officials.

Fourth, many contemporary research questions that have broad societal implications (and eventual applications) defy traditional disciplinary boundaries and must be approached instead by teams of investigators representing a broad range of fields and possessing a variety of skills. Problems such as AIDS, health care financing, cancer, and the ethics of organ transplantation offer new opportunities for scholars from across an entire university to work together in multidisciplinary inquiry, establish innovative interdisciplinary partnerships between disparate parts of the university, and build bridges between the university and government or corporate entities.

The vision and leadership required to exploit these research opportunities cannot be overestimated. Multidisciplinary research typically exists outside traditional departmental structures and so may need special "advocacy" mechanisms to ensure that they prosper within the academic enterprise. Devising organizational and fiscal structures conducive to the growth and development of multidisciplinary inquiry is one of the major administrative challenges faced by research universities today. Institutions may tend to allow proliferation of an endless array of new multidisciplinary centers or programs, with resulting high administrative overhead, rather than undertake the politically unpopular task of reorganizing existing departmental structures. University leaders need foresight, skill, and courage to devise the best means of addressing and periodically adjusting their universities' research and instructional agendas. And, changes must be made within institutions' administrative infrastructures so that more resources become available for redeployment, since one cannot count on there always being *new* infusions of resources to fuel organizational change and progress.

Fifth, the information age is upon us. Characterized by the dramatic explosion of knowledge in all fields and our enhanced capacity to move, merge, and manage information by means of computers and other electronic technology, the information age presents research universities and AHCs with new challenges. Never before in history has so much new information been generated at such a swift pace, and never before have knowledge bases experienced such rapid reorientation and turnover. In research universities, as in society, there is a high premium on the timely delivery of information and knowledge to those who need it, wherever they may be located.[11] Electronically networked mail systems already link scholars within and among universities[12]; they will soon link AHC-based health professionals, providing researchers with immediate linkage to laboratory-based colleagues and databases and giving clinicians ready access to the information they need to deliver state-of-the-science care. In time, decision support systems, computer-based patient records, computerized imaging systems, electronically networked scheduling systems, and other data- and knowledge-management systems will be integral parts of every AHC's clinical environment.[13] Such systems also will link the AHC with selected scholars across the university, with community-based health care practitioners, and with colleagues and knowledge bases around the world.

THE AHC AND INTERNAL ISSUES

Academic health centers today face daunting challenges in health sciences research, education, and service. In the last two decades, the scope of health care has broadened considerably beyond what it was for the previous 80 years. Formerly, medicine's primary domain was disease—that is, the pathology and pathophysiology of organs and organ systems—and the management and therapy of disease. Today, while this traditional mission remains, the domain of medicine extends from the molecular and cellular biology of health and disease, on the one hand, to the sociomedical issues of public health (including AIDS, substance abuse, and violence), prevention of disease and injury, health maintenance, wellness and fitness, health policy, and bioethics, on the other. In short, not only *disease* but any and all dimensions of *health* are now legitimate subjects for medical investigation and intervention. More of these changes affect the practice of surgery than may at first meet the eye.[14]

For an AHC to make progress across such a broad front of medical concerns is a dizzying prospect. Finding the funds to build and maintain adequate research space is but one aspect of the AHC's struggle to keep pace with developments in medicine.[15] No AHC will be able to pursue cutting-edge work in all fields, since resources simply will not be sufficient to mount first-rate efforts across the board. Indeed, to remain competitive while making do with limited resources, some AHCs may choose to pursue work in fields that have less costly technological requirements. Such developments may have disturbing implications for technology-dependent fields such as surgery. Even more disconcerting, however, is the prospect that the technological imperative in research and patient care will drive some AHCs to bankruptcy before more rational systems of resource allocation and cost containment can be instituted.[16]

Keeping pace with new developments in health sciences research and in health care is important too, since the AHC is responsible for the education and training of the next generation of health professionals. And how the education and training of future professionals is done will determine in part how effective our health care system will be into the twenty-first century. The academic enterprise at present owns too much of the students' lives in the early years of their professional training, and the specialty boards control too many prerogatives during the latter half of physicians' professional upbringing.

Indeed, looking toward the twenty-first century, health professional students and trainees need a much more flexible academic/training experience than has heretofore been generally available to them.[17] The typical young physician today moves from college to medical school to house staff training and finally to practice; this educational experience is not seamless, but it needs to be. Physician education must be integrated, continuous, and lifelong.

Medical education also needs to be oriented more to learning and the learner and less to teaching and the teacher. Students should be able to move quite freely among knowledge bases, back and forth between academic and clinical settings, and they must have ready access to the mentoring of experts throughout their educational/training experience. Additionally, they need to be exposed to and conversant with developments outside the traditional medical disciplines that stand to influence medicine and its practice in the years to come.

In contrast, surgery, like most medical specialties, presently overstructures its teaching opportunities, with one result being a reinforcing for the student of the traditional boundaries between medical specialties. This has the added effect of limiting the ability of surgeons to contribute their considerable talents across all of medicine. Such an approach breeds and perpetuates a well-intentioned but narrow "groupthink" mentality within each specialty.[18] Thus, in surgery, what it means to be a surgeon is narrowly defined as what it *has always* meant to be a surgeon rather than what it *could* mean to be a practitioner of this particular specialty. As a result, too few surgeons today are engaged in national debate on policy matters (health-related or not). It should be apparent from the discussion earlier in this chapter that some very important health-related policy issues urgently require the attention and debate of thoughtful, well-educated individuals; the nation and the health professions will benefit enormously if broadly informed expert clinicians engage these issues. There is no reason why more surgeons should not contribute meaningfully to fields tangential to surgery. Unfortunately, those surgeons who are now active and influential beyond the operating theater got where they are more often because of their own perspicacity than because they were exhorted to do so during their training years. Greater flexibility in training would increase the value of surgery (and other specialties) to other disciplines and to itself.

As another example, there is an urgent need today for clinicians who are competent health services researchers. Clinicians with skills in health services research can help determine the efficacy of existing and newly developed clinical strategies and biomedical technologies and assess the outcomes of their use.[19,20] Technology assessment is essential to continued progress in all branches of medicine, and we must devise better assessment tools in order to monitor the development, introduction, and proliferation of new technologies and to ensure the replacement of outdated ones.[22] Surgeons could play an important role in this process. Similarly, surgeons could contribute much to improving the science of decision making under uncertainty, much as specialists in radiology are now doing.[21] Unless in the course of educating and training surgeons (and all physicians) we encourage them to participate—indeed, to take the lead—in such vital health services research, we risk the future health and well-being of the very discipline that represents our life's work. With visionary leadership and educational reform, the AHC can help effect this shift of priorities in the training of the next generation of physicians.

Finally, AHCs are well equipped and well positioned to develop research and educational programs that link back to and capitalize on some of their newly recognized societal responsibilities. For example, many AHCs now have formal programs or centers devoted to health policy research and analysis. These programs draw on scholars from many sectors of the AHC and its parent university and examine such critical policy issues as malpractice and liability, Medicaid reform, and revisions in health care financing. Health policy programs have the potential to build serviceable bridges between the AHC, its parent university, and state and federal agencies and can be a valuable source of research grants and contracts.

A second opportunity for AHCs to undertake greater societal responsibility involves their developing, through teaching hospitals or professional schools, and then assessing the value of experimental models for providing and/or paying for health care services. For example, an AHC may choose to create and evaluate an integrated regional system of comprehensive health care for a defined population that depends on a coordinated network of AHC and community institutions, agencies, and practitioners. The AHC thus becomes an incubator for, and potential model of, health care reform even as it is devising institutional answers to its own peculiar problems in the delivery or financing of care.

LEADERSHIP AND ORGANIZATIONAL ISSUES

There is a dearth of research on the leadership of academic health centers (see Chapter 4). Cohen and March[23] have written one of the classic texts on university leadership, and it is a generally helpful study. Bolman and Deal[24] wrote a good introductory text on understanding organizations, and Kellerman's book on leadership is similarly helpful.[25] A recent Rand study by Williams et al.[26] points out some aspects of successful leadership through development of case studies of AHCs that have coped well in competitive environments. Badaracco and Ellsworth's book on leadership is particularly pertinent to the question of AHC leadership.[27] An analysis of leadership from a variety of perspectives, the book speaks to dilemmas that institutional leaders encounter within their organizations. Badaracco and Ellsworth's format is unusual, their discussion thought provoking. Finally, Bulger and Reiser[28] have edited a volume of essays that looks at the character, ethics, and values of institutions and how leadership can shape the moral character of the AHC.

As many of these texts point out, AHCs that have a clear sense of direction and are able to make flexible use of their resources are better positioned to meet and take advantage of the further changes that are coming. AHCs must develop greater structural and budgetary flexibility so that they can respond quickly to change, pursue reasonable new opportunities, and undertake appropriate new responsibilities. Rigid departmental lines with fully allocated budgets can all but prevent an institution from availing itself of important opportunities.

It is critical, too, that all components of the AHC be in reasonable synchrony with one another. The individuals who make up the entire organization—leaders, second-tier leadership, middle management, and employees in all constituent elements of the AHC—must share a common vision and understand where the AHC (and their particular unit as an integral part of it) is going and when and how it plans to get there. This requires clear and effective communication and coordination throughout the AHC. It further requires that the organization's senior leaders play a substantive role in policy discussions at the university, state, and national levels. In all this, the leader of the AHC must function as a coach more than as a director. The role of the leader is elaborated in more detail in future chapters.

PREPARING FOR LEADERSHIP

So how does one train for this coaching job? That is, how does one prepare to assume a leadership role in an AHC?[29] The ideal academic program would resemble the administrative medicine program at the University of Wisconsin at Madison.[30] This program is targeted to health professionals who seek to be effective managers working between full-time administrators and full-time clinicians. The program is linked to the American College of Physician Executives, a feature that makes the program quite attractive in terms of both content and colleagues. The Association of American Medical Colleges offers excellent short-term, intensive programs in executive management; persons attending these programs include faculty moving up into AHC leadership positions as deans or vice-presidents. Some persons interested in AHC leadership have elected to earn master's degrees in business administration or to enroll in intensive management institutes offered by graduate business schools.

Depending on your own interests and directions, there will be differences in the specific knowledge you will need for effective leadership. However, it is important to gain and maintain a fundamental understanding of a constellation of subjects bearing on academic health issues. These subjects include the macroeconomics of health, health policy, managerial accounting and financial management, health law, organizational behavior, group dynamics, negotiation and communication methods/skills, decision analysis, quality assessment, statistics and clinical epidemiology, human values and bioethics, medical informatics, strategic planning, and marketing. The list could go on, but this is at least a start. You must be conversant in the salient literature of each field and know its major contributors.

In addition to gaining academic experience and accumulating a specialized body of knowledge, as a prospective leader you need to take on whatever leadership opportunities present themselves, so that you learn to chair committees, set agendas, work with and through others, and cultivate listening, speaking, and negotiating skills. Developing pilot projects and, later, large permanent projects within an AHC gives you invaluable familiarity with the ease and difficulty of administrative innovation and institutional change.

Much of this chapter has focused on the nature of present and coming contextual or environmental realities and how these have affected and will continue to affect the AHC. Awareness of and sensitivity to the environment within which an institution lives and works is essential to good leadership. Even individuals who bring great ability, ambition, and energy to a leadership position need to know the environment or the "territory," as Professor Harold Hill in "The Music Man" put it. The successful leader knows how to scan the environment, how to read and interpret it, and then how to turn problems and challenges into opportunities. Leadership of a complex organization is said to be analogous to directing snow drifts by erecting snow fences: The leader controls neither the weather nor the road conditions, but, by directing the placement of fences, he or she can shift the drifts so as to open avenues that would otherwise be blocked.

We have established that every leader needs to know the basics of his or her chosen work. Every leader also needs to have an aptitude or feel for the work. To succeed, leaders need to understand themselves as well (or better) than they understand the others with whom they work. They also need to be able to discover joy and satisfaction in the work they do. Above all, though, nothing in the leadership preparation process matches the combination of keen interest, native ability, thorough preparation, and practiced—even perfected—practice. Through repeated practice, your raw abilities become refined capabilities, your actions bear the stamp of your own leadership style, and you learn to change not only yourself but your world. The good news is that even those of us who are less naturally gifted can, by working hard in creative environments with creative colleagues, make a real difference in our organizations and make life better for those we are committed to serve.

BIBLIOGRAPHY

1. Jones RF. (1989). *American Medical Education: Institutions, programs, and issues.* Washington, DC: Association of American Medical Colleges.
2. Blendon RJ & Donelan K. (1990). The public and the emerging debate over national health insurance. *New England Journal of Medicine, 323,* 208-212.
3. Rockefeller JD IV et al. (1990, September). *The Pepper Commission: U.S. Bipartisan Commission on Comprehensive Health Care* [Final report]. Washington DC: U.S. Government Printing Office.
4. Task Force on Academic Health Centers. (1985). *Prescription for change.* New York: The Commonwealth Fund.
5. American living standards: Running to stand still. (1990, November 10). *The Economist,* pp 19-22.
6. Shortell SM & McNerney WJ. (1990). Criteria and guidelines for reforming the U.S. health care system. *New England Journal of Medicine, 322,* 463-467.

7. Relman AS. (1990). Changing the malpractice liability system. *New England Journal of Medicine, 322,* 626-627.

*8. Desrochers LA & Detmer DE. (1990, Fall). From the ivory tower to the unisearchity. *Educational Record,* 8-14.

9. Searle J. (1990). The storm over the university. *New York Review of Books, 37,* 24-42.

10. Wilder LD. (1990, Fall). One governor's perspective of higher education. *Educational Record,* 42-46.

11. National Library of Medicine Board of Regents. (1989, August). *Improving Health Professionals' Access to Information* (long-range plan). Bethesda, Md: National Library of Medicine.

12. Rutkow IM, ed. (1989). *Socioeconomics of surgery.* St Louis: CV Mosby.

13. Arms C, ed. (1988, February). *Campus networking strategies.* Bedford, Mass: Digital Press.

14. Institute of Medicine, National Academy of Sciences. (1991). *The Computer-Based Patient Record.* Washington DC: National Academy Press.

15. Marshall E & Hamilton DP. (1990). A glut of "academic pork." *Science, 250,* 1072-1073.

16. Buchanan JM Jr. (1990, April). *Technological determinism despite the reality of scarcity: A neglected element in the theory of spending for medical and health care.* Little Rock: Philosophy of Science Lecture Series, University of Arkansas for Medical Sciences.

17. Detmer DE. (1986). A university perspective of graduate surgical education for the Information Age. *Current Surgery, 43,* 363-368.

18. Janis IL. (1972). *Victims of groupthink.* Atlanta: Houghton Mifflin.

19. Heithoff KA & Lohr KN. (1990). *Effectiveness and outcomes in health care.* Washington DC: National Academy Press.

20. Lohr KN, ed. (1990). *Medicare: A strategy for quality assurance.* Washington DC: National Academy Press.

21. Kuhns LR, Thornbury JR & Fryback DG (Eds). (1989). *Decision making in imaging.* Chicago: Year Book Medical Publishers.

22. Gelijns AC. (1990). *Modern methods of clinical investigation.* Washington DC: National Academy Press.

*23. Cohen MD & March JG. (1986). *Leadership and ambiguity* (2nd ed). Boston: Harvard Business School Press.

*24. Bolman LG & Deal TE. (1988). *Modern approaches to understanding and managing organizations.* San Francisco: Jossey-Bass.

*25. Kellerman B. (1984). *Leadership: Multidisciplinary perspectives.* Englewood Cliffs, NJ: Prentice-Hall.

*26. Williams AP Jr. (1987, October). *Managing for survival: How successful academic medical centers cope with harsh environments.* Santa Monica: The Rand Corporation [R-3493-HHS].

*27. Badaracco JL Jr & Ellsworth RR. (1989). *Leadership and the quest for integrity.* Boston: Harvard Business School Press.

*28. Bulger RE & Reiser SJ, eds. (1990). *Integrity in health care institutions: Human environments for teaching, inquiry, and healing.* Iowa City: University of Iowa Press.

29. Detmer DE. (1992). The physician-executive: Human being, manager, and juggler. In DA Kindig & T Kovner, eds. *The role of the physician-executive: Cases and commentary.* Ann Arbor: Health Administration Press, pp 23-31.

30. Detmer DE & Noren JJ. (1981). An administrative medicine program for clinician-executives. *Journal of Medical Education, 56,* 640-645.

*Asterisk indicates an article or book that is particularly informative and helpful.

CHAPTER 2

Dynamics of Institutional Interaction

George F. Sheldon • Jill Ridky

*There is nothing more difficult to take in hand, more perilous to conduct, or more
uncertain in its success than to take the lead in the introduction of a new order of things.
Because the innovator has for enemies all those who have done well under the old
conditions, and the lukewarm defenders in those who may do well under the new.
The coolness arises partly from the fear of the opponents, who have the laws
on their side, and partly from the incredulity of men, who do not readily believe
in new things until they have long experiences of them.*

MACHIAVELLI, *The Prince*

There is significant concern today about the future of the academic health center, given the present environment of health care in our country and the dynamics
of institutional interactions. Will AHCs survive such volatile times? Will they be
able to preserve and develop educational and research programs? Successful man-
agement of the AHC in the 1990s includes an awareness of the dynamics of institu-
tional interaction. We will address only a few relevant issues in this chapter; others
will be elaborated throughout the book. Some of these issues include the following:
- Economic shifts
- Organization
- Conflict
- Culture and change
- Focus
- Management roles
- Atmosphere

ECONOMIC SHIFTS

One of the major concerns for AHC managers is the economic shifts that occur,
requiring close observation of the political arena and private industry. Politically,
the areas of concern are funding and support of graduate medical education programs, legislative support of primary and specialist physicians, Medicare and Medic-

aid funding, and budget reduction and reimbursement levels. Regarding private industry, the manager must evaluate whether the private sector will continue to collaborate with the AHC, providing support for research, clinical, and educational studies. Will private-profit medical centers begin to develop their own research foundations, thus competing with AHCs for funding and contractual relationships? As academic health centers continue to rely extensively for funding strength from their clinical research and educational mission, economic shifts must be closely monitored by managers.

ORGANIZATION

The organization of a university AHC and teaching hospital is complex, as illustrated in Figures 2-1 and 2-2. The reporting structure is typically to a higher authority, such as the citizens of the state, or if a private medical school, even to the hierarchy of a religious group. The oversight responsibility is usually vested in a group of appointed or elected officials, usually governors. Typically there is a board of trustees and/or board of governors that oversees the university. While such appointments can be quasi-political, efforts have been made in recent years not to have the public oversight group directly tied to an elected or political office to reduce undue political influence on the academic environment. Nevertheless, such organizations are inevitably somewhat political, and managers must remain sensitive to that. The board of governors usually supervises the statewide organization for a specific university within a statewide complex. Authority is then vested in a board of trustees, which may be elected or appointed. These board members are usually private citizens who meet at intervals to review the overall operation of the university. Occasionally such highly sensitive issues as sexual harassment, affirmative action, and disability and the new public access laws are referred to the board of governors. The authority of the board of governors is usually relegated to a president of the university (which may be a whole statewide system). Usually individual campuses of the university have a chancellor, who functions as the on-campus day-to-day chief executive officer. The rest of the organization, then, performs a variety of administrative functions that form the nucleus of a central academic administrative staff.

University reporting to the chancellor is from a variety of subdivisions, from athletics to business and finance, academic affairs, the provost, graduate studies and research, health affairs, university relations, and others. A common model is for a vice-chancellor for health affairs to oversee the health sciences operations of an individual campus. Reporting to the vice-chancellor for health affairs would be the schools of medicine, pharmacy, nursing, dentistry, and public health. Obviously only a few schools in the United States have all of these professional health campuses. Under this model the vice-chancellor for health affairs is the immediate superior of the dean of each of these professional schools. In recent years there has been a tendency to consolidate the positions of the dean of the medical school and the vice-chancellor for health affairs, based on the feeling that there is enough authority overlap between the two to make their relative positions awkward. In campuses where the earlier model persists, usually the dean or the vice-chancellor has a somewhat more modest or limited authority, especially regarding the day-to-day management of the complex.

Academic health centers have been either a bane or a boon to many campuses. Usually they account for approximately 50% of the federal competitive research dollars and the indirect costs that come to the state and to the campus. The ability to generate income through academic practice plans places the clinical departments in an AHC in a somewhat favored position among the other departments of the university. Some conflict and jealousy are inevitable because of this special relationship. Usually a health affairs code is part of the overall structure of the AHC to deal with the expectations, policies, and regulations governing faculty who generate income within the health affairs department.

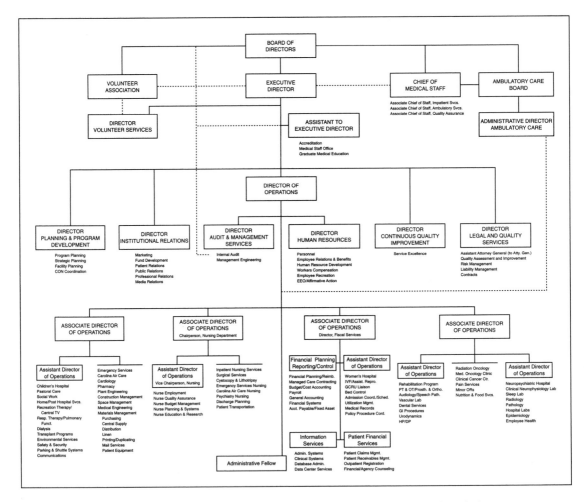

Figure 2-1. A representative organizational chart for a university hospital.

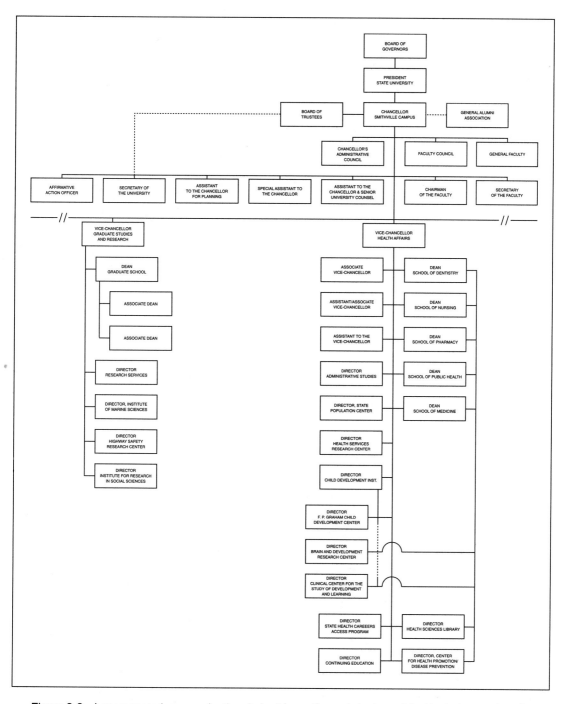

Figure 2-2. A representative organizational chart (a portion only is shown) that includes a university health sciences division.

Over the last decade the major growth of academic health centers has been through clinical departments. Thirty-seven percent of the revenue available to medical schools now comes from clinical practice plan revenues, allowing the growth on which they depend to support their mission of education and research as well as facility and program expansion projects.

The complexity of the academic clinical department is further illustrated by its relationship to a second, usually independent, organization—the university teaching or affiliated hospital. It is in the university hospital that the academic health science center teaches, practices, does research, and conducts professional activities. The hospital may be private, nonprofit, religious affiliated, or state affiliated. The particular board of organization responsible for the ultimate direction of the hospital is somewhat similar to a board of governors or a board of trustees. If the hospital is state affiliated, its ultimate responsibility and relationship will be to the state organization, including personnel and budgetary systems. A closer relationship to the operation of the hospital usually resides with a board of directors. This is usually a nonsalaried, appointed position, and the board members meet infrequently.

The power of the hospital resides in its budgetary status, which has, in the past two decades, been historically favorable to the teaching hospital. Over the years teaching hospitals have received extra funding through federal programs by virtue of several federal subsidies of graduate medical education. The first is the indirect medical education cost, which allows the hospital to bill Medicare at a higher rate if it has graduate medical education training programs. The second resource is the graduate medical education factor, which is designed as a direct cost based on the number of full-time resident equivalents (FTE) present in the teaching hospital. These combined salaries have been an extrabudgetary resource for many hospitals and have resulted (until recent years, when the prospective payment system was implemented) in teaching hospitals having financial advantages over nonteaching hospitals.

A teaching hospital generally has more revenue than do the other parts of the organization—that is, the medical school. The chief executive director of the hospital, regardless of title, is a powerful figure in these combined relationships. Usually, but not obviously, the departments relate directly to the hospital in a manner somewhat analogous to the academic system. The chair of a clinical department may in some cases also be the chair of the hospital department. In some hospitals whose main staff is private, a full-time director of education will often be employed by the hospital, and this individual may also be the program director or the training director but will not necessarily be chief of the department.

The relationship and duties with the hospital of a chair or chief of a clinical service are understandably different from those required of a chair or chief in an academic setting. The academic dimension for a chief of a clinical service in a university hospital will be to ensure graduate and undergraduate education, appropriate participation in the medical school, participation in curriculum and other committees, and research and clinical programs. The same individual's responsibilities to the hospital will relate to credentialing of staff, quality assurance, faculty discipline, and quality of care.

These complex organizational relationships work surprisingly well in practice. It is important, however, that the reporting structure and the relative imbalance of power and influence between the two organizations be understood. Academic health centers are funded by various sources. The basic science departments are often partially supported by state or other basic revenues from the medical school. The most successful basic science departments will have substantial peer-reviewed grant resources and can expand and enhance their mission through those resources. Clinical departments are often large and mostly dependent on clinical practice plan revenue for support. Some departments—traditionally internal medicine and pediatrics—will have substantial grant funding and a large number of faculty whose clinical obligations are minimal. Surgical departments, while having significant research activities, usually have more of a clinical tilt and a smaller faculty than the other organizations. The clinical departments usually include internal medicine, pediatrics, surgery, psychiatry, obstetrics and gynecology, anesthesiology, neurology, and emergency medicine. Some institutions have all of the specialty units in a large department. These would include the specialties of surgery: cardiothoracic, general (and its components), vascular, pediatric, plastic, neurosurgery, and so on. The structure and size of the department obviously depend on whether all components exist.

CONFLICT

The dynamics and complexity of roles and structure of AHCs are inevitably associated with some institutional conflict. One dimension of institutional conflict may also result from turf issues or the competition for control of resources. In an academic environment, with a majority of fixed resources, a perception exists among organizational members that if resources are gained by one department or program it will result in competition with others. It is assumed that the gain of one must occur at the expense of others.

In an academic health center turf issues exist in a variety of areas. The most obvious is within the funding body for the institution. Understandably, uneven distribution of resources exists in any organization. The reason for unequal distribution of resources is the program needs identified by leaders. Application of available monies stimulates growth and development, prevents deterioration, and has other salutary effects. Paradoxically, units that prosper more or less independently are often the most developed and innovative, and those may suffer somewhat because resources are applied to less successful units.

Common conflict areas external to a department in AHCs include the control over new therapeutic technology, such as lithotripsy for treatment of biliary and urinary calculi. The radiologist, gastroenterologist, and surgeon all may have some claim on an area that has traditionally resided entirely within a single academic department. As another example, for vascular and cardiac conditions, radiology or cardiology often will use indirect or noninvasive interventions to repair lesions that were traditionally treated by a surgical procedure. The emergency department has been a recent area of some conflict. The staffing of emergency rooms has been inadequate historically, with new physicians or inexperienced physicians often staffing these units. In recent years, emergency medicine has become the twenty-fourth of the American Board of Medical Specialties (ABMS Board), and emergency departments have become free-standing in many institutions. The roles of traditional specialties such as internal medicine and surgery have been redefined by the emergence of this specialty.

The intensive care unit is another area with the potential for conflict. In some institutions, hospital credentialing, spurred by individuals with Added Certification in Critical Care, established criteria with management, including order writing and patient care within units. This can result in fragmentation of patient care and has been and will continue to be resisted by practitioners in most traditional specialties who believe that total care is necessary for optimal patient care in most situations. In recent years some groups, through their certifying and accrediting organizations, such as the residency review committee of the Accreditation Council for Graduate Medical Education documents, have extended the scope of their specialty by defining it into training requirements. Internal medicine and pediatrics, for example, now cover burns and laceration treatment as part of internist training from cardiothoracic surgeons, cardiologists, pediatricians, general surgeons, and traumatologists. The emergency physician and the internist also have a claim to these clinical conditions.

In addition, the advent of new technology is bound to increase turf conflict in academic health centers in ways and areas that could not have been anticipated in the past. Such issues as interpretation of magnetic resonance images or ultrasonography are areas of conflict that could not have been anticipated before the development of technology.

Institutional conflict, especially over turf, requires compromise, because such issues can result in significant, nonproductive conflict that detracts from achieving the goals and growth of an institution.

CULTURE AND CHANGE

What does a manager in academics need to understand about the culture of the institution? What *is* institutional culture? According to *Webster's, culture* is an "integrated pattern of human behavior that includes thought, speech, action, and artifacts and depends on man's capacity for learning and transmitting knowledge to succeeding generations." Or, as some managers quickly assess, culture is "the way we do things here." Every AHC has its own institutional culture, and that culture is a very strong force for directing how things are developed and accomplished—or not.

Managers, especially in a new institutional setting, usually tend to initiate change. However, before initiating change, you must carefully consider the institutional culture. Every institutional culture has its attachment to heroes, legends, the rituals and rhythms of day-to-day life, and the ceremonies, symbols, and settings of the workplace. When change occurs, many of these rituals change. Often the hidden culture barriers to change are overlooked. Bergquist notes, "New directors may realign the organization, but in the process may unknowingly topple heroes that people have revered since the organization began. New initiatives may undermine important values that have guided an organization for years and years."[1]

Managers who have attempted change in academic organizations without understanding the institutional culture have found organizational members disgruntled with the changes, or they will seem to embrace the change but not implement it. The stronger the culture, the harder it is to change. Deal and Kennedy state, "Culture causes organizational inertia; it is, on the other hand, the brake that resists change, because this is precisely what culture should do: protect the institutional organization from fads and short-term fluctuations."[2]

Changing agendas and issues in an organization can push a strong culture into conflict with its environment. Understanding when to take on the challenge of change and when not to is a key to successful management. According to Deal and Kennedy, there are five situations in which management should consider the reshaping of a culture as something close to its most important mission[2]:

1. When the environment is undergoing fundamental change and the organization has always been highly value driven
2. When the environment is highly competitive and the environment changes quickly
3. When the organization is mediocre—or worse
4. When the organization is truly at the threshold of becoming a major top-ten academic program, department, or school
5. When the organization is growing very rapidly

Once the need to change is apparent, the next two important considerations are time and money; cultural change can be a very time consuming and very expensive endeavor.

AHCs have developed accepted actions or culture over decades that are now deeply entrenched in each institution. What conditions might cause academic health centers and institutional culture to change? There are several factors to consider. First, is there a major crisis in the culture, or a dramatic event? Examples include a nationally publicized lawsuit for sexual harassment, loss of accreditation of a residency program, and loss of a major funding source. Another factor is a change in leadership, such as the retirement of the institution's original chair or dean. This factor will provide an opportunity for change. A new leader, especially one who has been recruited externally, may be viewed by colleagues as bringing new and improved cultural values.

Another factor is the age of the institution. For example, a fairly new department or program will not have a very well–developed culture. The entrenchment of the culture is strongly related to the age of the organization. Naturally, culture in an older organization is more difficult to change. Changes in culture may also occur as an organization faces rapid growth, which will cause major adjustments to the organization's mode of operations. Change will also occur if academic programs are merged or separated. At such times a high premium is placed on the value of sponsoring orientation and educational sessions as a way of acculturating recent organizational changes, such as program additions or deletions.

Finally, there are several other observations of changes that organizational managers should consider. First, the argument from the dean or chief must be credible; second, time must be invested in the change program; third, if the change is simply not economical, it should not be implemented; and fourth, the manager must know which culture problems to attack and which ones to walk away from.

FOCUS

In today's volatile environment, academic health centers must renew the emphasis of clear and well-grounded missions. AHCs should and can be the leaders in national and global health care issues, research, and education. They are culturally rich, cutting-edge institutions with the ability to provide the best health care technology. Institutions need to develop network and satellite affiliations as well as outreach programs with other hospital systems and localities. To do this successfully, managers must recognize the issues and problems of institutional focus and consistently share this focus with all members of the organization.

The individual focus. A common institutional problem can be called *individual focus*. Examples are faculty members who are totally absorbed by their own goals, teaching endeavors, research, and clinical service and who neither value nor understand the total institutional activity or focus. Although these faculty members might see themselves as functioning in a well-established academic health center, they do not become a part of the environment or the institution's dynamics. If they think about it, they truly believe they can have little or no influence on the organization's dynamics. Such faculty or staff members come to work and focus completely on their job—often adequately or even superbly. Yet their inward focus leads to isolation from the institutional focus as they attempt to be nonreactive to institutional and environmental forces.

The "not-us" focus. Within institutional dynamics there is a natural propensity when something is wrong for programs or departments to place the blame on another internal or external organization or position, leading to a *not-us focus*. For example, the number of inpatient procedures in a surgery department is declining. The not-us syndrome would lead faculty to say that this is not related to the department of surgery but to the operating room. Similarly, an academic department or an investigator has a problem meeting grant submission deadlines; a not-us focus leads to blaming the research service program for their slowness in reviewing and approving the grant proposal. This problem can be an extension of the individual focus; when we have an individual focus, we do not see how the results of our own actions extend beyond the boundary of that position. When these actions have consequences that come back to hurt us, we misperceive these new problems as externally caused. Typically academic health centers place the blame or label the "enemy" as the state or private foundation that funds and supports the institution, the state bureaucracy, the rules and regulations. The "enemy" does not allow the department or program to achieve. While it may well be true that some state or foundation rules can be obstacles, the not-us focus creates an incomplete picture and does not lead to any constructive solutions. The total institutional system needs to be the focus, not just internal or external constituencies.

Proactive versus reactive approaches. Academic organizations are trying harder than before to function in a proactive mode rather than the more traditional reactive mode. Most want to anticipate problems, thereby avoiding crisis management or the reactive mode of operation. This often proves to be a dysfunctional approach. Many times the solution to a problem cannot be achieved by either a reactive or a proactive stance. Just as a reactive approach can come too late to solve problems, the proactive approach can come too early or be misguided. For example, a department of radiology was beginning to be considerably concerned about the potential loss of revenue resulting from changes in reimbursement legislation. The dean reacted proactively, developing a plan whereby all departments would contribute to offset radiology's loss of revenue. Several months later the reimbursement legislation was reversed and the plan was not implemented. However, in the process, many hours of productive committee time had been expended unnecessarily. Proactive or reactive, a reaction that is emotional rather than a logical, thinking approach to the problem is often counterproductive.

Event and cause. Event and cause is another type of institutional problem. Managers find themselves reacting to an event, perceiving organizational activity as a series of events in which for every untoward event there is a remediable cause. Institutional dynamics are typically filled with events: reappointments, promotions and tenure, a new clinical program, state budget cuts, increases in liability insurance, and so on. Managers in academics can spend countless hours in committee meetings discussing and sometimes agonizing over events. Some logical causes may be speculated, and solutions to the immediate problem may come from these meetings; however, they dilute the focus on charting the long-term trend of change behind the event and on understanding the cause of the trend. As Peter Senge has stated, "Today, the primary threats to our survival, both of our organizations and of societies, come not from sudden events but from slow, gradual processes; the arms race, environmental decay, the erosion of a society's public education system, increasingly obsolete physical capital, and the decline in design or product quality are all slow, gradual processes."[2] An institution should not invest all its energies in short-term projects. AHCs can benefit from sometimes slowing down the fast pace of academic activities and focusing attention on the subtle as well as the dramatic dimensions of their mission.

MANAGEMENT ROLES

The manager of an AHC assumes many roles over time, as shown in the box on p. 24. These various roles are not only difficult and tedious to juggle at any one time, but in an organization with multiple missions (teaching, research, patient care, administration) operating within a multifacility/multiorganizational institution, managers may quickly find themselves enmeshed in institutional dynamics and conflict. Sometimes the roles themselves within a department or program will be in conflict with each other, or the expectations of the faculty versus those of the dean will be at odds. Managers will find themselves making important and highly visible decisions, which will create dilemmas and will not always conclude with an easy solution. Of several highly visible decision areas, one is the allocation of resources. Whether financial, facility, or human resources are allocated, the solution typically will please no one and embitter almost everyone. A manager must remember during such times of visible decision making that his or her role or position is not to be popular. The

ROLES OF THE ACADEMIC HEALTH CARE MANAGER			
Decision maker	Clinician	Leader	Problem solver
Planner	Crisis manager	Evaluator	Appointer
Recruiter	Initiator	News bearer	Facilitator
Defender (2-ton gorilla)	Visionary	Cheerleader	Developer
Teacher	Arbitrator	Adviser	Researcher
Mentor	Delegator	Director	Allocator

manager and institution must establish priorities and expectations and follow them, thus creating the "sail" for the institution. Another visible decision area is assessment. Again, managers and the institution must establish levels of supervision and evaluation criteria and must support the productive, eliminating support from the nonproductive.

ATMOSPHERE

The institutional atmosphere in academic health centers is a critical component for building high-quality departments and programs. Academic programs, centers, and departments need to function in an atmosphere of trust and openness. Institutions must keep organizational members informed and must communicate the institution's expectations for all organizational members (faculty, staff, students, residents). An atmosphere of trust and openness with information, plans, and expectations will allow organizational members to share ideas and to seek advice, opinions, and direction.

Academic health centers are best served by utilizing the metaphor of a "family" for describing the organization. Many a chair relates to all of the organizational members in the course of a day as "life with all my children." Like families, all organizational members are important to the entire complex and institution. The institutional atmosphere should be such that members want to take an active part in what is happening institutionally. Their input should be welcomed and an invitation should be extended for their leadership, expertise, and knowledge in developing and managing the institution.

Within any academic health center there are, as in any workplace, satisfactions and frustrations. It requires the right ratio of satisfaction to frustration to either enhance or deteriorate an institution's atmosphere. Chairs or program directors can be instrumental in improving the institution's ratio by sharing information and expectations, and, what is more important, providing organizational members with the resources they require. Many ongoing interactions will also impact the satisfaction/frustration ratio. For example, faculty of a division or program may want autonomy and believe achieving this will bring them a high satisfaction level.

During the expression of frustration, demands are made for quick decision-making, and power, and authority will be sought.

AHC managers should focus attention on producing the best program, clinically, educationally, and in research, for all members of the organization. They should *not* focus on the popularity of a decision. A recent analogy describes the role of academic manager as that of "herding cats"—an allusion, obviously, to the complexity of directing the efforts of a group of highly intelligent, educated, and independent individuals toward a mutual goal. Management needs to continue to develop not in an atmosphere of a "business" but of a "family," an organization that will support itself, change when necessary, and evolve and develop in its environment. Barbara Tuchman has said, "Working together and using the new tools of management more self-consciously, scholars and executives can steer their institutions through the turbulent waters ahead and emerge even stronger and finer."[3]

BIBLIOGRAPHY

*1. Bergquist WH. (1992). *The Four Cultures of the Academy*. San Francisco: Jossey-Bass.
2. Deal TE & Kennedy AA. (1982). *Corporate Cultures*. Reading, Mass: Addison-Wesley.
3. Tuchman B. (1984). *The March of Folly, From Troy to Vietnam*. New York: Knopf.
4. Tucker A. (1992). *Chairing the Academic Department: Leadership Among Peers*. New York: ACE/Macmillan.
*5. Creswel JW, et al. (1990). *The Academic Chairperson's Handbook*. Lincoln: University of Nebraska Press.
6. Keller G. (1983). *Academic Strategy*. Baltimore: The Johns Hopkins University Press.

*Asterisk indicates an article or book that is particularly informative and helpful.

CHAPTER 3

The Productive Organization

Carole J. Bland • Shelley N. Chou • Thomas L. Schwenk

———————————————— ❧ ————————————————

At least 85% of [organizational] problems can only be corrected by changing systems (which are largely determined by management) and less than 15% are under a worker's control—and the split may lean ever more towards the system.

PETER SCHOLTER, on W.E. Deming's 85/15 rule*

In order to thrive, an organization needs well-prepared and motivated people—but this alone is insufficient.

A vital, productive organization—this is the goal of organizational leaders and members alike. All academic leaders, from department heads to university presidents, strive to develop and maintain organizations that provide excellent education, outstanding research, and quality service. Similarly, faculty members want to contribute to and affiliate with such organizations. However, university-wide conditions of the 1980s and 1990s—increased financial constraints, renewed emphasis on undergraduate education, removal of mandatory retirement, tenured-in departments, and expected faculty shortages—have raised concerns about universities' abilities to maintain teaching quality, research productivity, and service levels.[1-5] In the health sciences, additional conditions contribute to this concern, for example, decreasing hospital patient populations either from increased care for patients in ambulatory settings or decreased referrals, changing reimbursement mechanisms, and increasing numbers of managed care plans.

To meet this concern, academic leaders can no longer simply be scholars or clinicians and part-time caretakers of the organization. Today's administrators are

Portions of this chapter were previously published in Bland CJ & Schmitz CC. (1986). Characteristics of the successful researcher and implications for faculty development. *Journal of Medical Education, 61,* 22-31; and in Bland CJ & Ruffin MT IV. (1992). Characteristics of a productive research environment: Literature review. *Academic Medicine, 67,* 385-397. With permission. *(Academic Medicine* was previously *Journal of Medical Education.)*
*As quoted in Scholter PR et al. (1988). *The Team Handbook.* Madison, Wisc: Jorner Associates Inc.

full-time professionals overseeing sophisticated organizations that demand ever-changing management and leadership experience. Seldin[6] quotes the provost of a large midwestern university, who stated this succinctly: "The days of passive, laissez-faire management are over. Financial exigency has forced us to make selective cuts based on academic priorities and quality. Our involvement in managing the institution is far greater today than ever before."

Fortunately, over the last three decades studies and writings on effective leaders and organizations, and specifically on academic productivity, have provided some guidance to leaders and faculty members striving to maintain a vital, exciting organization despite external conditions. Most of these writings are on leadership and excellent organizations in general, such as the now-classic *In Search of Excellence* by Peters and Waterman[7] and *The Change Masters* by Rosabeth Moss Kanter.[8] But a growing body of handbooks[9-13] and newsletters[14,15] is developing specifically on academic leadership. In addition to reading this book, you are encouraged to seek out these references. They are "user friendly" and written for the busy academic administrator.

On the other hand, research articles on academic leadership and productivity are scattered across about 100 different journals and are less easy for the busy administrator to read and synthesize. Thus this chapter takes one area of academic productivity—research—and summarizes the individual, environmental, and leadership features that have been reported in the research literature to correlate with individual and group research productivity. We have deliberately grouped the findings into these three categories. While at a distance the productive research enterprise looks like a highly robust entity, on closer inspection it is revealed to be a delicate structure that is highly dependent on the existence and effective working of numerous individual, organizational, and leadership characteristics.

Of course, the mission in academic health centers is fourfold: patient care, research, education, and service. Patient care is frequently subsumed under the service category. But it is important to remember that academic faculty have, in addition to patient care, service opportunities and obligations such as service to the community, to the discipline, and to the governance of the institution. Although this chapter focuses on features that correlate with research productivity, these same features are frequently found to further other important missions (education and patient care). For example, studies have found that these features characterize quality teaching organizations[9] and effective organizations in general.[7,8]

This chapter closes with two case examples that provide a concrete illustration of how the features identified in the research literature play out in actual department settings. Dr. Shelley Chou, former associate dean and former head of neurosurgery at the University of Minnesota, describes how these features related to his leadership of a department for 15 years. Dr. Thomas Schwenk, head of family medicine at the University of Michigan, describes how these features relate to his transforming a training-oriented department into one that equally emphasizes research, teaching, and service.

Figure 3-1 depicts the components of a productive organization, as discussed in the pages that follow.

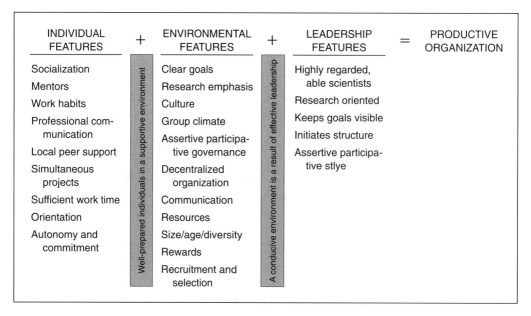

INDIVIDUAL FEATURES	+	ENVIRONMENTAL FEATURES	+	LEADERSHIP FEATURES	=	PRODUCTIVE ORGANIZATION
Socialization		Clear goals		Highly regarded, able scientists		
Mentors		Research emphasis		Research oriented		
Work habits		Culture		Keeps goals visible		
Professional communication		Group climate		Initiates structure		
Local peer support		Assertive participative governance		Assertive participative stlye		
Simultaneous projects		Decentralized organization				
Sufficient work time		Communication				
Orientation		Resources				
Autonomy and commitment		Size/age/diversity				
		Rewards				
		Recruitment and selection				

Well-prepared individuals in a supportive environment

A conducive environment is a result of effective leadership

Figure 3-1. Components of a productive organization. (Adapted from Bland CJ & Schmitz CC. [1986]. *Journal of Medical Education, 61,* 22-31; and Bland CJ & Ruffin MT IV. [1992]. *Academic Medicine, 67,* 385-397.)

INDIVIDUAL FEATURES

What is known from literature about the characteristics of productive researchers, their training, and their work environment? To answer these questions, Bland and Schmitz[16] searched the literature in faculty development and evaluation, career development, professional socialization, organizational development, and faculty vitality. These readings revealed a profile of a productive researcher as one who has in-depth knowledge in a research area, such as compliance, fibrocystic breast disease, or family systems. Further, the productive researcher has mastered fundamental methodological skills and advanced skills relevant to the researcher's area of investigation. These two attributes—content knowledge and skills—come as no surprise. But several other critical features of the productive researcher were revealed and deserve expansion. The manager or leader needs to consider these features when researchers are recruited and developed.

Socialization

The productive researcher is highly socialized to the academic profession. Daniel Wheeler and John Creswell[17] of the University of Nebraska, in a paper presented at the 1985 annual meeting of the Association for the Study of Higher Education in Chicago, reviewed the literature on research productivity. They found socialization to be fundamental in predicting scientific productivity. Socialization is used in this sense to mean the process by which a newcomer to academe learns the norms, expectations, and sanctions of a faculty career. This is critical knowledge, because common values, even more than common knowledge, bond a group into a profession and allow the members to work together effectively. Given a common understanding and common view of the world, it is easy for the group to agree on goals and means. The importance of professional values should not be underestimated; in highly developed professions these values undergird nearly every action. Thus knowing the underlying values allows faculty members to understand why persons in their profession behave as they do, to predict a colleague's behavior, and to behave in accordance with others in that profession.[18]

Corcoran and Clark[19] studied the socialization patterns of two groups of faculty members from various disciplines (physical and biological sciences, mathematics, social science, and humanities) at a large research university. One group consisted of 63 tenured faculty members who were judged "highly active" in teaching, research, and service. The second "representative" group had 66 tenured faculty members randomly selected but matched by rank, field, and faculty generation to the first group. Corcoran and Clark found striking differences in the socialization patterns of the highly active and representative group. For example, highly active faculty members said research attracted them to academic work, while representative faculty members said teaching was more appealing than research. Highly active faculty members said academic freedom and research were the most satisfying aspects of their work; representative faculty members said working with students was most satisfying. These differences suggest that the highly active group had more heavily embraced the mores of a researcher.

Professionals typically allot a significant amount of time to initiating new members. Although mentors or other representatives do not always articulate the profession's rules of conduct and thought for the novice, most professions consciously socialize newcomers through a period of apprenticeship. Clinical rotations and residency programs socialize future practicing physicians; attorneys spend years as junior or associate members of their firms; psychologists go through internships and supervised counseling. As for academics, most are Ph.D.s whose entire doctoral training, especially the dissertation, teaches them the values of the university professorate and the expected activities of faculty members.

Many physician faculty members are socialized to academe through postresidency fellowships (for example, the National Institutes of Health [NIH] New Investigator Programs) or through experience with a seasoned research team. Unfortunately, however, a significant number of physician faculty members receive no formal research training. The American Association of Medical Schools reports in their annual survey of all medical school faculty that only 56% have had 6 months or more of postresidency training in research.

Mentors

Productive researchers have had specific help before, during, and after training from advisers or mentors. Individuals who associate early with distinguished scientists or collaborate with them on research projects are more likely themselves to become productive researchers.[20] Blackburn wrote[21]: "Mentorship/sponsorship in the first years is critical for launching a productive career. Learning the informal network that supports productivity—the inner workings of professional associations and who the productive people are—is critical." Besides providing training and contacts, mentors often also provide important emotional support.[20]

In Corcoran and Clark's study[19] highly active faculty members reported learning how to behave from their advisers and had had many more research-related experiences (assistantships and fellowships) during graduate school. They also had tangible, specific help from their advisers or mentors after graduation; advisers helped them write grants, offered them positions, and collaborated on papers.. The representative group reported fewer instances of such help.

Work Habits

Productive researchers establish scholarly habits early in their careers. Lightfield[22] looked at publishing records of young sociologists in the first 5 and 10 years after completion of their doctorates. He found that frequent publications and numerous citations in the first 5 years predicted output in the second 5 years. He concluded: "Unless a person achieves a qualitative piece of research during the first 5 years as a sociologist . . . it seems unlikely that he will do so during the next 5 years—if at any time during his career." Studies in other disciplines, such as physics and chemistry, have similarly found that few researchers who start their careers slowly ever become highly productive.[23,24]

Professional Communication

Productive researchers maintain professional contacts with their research training peers and with colleagues outside their institutions. Academic work, especially research, is both a highly independent and dependent profession. Although the daily work of research is quite autonomous, performed alone or with a small team, researchers are very dependent on the work of others to build on and advance the body of knowledge. Also, researchers need other investigators to critique and replicate their work and to maintain the quality of work in the field through grant reviews, refereed journals, conference presentations, and critiques. Because of this interdependence, successful academics have a network of professional colleagues that is vital to their effective performance. These colleagues provide quick access to the most recent work in the area, serve as thinking partners when the researcher needs help, and open doors to peer review panels.[21,25]

For example, Pelz and Andrews,[25] in their work on scientists in organizations, found that highly productive scholars maintained frequent contact with colleagues and spent significant time communicating with them through personal correspondence, telephone conversations, visits, and exchange of reprints and unpublished papers. Corcoran and Clark[19] also found that the highly active faculty members maintained professionally meaningful relationships with their advisers and research training peers, whereas the representative group maintained only social relationships.

Local Peer Support

While socialization to the values and attitudes of research is important during and immediately after training, continued support and stimulation in the researcher's environment are critical. In studying chemists and psychologists, Braxton[26] found that the productivity of department colleagues indirectly influenced an individual's performance. That is, the same researcher published more when placed among productive researchers than when moved to a department where colleagues published less. Reskin[24] attributed high research performance to the immediate reinforcement that researchers received from colleagues and not to the recognition gained from citations alone. She also suggested that informal recognition may be more important than formal measures.

Studies of corporate research and development professionals also found that interest, praise, and recognition were among the most valued rewards possible. In a 1976 study, Gary Latham of the Weyerhauser Company, Tacoma, Washington, and Terence Mitchell[27] of the University of Washington asked research and development scientists and engineers to rank 30 rewards. The top 10 were seeing one's work applied, salary increase, work put to commercial use, recognition by supervisors, monetary bonus, promotion, profit-sharing, working in a group that is recognized as a top-flight group, recognition by management at the top of the company, and recognition by one's work group. A majority of these rewards involve some form of recognition.

Simultaneous Projects

Stinchcombe[28] suggested that by pursuing several projects simultaneously, faculty members were buffered against the disillusionment that can occur when tackling difficult research projects. Hargens[29] bore out this premise in his study of chemists, mathematicians, and political scientists. In these fields, faculty members who publish the most also work on multiple projects simultaneously. If one project stalls or fails, another may prove successful.

Sufficient Work Time

How much time should faculty members devote to research? A significant amount of uninterrupted time is needed for what Menkes[30] called "the dogged pursuit of clues . . . an unhurried sauntering of the mind." As to what is significant time, Knorr et al.[31] observed how numbers of publications, from scientists in university and industrial settings, varied in the amount of time allocated for research. They concluded that research time should not exceed 80% of all work time or fall below 10%; somewhere in the 40% range is probably ideal. Similarly, Reif-Lehrer in his book, *Writing a Successful Grant Application,*[32] stated that to compete successfully for an NIH grant, principal investigators need to commit at least 50% or more of their time to any proposed study.

Orientation

Prolific researchers are both externally and internally oriented; although they attend frequent national meetings and collaborate often with colleagues outside their institutions, they are not less committed locally.[21,33] In fact, Corcoran and Clark found that highly active faculty members were both active outside their institutions and heavily involved with internal institutional governance, major curriculum decisions, and similar activities.[19]

Autonomy and Commitment

The importance of autonomy to researchers in corporations and higher education is not surprising given that they are highly motivated by intrinsic factors of the work itself, such as challenge, creativity, and problem solving.[34] But their autonomy is matched by commitment to the organization. Several authors have discussed the importance of "tight-loose" relationships between seasoned, productive members and their organizations.[25,35] In a "tight-loose" relationship, faculty members enjoy academic freedom, plan their own time, and set their own goals. However, they also need affiliation and a meaningful role. They want to be valued as important contributors to the organization and to have their goals relate to the larger institutional mission. The only exception to this need for autonomy applies to new faculty members, who require close supervision and direction for at least 1 year. In fact, Katz[36] found that during a researcher's first year on the job, the most significant negative correlate with productivity is autonomy.

Supportive Environment

Finally, of all the factors that affect a researcher's productivity, none is as powerful as the environmental features of the work place.[37] G.R. Pellino et al., from the University of Michigan School of Education, in a 1981 monograph produced by the Center for the Study of Higher Education in Ann Arbor, found in higher education that "The place of employment is the single best predictor of faculty scholarly productivity. . . . Faculty [members] who come to productive surroundings produce more there than they did before they arrived and more than they will later if they move to a less productive environment. Resources, support, challenge, communication with producers on other campuses, all correlate with a professor's productivity."[38] Therefore, in the next section we describe the environmental features that correlate with research productivity.

ENVIRONMENTAL FEATURES

Studies in addition to Pellino's have revealed that environmental features are the most powerful predictors of research productivity.[39-43] For example, Long and McGinnis[40] studied scientists who had moved from one organization to another. They found that when changes in an organization take place, changes in research productivity occur also. These changes are not a result of training, mentors, values, or a national network of colleagues, since these remain the same. Rather, the organization emerges as the significant factor. Even the most productive scientists suffered decreases in productivity when the organizations to which they moved had a less research-conducive environment. This finding is not surprising. As Fox[44] articulately points out, research is a highly social and political process of communication, interaction, and exchange. Scientific creativity extends or revises existing knowledge. Scientists do this through publications and conference presentations, and even more informally in conversations in the laboratory, lunchroom, corridor, bathroom, and at after-hour gatherings. This is not to say that individual features are unimportant; rather, individual features are essential but insufficient by themselves. To be productive, it seems, researchers must have certain individual features and must work in an environment conducive to research. Just what are the features of such an environment? To answer this question, Bland and Ruffin[45] returned to the literature on research productivity, but this time, the focus was on environmental features that affect productivity. The literature review revealed several substantial and diverse bodies of literature that address the elements of a productive research environment. For example, the fields in which environmental features of productive organizations had been studied included mathematics, physics, chemistry, astronomy, life sciences, earth and space, agriculture, health sciences, technical sciences, and social sciences, although most were in the natural sciences. In spite of this diversity in investigating what organizational factors affect research productivity, Bland and Ruffin's analysis identified characteristics consistently found in productive research environments.[45] They are clear goals that serve a coordinating function, research emphasis, culture, group climate, assertive participative governance, decentralized organization, communication, resources, size/age/diversity, rewards, recruitment and selection, and leadership.

For purposes of explanation, a discussion of each of these follows. However, these factors do not operate in research groups as isolated characteristics. Rather, they are like delicate threads of a whole fabric: individual, yet when interwoven, providing a strong, supportive, and stimulating backdrop for the researcher and the entire organization. The following descriptions will occasionally point out connectors among characteristics. In the discussion section the authors return to the overarching feature of connectedness of these characteristics.

Clear Goals That Serve a Coordinating Function

Productive research groups have clear organizational goals; and the people within them have articulated personal goals compatible with the organizational ones. This characteristic resounds strongly from several bodies of literature. Bland and Schmitz[46,47] reviewed the last 20 years of research on faculty and institutional vitality across all of higher education and found that a vital organization is characterized by clear, coordinating goals.

This focus on organizational goals may appear inconsistent with the commonly held belief that a scientist needs autonomy. Yet in *Scientists and Organizations:*

Productive Climates for Research and Development, Pelz and Andrews[48] found coordination of the research group toward common goals clearly compatible with individual freedom. As one of the research leaders at Bell Labs told them, "Everyone must know what the overall goal is, so that within each person's area he or she can look for those solutions that are most relevant to the major goals." Another scientist put it like this: "The organization points out what mountain they want us to climb, but how we climb it is up to us."

Pelz and Andrews' look at freedom versus coordination revealed another interesting finding.[48] Their more productive scientists said many people had influenced their choice of research areas. In fact, productivity was greatest when a scientist reported that he or she had at least 30% of the weight in the decision, and no one else had more than 30% of the weight. Performance was low when few people had some influence on the decision, and lowest when the chief alone decided on what a researcher would work. Thus when a scientist had both high influence in a research direction and high involvement from several others, maximum performance resulted. It seems a combination of coordination and freedom is not only feasible but essential for high productivity of scientists.

This finding is reminiscent of *In Search of Excellence,*[35] which describes excellent, innovative companies as having a "tight-loose organization." But just how tight and how loose should a research group be? Again, Pelz and Andrews' work provides guidance.[48] They looked at levels of organizational coordination and found that in the more loosely coordinated groups, only the most personally motivated researchers continued to achieve. Complete autonomy usually resulted in low performance. This finding bears particularly on supervision of new scientists. Recall that Katz[49] reported that the "most significant negative correlate" on productivity in the first year is autonomy. Similarly, when Pineau and Levy-Leboyer[50] compared successful biomedical laboratories with less successful ones, they found the best laboratories were managed by heads "whose approach was moderately free but who did formally control" the team.

On the other hand, Pelz and Andrews[48] found that researchers in very tightly coordinated organizations were so constrained that it decreased their ability to be productive. Thus only in the middle-range situations were scientists most productive. The middle range they describe is an environment where high individual autonomy is accompanied by clear goals, the strong influence of others, and a setting flexible enough to allow these influences to improve performance. Balancing this mix is a leader who keeps the goals of the organization in the minds of all the scientists. Also, as described in the communication and governance sections that follow, the leader ensures open and frequent communication so that people talk to each other about their work and celebrate each others' achievements.

Research Emphasis

A research-conducive environment places priority on research productivity, or at least puts priority on research equal to that on other missions.[2,39,51-53] Bean's causal model of faculty members' research productivity in institutions defines "research emphasis" as the weight given research criteria in promotion and tenure decisions.[54] Within research-oriented universities, Blackburn and colleagues[39] found productivity highest among faculty in universities where the educational emphasis was on graduate students, followed by progressively less productivity as the institution increases focus on undergraduate students. Research productivity also diminishes when a unit focuses on applied graduate training versus academic graduate training. Baird's study of 74 chemistry, history, and psychology departments found that those with clear, dominant goals of research were more productive.[51] Effects of not having a research emphasis were illustrated by psychology departments that emphasized training practitioners and were less productive in research. Similarly, other departments or disciplines that place a high priority on practitioner training and service, such as family medicine or nursing, generally have had low research productivity.[42,55]

Other studies underscore the importance of an emphasis on research by showing the negative impact of *not* having it. Drew[53] and Clark and Lewis[2] report a significant barrier to research productivity is lack of institutional commitment to it as evidenced by lack of time, resources, finances, and facilities for research. Commitment to research is very important, as Kapel and Wexler[52] confirmed in their study of a university's transition from a primarily educational mission to a joint mission of education and research. This institution found it insufficient that faculty and administration recognize the need for and value research. Rather, productive research environments have administrators and faculty who are highly committed to research and allocate resources accordingly. Occasionally a discipline or department has high research productivity even though it is part of a larger institution that does not emphasize research. Most often these are disciplines that Biglan[56] and others [57,58] describe as pure life science with a highly developed paradigm. These disciplines have high levels of connectiveness, multiple collaboration in teaching and research, and high commitment by individual faculty within the local group and across the nation that provide an "across-institutions environment" with a research emphasis.

Culture

Rice and Austin's studies[59,60] of faculty morale at U.S. colleges found one feature foremost in the nation's colleges with the highest morale: "Distinctive organizational cultures that are carefully nurtured and built upon."[59] Organizational culture is the distinctiveness that sets an organization apart from other similar organizations, and it is a distinctiveness that everyone within the organization understands, shares, and values. A clear organizational culture, writes William Tierney,[61] "ensures that everyone is on the same boat, and they know where the boat is headed. . . . Identity provides the framework for participants to deal with the existential issues of their own worth and meaning in the organization. Because new people join the institution every year, and the institution changes constantly, a strong sense of identity must be cultivated, tended, and frequently revisited."

The corporate literature frequently talks about the importance of an organizational culture to productivity. IBM, for example, is known for its organizational culture—the IBM look, the IBM ideals, the IBM business ethic. In addition, IBM has been consistently cited as the company that has built uncommon commitment from staff by emphasizing the management of human resources.[62,63] In the IBM culture, support for the individual and achievement of excellence are common basic beliefs. Other authors[63,64] have further noted that the culture of a group is not self-preserving. Culture requires symbolic management and social organizations to keep it sustained and growing.

Organizational culture, though seldom formally articulated, plays an important role in building and bonding a group by giving the group an identity, a safe home base in which to experiment and thereby be productive. In highly productive research groups, the culture is usually characterized by shared values about academic freedom and the ways to establish truth through that discipline's scientific method.[65] These research groups often have "war stories," sagas, tales, or rituals that make up their distinct culture.[66] Common examples of distinctive histories being retold by the members of productive research groups are the stories of the founders of Johns Hopkins or Stanford Universities, known to all members of these communities. Recently, President Kennedy of Stanford University related his repositioning plan to the original vision of Jordan and the Stanfords as a means of evoking acceptance of the plan from Stanford faculty.[67] Organizational culture is often communicated and maintained through rituals. Rituals are patterned social activity that expresses and articulates specific meaning to the group's members. They need not be the formal recognition events but can consist of paper cups of champagne at the end of a long project, cutting the ivy at Greenville College, or the yearly recognition of excelling junior members of the group.[59,68]

Group Climate

Most studies investigating the possible link between group climate and research productivity found a positive correlation.[69-72] Andrews[69] measured group climate via scientists' ratings: a spirit of innovation in the unit, dedication to work, degree to which new ideas were given consideration, degree to which ideas from junior members are given consideration, degree of cooperation, and frequency of staff meetings. Aggregate ratings of these items correlated positively and directly with group productivity.

Another example of the relationship between group climate and productivity is found in Birnbaum's study[72] of 84 academic research projects randomly drawn from 14 U.S. universities and one Canadian university. The U.S. institutions were among the top 22 U.S. universities in terms of federal grant dollars. This study found article and book publication rates were higher from projects with low faculty turnover, good leader-member relationships, and a habit of open discussion of disagreements.

The importance of good group climate to productivity is also suggested by our previous discussion on goals. Recall that productive group members are influenced by their co-workers. Such influence would more likely take place in an organization characterized by mutual respect and esprit de corps. Schweitzer's study[70] of 49 "top researchers" in mass communication found that 97% of this group rated "personal relations" as an important to very important factor in their productivity. Sixty-seven percent also rated "stimulation and encouragement from colleagues" as very important. Responses to open-ended questions on factors influencing their productivity most frequently referred to research-oriented colleagues and a supportive environment.

Assertive Participative Governance

One of the most persistent findings in the literature is the correlation between participative governance and research productivity.* Rice and Austin[59] began their study of high-morale colleges with the hypothesis that effective leadership contributes to high morale. They assumed that "a variety of leadership approaches would work, but that what was important was managerial competence." Faculty morale was surveyed in more than 100 colleges. The top 10 high-morale colleges were then site-visited and studied in depth. The conclusion: None of the 10 case studies supported the hypothesis about effective leadership; rather, "Every one of the 10 colleges with high morale and satisfaction had leadership that was aggressively participatory in both individual style and organizational structure."[59]

Another example comes from Pineau and Levy-Leboyer's study, "Managerial and Organizational Determinants of Efficiency in Biomedical Research Teams."[50] After studying all 155 laboratories in the Paris area, they concluded, "The best laboratories were characterized by participatory working relations: more meetings, the technicians were personally involved in the results, and more interpersonal relations between the researchers and the heads." Kerr[77] puts it bluntly: "Literally hundreds of studies have incontestably demonstrated the superiority of participative leadership and group decision making." Although he points out that there are certainly times when participative leadership is not the best governance approach, in research organizations it is usually preferred. He suggests that participative leadership is most effective for the following reasons: (1) the requisite knowledge may be too extensive, the conglomeration of needed skills too complex, or the simultaneity of the decisions too considerable for anything but participative leadership; (2) such leadership heightens members' morale and self-esteem; (3) it allows for diversity of perspective and variety of competencies that no one leader can possess; (4) it accords opportunity to focus on and develop commitment for the task at hand; and (5) it allows subordinates to have information that increases their abilities to contribute, and it reduces the opposition to decisions.

Decentralized Organization

Another expression of the positive impact of participatory leadership is the finding that flat and decentralized organizational structures correlate with highly productive units.[54,59,73,78] For example, Birnbaum[72] looked at predictors of long-term research performance in his sample of 84 academic research projects drawn from 15

---

*References 48, 50, 59, 65, 68, 69, 73-76.

universities, of which the 14 U.S. institutions were among the top 22 universities in federal research support. The study, conducted in 1975 and again in 1977, examined research productivity in 50 widely varied areas (some subjects: electrical properties of bone, epilepsy, off-shore drilling, arms control, urban transportation). Birnbaum found that *horizontal differentiation,* his term for a decentralized, flat organizational group structure, was a significant predictor of research productivity. Okrasa[73] also found that research units with a decentralized structure have both greater overall research productivity and more consistent research productivity across members.

Decentralization, it should be noted, does not mean anarchy. Recall that effectiveness of decentralization was found in the context of leadership that uses aggressive participative governance and where there are clear, commonly understood goals. And, as Steiner[76] described in his book, *The Creative Organization,* a decentralized organization needs feedback systems that allow leaders to track the performance of the quasi-autonomous parts.

Communication

Communication process includes giving or exchanging information, supportive and sympathetic relationships, physical connections and contacts, and access to the larger network of colleagues. These communication processes need to occur between the leader and the team, among team members, and between team members and their external network of colleagues.

The previous section on governance and a later one on leadership describe communication between the leader and team members. Communication among internal and external colleagues, our focus here, has been found to predict individual research performance and to be important to all staff levels to maintain productivity.[44,48,71,79,80] In fact, Visart[81] found that communication between (and within) units explained as much as 31% of the variance in the number of published written products among research groups in six countries. In addition, Saxberg and Newell[82] reported that it was the unanimous opinion among members of interdisciplinary research teams they polled that communication with consideration for all parties and all dissenting viewpoints was critical to group success.

Several researchers have looked at the features of the communication activities among colleagues. As mentioned earlier under individual features, Pelz and Andrews[48] found that researchers with the highest productivity levels had frequent contacts with colleagues, spending up to 8 to 15 hours per week in a communicative activity. Similarly, Sindermann[68] found extensive references to communication and networking in his interviews with successful scientists. These scientists communicated and maintained their communication network predominantly through regular and frequent discussions with peers; including these same peers in planning for workshops, symposiums and conferences; frequent late evening, small-group conferences in offices, hotel rooms, or poolside; and requests to peers for preliminary reviews and comments about research projects. In addition, these scientists identified communication channels or networks as a mutual activity that can be professionally managed and that requires periodic purging.

Finkelstein[83] developed four prototypical profiles of collegial communication patterns among faculty members. These profiles include the classic locals, departmental-anchored cosmopolitans, unanchored cosmopolitans, and social and emotional supported colleagues. Highest publication rates were associated with the departmental-anchored cosmopolitan communication pattern, one that is relatively insulated from campus colleagues outside the department while strongly tied to departmental and off-campus colleagues. This communication pattern was the most common among university faculty and the most prevalent among faculty with a research orientation regardless of the setting. The importance of this pattern of communication is confirmed by Schweitzer's finding that the second most important reported extrinsic factor contributing to a researcher's productivity was the stimulation and encouragement of colleagues at other schools.[70] In short, it seems the research-conducive environment encourages and facilitates a variety of frequent communications among internal and external colleagues and between the leader and team members.

Resources

Resources to accomplish a task or achieve a goal are essential for any endeavor, including research. Essential research resources are defined as those the individual perceives as necessary to carry out a research program.[54] *Perceives* is an important word in this definition, which we will return to at the end of this section. The following describes the commonly identified essential resources: human resources (colleagues, assistants, technical consultants, graduate students, research-knowledgeable leader), time, funding, research facilities, and libraries.[35,53,84,85]

The previous section on communication notes the importance of colleagues as a resource, wherever those colleagues are located. Several studies address more specifically the importance of having able colleagues and other human resources easily accessible within the unit. Andrews,[69] looking at the impact of major resources (workspace, equipment, colleagues, leader, library sources) on research productivity, found that satisfaction with human resources (including colleagues) in a research unit was the resource type explaining the largest amount of the variance in the unit's performance. Others note that frequent face-to-face contacts help provide ideas, catch errors, stimulate development, and provide support.[35,48,70] It further helps to have colleagues physically and conceptually close together. An MIT study[39] found that the probability of communicating at least once a week was only 8% to 9% if people's offices were 10 meters apart, versus 25% when 5 meters apart. As for conceptual distance, Blau's study of theoretical high-energy physicists found the best departmental environment to be one in which the physicist has a few colleagues working in the same specialized area and many in other areas who share the same theoretical orientation.[79]

Productive colleagues provide an additional, less specific resource role through the ambiance they create in a department. Braxton[86] found that the productivity of departmental colleagues indirectly influenced an individual's performance. That is, the same researcher published more when working among productive researchers than when moved to a department where colleagues published less. Similarly, Long and McGinnis[40] found that for scientists who changed institutions, changes in productivity levels correlated with the productivity of colleagues in the new department. Reskin[87] attributes high performance to the immediate reinforcement that researchers receive from colleagues in productive environments and not to the recognition gained from citation alone. Thus faculty colleagues not only serve as a source of knowledge, skill, expertise, emotional support, and stimulation, but they also nurture the individual's "spark" or commitment to research, thus building a culture in which to survive and prosper. The lack of research-oriented colleagues has been shown to drain energy and extinguish the spark from even the most skilled and talented researcher.[42,43]

Graduate students or, occasionally, undergraduate research assistants are another important resource. Blackburn and colleagues[39] found that faculty teaching graduate students were six times more likely to have produced five or more articles over a 2-year period than those teaching only undergraduates. Additional support for this observation comes from the common finding that doctoral-granting institutions consistently have higher levels of research output than other types of institutions.[40,85,88-92]

Sindermann's case histories[68] highlighted the importance of support staff, as in these quotes from researchers describing ingredients of a good research group: "a secretary who knows how to wash test tubes and a technician who can type" and "obvious research progress during prolonged and frequent absence of the principal investigator." Pineau and Levy-Leboyer[50] also found that among the 151 biomedical teams investigated in their research, the least productive teams had no or few full-time technicians and the most productive teams had 10 or more full-time technicians.

With regard to funding, Harrington's evaluation of dental school research productivity[93] found the combination of external funding, student-faculty ratio, and number of library books accounted for one third of the variance in research productivity. The relationship among these variables was that as funding and library books increased, the student-faculty ratio decreased and research productivity increased. Similarly, Clark and Lewis[2] found the second most frequently cited institutional condition supporting research success was research funding availability. In addition, the institutional conditions hindering research success were heavy teaching/administrative responsibilities and lack of funding. Culpepper and Franks[94] found the common major impediments to research reported by family medicine university units were, in rank order: lack of time, lack of funding, lack of research skills, and lack of role models. In short, the inadequate availability of money is commonly found as a barrier to research.[84,85,95]

Finally, although the resources described above are essential for research productivity, it is not enough that they exist in a unit; they must also be obviously accessible. Pelz and Andrews[48] found actual resources correlated less highly with productivity than did resources that researchers perceived they could access. This distinction may explain some of the correlation between unit productivity and having a research-knowledgeable leader and having a decentralized organizational structure. A knowledgeable leader probably understands the need for appropriate resources and not only provides them but also makes them easily accessible. Further, departments or units that have an organizational structure with vertical differentiation or a high number of hierarchical decision-making levels may have reduced productivity if faculty perceive access to resources difficult.[72]

Size/Age/Diversity

In general, performance increases as group size increases. Size positively correlating with productivity was found in studies on groups, departments, schools (e.g., dentistry) and institutions (e.g., university).[39,50,51,93,96-99] This finding follows points noted above in that one would expect more opportunities for contact, stimulation, and resources in a larger group. As for age of the group and its relation to productivity, Pelz and Andrews[48] found it helps to have a group that has been together for quite a while. They found some evidence, however, of group productivity dropping after the group has been together for more than 7 years, although this drop was not consistently found. Rather, they found creativity dropped when older groups lost their atmosphere of high standards, group cohesion, and enthusiasm. Andrews describes the demanding yet cohesive and enthusiastic atmosphere found in productive groups as "creative, supportive tension."

More recent research on age of the group has been less consistent; the inconsistency may be explained by ageism. That is, if one uses supervisors' ratings of a group's usefulness, performance in older groups appears to decline. When group performance is assessed with respect to actual scientific products (for example, patents or papers), however, the trend in productivity is more likely steady state or steady increase with age of group.[100]

Studies on diversity looked at the effects on productivity of differences among group members in disciplines and level of terminal degree. Generally, the trend is toward more productivity when diverse approaches to problems are represented in the group.[48,65,76,79,101] Pelz and Andrews[48] do point out that diverse approaches need to be balanced with common values and goals.

Rewards

Latham and Wexley[102] conducted an experimental study assessing the effect of various rewards on the performance of research and development scientists. Managerial praise (from specifically trained managers), public recognition, and monetary bonuses were given to research and development professionals judged to have performed effectively. Performance was assessed by specially trained supervisors who observed and rated each professional using a behavioral observation scale. All three rewards had impact; money and praise ranked one and two, respectively. Latham and Wexley reported, however, that "the increase in performance due to the money over praise was so small as to be practically insignificant. Thus, from a cost/benefit viewpoint, it is most effective to give praise."

What is it about praise that increases productivity? McKeachie,[103] a longtime scholar on faculty vitality, suggests that praise, prestige, salary, and promotions are important not so much for the material gains they provide but for their ability to recognize the researcher's special expertise, intellectual ability, and value to one's colleagues. Support for this view is amplified in another study by McKeachie[104] that looked at events that lowered faculty productivity. The events most often cited were critical department heads or administrators who seem not to appreciate good work, incompatible colleagues, and lack of respect from others for one's research.

Money, it seems, increases productivity or is a motivating factor only under limited circumstances and only for a small subset of members.[105,106] The circumstances in which money rates as a preferred reward are very low salaries in comparison with other members in the unit or for a whole unit compared with other units. For example, Gustad[107] surveyed faculty members about their job satisfactions. He reported faculty valued opportunities for responsibility, achievement, independent thinking, and intellectually stimulating activities. The top three answers to his question about what is most rewarding were research, stimulating colleagues, and salary. Respondents with low salaries rated salary highest. Eckert and Stecklein[108] looked at job satisfaction of faculty members at Minnesota. They found that social significance of work and intellectual interest were most important.

Researchers in corporate settings, like their university counterparts, report preferred rewards are challenging projects, stimulating colleagues, and recognition, as well as money. For example, when Latham and Mitchell[27] had research and development scientists rank-order 30 rewards, the rank-order result was as follows: seeing one's work applied, salary increase, work put to commercial use, recognition by supervisors, monetary bonus, promotion, profit sharing, working in a group that is recognized as a top flight group, recognition by management at the top of the company, and recognition by work group. Similarly, the 63 "highly active" faculty in a major research-oriented university interviewed by Clark and Corcoran[109] reported the following situations or factors that support success: stimulating colleagues, strong academically oriented administration, recognition by administration and colleagues, and resources.

Although salary, awards, promotions, and the like are important rewards, what most motivates researchers are the intrinsic pleasures of challenging work, intellectual accomplishment, stimulating colleagues, and being valued by one's colleagues, local and national. It is important to note that the most effective combination of these rewards varies for each individual and for an individual over a lifetime.[105,106] McKeachie,[103] for example, uses Levinson and colleagues' theory of stages of adult development to suggest how preferred rewards are likely to change over a lifespan.[110] He also notes, as have others,[2] that research productivity does not predictably decrease with an individual's age. It appears, then, that research-conducive environments not only offer the preferred rewards described but also enable researchers to obtain the rewards they prefer when their needs change.

Recruitment and Selection

Dill[111-113] found that highly productive research and development units were distinguished by their concentration on hiring talent. These units spent extraordinary amounts of time recruiting people with the specific talent—skills and socialization—

wanted. Particularly important was socialization—the values and commitment that fit in their organization. These characteristics are largely determined by a person's training and mentors.[40,80,111] For example, Zuckerman[114] identified the training program as critical to achieving high performance since this is the setting where knowledge, skills, and competencies relevant to research are developed and where norms and values are cultivated. The most prestigious research universities systematically recruit new faculty with proven commitment to research from the same select group of elite institutions.[115-117] This recruitment and selection process concentrates talented faculty in a department with a culture and collegial climate strongly supportive of research.

An emphasis on recruitment echoes some of the characteristics previously mentioned. When one knows the organization's goals, knows too that it has a positive climate and an organizational culture one is trying to build and maintain, then one is able to recruit very carefully.

LEADERSHIP FEATURES

Without question, leadership is the most influential organizational variable the literature review uncovered. It is the one variable that affects all of the other organizational characteristics, which in turn influence research productivity.

To quote Blackburn,[95] "Nearly every positively correlated factor [with research productivity] resides in administrative hands." Studies examining the characteristics of the leader of productive units consistently conclude that the leader must be perceived as a highly skilled scientist.[53,63,68,69] Dill,[111,113] for example, studying the effectiveness of research and development units in Europe, found that the most significant predictor of success over time in these units was the leader. Further, he found that the leader's level of professional expertise as a scientist before assuming the managerial position most predicted the unit's productivity. Dill maintains that it is this experience that enables a unit director to influence members' knowledge and values, to facilitate contacts and networks, to attract other competent researchers, to help colleagues who are blocked or stopped in their research efforts, and so on. In addition, this experience establishes a basis of power or influence built on competence, experience, and admiration of the group members. Pineau and Levy-Leboyer[50] found biomedical research teams were more successful when the "relations between the head and the researchers were based on mutual confidence." Power based on competence has also been found to be the most effective base in studies conducted in business. These studies often use French and Raven's categories of power bases to look at kinds of power between individuals.[118] For example, Bachman, Smith, and Slesinger[119] looked at the relationship of workers' job satisfaction to the power bases their office managers use. They found worker satisfaction positively associated with managers whose power was based on competence and experience, or based on personal admiration. Dissatisfaction coincided with influence, or power based on "legitimate rights" of supervision, or based on positive and negative sanctions. This outcome is echoed in Andrews' finding that the quality of the leader correlated highly with group climate.[69] The quality of the leader was measured by scientists' ratings of the leader's technical competence, knowledge of the field, personality and character, amount of work he or she does, and level of support he or she gives others' research. Leaders who had more of these characteristics ran groups that had higher group climate and in turn had higher productivity.

Given the previous characteristics of a research-conducive environment, it is easy to understand how other studies found that leaders of productive groups were highly research-oriented,[53] internalized mission and kept research emphasis clear to the group,[120] and exhibited the behaviors one would expect of a leader with a participative governance style. These behaviors include frequent meetings with clear objectives, good leader-member relationships facilitating open communication, allowing expressions of all points of view, complete sharing of information, and vesting ownership of projects with all group members.*

This profile of the effective research leader—one who facilitates group productivity through the pairing of common goals and some structure with highly participative governance—is echoed in the research on effective university department chairs and deans.[10] This body of research differs from the others described earlier. But since many research leaders also serve these roles, it is important to note that the same behaviors that are effective in the role of research leader also best serve the roles of chair and dean.

Bensimon and colleagues[123] synthesized the work on higher education leadership into these categories: trait theories, power and influence theories, behavioral theories, contingency theories, and cultural and symbolic theories. The third category of studies, behavioral theories, applies here. These investigate leadership by "examining patterns of activity, managerial roles, and behavior categories of leaders— that is, by considering what it is that leaders actually do." Typically, in these studies, chair or dean behaviors and performance are rated on all major job tasks, not just facilitating research, usually by faculty. Often these ratings are then correlated with a global indicator of leader, department, or college success. The overall conclusion from these studies is that two major constructs relate to effective leadership: initiating structure, and using considerate behaviors.[123-127]

Initiating structure includes the characteristics described above under establishing clear goals that serve a coordinating function. Considerate behavior includes the characteristics of leadership described in this section and those under assertive participative governance. For example, Knight and Holen[127] investigated whether there was a significant relationship between department chair behaviors (defined as faculty perception of the chair's initiating structure activities and use of considerate behaviors), and faculty's perception of the chair's accomplishment of typical responsibilities, which included facilitating research. This study included the ratings of 458 chairs by 5830 faculty members in 65 colleges and universities across the United States. The results across these sites were consistent, strikingly so. Chairpersons rated high on both initiating structure and using considerate behaviors were also rated highest in effectively accomplishing and performing all 15 common

*References 48, 50, 72, 78, 111, 112, 121, 122.

responsibilities of a chair. Conversely, chairpersons rated low on both dimensions received the lowest ratings with regard to how well they accomplished their responsibilities. In summary, it appears that department chairs who are good at both initiating structure and using considerate behavior impress their faculties as being most effective at fulfilling their responsibilities.

Skipper[128] also conducted several studies investigating higher education administrators' use of initiating structure and considerate behaviors. He consistently found that at the dean's level and above, most effective administrators were characterized by high scores on both constructs. Interestingly, Hoyt and Spangler[124] report that Fleishman and Harris's review of the literature on department leadership[129] found inconsistencies in the desirableness of leaders initiating structure or exhibiting consideration behaviors. But, they found these inconsistencies were explained by noting that under low consideration climates, high structure is seen as threatening and restrictive. But under high consideration climates, these same structures are seen as supportive and helpful.

CONCLUSIONS AND IMPLICATIONS

The productive research organization, then, is composed of critical individual, environmental, and leadership features. The environment must contain individuals who possess a commitment to research, content knowledge in their research areas, and basic and advanced methodological research skills relevant to their areas of investigation. Further, these members must be socialized to the academic profession, have had effective mentors, have scholarly habits, have a network of colleagues with whom they communicate frequently, work on several projects simultaneously, commit a significant proportion of their professional time to research, value both their autonomy and their commitment to their organization, and maintain an active interest in internal and external matters.

However, possessing these individual characteristics is insufficient to allow a researcher to be productive: The productive researcher must be part of a productive organization. A productive organization has clear organizational goals as well as individual goals that relate to the organizational ones, emphasizes research, has a distinctive culture, has a climate of respect paired with intellectual jostling, and consciously socializes new members. The productive organization has a critical mass of scientists who are well seasoned, but not so seasoned that they do not convey excitement through a great deal of communication among each other and to other groups. The productive organization has sufficient resources, particularly human, but what is more important, has resources that group members perceive as accessible. Finally, it has a flat organizational structure with a leader who facilitates group productivity through participative governance, who is experienced in research and plays an important though not predominant role in an individual researcher's planning, who keeps the organizational goals visible, and who carefully attends to recruitment.

The characteristics reported in this chapter were culled and synthesized from a very broad range of literature; these characteristics consistently emerged, almost regardless of discipline or research setting (e.g., academic or corporate). However, there may be additional characteristics unique to specific disciplines that were not revealed in this wide, sweeping look at research-conducive factors. As Burton Clark eloquently pointed out in *The Academic Life: Small Worlds, Different Worlds,*[130] "The discipline has become everywhere an imposing, if not dominating, force in the working lives of the vast majority of academics. Organized around individual subjects, the disciplines have their own histories and trajectories, and their own habits and practices."

Also the impact of these factors may vary by gender. The studies reviewed here looked at research groups composed mostly of men. Recent work on women in the scientific community suggests women scientists do not thrive as well as do their male counterparts in the same environment.[131]

Many of the characteristics described of the productive individual, the effective leader, and the research-conducive environment are not surprising. They are similar to the factors found in the management and organizational development literature that relate to employee productivity in business settings, particularly when the employees are professionals or "gold collar" workers.[71] One would expect an organization that emphasizes research or that has a leader with research skills to be more research productive than one without these features.

Less intuitively obvious are other findings: that participative governance is a consistent form of leadership that correlates with productivity and that perceived resource availability correlates more with productivity than actual resource availability.

It may also not be obvious, particularly to emerging disciplines, how to build these characteristics into a group. Fortunately, just identifying the characteristics implies some strategies: locate research members in close proximity; provide mechanisms for frequent professional communication among group members and across groups; and select leaders who are (or were) accomplished researchers. Naming a strategy, however, is easier done than effectively using one. Take assertive participative governance, for example. Chris Argyris,[132] one of the most prolific researchers and writers on organizations, found that leaders of research organizations tend to be blind to the extent they truly encourage participation. For example, in a study of technical problem solving meetings led by more than 250 research and development supervisors, 85% of the supervisors described their leadership style as facilitating autonomy, openness, risk taking, innovation, and self-responsibility. However, when tapes of these meetings were reviewed and careful count was made of the supervisors' behaviors, the researchers did not find many participative leadership behaviors used. In fact, the opposite was found. Thus a few recommended strategies for acquiring the characteristics may be helpful.

Recommended Strategies

1. Practicing effective participative governance as either a leader or a member is a learned skill; therefore, provide formal training for it. Particularly in disciplines in which the "natural" governance structure is hierarchical (medicine, for example), formal training would speed up and ease members' learning how to use a second governance approach.

2. Many of the characteristics are subjective, such as culture, positive climate, perception of resource accessibility, and feelings of worth of one's work. Thus the effective leader should systematically monitor and attend to these "soft" aspects of group environment.

3. It is difficult for a group to know how to find and recruit new members who have the research skills and socialization the group wants but does not now have. In this case, Dill[112] points out that the active, successful researcher in an affiliated field is more capable of assessing the capacity of a candidate for research and commitment to scholarly activity than is an inactive researcher in the target field. Thus fields or departments just initiating research programs could call on faculty outside their department or field to help identify and assess new members.

THE INTERWOVEN WHOLE—
CASE STUDIES OF PRODUCTIVE ORGANIZATIONS

We described the individual, environmental, and leadership features as separate characteristics. As mentioned before, however, in a productive organization these features get interwoven and fused together into a whole that outsiders see as a productive organization and insiders feel as a stimulating, vital workplace (see Figure 3-1). The following case examples describe workplaces where the features are well woven together but in which the informed reader can now also see the essential individual, environmental, and leadership threads.

&ea; Case Example: University of Michigan — *Thomas L. Schwenk*

The Department of Family Practice at the University of Michigan was established in 1978 following a planning process of several years. I joined the department in 1984, became interim chairman in 1986, and permanent chairman in 1988. Support for the department's establishment originated primarily with the state legislature and the Michigan Academy of Family Physicians, and the emphasis in this support was primarily on resident training. By far the youngest department in an established, traditional, research-intensive tertiary care academic medical center, the department lacked both the research tradition and the inpatient subspecialty clinical support typical of other medical center departments. Subsequent department development built on the original political support by creating a strong university-based residency program supported by a vigorous clinical practice. After several years of work in establishing the department's clinical and graduate education programs, attention turned to the development of equally strong research and medical student teaching programs.

The original group of about eight clinician-teacher faculty members maintained their focus on residency training and clinical practice, while a faculty cohort of approximately equal size was recruited in 1989-1990 to build a critical mass of tenure-track, research-oriented faculty. Another cohort of clinician-teacher faculty has since been recruited to expand the clinical operations into new primary satellite health centers to build the department's clinical base for medical student teaching and clinical research. The department now comprises 26 residency-trained, board-certified family physicians, seven Ph.D. faculty members in the behavioral and educational sciences, and more than 80 clinical and academic support staff members. The department administers an 18-resident training program (more than 60 graduates to date), accounts for over 58,000 patient visits annually, and has seen research and training grant support increase in total direct costs from $460,000 in 1987-1988 to $1,100,000 in 1992-1993 (estimated). The total budget for the department in 1992-1993 is about $6,500,000.

The primary growth in the department in the last few years has been in funded research programs, unfunded scholarly productivity (clinical reviews, case reports, book chapters, and editorial appointments), and clinical programs, with significant new responsibilities anticipated in medical student clerkship teaching in 1993. I will address specific examples of the way in which the factors associated with research productivity are manifested in these recent changes. In this case study the factors will be compressed into four: (1) *socialization* (including the influence of mentors, a research emphasis, group climate, work habits, and size/age/diversity issues), (2) *communication* (including local peer support and clear department goals), (3) *resources* (including work time and rewards), and (4) *leadership and governance* (including a decentralized organization, assertive participative governance, autonomy and commitment, and recruitment and selection issues).

Socialization. Inculcating and maintaining a research-conducive culture in the department is what I call *socialization*. Socialization within the department is fostered through the provision of a relatively sacred faculty and research development committee, which meets when faculty members do not have regularly scheduled clinical responsibilities. These meetings occur despite strong institutional pressure to generate clinical revenue to support fixed clinical overhead expenses. Establishment and support of a strong research development committee have provided a form of multiple mentorships through research plan critiques, shared work-in-progress, and extensive sharing of manuscripts for editing and comment. Socialization outside the department is encouraged through extra budget support for travel to research meetings, especially in the first 2 years of appointment, encouragement to submit pilot studies and work-in-progress to regional research meetings, permission and encouragement to seek mentoring with senior faculty members outside the department (such as the School of Public Health and the Cancer Center) or outside the institution, and enthusiasm for the development and submission of various investigator award and fellowship award applications (despite the fact that they usually represent a net cost to the department through matching support provisions). Senior faculty members, including the chair, have set a department-wide expectation for collaboration and have supported that expectation through personal role modeling. There was a strong bias toward innovation and autonomy in research themes in the recruitment of the original cohort of research-oriented faculty members. However, future faculty recruitment will seek faculty with identified research interests that will allow the department to achieve a critical mass in certain content areas, and we will seek individuals with compatible professional styles so as to foster group camaraderie and identity. In recruiting faculty members, we discuss the extremely high institutional expectations for research productivity with clarity and honesty. Only those candidates with the fellowship and graduate degree credentials likely to predict success are offered positions, despite the temptation to sometimes fill positions in a more expedient fashion. This demanding level of recruitment has been successful to a large extent as a result of the resources described, and to the national visibility and aura of success that results from the travel and support afforded current faculty members in the department.

Other examples of socialization include strong support for a faculty member's working at home as long as productivity supports the value of this work habit. Also, we have a long-standing department tradition of bringing a cake to be shared at faculty meetings whenever a major grant funding success is announced. This tradition has recently been extended for recognition of notable academic and scholarly achievements of other types (for example, successful achievement of a certificate of Added Qualification in Geriatrics).

Diversity in age has been difficult to achieve because of the paucity of family physicians with academic interests and skills, but recent and anticipated successes in promotion and tenure have helped considerably.

Communication. By its very nature, research is often the most hidden or invisible aspect of daily department life. Several specific steps have been taken to make research work more visible. The department has set high standards for the quality of teaching in general, and the quality of didactic presentations in particular. These standards are applied to research presentations, resulting in more effective communication of research work and progress to all faculty. The expectation that all papers will have benefited from significant sharing and editing within the department has the added value of enhancing the visibility of research accomplishments. Weekly faculty meetings have a monthly cycle of general areas of emphasis, of which one is research development, including papers about to be presented, work-in-progress, and descriptions of recently funded grants. The abstract pages of all published papers are attached to the weekly faculty meeting minutes, which are distributed to a wider audience of residents and staff as well as to faculty. A department newsletter is published twice yearly, ostensibly for alumni and other department friends (the mailing list currently contains about 2000 names). This newsletter lists (in addition to many other articles and notices about clinical and educational programs) notable research and grant achievements, papers published, presentations made, meetings attended, and grants funded. The newsletter probably has as much value to internal as to external communication.

The department has made a strong and unambiguous commitment to the importance of research development in a balanced department in an institution such as the University of Michigan. The interlocking benefits of research success to the missions of patient care and teaching are an important part of this commitment, which requires frequent vigorous repetition and reinforcement by the chair.

Resources. Resources include additional faculty members, equipment, support personnel, time, and money, in one form or another. The department made an explicit decision to build a strong research infrastructure, including support staff, research assistants, a Macintosh computer network (now totaling about 60 PCs for 130 faculty and staff), and a sophisticated clinical research data system, as soon as it was apparent that there would be a critical mass of research-oriented faculty members with the skills to make use of such resources. This infrastructure was built with training grants, general funds, and clinical revenue. Generous travel allowances and seed money for research (both distributed somewhat competitively in response to requests and opportunities) are available, funded through general funds and clinical revenue. Providing research office space in an on-campus building away from the off-campus clinical facilities has increased travel time but created a research-oriented environment with a critical mass of highly trained research faculty (both M.D.s and Ph.D.s) who enjoy close proximity for the development of collaborative working relationships. The university has a vigorous program of funded summer medical student research, which, in addition to work-study students and paid research assistants, has enhanced the productivity of the faculty. Subsequent additions to the infrastructure have been made as close to the time of need as possible (similar to the "just-in-time" inventory approach of automobile manufacturers) so as to minimize expense and allow the affected faculty members to participate in the planning and implementation of the particular resources.

An early department policy established a generic allocation of faculty time for all tenure-track positions: 30% to 40% clinical work, 10% to 20% core clinical teaching, and 40% to 50% research development. This allocation is similar to that in many medical school departments but requires a financial commitment that strains even the best of intentions and that is infrequently met in many family medicine departments, at least according to several recent studies. Long-term strategic planning for the department has maintained a commitment to this policy of time allocation in the face of significant clinical revenue pressures. This time allocation is aggressively adhered to with new faculty members for at least 3 years in the belief that it will be this long before external funding is even moderately likely.

Leadership and governance. Some of my fundamental principles of departmental governance include the following:
- Emphasis on fostering individual faculty autonomy
- Emphasis on enhancing faculty strengths rather than confronting weaknesses as a way of encouraging faculty-centered individual and department growth
- Matching faculty strengths to department needs by providing opportunities rather than making assignments

The department has experienced an inexorable and desirable evolution from centralized to decentralized planning and implementation as the experience, seniority, and maturity of the faculty warrant. The current status of this evolution is one of a high level of participative involvement in the implementation of department programs combined with more centralized strategic planning and policy setting. However, even now strategic planning and policy setting is gradually shifting to more decentralization and participation as faculty experience allows and opportunities arise.

The department has from the outset avoided the temptation to set department research themes and agendas that run counter to the interests and expertise of individual faculty members. This value choice has preoccupied the discipline of family medicine since its inception, but the department has never wavered from its commitment to individual faculty autonomy in setting research development directions. On the other hand, as faculty members mature, natural collaborations and themes emerge that can be more naturally supported through future faculty recruitment. Faculty members are provided with extra monitoring and supervision early in their appointment, but with a defined transition time to greater autonomy. Such autonomy in research development is sometimes disruptive to core clinical and teaching responsibilities (for example, clinic schedules are set 3 months in advance, but unexpected grant deadlines or multidisciplinary project opportunities have necessitated schedule changes) but is supported within reason if it can be accomplished without undue disruption to the work of other faculty members or the needs of medical students, residents, and patients.

I use a mixed style of leadership, depending on the type of program concerned: clinical and educational programs require stronger hierarchical administrative styles, whereas research development benefits from a more collegial academic and professional leadership style. For example, I have not appointed a director of research, an appointment common in many family medicine departments, as is the presence of a division of research. Such appointments and organizational structures suggest that research can be commanded, or that it is the province of only a few members of the faculty, neither of which are felt to be true by me or by faculty members. Promotion of individual growth and success within the context of broad department missions, on the assumption that "what is good for individual faculty members is usually good for the department," is one of the strongest and most ingrained values of the department.

Characteristics of the chair that may contribute to the research success of department faculty members include (1) the presence of a selective but consistently productive externally funded personal research program that includes collaborative scholarly relationships with several department faculty members, (2) expertise and visibility in national faculty development programs, (3) enthusiasm for promoting the success and growth of department faculty member careers, (4) a history of commitment to an annual career development process that promotes the development of clear career goals and encourages explicit negotiations for the resources necessary to bring those goals to fruition, and (5) expertise in academic time management that serves as a role model for other faculty members.

Finally, two methods of rewarding faculty members deserve mention. First, in 1990 the department established an incentive system in which faculty members who succeed in gaining external grant funding receive, in personal income or professional development support, an amount equal to 10% of existing department salary expenses supported by new grant funds. Second, I am famous within the department for sending what are affectionately known by faculty members as "love notes." These are handwritten expressions of support, congratulations, or thanks (often written in the margins of memos, on copies of letters of acceptance, or on small scraps of note paper) to faculty members who have achieved distinction, whether large or small. I received feedback that this seemingly small effort has a significant positive effect on faculty morale. It also gives me great pleasure to send them!

❧ Case Example: University of Minnesota — *Shelley Chou*

To the extent possible, I will relate this case study of the Department of Neurosurgery at the University of Minnesota to the characteristics described earlier in this chapter. In practice, however, the characteristics are interwoven and not easily described separately. The following is merely an example, and should not be interpreted as the only correct way. As they say, "There are many roads to Rome." This is the one we traveled. First, however, let me describe the department and my tenure as its head.

The Division of Neurosurgery as an academic unit began at the University of Minnesota in 1937, with W.T. Peyton, M.D., Ph.D., as its director. Dr. Peyton's Ph.D. was in anatomy, and it was natural for him to collaborate with Dr. A.T. Rasmussen, Professor of Neuroanatomy. There was also collaboration with the departments of neurology, neuropathology, and radiology (neuroradiology did not exist as a separate specialty until after World War II). Dr. Lyle French joined the division and became the director in 1960, on Dr. Peyton's retirement. I completed my training in 1955, under Drs. Peyton and French, and was invited to join them that same year. Dr. French and I agreed that I should spend some time free of clinical obligations at NIH to work on electrophysiology, which I did before my return to Minnesota. I was able to use that research as part of the work to obtain my Ph.D. in 1964. Thus from the beginning in this division there has been interdisciplinary collaboration, emphasis on research, and the recognition of the importance of formal research training.

The Department of Neurosurgery was established in 1968, and activities in research, education, and patient care continued to expand. The number of faculty members and residents gradually increased as well. Dr. French became the first vice-president for health sciences at the University of Minnesota in 1971. At that time, I was selected to take over as head of the department, which I held until 1989. My successor, Dr. Roberto Heros, was the first recipient of the endowed Lyle A. French chair. The funding of the chair from friends and former residents took approximately 3 years to develop under my tenure. At the present time, the department has 10 full-time and three part-time faculty members (three Ph.D.s who hold joint appointments in basic science departments, four neurosurgeons with Ph.D.s, and the rest neurosurgeons with M.D.s). In addition, four faculty members from other departments hold joint appointments in neurosurgery. There are 12 residents, nine research fellows or associates, six nurse clinicians, 13 secretaries at all levels, one computer technician, and several other helpers. The departmental office space is approximately 4000 square feet, and the research laboratory space is approximately 9000 square feet. In our medical school this is by no means a large department, but it is not a small one either. With that as the background, let us now look at some of the "characteristics."

Research emphasis and interdisciplinary collaboration. Unquestionably the department has had a long tradition of research and of interdisciplinary collaboration, as evidenced by Dr. Peyton's collaboration with other disciplines. As the years passed, we progressively enlarged our collaborative efforts with neurophysiology, neuropsychology, endocrinology, biophysics, orthopaedics, and more recently with transplant biology/immunology and tumor biology.

Our research directions in the department are a result of our continuing search to serve patients better; thus for the most part research is patient driven. Clinical problems have often required laboratory investigation to seek new insights that may point to new therapeutic opportunities. For example, our early investigation using radioisotopes to localize brain tumors (before the advent of CT and MRI scanning) and to study the dynamics of cerebrospinal fluid required that we work closely with the radiology and biophysics departments. Our long-term interest in understanding and finding new ways to combat cerebral edema called for working with ultrastructure anatomists and membrane biologists. Dexamethasone, a powerful agent for combatting cerebral edema, was first introduced at the University of Minnesota, and it has continued, for the past three decades, to be a universally used agent. More recently, our interest in brain cell transplant led us to organize a group of neurobiologists to work on a number of investigations in the laboratory.

The practice of collaborating is introduced early to residents. Residents participate extensively during their dedicated research time (without clinical obligations) on all department projects. Regularly scheduled conferences on research keep almost everyone informed of the projects and the progress in the laboratory. Impending presentations at national or international meetings are reviewed at such conferences, and critiques are generously delivered. Priorities are established for residents to attend national meetings on the basis of their oral and poster presentations. As neurosurgery becomes progressively subspecialized, staff are encouraged to focus on their areas of expertise and most are nationally well known. Likewise, the department invites a number of visiting professors throughout the year to spend time with the staff, particularly with the residents. Most of them are of national or international status; their names appear constantly in the literature. The positive impact on the residents and others in the department is significant.

Rewards. In addition to timely, informal recognition given for excellent work, research productivity is formally rewarded through support for travel to make presentations and through other formal events. For example, I was extremely gratified that at my retirement as the head of the department my colleagues established an annual lecture in my honor. Again, the lecturers are international figures. They give two to three lectures, which are open to the public, on subjects reflecting their lifetime experience. During the banquet portion of this event, the name of the resident chosen on the basis of academic accomplishment, clinical excellence, and humanistic qualities by a committee representing the staff and peer residents, to receive the Zhao Zi-Zhen Award, is announced. This annual award, as a memorial to my late mother, was endowed by my wife and me.

Resources. The department has been competitive and receives funding from the NIH, NSF, and other national agencies. Dr. French and I received our first award from the Atomic Energy Commission for research using radioisotopes in 1953, and an NIH R01 award in 1960. In the mid-1960s to the mid-1970s we received training grants from the NIH, which greatly enhanced our resources for research and training. This trend has continued to the present; currently we have principle investigators in the department with R01, program project, and training grants. Moreover, the department has always committed a significant allocation from the faculty practice plan to fund a variety of academic activities, including salary items of residents and technicians in the research laboratory.

Communication. To stimulate motivation and interest in research and to assist in maintaining colleague networks, an exchange resident research conference was established with the division of neurosurgery at the University of Iowa about 10 years ago. We visit each other's campus on alternate years, and the residents present their current research with the staff of both institutions attending to discuss these papers. We also have a golf competition on Saturday afternoon, followed by a dinner. These conferences are annual highlights.

Culture and group climate. Because the department is relatively small, certain activities can be scheduled at faculty members' homes. For many years we held Journal Club on two Thursday evenings per month during the academic year. The residents were scheduled to present summaries of articles in clinical, and less often, basic neuroscientific journals. The aim, of course, was to keep abreast of what others in the discipline have been working on and what trends one could perceive. Attention was not only paid to the content of the articles, but also to the design, results, and analysis, and whether the conclusions were sound. Also, those who had attended national meetings were required to report on a number of key papers for discussion. Each Journal Club lasted approximately 2 hours. Soft drinks, beer, and simple hors d'oeuvres were served. The atmosphere was relaxed and enjoyable. In the winter there was a fire in the fireplace, and the sense of tranquility reflected by the snow-covered lawn during the conversation made most feel very much at home. Unfortunately the Mideast oil embargo in the 1970s caused gasoline prices to soar, and for conservation reasons, we reluctantly moved these sessions onto campus.

Other traditional social get-togethers continue to be held at faculty homes. These include year-end holiday dinners for the staff and residents and their families, luncheons for the secretarial and technical staff, and a departmental cookout each summer. Everyone is invited, including children. There are volleyball games, water-skiing, swimming, canoeing, and relaxed visiting.

In 1959, just before Dr. Peyton's retirement, all of the former residents and their spouses returned for a reunion. It was a 2-day scientific and social occasion, which was the beginning of the William T. Peyton Society. Since then, we have had such meetings every fifth year. Now we have members all over the United States, some in Asia, Europe, and Latin America. Many members give a yearly contribution to the Peyton Fund, which is used for the residents' benefit, including funds for travel to national meetings. It is an excellent example of support of the next generation by those who have benefited in the past under similar circumstances.

At the annual meeting of the American Association of Neurological Surgeons, there is a reception sponsored by the department, using practice funds, for all members of the Peyton Society and other friends attending the meeting. The reception facilitates a great deal of reminiscence and nostalgia, as well as opportunities for new ideas and critical discussion.

Governance and leadership. Again, due to the relatively small number of faculty and residents, a sense of family prevails in the department. Communication occurs frequently and easily. However, faculty have at least two "business" dinners monthly, which usually take place before the Journal Club meetings. During these occasions, important departmental matters are discussed. Such items can be broadly grouped into graduate education, resident evaluation and rotation, medical student matters, ongoing and direction of research, professional and practice activities, matters relating to other departmental personnel, and fiscal considerations. An agenda is usually preset.

Other departmental meetings are held; the chief resident, who represents the resident group, participates in those meetings. In administrative areas, different faculty members have identified responsibilities, such as education, research, and fiscal concerns. Opinions are sought and a consensus reached. We seldom use the voting procedure. During my tenure, I chaired the meetings, and short but concise minutes were kept by one faculty member designated as the secretary. With faculty support, I could fully implement the decisions. Once in a great while, I chose to act contrary to the faculty position. In these instances, I took the time to explain to them why I did so, and usually I got their support.

Residents are asked to give their input twice per year regarding the quality and effectiveness of each faculty member as their mentors. They complete a form that asks residents to rate faculty based on a set of questions and to provide additional comments. This information is placed in each faculty member's file, and the information, positive or negative, is confidentially shared with each faculty member. We take the feedback from residents very seriously.

On the whole, the selection, education, counseling, and supervision of residents, patient care and research activities, as well as joint evaluation of residents by the faculty, take a great deal of time, particularly when disciplinary actions need to be taken. However, considering that each resident spends 6 years in the program and that there are 12 residents, the number of resident years under our guidance is daunting. It means that they put their trust in the faculty, not only regarding their training but also regarding the future of their careers, and the faculty need to respond to this trust very seriously, carefully, and with compassion. Junior faculty members also receive significant mentoring, review, and feedback. They are only a few years ahead of the residents in their careers.

•   •   •

A department and a training program are only as good as their products. Over the years we have trained close to 100 people. At the most recent count, we have produced 12 department chairpersons, and approximately 50% of the graduates have undertaken academic positions. Those who are in the private sector are successful as well, and many of them have assumed leadership roles in their own communities and nationally. The department has also consistently produced significant research and provided excellent clinical care.

In addition, the faculty work in an environment where work is enjoyable and is appreciated. They enjoy a fine reputation and are active nationally as well. They are reasonably well compensated financially, although quite a bit below the private sector level. Their additional rewards, though, include providing outstanding care, furthering knowledge, working with stimulating and appreciative colleagues, and the privilege and opportunity to mentor residents, which is always a stimulating, challenging, and satisfying encounter with excellent young people.

As in all units in academic health centers, the decline in research and education funding, the competitive environment in accessing patients, and always the shortage of space have been and will be major problems. Further explosions of technology will continue to add ethical dilemmas in patient care, as well as in research. Innovative planning is essential to resolve or diminish these difficulties.

Above all, I have viewed my job as that of ensuring an environment in which department members can continue to render excellent care, to educate students, residents and others, and to generate and communicate new knowledge. This proverbial three-legged stool is becoming increasingly difficult to balance. To make it work, we need sufficient resources, faculty with complementary talents, and a conducive departmental environment.

BIBLIOGRAPHY

1. Bowen WG & Sosa JA. (1989). *Prospects for faculty in the arts and sciences*. Princeton, NJ: Princeton University Press.
2. Clark SM & Lewis DR, eds. (1985). *Faculty vitality and institutional productivity: Critical perspectives for higher education*. New York: Teachers College Press.
3. Bowen HR & Schuster JH. (1986). *American processors: A national resource imperiled*. New York: Oxford University Press.
*4. Schuster JH & Wheeler DW. (1990). *Enhancing faculty careers: Strategies for development and renewal*. San Francisco: Jossey-Bass.
5. Grassmuck K. (1990). Some research universities contemplate sweeping changes, ranging from management and tenure to teaching. *Chronicles of Higher Education, 37*(2), A29-A31.
6. Seldin P. (1988). *Evaluating and developing administrative performance*. San Francisco: Jossey-Bass.
*7. Peters TJ & Waterman RH. (1982). *In search of excellence*. New York: Random House.
8. Kanter RM. (1983). *The change masters*. New York: Simon & Schuster.
9. Seldin P et al. (1990). *How administrators can improve teaching*. San Francisco: Jossey-Bass.
*10. Cresswell JW et al. (1990). *The academic chairperson's handbook*. Lincoln, Neb: University of Nebraska Press.
11. Tucker A. (1984). *Chairing the academic department: Leadership among peers*. New York: American Council on Education–Macmillan Publishing Co.
12. Morris VC. (1981). *Deaning: Middle management in academe*. Urbana: University of Illinois Press.
13. Fischer JL. (1984). *Power of the presidency*. New York: American Council on Education–Macmillan Publishing Co.
14. *Academic leader*. (1986). Madison, Wisc: Magna Publications, Inc.
15. *Administrator*. (1986). Madison, Wisc: Magna Publications, Inc.
16. Bland CJ & Schmitz CC. (1986, January). Characteristics of the successful researcher and implications for faculty development. *Journal of Medical Education, 61,* 22-31.
17. Wheeler D & Creswell J. (1985). *Developing faculty as researchers*. Paper presented at the Annual Meeting of the Association for the Study of Higher Education. Chicago, March 15-17, 1985.
18. Lewin K. (1958). Group decisions and social change. In EE Maccoby, TM Newcomb & EL Hartley, eds. *Readings in social psychology*. New York: Henry Holt, pp 197-211.

*Asterisk indicates an article or book that is particularly informative and helpful.

19. Corcoran M & Clark SM. (1984). Professional socialization and contemporary career attitudes of three faculty generations. *Review of Higher Education, 30,* 131-153.
20. Cameron SW & Blackburn RT. (1981). Sponsorship and academic career success. *Journal of Higher Education, 52,* 369-377.
21. Blackburn RT. (1979). Academic careers: Patterns and possibilities. *Current Issues in Higher Education, 2,* 25-27.
22. Lightfield ET. (1971). Output and recognition of sociologists. *American Sociologist, 6,* 128-133.
23. Cole S & Cole J. (1967). Scientific output and recognition: A study in the operation of the reward system in science. *American Sociological Review, 32,* 377-390.
24. Reskin BF. (1977). Scientific productivity and the reward structure of science. *American Sociological Review, 42,* 491-504.
25. Pelz DC & Andrews FM. (1966). *Scientists in organizations.* New York: John Wiley & Sons.
26. Braxton JM. (1983). Department colleagues and individual faculty publication productivity. *Review of Higher Education, 6,* 125-128.
27. Latham GP & Mitchell TR. (1976). *Behavioral criteria and potential reinforcers for the engineer/scientist in an industrial setting.* Washington, DC: American Psychological Association.
28. Stinchcombe AL. (1966, Winter). On getting "hung-up" and other assorted illnesses. *Johns Hopkins Magazine, 28,* 25-30.
29. Hargens LL. (1978). Relations between work habits, research technologies and eminence in science. *Sociology of Work and Occupations, 5,* 97-112.
30. Menkes JH. (1981). The physician-scientist: Past, present and future. *Johns Hopkins Medical Journals, 148,* 175-178.
31. Knorr K, Mittermeir R, Aichholzer G & Waller C. (1979). Individual publication productivity as a social position effect in academic and industrial research units. In FM Edwards, ed. *Scientific productivity: The effectiveness of research groups in six countries.* Cambridge, Mass: Cambridge University Press, pp 55-94.
32. Reif-Lehrer L. (1982). *Writing a successful grant application.* Boston: Science Books International.
33. Finkelstein M. (1984). *The American academic profession.* Columbus: Ohio State University Press.
34. Turney JR. (1974). Activity, outcomes, expectancies, and intrinsic activity value as predictors of several motivational indexes for technical professionals. *Organizational Behavior and Human Performance, 11,* 65-82.
35. Peters TJ & Waterman RH Jr. (1982; rev 1988). *In search of excellence: Lessons from America's best-run companies.* New York: Harper & Row.
36. Katz RL. (1978). Job longevity as a situational factor in job satisfaction. *Administrative Science Quarterly, 23,* 204-223.
37. Long JS & McGinnis R. (1981). Organizational context and scientific productivity. *American Sociological Review, 46,* 422-442.
38. Pellino GR et al. (1981). *Planning and evaluating growth programs for faculty.* (Monograph Series 14). Ann Arbor, Mich: Center for the Study of Higher Education.
39. Blackburn RT, Behymer CE & Hall DE. (1978). Research note: Correlates of faculty publications. *Sociology of Education, 51,* 132-141.
40. Long JS & McGinnis R. (1981). Organizational context and scientific productivity. *American Sociological Review, 46,* 422-442.
41. McGee GW & Ford RC. (1987). Faculty research productivity and intention to change positions. *Review of Higher Education, 11,* 1-16.
42. Perkoff GT. (1986). The research environment in family practice. *Journal of Family Practice, 21,* 389-393.
43. Bland CJ, Hitchcock MA, Anderson WA & Stritter FT. (1987). Faculty development fellowship programs in family medicine. *Journal of Medical Education, 62,* 632-641.
44. Fox MF. (1991). Gender, environmental milieu, and productivity in science. In H Zuckerman, JR Cote & JT Bruer, eds. *The outer circle: Women in the scientific community.* New York: WW Norton, pp 188-204.
*45. Bland CJ & Ruffin MT IV. (1992). Characteristics of a productive research environment: Literature review. *Academic Medicine, 67,* 385-397.

46. Bland CJ & Schmitz CC. (1988). Faculty vitality: Retrospect and prospect. *Journal of Higher Education, 59*, 190-224.

47. Bland CJ & Schmitz CC. (1990). An overview of research on faculty and institutional vitality. In JH Schuster & DW Wheeler, eds. *Enhancing Faculty Careers: Strategies for Development and Renewal.* San Francisco: Jossey-Bass, pp 41-61.

48. Pelz DC & Andrews FM. (1966). *Scientists in organizations: Productive climates for research and development.* New York: John Wiley & Sons.

49. Katz RL. (1976). Job longevity as a situational factor in job satisfaction. *Administrative Science Quarterly, 23*, 204-223.

50. Pineau C & Levy-Leboyer C. (1983). Managerial and organizational determinants of efficiency in biomedical research teams. In SR Epton, RL Payne & AW Pearson, eds. *Managing Interdisciplinary Research.* New York: John Wiley & Sons, pp 141-163.

*51. Baird L. (1986). What characterizes a productive research department? *Research in Higher Education, 25*, 211-225.

52. Kapel DE & Wexler N. (1970). Faculty attitude toward research in an emergent college. *Journal of Experimental Education, 38*, 44-47.

53. Drew DE. (1985). *Strengthening academic science.* New York: Praeger.

54. Bean JP. (1982, March). *A causal model of faculty research productivity.* Paper presented at the Annual Meeting of the American Educational Research Association, New York.

55. Barley ZA & Redman BK. (1979). Faculty role development in university schools of nursing. *Journal of Nursing Administration, 9*, 43-47.

56. Biglan A. (1973). Relationships between subject matter characteristics and the structure and output of university departments. *Journal of Applied Psychology, 57*, 204-213.

57. Smart JC & Elton CF. (1975). Goal orientations of academic departments: A test of Biglan's model. *Journal of Applied Psychology 60*, 580-588.

58. Creswell JW & Bean JP. (1981). Research output, socialization, and the Biglan model. *Research in Higher Education, 15*, 69-89.

59. Rice RE & Austin AE. (1988). High faculty morale: What exemplary colleges do right. *Change*, 50-58.

*60. Rice RE & Austin AE. (1990). Organizational impacts on faculty morale and motivation to teach. In P Seldin, ed. *How administrators can improve teaching: Moving from talk to action in higher education.* San Francisco: Jossey-Bass, pp 23-42.

61. Tierney W. (1987). Facts and constructs: Defining reality in higher education organizations. *Review of Higher Education, 11*, 61-73.

62. Pascale RT & Athos AG. (1981). *The art of Japanese management.* New York: Simon & Schuster.

63. Dill DD. (1982). The management of academic culture: Notes on the management of meaning and social integration, *Higher Education, 11*, 303-320.

64. Zisbet R. (1971). *The degradation of the academic dogma.* New York: Basic Books.

65. Pelz DC. (1967). Some social factors related to performance in a research organization. *Administrative Science Quarterly, 11*, 311-325.

66. Pettigrew AM. (1979). On studying organizational cultures. *Administrative Science Quarterly, 24*, 570-581.

67. Eisenberg J. (1990, April 6). Kennedy at Stanford's second century: Emphasis on teaching, streamlining. *The Stanford Daily, 197*, 1-2.

68. Sindermann CJ. (1985). *The joy of science: Excellence and its rewards.* New York: Plenum Press.

69. Andrews F, ed. (1979). *Scientific productivity: The effectiveness of research groups in six countries.* Cambridge, England: Cambridge University Press.

70. Schweitzer JC. (1980, July). *Personal, organizational and cultural factors affecting scholarly research among mass communication faculty.* Paper presented at the 71st Annual Meeting of the Association for Education in Journalism and Mass Communication, Portland, Oregon.

71. Kelly ME. (1986). Enablers and inhibitors to research productivity among high and low producing vocational educational faculty members. *Journal of Vocational Education Research, 11*, 63-80.

72. Birnbaum PH. (1983). Predictors of long-term research performance. In SR Epton, RL Payne & AW Pearson, eds. *Managing interdisciplinary research.* New York: John Wiley & Sons, pp 47-59.

73. Okrasa W. (1987). Differences in scientific productivity of research units: Measurement and analysis of output inequality. *Scientometrics, 12,* 221-239.

74. Bagenstos NT. (1988, April). *Preparing minorities and women as researchers: Have we learned anything?* Paper presented at the Annual Meeting of the American Educational Research Association, New Orleans.

75. Brief AP. (1984). *Productivity research in the behavioral and social sciences.* New York: Praeger.

76. Steiner GA, ed. (1965). *The creative organization.* Chicago, Ill: University of Chicago Press.

77. Kerr S. (1984). Leadership and participation. In AP Brief, ed. *Productivity research in the behavioral and social sciences.* New York: Praeger, pp 229-251.

78. Epton SR, Payne RL & Pearson AW, eds. (1983). *Managing interdisciplinary research.* New York: John Wiley & Sons.

79. Blau JR. (1976). Scientific recognition: Academic context in professional role. *Social Studies of Science, 6,* 533-545.

80. Aran L & Ben-David J. (1968). Socialization and career patterns as determinants of productivity of medical researchers. *Journal of Health and Social Behavior, 9,* 3-15.

81. Visart N. (1979). Communication between and within research units. In F Andrews, ed. *Scientific productivity: The effectiveness of research groups in six countries.* Cambridge, England: Cambridge University Press, pp 223-252.

82. Saxberg BO & Newell WT. (1983). Interdisciplinary research in the university: Need for managerial leadership. In SR Epton, RL Payne & AW Pearson, eds. *Managing interdisciplinary research.* New York: John Wiley & Sons, pp 202-210.

83. Finkelstein M. (1982, March). *Faculty colleagueship patterns and research productivity.* Paper presented at the annual meeting of the American Educational Research Association, New York.

84. Meltzer L. (1956). Scientific productivity in organizational settings. *Journal of Social Issues, 12,* 32-40.

85. Creswell JW. (1985). *Faculty research performance: Lessons from the sciences and social sciences.* Washington, DC: Association for the Study of Higher Education.

86. Braxton JM. (1983). Departmental colleagues and individual faculty publication productivity. *Review of Higher Education, 6,* 125-128.

87. Reskin BF. (1977). Scientific productivity and the reward structure of science. *American Sociological Review, 42,* 491-504.

88. Allison PD & Stewart JA. (1974). Productivity differences among scientists: Evidence for accumulative advantage. *American Sociological Review, 39,* 596-606.

89. Fulton O & Trow M. (1974). Research activity in American higher education. *Sociology of Education, 47,* 29-73.

90. Crane D. (1965). Scientists at major and minor universities: A study of productivity and recognition. *American Sociological Review, 30,* 699-714.

91. Astin HS. (1978). Factors affecting woman's scholarly productivity. In HS Astin & WZ Hirsch, eds. *The higher education of woman.* New York: Praeger, pp 133-157.

92. Blau PM. (1973). *The organization of academic work.* New York: John Wiley & Sons.

93. Harrington MS. (1987). Organizational characteristics of dental schools associated with research productivity. *Journal of Dental Education, 61,* 583–588.

94. Culpepper L & Franks PF. (1984). Family medicine research: Status at the end of the first decade. *Journal of the American Medical Association, 249,* 63-68.

95. Blackburn RT. (1979). Academic careers: Patterns and possibilities. In *Current issues in higher education.* Washington, DC: American Association for Higher Education, pp 25-27.

96. Smith SL, Baker DR, Campbell ME & Cunningham ME. (1985). An exploration of the factors shaping the scholarly productivity of social work academicians. *Journal of Social Service Research, 8,* 81-99.

97. Manis JG. (1951). Some academic influences upon publication productivity. *Social Forces, 29,* 267-272.

98. Jordan JM, Meador M & Walters S. (1988). Effects of department size and organization on the research productivity of academic economists. *Economics of Education Review, 7,* 251-255.

99. Wispe LG. (1969). The bigger the better: Productivity, size, and turnover in a sample of psychology departments. *American Psychologist, 24,* 662-668.

100. Smith C. (1970). Age of R and D groups: A reconsideration. *Human Relations, 23,* 81-96.

101. Smith CG. (1971). Scientific performance and the composition of research teams. *Administrative Science Quarterly, 16,* 486-496.

102. Latham GP & Wexley KN. (1981). *Increasing productivity through performance appraisal.* Reading, Mass: Addison-Wesley.

103. McKeachie W. (1979). Perspectives from psychology: Financial incentives are ineffective for faculty. In D Lewis & W Becker, eds. *Academic rewards in higher education.* Cambridge, Mass: Ballinger, pp 3-20.

104. McKeachie WJ. (1963). Faculty as a renewable resource. In Creswell JW, ed. *New directions for institutional research—measuring faculty research performance.* San Francisco: Jossey-Bass, pp 57-66.

105. Lewis DR & Becker WE, eds. (1979). *Academic rewards in higher education.* Cambridge, Mass: Ballinger.

106. Blackburn RT & Pitney JA. (1988). *Performance appraisal for faculty: Implications for higher education.* Ann Arbor: National Center for Research to Improve Postsecondary Teaching and Learning.

107. Gustad JW. (1960). *The career decisions of college teachers.* Washington, DC: US Department of Health, Education and Welfare.

108. Eckert RE & Stecklein JE. (1961). *Job motivations and satisfactions of college teachers: A study of faculty members in Minnesota colleges.* Washington, DC: US Government Printing Office.

109. Clark SM & Corcoran M. (1965). Individual and organizational contributions to faculty vitality: An institutional case study. In SM Clark & DR Lewis, eds. *Faculty vitality and institutional productivity: Critical perspectives for higher education.* New York: Teachers College Press, pp 112-138.

110. Levinson DJ, Darrow CM, Klein EB, Levinson MH & McKee B. (1976). Periods in the adult development of men: Ages 18 to 45. *Counseling Psychologist, 6,* 21-25.

111. Dill DD. (1986). Research as a scholarly activity: Context and culture. In Creswell JW, ed. *New directions for institutional research—measuring faculty research performance.* San Francisco: Jossey-Bass, pp 1-23.

112. Dill DD. (1986, April). *Local barriers and facilitators of research.* Paper presented at the annual meeting of the American Educational Research Association, San Francisco.

113. Dill DD. (1985). Theory versus practice in the staffing of R&D laboratories. *R&D Management, 15,* 227-241.

114. Zuckerman H. (1977). *Scientific elite: Nobel laureates in the United States.* New York: Free Press.

115. Thompson F & Zumeta W. (1985). Hiring decisions in organized anarchies: More evidence on entrance into the academic career. *Review of Higher Education, 8,* 123-138.

116. Helmreich R, Spence J, Beane W, Locker G & Matthews K. (1980). Making it in academic psychology: Demographics and personality correlates of attainment. *Journal of Personality and Social Psychology, 39,* 896-908.

117. Smelser JM & Content R. (1980). *The changing academic marketplace: General trends and Berkeley case study.* Berkeley: University of California Press.

118. French JRP & Raven B. (1959). The bases of social power. In DI Cartwright, ed. *Studies in social power.* Ann Arbor: Research Center for Group Dynamics—Institute for Social Research, University of Michigan, pp 150-167.

119. Bachman JG, Smith CG & Slesinger JA. (1966). Control, performance, and satisfaction: An analysis of structural and individual effects. *Journal of Personality and Social Psychology, 4,* 127-136.

120. Minckley BB & Punk SN, eds. (1981). *Creating research environments in the 1980s.* Indianapolis: Midwest Alliance in Nursing, Inc.

121. Hoyt DP & Spangler RK. (1979). The measurement of administrative effectiveness of the academic department head. *Research in Higher Education, 19,* 291-304.

122. Locke EA, Fitzpatrick NW & White FM. (1983). Job satisfaction and role clarity among university and college faculty. *Review of Higher Education, 6,* 343-365.
123. Bensimon EM, Neumann A & Birnbaum R. (1989). *Making sense of administrative leadership: The "L" word in higher education.* Washington, DC: Association for the Study of Higher Education.
124. Hoyt DP & Spangler RK. (1978). *Administrative effectiveness of the academic department head: Correlates of effectiveness.* Report of the Office of Educational Research. Manhattan, Kan: Kansas State University.
125. Hemphill JK. (1955). Leadership behavior associated with the administrative reputation of college departments. 3. *Educational Psychology, 46,* 385-401.
126. McCarthy MJ. (1972). *Correlates of effectiveness among academic department heads.* Report of the Office of Educational Research. Manhattan, Kan: Kansas State University.
127. Knight WH & Holen MC. (1985). Leadership and the perceived effectiveness of department chairpersons. *Journal of Higher Education, 56,* 678-690.
128. Skipper CE. (1976). Personal characteristics of effective and ineffective university leaders. *College and University, 51,* 138-141.
129. Fleishman EA & Harris ES. (1962). Patterns of leadership behavior related to employee grievances and turnover. *Personnel Psychology, 15,* 43-56.
130. Clark BR. (1987). *The academic life: Small worlds, different worlds.* Princeton, NJ: The Carnegie Foundation for the Advancement of Teaching, p 25.
*131. Zuckerman H, Cole JR & Bruer JT, eds. (1991). *The outer circle: Women in the scientific community.* New York: WW Norton.
132. Argyris C. (1968). On the effectiveness of research and development organizations. *American Scientist, 56,* 344-355.

&❧ Part Two ❧

_____

DEVELOPMENT

When a man knows he is to be hanged in a fortnight,
it concentrates his mind wonderfully.

SAMUEL JOHNSON

CHAPTER 4

Leadership in Academic Health Centers

Jill Ridky • George F. Sheldon

———————————— ૨ふ ————————————

Men made history and not the other way round. In periods where there is no leadership, society stands still. Progress occurs when courageous, skillful leaders seize the opportunity to change things for the better.

HARRY S TRUMAN

People cannot be managed. Inventories can be managed, but people must be led.

H. ROSS PEROT, Founder, Electronic Data Systems

Abigail Adams, in a 1790 letter to Thomas Jefferson, wrote, "These are hard times in which a genius would wish to live. Great necessities call forth great leaders." In the 1990s life in academic health centers calls for great leaders. AHCs are faced with volleys of budget reductions and fiscal, staffing, and resource constraints and severe cost containment measures. Profound changes will continue in academic health centers, and with these changes comes the moment for visionary leaders to look beyond today and to devise plans for tomorrow.

As faculty members develop, they often segregate into high-maintenance faculty and low-maintenance faculty. High-maintenance faculty are ones who require a considerable amount of the manager's time to keep them focused on their ultimate goal and development. High-maintenance faculty can develop a type of dependency that moves most of their problems into the leader's domain. Obviously, this can become counterproductive.

Paradoxically, low-maintenance faculty can be equally problematic. They may require or request very little time, and it is often tempting to allow that type of informal relationship to be the ongoing pattern. Frequently, however, such faculty members will come to a crisis point either in their career or in their own micro-organization, involving the chair of the department only at a point when the problems are quite advanced.

The following case highlights an example of a high-maintenance faculty in a department in an academic health center. It is a true situation, with details altered.

❧ Case Example

The pathology department at Charles University had a long history of being dysfunctional. While it had served the institution reasonably well, it usually was at cross purposes with parts of the organization. There had been instability within the faculty, with considerable faculty movement. The residents were of a variable quality, and the approach to the department, the university, the hospital, and indeed, the region was usually confrontational. The leadership patterns that had evolved in the organization were confrontational as well. Because of their extremely heavy workload, the faculty developed an internal group ethic that fostered the notion of "them against the institution."

Dr. Bak, the department chair, was a person of international distinction. His travel schedule, however, was such that he was infrequently available for the junior faculty. When he would return from national or international obligations, the complaints would be so severe that lengthy letters of complaint would be sent, with multiple copies distributed. This dysfunctional situation, as it reached the severely problematic point, was compounded by the abrupt resignation of Dr. Bak when he accepted appointment at a neighboring institution. The organization was additionally demoralized by several lawsuits and other problems.

The faculty of the group and the organization obviously were "high maintenance." They were disenfranchised from good feelings about themselves and about the institution. Clearly, while Band-aid types of approaches were taken to try to acculturate them to the organization, new leadership of a strong nature was required. A national search was undertaken, and when an outstanding individual was recruited the entire tone of the unit quickly changed. During the interim, however, as the national search was evolving, the group decided to cancel all student lectures so that they might go to a national meeting. When told that was unacceptable and that other ways of addressing the national meeting would have to be instituted, a near-rebellion occurred. The dean met with each member individually and let it be known that unwavering commitment to maintaining the student lectures/seminars that were scheduled would be insisted upon. The group balked further, and the dean held a meeting with the open group. That meeting was confrontational, but not hostile. The problem was eventually solved in the acute phase by allowing a face-saving maneuver, with partial coverage of the academic obligations by both the group and by someone external to the group. Clearly, however, the overall dysfunctional nature of the unit could only be solved by recruitment of new leadership to the unit. With this new leader in place, many of the problems have disappeared.

THE ROLE OF A LEADER

How do we begin to define the role of a leader in AHCs? Leaders are known for their ability to turn a dream, a vision of a desired state, into reality. The ability to do this requires the strong development of and willing cooperation from the human resources of the organization. Leaders must inspire followers to new levels of achievement by showing them how each individual's work contributes to a worthwhile end. Harry S Truman defined a leader as one who has the ability to get other people to do what they do not want to do—and like it.

The true leader does not see a need to merely perpetuate an existing set of regulations. Leaders are innovative, rely less on accepted principles, and, when necessity demands it, defy or question basic management tenents. As Abraham Zaleznik states, "Great leaders furnish not just vision but intellectual capital and ideas that work."[1] Consider the vision of David Sarnoff of RCA and Disney's Michael Eisner. Brilliant leadership and vision are just that—brilliant.

Leadership is one of those amorphous concepts, like *quality,* that can be defined in myriad ways. Many times the definitions of *leader* and *manager* are muddled together. However, leaders and managers, in the corporate world, have become increasingly separate with distinct functions. *Managers* plan, organize, allocate, and oversee within the organization's system; they work toward implementation and development of new policies and operating procedures. All of these functions ultimately produce improvements in the organization's productivity, effectiveness, and efficiency. Clark Kerr, lecturing at Harvard, noted that "the university has become the multiversity," where a *leader* must be "educator, wielder of power, pump . . . caretaker, inheritor, consensus seeker, persuader, bottleneck. But he is mostly mediator."[2]

In this chapter we will consider the characteristics of a leader and the challenges facing leaders in academic health centers today.

Speaking frankly, a number of us are worried about
a serious leadership vacuum.

LEADERS AND VISION

What are the leadership qualities needed to bring academic departments out from their current survival mode to increased levels of success and achievement? To lead an academic department today you must be a creative person, one who can decide and act, one who can operate a continuously learning organization. (The concept of the learning organization is discussed in more detail in Chapter 19.) You must have courage, and you must be able to stimulate, inspire, and motivate others. The leader must be a visionary able to master present challenges while planning growth for the future.

Developing vision is not something mysterious, just as developing good business direction is not magical. "Most discussions of vision have a tendency to degenerate into the mystical," Kotter notes.[3] "The implication is that vision is something mysterious that mere mortals, even talented ones, could never hope to have. But developing good business direction isn't magical. It is a tough, sometimes exhausting process of gathering and analyzing information. People who articulate such visions aren't magicians but broad-based strategic thinkers who are willing to take risks." To paraphrase Satchel Paige, academic leaders cannot afford to look back, since the future is increasingly gaining on all educational institutions. Successful programs must continue to be guided and nurtured with leadership. The leadership role and function is never done. Reverend William J. Rework, S.J., President at Santa Clara University, after a presentation on the facility and growth plans for the university, said, "Vision needs management, electricity and concrete. Grand dreams cannot become significant realities with élan alone. Leaders must have detailed plans. They must steer projects along the course, measure performance, raise funds, and take corrective action. Many conventional management practices are certainly useful. Yet there is an even more demanding leadership task if a person is to direct the course of action: The leader must model the way."[4]

LEADERSHIP STYLES

Within academic departments several types of leadership roles have emerged. The first is the academician, a full-time chair or faculty member whose primary responsibility is to direct a department, division, or program. The second type is an academician who is a part-time teacher, instructor, and/or researcher as well as part-time director of a program or department. In addition is the newer model of the full-time professional leader or manager without any primary commitments to clinical, educational, or research functions. All of these leadership models are functional, yet very different, especially in terms of the competencies required. Adequate professional and educational preparation and experience are required for each of these roles.

In Maccoby's *The Gamesman,*[5] four types of leadership styles are described that can be observed in the academic environment (Figure 4-1). First is the *spectator*. The spectator is a passive leader, one who does little, is nonactive, and places the majority of energy on trying to maintain a trouble-free environment. The spectator is typically the chair or director who turns power and decisions over to blue-ribbon task forces or committees. A second type is the *technician*. The technician is a loyal bureaucrat, an expert on rules, policy, and regulations. The technician focuses energy on operating the department within approved and accepted principles and procedures. A third type is the *jungle fighter*. This leader wants to move the department into the rankings, to be recognized as a top program. He or she is progressive and determined and may sometimes be referred to as the department's "two-ton gorilla." The jungle fighter is capable of vision and can be a great agent for change in the organization. A fourth type is the *gamesman*, a leader devoted to administration and the concept of improvement. This leader is a strategist with a leadership style that is strong but flexible. The gamesman tries to reduce the number of times the department's goals are perceived to be at odds with the institution's goals. This is accomplished by convincing others that everyone's best interests are served.

In reality, the chair or director in an AHC is typically a blend of these types at times. Each of these may be a valid style, but all types of leaders must guide their institutions to new levels of success and fulfillment. AHC leaders must not only understand the current operation and make appropriate revisions but must also develop a future vision. Leaders must correct inefficiencies, sometimes pursuing causes

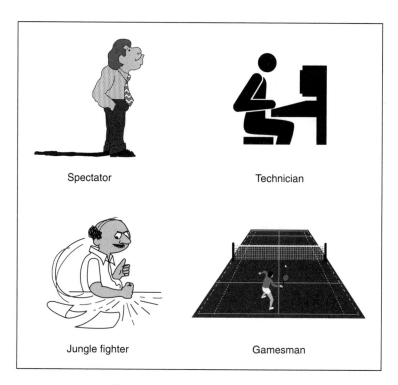

Figure 4-1. Four types of leaders.

that may be perceived as ruthless by those more comfortable with what is familiar and known, though possibly outmoded or inefficient. With internal inefficiencies exposed, previously hidden redundancies can also be eliminated as the program is streamlined.

THE CHALLENGES OF LEADERSHIP

Academic leaders of all types must continue to identify and eliminate system inefficiencies and programs that are no longer beneficial. However, the days of one leader who learned *for* the organization, like Ford's Henry Ford and IBM's Tom Watson, are gone. In an increasingly dynamic, interdependent, and unpredictable world, it is simply no longer possible for anyone to "figure it all out at the top." The old model, "the top thinks and the bottom acts," must now give way to integrating thinking and acting at all levels. All members must be encouraged to trust that their creative problem-solving efforts will be acknowledged and valued. While the challenge is great, so is the potential payoff. According to former Citibank CEO Walter Wriston, "The person who figures out how to harness the collective genius of the people in his or her organization is going to blow the competition away."[4] As will be discussed further in Chapters 6 and 19, the old hierarchical model in which the top leads and the bottom follows must now give way to leading and thinking throughout the organization.

The organizational challenge for academic departments today is to find innovative ways to evolve and make significant strides with cost-effective methods. The expectations on AHC leaders are high, and academic departments must present the leadership challenge to all organizational members, from faculty to residents, students, staff, and board members. Henry Kissinger faced this dilemma when he was Secretary of State. His solution: "We really cannot plan on having large numbers of brilliant people salted all across the state departments and embassies of the world. What we really need to do is figure out ways to make organizations work so that ordinary people can do extraordinary things." Leaders in academic organizations need to harness the collective energy and insight of organizational members to build shared vision. Leaders *became* leaders because they were acknowledged to be dynamic designers, creators, and teachers. It takes knowledge, expertise, and insight to have vision and courage to face difficulties despite doubt, the ability to say it isn't good enough, the ability to learn from losses. A clear vision is very important—it is a force. Kouzes and Posner state: "When leaders clearly articulate their vision for the organization, people report significantly higher levels of job satisfaction, commitment, loyalty, esprit de corps, clarity of direction, pride, and productivity. It is quite evident that clearly articulated visions make a difference."[4]

Being a *visible* leader is not easy; it is much easier to come to the office and stay behind a desk or in the office. It is tempting not to venture away from the safe and secure. The "paper chase" of management can seem never-ending, and the minutia of administrative detail can all too quickly absorb your energies, obscuring the needs of your faculty and staff. One solution is to employ the concept of "management by

```
                   THE PURPOSE OF MBWA

To find out what is going on
To find out what is bugging members
To find out about accomplishments and happenings and to celebrate
To convey your value set
```

walking around," also known by the acronym *MBWA* (see the box above). Peters and Austin observe, "The effective leader wanders, coaches, develops and engenders."[7] As you begin to walk around, you will quickly become an active listener, teacher, and facilitator, as shown in the following example.

⮞ Case Example

Dr. Janet Erickson, chair of the neurology department, walked over to her department's research area. In the process, she learned through various discussions of the urgent need for 250 square feet of research space in order to finalize a research study to provide preliminary data for an NIH grant. By the next day Dr. Erickson was able to allocate a laboratory temporarily for the study and to provide equipment support from a shared equipment laboratory. Dr. Michael Watts, clinical program director, utilized the MBWA concept in the pediatric clinic. During his MBWA he discovered an overfilled morning clinic, with irate parents and overactive children. In a quick session with his clinic manager, he discovered that the manager had already formulated a solution to the problem, which included turning an office/storage area into an extra examination room. Both suggestions would cut patient wait time and improve patient service—the manager was just waiting for approval to proceed with the plan. Leaders can relieve these crises on the spot, but only if they are *there*. MBWA is important, even if it consists of a 10-minute drop-in.

Managers and leaders in AHCs typically have overfilled daily agendas. They are attending to numerous administrative needs, "putting out fires," chairing meetings, recruiting, presenting at national meetings, and performing the countless other roles of chairs or directors (see Chapter 2). The overall success of MBWA depends on delegating some walking-around responsibilities to other members. Leaders must know what is going on and have sources that keep them well informed. The delegation must be to organization members who will not be "bulls in the china shop," doing more harm than good. The delegated individuals must be able to infuse programs, divisions, and clinics with the department's values. MBWA should be used to learn what is going on in the various offices, laboratories, and clinics, to learn what is bugging department members, to learn about accomplishments, organizational and professional happenings, to celebrate accomplishments, and to convey the organization's value set. You should be cautious, however, not to turn your

MBWA questioning into commands, because this is counterproductive, and members will begin to fear the MBWA approach. Organization members "require the freedom to try more things within the parameters of the vision."[7]

Leaders are also challenged to be counselors. According to Tom Peters and Nancy Austin, this means "caring enough to let someone know in a timely fashion when performance is off track. It takes self-confidence and skill to lead people to recognize problems as well as successes in a constructive way."[7] If a leader or manager in an AHC observes an organization member not performing up to the same level he or she once did or being an obstructionist rather than a service-oriented team player or a facilitator, it is cruel and unfair to the member that he or she be allowed to continue without counseling.

One of the keys to effective counseling is to know when to confront an organizational member. Peters and Austin give some guidelines for leaders in their book, *Passion for Excellence*. These are listed in the box below. Confrontation is one of the hardest leadership challenges, because most people wish to avoid conflict or disharmony. However, as a leader you must consider the negative impact on the organization if problems are not addressed in a timely fashion. "That's the crime of refusing to act, and act quickly," Peters and Austin note. "Nothing reduces the manager's credibility faster than the unwillingness to address an obvious problem. People rightly will ask, 'What in the hell is she or he waiting for?'"

You can avoid creating hostile or threatening confrontations and instead, arrange amicable meetings at which the problems and issues are reviewed and solutions and a plan for improvement are developed. The purpose of the meeting is for everyone to recognize that things are not going as well as expected and that a plan for change is required.

Leaders must build positive self-regard and demonstrate complete confidence in organizational members. Bennis and Nanus[8] report that "Coach John Robinson of the Los Angeles Rams said he never criticizes his players until they are convinced of his unconditional confidence in their abilities. After that is achieved, he might say, 'Look, what you are doing is 99% terrific, but there is that 1% factor that could make a difference.'"

It's possible to find numerous excuses for not initiating a counseling session. Excuses range from not having enough time today, to this is just not the right time,

---

WHEN TO COUNSEL ORGANIZATIONAL MEMBERS

When performance falls below expectations

If the member seems unhappy and unable to perform

When behavior is disrupting the team's performance

To review the consequences of continued inappropriate behavior or low performance

From Peters T & Austin N. (1985). *Passion for excellence*. New York: Random House.

to the member is not in a very important position and therefore the problem will not greatly affect the organization. However, all such counseling sessions are important and should be initiated as quickly as possible. Counseling, particularly in disciplinary matters, does not always end on an upbeat note. Try to find a positive comment to end with, and recognize that if the session allows the counseled individual to retain his or her dignity and self-worth, in the long run it will make that person's performance much better, ultimately benefitting the whole organization.

Leadership implies working with people to accomplish certain personal or organizational goals. The importance of a leader's diagnostic ability cannot be overemphasized. Edgar H. Schein expressed it well when he said that the successful manager and leader must be a good diagnostician and must value a spirit of inquiry. If the faculty and staff under the leader have varied abilities, they must be able to recognize and understand the differences. An organization will thrive and grow with leadership that recognizes talent, skills, and expertise.

COMPONENTS OF LEADERSHIP

There are many varied and important components to leadership (see the box below); some of the major components are highlighted as follows. The first is competence and credibility. The leader must be a competent and knowledgeable practitioner of the "heart" of the organization. The level of the organization's complexity will determine the knowledge required of the leader. The less complex the organization, the more readily the organization can accommodate a simpler form of leadership. On the other hand, an organization may have modest goals, but with proper leadership may have the potential to expand into different markets or offer expanded services. In AHCs, as in other parts of university management, familiarity and competence with the "delivery" end of the field add to the faculty and staff's support and willingness to follow. If you are willing to "get your hands dirty," you will find that faculty will expend the extra effort required for the department to excel.

The long-standing response to the question "How can the chair or director of an academic clinical department have time for clinical care as well as leadership?" has been "The head of General Motors doesn't work on the assembly line." In aca-

---

COMPONENTS OF LEADERSHIP

A leader has: Competence and credibility
                Accessibility
                Commitment
                Communications skills
                Awareness of the academic environment
                Vision

demic health centers, however, it might well be stated that front-line, in-the-trenches contact of a constant and continuing nature is one of the elements that keeps you informed and current as a leader, and what is perhaps even more important, keeps you credible and legitimate as a leader.

A second component of leadership is commitment, especially a commitment of time. You must be an example, a role model, and should stand ready to work harder and longer than other members of the organization. Department members will respond to your energy and drive in achieving organizational goals. Time commitment is one of the best statements of how a leader communicates values to the organization. Time spent in dealing with specific sets of problems or in accomplishing tasks communicates your values as a leader.

As leadership evolves in a dynamic organization, another component is delegation. Leaders may initiate or identify then delegate its implementation to another individual. Delegating is difficult for many leaders; it sometimes seems more efficient to simply do it yourself—and you are more certain that you will be satisfied with the result. Delegation is always a complicated process as individuals are selected to take on new responsibilities. Although you may not be pleased with a particular individual's initial performance, delegation is essential to free the leader to develop visionary new programs.

Another component of leadership is communication. When he placed the famous sign on his desk, "The buck stops here," President Harry S Truman communicated a definite message to his staff that he would act and take responsibility for his own actions and expected the same from his associates. Once plans and visions are formulated, communicating them is all-important. Unless everyone is clear about what the goals are, confusion will occur about how to implement them. One reason for the success of Japanese management has been managers' ability to communicate their belief in corporate decisions throughout the organization, so that everyone feels responsible and involved in carrying out the plan. As seventh-century Chinese sage Lao-Tzu said, "When the best leader's work is done, the people get on with their responsibility. This means making mistakes but in the process also letting people achieve." Lao Tzu also noted, "Fail to honor people, they fail to honor you; of a good leader, who talks little when his work is done, his aim fulfilled, they will all say, 'We did this ourselves.'"

Awareness of the environment is another component of leadership. Even those with great ambition, ability, energy, and vision need to "know the territory." The successful leader knows how to scan the environment and turn problems and challenges into opportunities. Leadership in complex organizations is said to be analogous to directing snow drifts by erecting fences: The leader can control neither the weather nor the road conditions, but by directing the placement of fences, he or she can shift the drafts and open avenues that would otherwise be blocked. In AHCs many of the departments (such as emergency medical services) or programs (such as magnetic resonance imaging, ultrasonography, and geriatrics) did not exist 15 years ago. Leaders must be bold and willing to explore and incorporate new technologies. Sticking to what you know, not venturing into the unknown, will not lead to fulfilling your promise as a leader. You must think innovatively, not merely falling back on what has succeeded in the past. As André Gide noted, "One doesn't discover new lands without consenting to lose sight of the shore for a very long time."

Finally, leaders must concentrate on when to react and what level of decision making is appropriate. Leaders in AHCs are faced daily with crises, many times with organizational members pushing leaders toward quick responses and action. But a leader cannot afford to always be in a reactive mode. He or she needs to be knowledgeable enough about the environment and organizational issues to know when an immediate proactive response is required, or whether it is best to wait, or whether it is best not to act or react at all.

🍂 Case Example

The director of the pediatric orthopedic program had recently been recruited by another institution. Dr. John Davidson, chair of pediatrics, was receiving concerned calls from institutional members regarding the recent decline in referrals to the pediatric orthopedic service. Colleagues were coaxing Dr. Davidson to take some type of immediate action to prevent any further decline from occurring. His colleagues believed referring physicians had been alerted to the departure of the director and were now referring cases to another institution. Dr. Davidson decided not to react immediately to the crisis situation his colleagues feared. As the department chair, Dr. Davidson was well aware that pediatric orthopedics had been a hallmark service over the past several years, with some tremendous volume increases. The service had increased to such a significant level that they were recently experiencing a leveling off of volume. Dr. Davidson believed the leveling off trend was the major factor responsible for the decline of referrals to the service, not the departure of the director. Dr. Davidson did decide, however, to take some corrective measures by corresponding with the referring physicians, introducing the new director of the service. In addition, the news bureau published an article on some of the advances utilized by the pediatric orthopedic service.

Leaders must develop the ability to know which occurrence is a crisis, which is important or critical. As Peter Drucker says, "Effective executives do not make a great many decisions. They concentrate on the important ones."[9]

LEADERSHIP PHASES

Every individual who has had an academic appointment has considered the potential of becoming a leader of one of the units or divisions of the department, or of filling other leadership roles in the institution. Many examine and reject such a role for reasons of their own, ranging from lack of interest to an unwillingness to devote the time required. Nevertheless, everyone in the organization probably has some understanding of the complexity of leadership. Once an individual has crossed the boundary to leadership, a variety of developmental stages will occur. These stages can be divided into several time periods.

The first is the honeymoon period, when individuals in the organization are attempting to determine what type of relationship they will have with the new leader. The new leader in turn is making a similar assessment, but usually with incomplete information about all aspects of the organization. Leaders should spend the honeymoon period wisely, because it will set the stage for the future. The honeymoon period is the ideal time for leaders to negotiate for needed resources. The honeymoon period presents a unique window of opportunity during which institutional members are willing to provide support quickly, and with a minimum of complexity or delay. For example, in the first year after Dr. Harvey Bohlen began as the new program director for periodontics, he requested and was granted additional clinical and research space. As the years went by, however, Dr. Bohlen discovered that his requests were far more difficult to have fulfilled than in early days. He felt fortunate to have made his needs known so early in his appointment.

During this period the new chair or leader will become acquainted with the people, resources, and potential goals of the organization and the potential impact that actions and new developments will have. They will also learn of hidden agendas and environmental resistance to change, of individuals who are threatened by new developments, and potential turf struggles and competition for resources. Sometimes an area that is obviously in need of development has not been completed because of some of these environmental factors and personalities. This means that the political process needs to be exerted before such projects can be completed. Inevitably, during the honeymoon period, problems will surface that were not anticipated when the new leader was recruited. Often as you begin to uncover the details of the new job, you may develop a certain defensiveness because you were not informed of some of the existing problems. It is best to have constructive discussions with the appropriate people as such unexpected issues surface. You can develop a "don't look back" attitude, working with the resources and problems as they are identified.

During the honeymoon period there are a number of areas where change may be useful; these should be examined and plans established. These include administrative structure, budget planning, teaching conferences, research goals, clinical program development and others. It can be productive to approach these with the faculty as if you were in a case study situation, thus not giving the impression that you are unilaterally imposing a whole new set of values and goals on the organization all at once. Often there will be a core of people whose values and energy will correlate with your own. If that is the case, these individuals will become instant allies in the development of the department.

The next phase is implementing the changes deemed appropriate. This may require some change in the physical plant, some remodeling, and some recruitment of personnel; thus a timeline and budgetary considerations must be evaluated. Furthermore, a period of time may be required during which other parts of the organization accept the advisability of implementing such a plan.

The next phase is development and recruitment. The recruitment/implementation phase evolves from the honeymoon period. Recruiting becomes one of the key duties of the leader; this is discussed in more detail in Chapter 9. Not surprisingly, when you talk to potential chairs or directors, one of their greatest concerns is their ability to recruit. When you have determined what areas are to be developed and what recruitment is necessary, then you move on to obtaining the resources, human and otherwise, to make the goal a reality. By the time this is initiated, all of the objections should have surfaced and been dealt with as successfully as possible. Sometimes members of the organization will not be supportive; nevertheless, you must move ahead with the implementation with an expectation that support from the institution will come later. Obviously, however, it is preferable to gain the support early on rather than at a later stage.

PREPARING FOR THE LEADERSHIP ROLE

How can you prepare for a leadership role in an academic environment? There are some academic management programs at universities targeted at health professionals who seek roles as effective managers and leaders; these are primarily for those who serve both as full-time administrators and full-time clinicians. One program, based at the University of Wisconsin–Madison, is linked to the American College of Physician Executives. The Association of American Medical Colleges has offered excellent executive management programs for many years. Some persons interested in academic medical leadership have elected to earn a master's degree in business administration (MBA).

Depending on an individual's interests and directions, there will be differences in the specific bodies of knowledge needed to prepare for leadership. It is important to gain and maintain a fundamental understanding of a constellation of subjects bearing on academic health issues; one must be able to read the literature of each field and know its major contributors. Topics of importance to the academic leader include macroeconomics of health, health policy, managerial accounting and financial management, health law, organizational behavior, group dynamics, negotiation and communication methods and skills, decision analysis, quality assessment, statistics and clinical epidemiology, values and bioethics, medical informatics, strategic planning, and marketing.

In addition to gaining academic experience and building a body of knowledge, you should welcome any leadership opportunities that present themselves—learning to chair committees, set agendas, work with and through others, and cultivating your listening and speaking skills. Developing pilot projects and, later, large permanent projects within an AHC yields invaluable experience about the ease or difficulty of academic management.

Leaders can be effective only if their efforts are viewed as moving the organization forward. If their own ego needs are such that they accept credit for every accomplishment within the organization, then ultimately their leadership will be less effective. Similarly, while visibility is useful in some regards, a leader can become so "high profile" that the entire organization is functioning in a fishbowl. If an objective or goal can be accomplished without too much visibility, that is preferable—unless visibility is essential to achieving the goal, as with striving for increased funding based on the results of important research findings by a department member. The most effective, sustained progress for the department should be manifest as a series of accomplishments by individual members or the organization rather than as a special accomplishment credited to the leader.

BIBLIOGRAPHY

*1. Zaleznik A. (1989, July 24). Managerial mystique—so many managers, so few leaders. *Business Week.*

2. Kerr C. (1963). *The uses of the university.* The Godkin lectures. Cambridge, Mass: Harvard University.

3. Kotter JP. (1990, May-June). What leaders really do. *Harvard Business Review,* p 105.

*4. Kouzes JM & Posner BZ. (1987). *The leadership challenge.* San Francisco: Jossey-Bass.

5. Maccoby M. (1977). *The gamesman.* New York: Simon & Schuster.

6. Senge PM. (1990, Fall). The leader's new work: Building learning organizations. *Sloan Management Review.*

7. Peters T & Austin N. (1985). *Passion for excellence.* New York: Random House.

*8. Bennis W & Nanus B. (1985). *Leaders: The strategies for taking charge.* New York: Harper & Row.

9. Drucker P. (1967). *The effective executive.* New York: Harper & Row.

10. Hershey P & Blanchard K. (1982). *Management of organizational behavior: Utilizing human resources.* Englewood Cliffs, NJ: Prentice-Hall.

ADDITIONAL RESOURCES

Badaracco JL Jr & Ellsworth RR. (1989). *Leadership and the quest for integrity.* Boston: Harvard Business School Press.

Bolman LG & Deal TE. (1988). *Modern approaches to understanding and managing organizations.* San Francisco: Jossey-Bass.

Cohen MD & March JG. (1986). *Leadership and ambiguity* (ed 2). Boston: Harvard Business School Press.

*Creswel JW, et al. (1990). *The academic chairperson's handbook.* Lincoln: University of Nebraska Press.

*Detmer DE & Noren JJ. (1981). An administrative medicine program for clinician-executives. *Journal of Medical Education, 56,* 640-645.

Kellerman B. (1984). *Leadership: Multidisciplinary perspectives.* Englewood Cliffs, NJ: Prentice-Hall.

*Tucker A. (1992). *Chairing the academic department: Leadership among peers.* New York: Macmillan.

Williams AP Jr, et al. (1987, October). Managing for survival: How successful academic medical centers cope with harsh environments. The Rand Corporation, R-3495-HHS.

*Asterisk indicates an article or book that is particularly informative and helpful.

CHAPTER 5

Organizing for Effectiveness

Jill Ridky • Richard S. Blackburn

We must all hang together, or assuredly we shall all hang separately.

BENJAMIN FRANKLIN

All academic health centers attempt to gain results through people; people are the quintessential resource for the successful accomplishment of objectives and for the efficient use of resources. C.I. Bernard maintains, "Essential to the survival of an organization is the willingness to cooperate, the ability to communicate and the existence and acceptance of purpose."[1] Organizational design is a decision process to bring about a coherence between the goals or purposes for which the organization exists. How can AHCs optimally mobilize human resources and energy to achieve the organization's mission and at the same time maintain a viable, growing organization of people?

The changes within AHCs over the past decades have been breathtaking. They have progressed to professionally staffed organizations with impressive programs, departments, and centers. The AHC is an organization of people serving and producing for people. But how should academic health centers be designed? What are work teams? What is the role of team leaders? How can they evaluate effectiveness?

Human resources, faculty, students, and staff should be organized in such a way as to enable them to make the maximum possible productive contribution. Organizational members must know what is expected of them in advance and in detail, through a clear communication of expectations. Anthony and Herzlinger note, "If the facilities and personnel are available to provide a service, and they are not used, the revenue from that capability is lost forever."[3] Most AHC managers have encountered the staff member who reports to work but does not produce and the staff member who becomes incompetent in order to be shielded from additional responsibilities. Human potential needs to be considered. "If you place individuals into a rational system and give them some understandable signals, you can effectively utilize this resource. It is a shame to waste it."[3]

But how do we know if our organizational members are productive? As Peter Drucker observes, "Most of American management and practically all of our public

Good morning, human resources!

organizations pay no attention to white collar productivity. For the rest of the century and far into the next one, the competitive battle will be won or lost by white-collar productivity."[4] Few managers, however, seem concerned with this issue; the excuse is, "No one knows how to measure it."[4] Chapter 15, Understanding the Numbers, outlines some instruments and trends for managers to develop and review. The results of the reviews will allow you to identify any shortfalls or ineffectiveness and whether your organization is losing or gaining ground. A competitive advantage for AHCs lies in making productive one of its abundant resources—people—people with long years of academic study and experience.

What is a productive organizational size, given an organization's goals and mission? How many levels or layers of management are needed for a given output? Should the levels of management increase with an increase in the volume of service? How should the organization be designed to promote efficiency and productivity?

There is a growing tendency to eliminate the extensive organizational structures bloated with redundant groups and middle management. In addition to being too costly, this situation means that most managers really do not know what is going on, because they are so far removed from the action. All AHCs need to keep pace and to carry out new and special projects, but this can often be accomplished with a much smaller group. You should be alert to the numerous structures and hierarchies that may be found in AHCs and to the possibility of multiple hierarchies within "single organizations."

❧ Case Example

The Department of Family Practice at the University of Tulsa Medical Center operated for decades with an ambulatory care practice at the Family Practice Center. In recent years, however, the program, in order to develop its services and its educational dimensions, expanded the ambulatory care practice to four separate clinical locations.

Julie Kennedy, R.N., the practice's clinic manager for the past 8 years, recently resigned to accept a career advancement opportunity. The program director, Dr. Tapp, found it timely to examine the clinic's organizational structure before recruiting to fill the position.

After the review, Dr. Tapp developed two organizational options. One was to recruit a replacement for Julie Kennedy who would have management responsibility for all four clinics. Another option was to decentralize and to appoint a nurse clinic manager for each site and to eliminate Julie's position. Dr. Tapp's review of the clinics found that it was getting difficult for Julie to manage all four clinics from a distance. Her position had evolved to that of a middle manager. If a clinic had a problem, they would contact Julie, who then would review the problem with Dr. Tapp and the newly formed family practice ambulatory care committee. Dr. Tapp believed the decentralized option would eliminate a middle manager position and each location would designate a nurse as the manager. The four nurse managers would work together on staffing and coverage needs. Any problems that could not be resolved by the nurse managers would be relayed to Dr. Tapp to be discussed and resolved at the monthly committee meeting. Dr. Tapp and the committee favored the decentralized option.

After the plan was implemented they also found the decentralized option to be less costly, since it eliminated a position, and on-site management was greatly improved. For example, the on-site managers were keenly aware of patient wait time and made suggestions for patient scheduling and room utilization. The four nurse managers have worked well together as a team and facilitate staffing rotations, which has reduced the budget line for nursing temps. In addition, the nurse managers have presented plans for improvements and openly share problems with Dr. Tapp and the committee.

Hierarchical organizational charts are still commonplace in academic health centers (Figure 5-1; see also Figures 2-1 and 2-2). This is a classic structure of bureaucracy that Max Weber (1946) discussed in his essays. Weber delineated what he considered to be the distinctive features of bureaucracies: division of labor and hierarchy of authority such that each official has one and only one superior. Originally hierarchies were formulated because no alternative ways had been discovered during the industrial era to cope with the problems of organizing large numbers of people to perform complex tasks to produce goods and services efficiently. The organizational structure considered to be appropriate was the pyramid, in which power and authority reside at higher levels. The pyramid design was accepted not on the basis of scientific theory but on some very bold propositions, such as: most persons lack expertise and experience and must be directed by the "top few"; most persons will expend the least amount of effort; and procedures should be developed by the top few. Drucker believes that multiple levels of management and staff place an overall drag on the effectiveness of the organization. Peters and Waterman, in

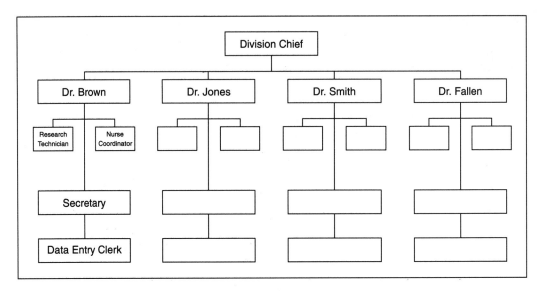

Figure 5-1. A representative hierarchical staff structure.

In Search of Excellence, found "less obvious structure and layering at the excellent companies."[5] Excessive layering can ultimately produce a slow-moving, rigid organization that cannot function in a changing and unstable environment. Layering also can complicate the communication flow and discourage fluidity and flexibility.

There are many types of organizational design options—hierarchical, matrix, spherical (see Figures 5-2 and 5-3). Whatever design is selected, AHCs require a functional design for achieving specific organizational objectives. The design should place human resources in a composite that eliminates the role of the subordinate and promotes the role of all individuals working together. The design should not stifle innovation or cause stagnation; the design should be flexible and responsive. As John Millet stated, "Management should be achieved not through a structure of subordinations of persons and groups, but through a group dynamic work consensus."[6]

DEVELOPING WORK TEAMS

One approach to developing individuals working together is the concept of *work teams.* Many studies have concluded that staff members work harder and more diligently in small teams than by themselves. Rosabeth Moss Kanter, a Harvard professor, reported in her book, *The Change Masters,* that "The few projects in my study that disintegrated did so because the manager failed to build a coalition of supporters and collaborators."

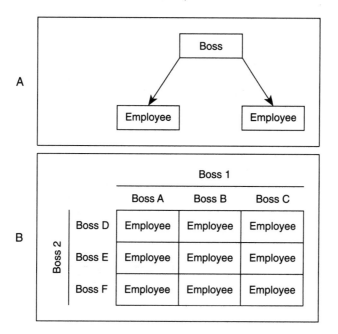

Figure 5-2. **A,** Hierarchical and **B,** matrix organizational designs.

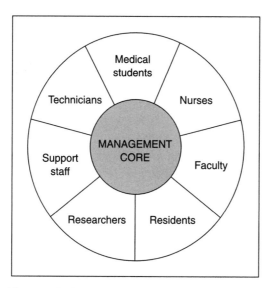

Figure 5-3. The spherical organizational design.

Over time, many AHCs have assembled too many committees and task forces that have not been as productive or effective as expected. This rather limited record with successful committees now causes management to associate the suggestion of developing work teams with further delays, and nonproductive or ineffective efforts. Before establishing a team, you must decide whether the issue or problem at hand really requires a team. If the problem is best served by the attention of a single experienced and knowledgeable organizational member, then the manager should assign resolution of that problem to that individual. Although teams, if developed appropriately, can be very effective, they can also be expensive in terms of the time and effort needed. Think of some AHC committees with five or more faculty members devoting time and effort at salary levels greater than $90,000. Hershey and Blanchard note, "Meetings are costly in terms of people's time (a 2½-hour meeting of eight people consumes 20 person hours, the equivalent of half a work week."[8] It is easy for AHCs to assemble very expensive teams; this point needs to be noted and the individual assignment method utilized whenever appropriate.

Although an individual assignment to issues should be employed, the nature and objectives of AHCs are usually accomplished by working with other organizational members. Most of the work in AHCs is conducted with multispecialty teams rather than individuals. In the day-op or operating room, for example, the clinical mission is accomplished by a team of nurses, technicians, surgeons, anesthesiologists, and others. Likewise, medical students are educated and trained by teams of residents and clinical and research faculty.

Team spirit can create organizational solidarity and the willingness of all members to participate in goal setting. When organizational members work within a group, their attitudes and behaviors result from two different sets of motives. Each group evaluates its own performance and will tend to view the results not as another piece of interesting information but as a source of satisfaction or dissatisfaction that should not only promote workers' involvement but also lead to better communication, feedback, and discussions on ideas for improvements. Team building should promote group success and provide organizational members with success experiences. Many studies have also revealed that organizational members are more productive in smaller groups because they feel as though they are an important part of the organization and that they are in control of their destiny. As Deal and Kennedy maintain, "Small is beautiful, small and semiautonomous, because it best serves not just the needs of the organization, but also the needs of the people."[9]

Especially in the knowledge-creating organization, which will be discussed in Chapter 19, teams are important because they provide a mechanism for organizational members to interact with each other and engage in an ongoing dialog of issues, which makes the organization more effective. New and different views are presented through communication and dialog. Information may be pooled and examined much like a Rubic's cube for new angles and ideas. This dialog can sometimes involve considerable conflict and disagreement; however, it is this type of conflict that will lead organizational members to question existing premises and view problems and issues in a new way. This creates a fine line for management: too much conflict or disagreement can be counterproductive; not enough, and beneficial changes will not happen.

One of the keys to teamwork is for the group or groups to understand and share the team's mission goals and objectives. As Jon Katzenbach and Douglas Smith, authors of *The Wisdom of Teams,*[10] stress, teams are a means to an end, an accomplishment greater than individual organizational members could have achieved independently. Teams require a meaningful purpose that will provide the proper direction, energize the group, and enable them to develop the commitment required. When goals are established for teams they should be specific and reasonable—such as discharging patients by noon every day, answering all referring physician calls within 10 minutes, or applying for an NIH grant within the first quarter of the fiscal year. These specific goals, rather than vague ones such as "improve patient discharges," "improve referring physician response time," or "increase NIH research proposals," are essential. Such specific goals provide a tangible target and focus for the team.

Productive teams must also be recognized and rewarded. Every accomplishment should be recognized. The entire organization should be made aware of significant accomplishments and successes via departmental newsletters, division chiefs or faculty/staff meetings, or postings on bulletin boards. Other forms of recognition include official letters, simple handwritten notes, or verbal praise. Team recognition will also improve the group's cohesion, since organizational members will want to be associated with a "can-do" team. In addition to team recognition, the department program or institution should also be recognized.

THE ROLE OF THE TEAM LEADER

Team leaders are selected and developed to recognize, unify, maximize, and focus the expertise and talents of team members. The team leader and members will attempt to transform the organization's vision into a reality. The team leader must be empowered—and be viewed by the team as empowered—to make significant decisions within the department structure that relate to team functioning.

In all AHCs one finds members with a wide variety of personalities, characteristics, strengths, and weaknesses. In recruiting team members, the team leader should consider candidates who have the best blend of talents and expertise. It is only natural to want to recruit team members who will be compatible and contribute to team harmony. However, successful teams contain some level of conflict. A "healthy" level of conflict can have a galvanic effect on team members, leading to innovative and creative thinking and accomplishments.

What is important is not for the team to share common personality traits but common goals and objectives. According to Hershey and Blanchard, "It is often more appropriate for managers to recruit team members who can compensate for areas in which there are shortcomings rather than to surround themselves with team members who are alike."[8] The team leader should also promote feedback. Both team and leader will learn and grow from continuous feedback and evaluation. Leaders should encourage team members to "tell it like it is."

Another role of a team leader is to understand the types of team roles. Within teams, a leader must be able to understand the roles of task and maintenance. Every team is focused not only on getting the job done (*task*), but also on continuing as a viable group (*maintenance*). The team leader must determine early on the nature of the group. Is the team a high-maintenance group, requiring much direction and support from the team leader? Is the group task-oriented, or completely focused on the tasks assigned? Or is the group floundering, not accepting tasks or maintenance activities and thus not being effective? In this role team leaders can be very important in moving the group toward being a team in which they focus on the task and on team cohesiveness.

Dysfunctional organizations are found to have inflexible organizational members, hierarchical structure, divided allegiances, poor quality standards, and a lack of purpose, goals, or a driving force. On the other hand, functional organizations exist with working team members who are flexible and who understand and are committed to the organization's goals, objectives, and mission. Once AHCs have a workable organizational design and have developed the team approach, how can they evaluate the level of their organizational effectiveness?

EVALUATING EFFECTIVENESS

Dr. Jane Wooten was appointed chair of the dermatology department 2 years ago. The appointment was for a 5-year term and required a review and recommendation for reappointment at the end of the fifth year. Dr. Wooten wanted to be reappointed but was concerned about assessing her department's accomplishments at the end of her fifth year. In her role as chair, how should Dr. Wooten conduct her evaluation of the performance of the department of dermatology?

Just as it is difficult to conduct staff, resident, and faculty evaluations, there are equal difficulties in evaluating organizations. What should be the basis for such a departmental evaluation? The number of patient visits? The number of patient referrals? The number of research grants? A positive year-end budget balance? These data may be useful and over time could provide useful information about performance trends. They would also be useful in making departmental comparisons. However, information of this sort does not always correlate positively with the effectiveness of the department. For example, a department could treat large numbers of patients, but large numbers may mean that each individual patient is not receiving high-quality care. Or a year-end budget deficit for a department with a low year-end collection rate might lead a review committee to believe the department was ineffective. However, what the committee might fail to appreciate is that three nationally prominent faculty members were successfully recruited by the department. The recruitment required a substantial monetary investment from the department, yet the faculty members have already attracted a number of new referring physicians. The collection rate is also low as a result of the increase in charges generated by these new patients and the usual delay in payment.

Although the department of dermatology may have closed its books with a year-end deficit, the chair was actually investing in the future of the department. In fact, the deficit could have been greater had the chair not actively managed the clinical budget and used other funding sources for recruitment and development expenses. On the other hand, the fiscal performance of another academic clinical department might look extremely good for a particular year. But did the chair defer some important and needed expenditures to the next fiscal year, creating unnecessary levels of stress among employees and subsequent high levels of turnover? It should be clear that financial measures alone should not be the sole indicators of how well a department is doing.

It might be useful to distinguish between *organizational efficiency,* which means operating a department with minimal resources, and *organizational effectiveness,* which means accomplishing the organization's objectives, regardless of resource usage. Thus an important question becomes: What criteria should an academic health organization use to determine its level of performance? Given the preceding discussion, some suggested criteria might be level of staff morale, employee stability, goal consensus and accomplishment, extent of participative decision making, turnover rate, rate of growth, and quality of planning and goal setting. It should be clear from this discussion that focusing on the bottom line issues of a work unit's performance may yield an overly narrow assessment and not provide an adequate picture of what is going on behind the numbers.

MODELS OF ORGANIZATIONAL EFFECTIVENESS

Over the years experts have developed several models that can provide an academic health center manager with a variety of perspectives with which to evaluate his or her organization's effectiveness. The *systems resource* model emphasizes the organization's ability to obtain resources from important sectors of the environment. Thus the extent to which an AHC can acquire faculty and staff, monetary support, necessary capital equipment and space, and patients would reflect its effectiveness from this perspective. While such an analysis may provide useful information, simple acquisition of resources tells a unit manager little about how or how well these resources are being used to accomplish the organization's goal.

For this reason, the chair or program director might also want to evaluate the unit's effectiveness by using the *internal process* approach. This model suggests an examination of the processes by which the unit's inputs are used to accomplish the unit's goals. Measures of effectiveness from this perspective might include employee satisfaction levels, quality of decision making, communication, conflict management systems, and/or equipment or space utilization rates. Evaluating a unit's effectiveness solely with this model can also be deceiving, however, particularly if the processes employed are directed at inappropriate goals or outcomes. To ensure that this does not happen, many organizations evaluate their effectiveness from the perspective of goals they would like to achieve. The *goal-centered* model recommends the evaluation of the organization's ability to meet its various goals. By definition, the better an organization can accomplish its goals, the more effective it is. In the AHC such goals might be educational (such as achieving accreditation for a residency program) or clinical (such as establishing a transplantation program). This model can be useful if managers can identify important goals and can assess the extent to which those goals have been achieved. Of course, when used in isolation, such a perspective of effectiveness does not address the ways in which certain goals were pursued or achieved, leading to some of the distortions in evaluation described when only financial goals are used to assess unit effectiveness.

Finally, a fourth approach suggests that an AHC's effectiveness might be best evaluated by seeking input from *strategic constituencies* served by the unit. These important sectors of the environment could include internal units with which the focal department interacts as well as important external organizations. Thus evaluations of the unit could be sought from patients, suppliers, laboratories, employees, regulators, legislators, administrators, and so on. Such an approach is particularly appropriate if the unit's survival depends on the favorable evaluation of the unit by these significant players.

Given the strengths and weaknesses inherent in each of these approaches, it is preferable that AHC managers develop multiple effectiveness criteria from each of these four perspectives. This *combination model* should provide a more well-rounded picture of the center's performance—assuming, of course, that the individual or body interested in the center's performance has not already expressed a strong preference for one particular approach to evaluation. Even if such was the case, the knowledgeable manager would still want to develop these multiple criteria for internal analysis.

A somewhat more sophisticated model of organizational effectiveness takes a diagnostic approach. Applicable for use within any of the models discussed above, this model assumes that an organization's evaluation will be adequate and accurate only when certain decisions about evaluation are made in advance of the actual evaluation process. The box on p. 87 lists six diagnostic questions that a manager should answer in advance of the actual evaluation.

Answering the first question makes clear the objective, activity, or set of activities to be evaluated at any one time. This knowledge ensures an appropriate focus for the evaluation efforts and eliminates the generic evaluation effort.

AHC leaders must determine the focus of the evaluation of their organization. The answer to the second question determines whether the evaluation's focus should be on internal performance measures, external evaluations by key constituents, or both. Deans, vice-chancellors, chairs, and so on may be interested in the internal performance of a particular academic health center. Externally, regulatory boards such as the Residency Accreditation Program, Joint Commission on Accreditation of Healthcare Organizations (JCAHO), and the Graduate Medical Education Council could be interested in very different indicators of a center's effectiveness.

Answers to the third question identify the levels at which effectiveness should be assessed—individual, group, divisional, or departmental. Information at each of these various levels provide differing snapshots of how well a work unit may be functioning. Effectiveness at one level may not reflect effectiveness at another level. Finding strong group performance, but at the cost of individual morale, provides a different picture of effectiveness than if only group performance had been examined. Similarly, high levels of individual performance may not translate into high levels of group performance if group cohesiveness is low and group interactions are required. In addition, measuring individual performance requires criteria and techniques other than those for assessing departmental or divisional performance.

The fourth question seeks identification of the time frame for determining effectiveness. American managers have generally been chastised for their fixation on

---

EVALUATING ORGANIZATIONAL EFFECTIVENESS: QUESTIONS PRIOR TO EVALUATION

1. Which major organizational objectives should be the focus of the evaluation?
2. What perspective should be taken?
    Internal?
    External?
    Both?
3. At what level should effectiveness be assessed?
    Individual?
    Divisional?
    Departmental?
    Combination?
    All levels?
4. What time frame should be used?
    Short-term (weekly, monthly, quarterly, annually)?
    Mid-term (1–2 years)?
    Long-term (5 years)?
    Some combination?
5. What kind of information about organizational effectiveness should be used in the evaluation?
    Subjective?
    Objective?
    Both?
6. What standards should be used to determine the level of organizational effectiveness?
    Comparisons with other comparable departments?
    Norms or "ideals" established internally or externally?
    Organizational goals?
    Improvements over time?
    Organizational traits?
    Some combination?
    All of the above?

quarterly earnings. AHC managers must make similar decisions about the length of time over which effectiveness would be assessed. For example, budget performance may be evaluated on a quarterly, semiannual, annual, or biannual basis. Turnover may be examined on a monthly basis. Individual performance might be evaluated annually, while the success of capital expenditures may require a longer-term time perspective.

The fifth question focuses on the type of information that will form the basis for an evaluation. Subjective information can be gathered from employees, other chairs, key administrators, or key constituency representatives on their *perceptions* of how well the organization is doing in certain areas. Objective information uses data gathered from departmental records or from reports available outside the organization (for example, residency program committees). It must be remembered, however, that just because data are reported numerically does not necessarily mean these "objective" data are more "valid" than perceptual data.

An answer to the sixth and final question is essential to provide a context for the results of an evaluation process. If an academic health department manager argues that his or her department is effective, this begs the question, "Effective relative to what?" The standards against which performance will be compared must be made known. Absent such knowledge, an assertion of effectiveness is meaningless. To assist with this process, there are five bases for making effectiveness evaluations.

Comparison. Results from one academic organization can be compared with results from a similar organization. Caution must be exercised using a comparative standard to ensure that apples are not being compared to oranges. AHCs are complex structures, and their organizational structures and modes of operation can vary widely. Comparative evaluations are beneficial only when the organizations function in a similar environment with similar measurement and reporting procedures. If these similarities are not present, comparative judgments are inappropriate.

Norms. Rather than comparing the performance of two organizations, results can be compared with some "ideal" level of performance established by top management or with performance norms developed by regional or national health care associations. This "ideal" standard reduces the need to gather information about other academic organizations—which is sometimes difficult to obtain. Of course, using norms as a basis for determining the effectiveness of a unit requires an academic manager to utilize a "realistic" norm. Using regional or national norms as a basis is relatively easy as long as the apples-and-oranges issues are not ignored.

Goals. The extent to which an organization achieves its predefined goals is another option for determining the level of effectiveness. This standard was discussed in some detail earlier.

Improvement. A work unit's own performance at some previous time can also serve as the basis for comparison, particularly the extent to which there was improvement in performance over that period. This approach assumes that measurement procedures are comparable at the different points in time and that *how* such improvement was achieved is not of primary importance.

Trait. The trait perspective requires managers of academic organizations to identify and then measure organizational success on the basis of an accomplishment of some set of important traits. For example, an academic organization that is innovative, creative, frugal, or flexible could be defined as effective. The difficulty with using this particular standard is developing instrumentation that allows for the valid assessment of these traits.

· · ·

The use of this diagnostic evaluation process should allow top managers to select the particular evaluation approach best suited to their academic organization. The model chosen by an academic organization, department, or program will most likely depend on the major mission areas of the organization, the extent to which internal and external constituencies are important, and the ease with which information can be gathered, processed, and reported.

As an academic organization evolves, so will management's need to develop approaches to evaluating effectiveness. With a new program or newly founded department, the approach to effectiveness may focus more on resource development and goal-centered approaches. As the academic organization matures and experiences growth and increased environmental complexity, the strategic constituencies approach may be added to the evaluation mix. In fact, where an academic organization is in its development will likely influence the nature of the responses to the six diagnostic questions. Choice of focus, points of view, levels of analysis, timeframes, data type, and standards can change as an organization becomes more mature and complex.

In the end, managers must realize that like art, the judgment of organizational effectiveness lies in the eye of the beholder. The key message to understand is that like individual performance, organizational effectiveness and performance must be multidimensional and multifaceted. One of the few truisms of management is that what gets measured, evaluated, and rewarded is what gets done. If a manager evaluates only the financial performance of the unit, that is what employees will focus on, possibly to the detriment of other equally (or more) important outcomes, such as quality patient care. A single snapshot of a unit's performance from a single perspective provides limited insight into what the unit has done or is doing. A series of pictures gives the manager and other interested parties a much more panoramic view of the work unit's effectiveness.

The greatest challenge for AHCs is to "make it happen." The challenge is greatest now, as we operate, manage, and lead during volatile times. The AHC's accelerating pace has outstripped the bureaucratic structure. AHCs now require adaptive, flexible, organizational structures. Organizing for effectiveness is a continuous process, one of adjustment of processes, structures, responsibilities, rewards, and evaluation modes. The future of an academic health center ultimately depends on the effectiveness of that organization.

BIBLIOGRAPHY

 1. Sink DS. (1983, October). *Much ado about productivity: Where do we go from here? IE,* p 638.
 2. Wall Street Journal, February 13, 1986.
 3. Anthony RN & Herzlinger RE. (1980). *Management control in non-profit organizations.* Homewood, Ill: Richard D. Irwin.
 4. Drucker P. (1985, November 26). How to measure white collar productivity. *Wall Street Journal.*
 5. Peters T & Waterman R. (1982). *In search of excellence.* New York: Harper & Row.
 6. Wilson MP & McLaughlin C. (1984). *Leadership and management in academic medicine.* San Francisco: Jossey-Bass.
*7. Kanter RM. (1982). The middle manager as innovator. *Harvard Business Review, 60,* 95-105.
 8. Hershey P & Blanchard K. (1982). *Management of organizational behavior,* 4th Ed. Englewood Cliffs, NJ: Prentice-Hall.
 9. Deal TE & Kennedy AA. (1982). *Corporate cultures.* Reading, Mass: Addison-Wesley.
*10. Katzenbach J & Smith D. (1992). *The wisdom of teams.* Cambridge, Mass: Harvard Business School Press.

ADDITIONAL RESOURCES

Bradford DL & Cohen AR. (1984). *Managing for excellence.* New York: John Wiley & Sons.
Dyer WG. (1987). *Team building.* Reading, Mass: Addison-Wesley.
Hackman JR & Walton RE. (1985). *The leadership of groups in organizations.* New Haven, Conn: Yale University Press.

*Asterisk indicates an article or book that is particularly informative and helpful.

CHAPTER 6

Managing Creativity in Academics

Richard S. Blackburn

*Creativity requires the freedom to consider unthinkable alternatives,
to doubt the worth of cherished practices.*

JOHN W. GARDNER

Introductory Exercise. Figure 6-1 presents a drawing of a new design for a wheelbarrow. It is certainly not like most wheelbarrows currently on the market. Take a few minutes now and write your reactions to this design on a piece of paper. Your remarks need not be lengthy; single words or short phrases will suffice, but do jot down some comments now. This will make material in the remainder of the chapter more relevant.

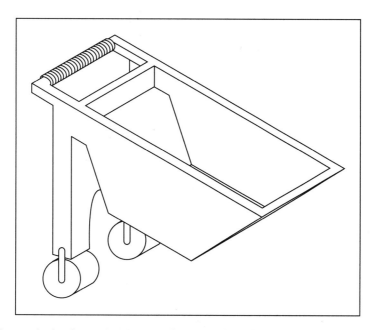

Figure 6-1. A new design for a wheelbarrow. (Redrawn from Campbell D. [1977]. *Take the road to creativity and get off your dead end.* Chicago: Argus Communications.)

An academic environment constantly bombards its managers with demands to take actions, make decisions, and solve problems. Actions, decisions, and solutions develop by the way one views the world (within and without the department or institution). Individuals prefer certain ways of managing by virtue of their education, experience, and previous reinforcement. Confronted with problems or opportunities demanding decisions and actions, managers fall back on those approaches that worked well in the past when similar situations arose.

Such a managerial approach is effective in a stable environment, where traditional ways of dealing with issues usually work over time. But the environment is no longer stable, particularly in the academic department. Tom Peters, in his book *Thriving on Chaos,*[21] talks about managing in times of chaos. Peter Vail describes the current managerial environment with a compelling metaphor; he argues that managing now resembles piloting a raft in "permanent white water." While the banks of the river may contain the raft's movement, and while the pilot knows the goal at the end of the river, the actual route chosen and the actions taken in going down the river are extremely difficult to plan. Each bend in the river offers new and different demands. The route taken at low water may not be appropriate when water levels are high. And while the location of the rapids remains constant, waves, eddies, and whirlpools form and reform, pulling the raft in a variety of directions.

To be successful in such an environment requires what Robert Quinn[20] calls *master managers*—those individuals able to confront and control a number of these new and frequently competing forces. Some managers regularly argue that people are their most important resource, but the same managers may argue that results make the difference. There are constant calls for more autonomy and flexibility in the workplace, but simultaneously managers realize the need for some measure of control in their departments or institutions.

Quinn argues that the master manager, rather than viewing the world from a single perspective (e.g., the human relations manager, the bureaucrat, the hard-charger, the politician), is able to confront issues from a variety of perspectives. Quinn labels the framework underlying this multiperspective approach to managerial issues as the competing values model (Figure 6-2). He proposes that all managerial efforts can be understood as attempts to resolve competing issues along two dimensions, reflecting the basic paradoxes that today's managers confront. Managers must balance departmental flexibility (enabling quick response to problem areas) with control (ensuring departmental stability). Additionally, the focus of managerial issues can be either internal to the department or external and focused outside departmental boundaries.

Crossing those two dimensions produces four perspectives on managing departmental issues. The upper left quadrant in Figure 6-2 houses the human relations model. Action here fosters the development of individuals and teams, placing an emphasis on people. Actions in this quadrant frequently compete with those appropriate for the rational goal model (lower right-hand quadrant). Here, managerial emphasis is on direction and productivity. In the lower left-hand quadrant is the internal process model, emphasizing control, stability, and structure within the department. Actions in this quadrant frequently compete with those appropriate for the open systems model (upper right–hand quadrant), where flexibility and interaction with the external environment are valued.

From a competing values perspective, master managers can view situations from the four perspectives simultaneously, but to do so requires the development of several managerial competencies. For the purposes of this chapter, we will consider the manager's ability to appreciate the insights afforded by the open systems perspective. To use the open systems model to its fullest, to be sufficiently adaptable to the chaos confronted in the departmental white water requires the ability to be innovative and creative. The environment also demands the abilities necessary to help others within your department use their creativity and innovativeness.

Unfortunately, many managers dismiss creativity as interesting but not terribly useful in resolving important departmental issues. In their minds, creativity resides in the hearts and minds of artists, musicians, sculptors, novelists, architects, designers, etc. Creativity is not (and some would say should not be) within the purview of the practicing manager. To this I say, BUNK!

In an environment where departmental survival may require flexibility and adaptability, the demand for creative solutions to managerial problems is greater than ever. Old ways of dealing with problems or opportunities may offer some guidance, but managers who develop new, innovative, and creative solutions for such issues will reap the benefits of these labors.

To that end, this chapter offers a brief definition of creativity, distinguishing between creative ability and creative behavior. This is followed by a discussion of the creative process. Reviewing the work of those labeled creative suggests that most followed a "systematic" approach out of which creative ideas emerge. An examina-

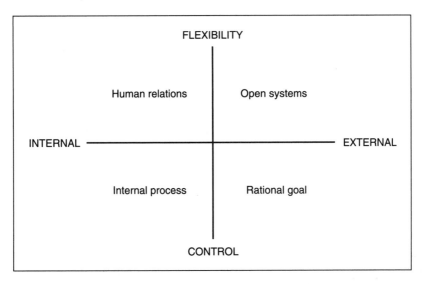

Figure 6-2. Competing values model. (Adapted from Quinn R. [1988]. *Beyond rational management.* San Francisco: Jossey-Bass.)

tion of one such model offers insights into potential obstacles that can arise to inhibit creativity. Given the identification of potential roadblocks to creativity, as a final step a series of suggestions for overcoming those obstacles are offered, looking at both individual and departmental factors that encourage creative thought and action.

CREATIVITY: WHAT IS IT?

Getting a handle on creativity is not an easy task. There are as many definitions of creativity as authors who consider the topic. For example, creativity has been defined as "looking at a problem . . . in a different way from somebody else and seeing something that they missed" or as "a battle against fixed attitudes."[22] To me, creativity means the generation of new or different ideas. These ideas can be stunning or mundane, as long as they are new or different to their creator. Limiting this discussion to personal creativity only, any new or different idea may be proposed. Once an organizational context is imposed, however, the definition must be modified a bit. From an organizational perspective, creativity must refer to the development of new or different ideas that are *useful* to the organization. Individuals can develop any number of new and different ideas, but if those ideas are not useful to the department, then they offer little assistance to the solution of departmental problems. As we will see later in this chapter, how one defines "useful" and who supplies that definition can either encourage or discourage creativity.

Taking this a step further requires a definitional distinction between two facets of creativity: creative ability and creative behavior. The former refers to one's capacity to develop new (and possibly useful) ideas; the latter refers to the actual production of those same ideas. Thus, creative ability is a necessary, but not sufficient, condition for creative behavior.

Perhaps a metaphor will clarify this distinction. Imagine a source of light representing creative ability. Now imagine that the light is reflected through a prism. On the other side of that prism a wondrous rainbow of colors appears, the result of turning capacity into creative productivity. Using one's creative ability to develop creative behaviors fosters the same type of dramatic transformation.

But what happens when the intensity of the light weakens? The magnificent transformation of white light to a rainbow of colors does not occur. Similarly, a lack of creative ability undermines creative behavior. Equally disturbing from a managerial perspective, one's creative capacity can remain strong, but external factors (an opaque prism) can also prevent the transformation of capacity into creative behavior.

A lack of creative ability is usually not the problem that managers must address. We all have within us the innate capacity to be creative. Despite possible protestations to the contrary, you, the reader, possess creative ability. For some that ability frequently translates into creative behaviors. Unfortunately, for others that translation occurs only rarely. There are both internal and external factors that inhibit this transformation, and these factors are best considered in light of how they affect the creative process.

A CREATIVE PROCESS

In attempting to identify the factors that act as inhibitors of creativity, it is useful to think about the transformation of creative ability into creative behavior as a process. The exact nature of the creative process is unknown. What we do know is that history's most creative products emerged from some type of creative process.

There have been many creative processes proposed, and any one is probably as valid and adequate as any other. Note that the title of this section begins with an indefinite and not a definite article. For our purposes, the creative process contains the six stages arrayed in Figure 6-3. A brief discussion of each stage follows.

Motivation

Creative behavior is like any other behavior; to engage in any activity there must be the internal drive or *motivation* to accomplish the task. This is the case with creativity. Think about a recent creative activity of your own. This could be something as mundane as taking a new route to work or something as exotic as composing a piece of music. As you reconstruct that creative activity, think about *why* you undertook the action you did. Was it to make money, to do something in an easier way, to solve a problem, to sell a product or service, to counteract boredom, or just to prove to yourself that you could do something differently? Any of these reasons encourage thinking about doing things in ways never done before. Without motivation there will be no creative efforts. Motivation is an absolute requirement for creative behavior.

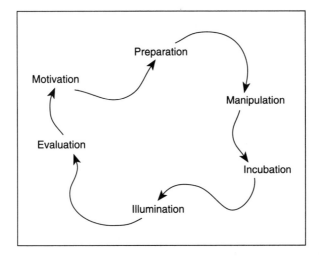

Figure 6-3. Creativity is a dynamic, nonlinear process.

Preparation

Motivation is a necessary but not sufficient condition for creative behavior. As with any behavior, motivation is only half the battle. Without the requisite skills and abilities in a given area, one can try, but acceptable behavior will never occur. To be successfully creative one needs the necessary *preparation* or knowledge about a particular area within which one hopes to exercise creativity. Some minimal level of technical knowledge is necessary to be creative in a task. For instance, an academic manager in a law school might find it extremely difficult to be creative in the fields of botany or medicine.

This second stage in the creative process can best be described as the step in which one "makes the strange familiar." From a professional perspective, most managers have sufficient levels of job-related knowledge to deal creatively with job or departmental issues. The problem arises when one must take the known and examine this knowledge from a variety of perspectives. Or one must take a series of known elements about a job or department and rearrange these in new ways. This requires the ability to manipulate information successfully.

Manipulation

The process of examining existing ideas, facts, and approaches from alternate perspectives and putting them together in new, different, and useful ways occurs by *manipulation*. If in the previous step one makes the strange familiar, then in this step one "makes the familiar strange." This is the point in the process where creativity truly occurs. For it is at this point where one disrupts the conventional, where the usual is viewed from unusual angles, and where the new arises from the old. Rosabeth Moss Kanter[15] argues that this step demands "kaleidoscopic thinking . . . that allows people to shake reality into a new pattern."

Consider the development of instant photography, an old technology now, but at the time a technological feat. Edwin Land manipulated well-known information and ideas about photochemistry and camera technology to develop a "photo store inside a camera." Art Frye of 3M manipulated his knowledge of adhesive application and his awareness of a "failed" adhesive to develop those now-ubiquitous Post-it notes.[13]

Incubation

Many individuals can look at disparate facts and information and readily manipulate these into creative ideas and outcomes (I am not such an individual). Others (like me) need time to think about the possible combinations and permutations of ideas to allow a creative solution to bubble to the surface of conscious thought. For some, this thinking process, though lengthy, is a conscious process. They develop the desired creative outcome through sheer perseverance. For others, continued, conscious attempts at developing creative outcomes are inhibiting. The more intense the effort to develop creative ideas, the more difficult the task becomes. I have heard this problem described as "paralysis by analysis." For these individuals, the best solution to the problem is to shift manipulation from the conscious mind to the subconscious mind.

This subconscious analysis of issues is called *incubation*. Ideas, facts, and information simmer in the mind's inner reaches, while the conscious mind directs its efforts at other, more mundane activities. These tasks could be work-related, but more likely would include non-work-related actions, like walking, reading, jogging, driving, or sleeping. The goal is to remove the creative attempt from conscious concern, allowing the less restricted subconscious mind to play with the information at hand. The reader probably has a favorite activity (or nonactivity) that best allows ideas to incubate. Over time, individuals develop insights into how best to support the incubation process.

Illumination

Illumination is the *Eureka!* event or the *Aha!* experience. After some period of incubation, the creative light bulb goes on, and the creative solution once barely visible is now fully illuminated. The creative answer is now so painfully obvious that one wonders why it took so long to discover. For each individual, illumination can occur in many settings. I have talked with managers whose best ideas surface while driving to the office, watching TV, running, taking a shower, shaving, or during those brief moments between sleep and wakefulness in the morning or evening. Each of us has our own favored locale for such illuminating experiences. They do occur, and with their occurrence one stumbles headlong into a period of creative behavior.

Evaluation/Verification

If the attempt to translate creative ability into creative behavior is a strictly personal one, then the poem or picture or gourmet meal does not require evaluation by anyone else (except perhaps family members or friends). Developing creative solutions for departmental problems requires a final and important stage in the creative process called *evaluation/verification*. As a wise person once said, "It takes courage to be creative. Just as soon as you have a new idea, you are in a minority of one." In this stage, the creative idea must be held up to the scrutiny of others. They must evaluate the idea, decision, solution, product, or service and verify its worth. Having a creative idea is only part of the battle in a departmental setting. Defending that idea and getting it accepted and implemented is an important and often difficult undertaking.

Summary

The six-stage process illustrated in Figure 6-3 represents only one description of how creative ideas may come to fruition. Other models have been proposed with more or fewer steps, but this one provides several leverage points to examine possible obstacles to creative behavior. The figure attempts to illustrate the nonlinear nature of the process. The two-dimensional page and the quest for clarity prevent the diagram from doing justice to the multiple, recursive, and/or parallel relationships usually at work in such a process. Kanter notes that such models "do not always adequately capture the give-and-take of innovation, and they risk artificially segmenting the process."[13]

Thus there will be times when we encounter dead ends and illumination fails to occur. Here, a return to the motivation, preparation, or manipulation stages may be needed. There may be times when stages can be skipped and manipulation or illumination occurs instantaneously. The process is dynamic and nonlinear, and for various issues or opportunities, individuals and departments may have to manage different stages in the process simultaneously.

OBSTACLES TO CREATIVITY

The model in Figure 6-3 provides a framework within which to think about where the creative process might get derailed, and what might cause creativity problems. An entire volume could be devoted to creative roadblocks. For brevity's sake, this discussion is limited to 10 possible obstacles to creativity (see the box on p. 99). These barriers to creativity have been called "killer phrases" (they kill creativity in an individual or department) or "mental locks" (they lock individuals into traditional, noncreative approaches to issues). I prefer to call these obstacles the "big buts," because the phrases are heard most frequently following the word "but" in such sentences as, "I think it is a good idea, *but* . . . ," or "That is an interesting idea, *but* . . .". Of course, our less creative (and less charitable) superiors, peers, or subordinates may omit the initial clause and conjunction. These 10 comments are voiced as imperative statements.

We've always (never) done it this (that) way! Departmental traditions or individual habits comprise one of the biggest obstacles to creative behavior. To assert that a department *always* operates in some way or *never* operates in the proposed, creative way becomes sufficient reason to continue with the time-honored approach. Of course, such responses provide one possible explanation of why Kodak did not invent the Polaroid camera, or IBM did not invent the personal computer.

That's not your (my) area of expertise! Occasionally, those outside a particular departmental area develop the most creative responses to departmental problems. Traditions, habits, and the old way of doing things do not hamper them. Unfortunately, the "not-invented-here" syndrome can prevent the acceptance of others' ideas particularly ideas of those located outside the area or department. It also may prevent the offering of potentially creative solutions to other areas or departments.

This better not cost me! The costs associated with creative ideas are difficult to assess. That an idea is new suggests difficulties in determining the financial costs associated with implementation. Such concerns can derail creative solutions. Nonfinancial costs also can wreck havoc with creative ideas. When individuals talk about potential costs of a creative solution, they may be including psychological costs associated with losing power, authority, status, or face. The maintenance of the psychological status quo may be a more substantial obstacle to creativity than financial concerns.

THE TEN BIG BUTS
THAT HAMPER CREATIVITY

"This is an interesting idea, *but* . . . "

1. We always/never do it this/that way.
2. That's not your/my area of expertise.
3. This better not cost me anything.
4. We don't have enough _____.
5. Be sure to follow the rules.
6. Let the experts look at it.
7. We only reward _____.
8. We/You/I must assume that _____.
9. To err is wrong!
10. You are /I am not creative.

We don't have enough _____*!* Real or alleged resource constraints can serve as the basis for rejecting new ways of doing things. Constrained resources might include money, personnel, time, and capital equipment. The unstated (and usually untested) assumption in using this rationale for rejecting a creative proposal is that the new way demands more resources than are available. But such rejections frequently view the creative proposal as a short-term cost rather than as a long-term investment with more appreciable returns accruing to the creative solution. Difficult times frequently demand creative solutions to ensure survival. Some managers manufacture resource crises to force subordinates to use new approaches to resolve these problems.

Let's be sure we (you) follow the rules! Want to kill off a creative idea? Force it (or its champion) to wend its (his or her) way through the departmental or institutional bureaucracy. Sending a creative idea to a committee for review can result in the idea's premature demise. Such review committees become creative "black holes": Creative ideas go in and are never heard from again. Requiring individuals with a creative bent to have all the *i*'s dotted and all the *t*'s crossed before considering their proposal also quenches most creative fires. Similarly, organizational or departmental rules that mandate specific work hours, reporting relationships, or resource allocations can stifle creativity. Some of your staff's most creative work might well occur outside regular work hours when they are not attending to the constant interruptions that mark every academic department.

Let's have the experts look at it! In spirit, this may seem a good idea, but only after a creative proposal is accepted in its general form. By definition, experts know a great deal about a narrow area. An expert's ability can limit creative thought and few creative ideas outside the area of expertise will appear "feasible."

Remember, we only reward _____*!* Fill in the blank space with such phrases as "creative ideas that prove profitable," or "creative ideas that succeed." The converse to the entire phrase may also be heard, as in "We punish creative ideas that fail." The department's reward system can have a substantial impact on the development of creative ideas. Consider the nature of creative ideas that arise when management rewards only profitable ideas and severely punishes ideas that don't work. With such a reward system, new ideas become conservative; marginal changes in already successful approaches. Television and movie productions reward efforts in this fashion. The results are spin-offs of successful TV shows and sequels of popular movies. How many iterations of "Rocky" or "Friday the 13th" must we see to appreciate the impact that such reward systems have on creativity.

Similar pressures arise when the reward system ignores *how* the creative outcome was achieved, and rewards (or penalizes) creative outcomes only. Such a system ignores the effort required to work through the entire creative process, and likely results in the development of marginally creative ideas.

We (you) must make the following assumption(s)! Many new and creative ideas never survive because their potential creators or those who define the parameters of acceptable creative actions operate under a variety of *assumed* constraints. Unquestioned acceptance of constraints that may not be real (only assumed) may constrain potentially creative solutions. The brain teaser illustrated in Figure 6-4 provides a classic example of how assumed constraints can prevent creative solutions. In Figure 6-4, can you connect the nine dots with four straight lines drawn without lifting your writing instrument? Try it! If one assumes that the exterior dots represent a

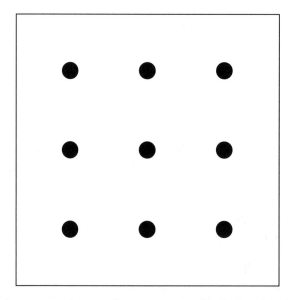

Figure 6-4. Challenging assumed constraints: test yourself with the nine-dot problem. (Solution on p. 114.)

boundary outside of which the lines could not go, this is an impossible task. Challenging this assumed constraint (the instructions made no such assumption), makes solution much easier. (The solution is shown in Figure 6-8 on p. 114). As a further challenge, what additional constraints must be dropped to allow the dots to be connected with three straight lines? With one straight line?

To err is wrong! Our previous discussion of how reward systems inhibit creativity is germane here. Most of us grow up with a tremendous fear of failure. Educational training at all levels stresses the downside of making mistakes—lower grades, parental concern, fewer attractive job opportunities, etc. The educational system is predicated on the belief that each problem or question has but one right answer, the answer the teacher has and that the student must discern. Failure to provide this correct answer is wrong and undesirable. Competent people simply do not make mistakes. Making mistakes indicates a lack of competence. The student's goal, therefore, is to find the one right answer. (This also makes it much easier for the teacher to grade assignments and tests.) On the other hand, creativity is an inherently risky venture. Creative ideas are new and may illustrate a second, third, or even fourth right answer to a problem. But a few teachers reward students for these other "correct" answers. Such answers are "wrong," and students receive no credit for their creative solutions. They fear failing more than they want to provide creative answers to their instructor. This lack of reinforcement and fear of failure inhibit the creative capacity as we grow older.

You're (I'm) not creative! The most creative individuals that we regularly see are small children. But as children grow they spend increasing amounts of time in our major social institutions: schools, churches, the military, work organizations. As discussed above, most of these institutions reward their charges for conformity. They choose the answer that the instructor or supervisor wants, even when the student or employee develops a more creative answer. From a creativity perspective, if enough of these experiences occur, the student/employee eventually comes to the conclusion that he or she is not creative. This critical evaluation can be directed both internally and externally. Thus, we never allow our own creative ideas to surface because of our conditioning to believe we lack creativity. We censor our own creative ideas before they can be publicly evaluated. When others attempt to offer their creative ideas we respond in our teacher/supervisor mode and not allow other potentially correct answers to be selected for implementation. This predisposition toward the critical evaluation of our own and others' new and different ideas is a remnant of the training in many of our major institutions.

Summary

These ten "buts" provide a bleak background against which to paint creative and innovative pictures. Take an inventory of the number of times these comments surface when a new and original way of dealing with a situation has appeared in your department. Where does your department stand relative to these ten roadblocks to creativity? When others offer creative ideas to you, how many of these comments reflect your typical reaction to such suggestions?

In settings where such comments are frequent, creativity has little chance of survival. Still, organizations in this country and the people they employ are among the most creative in the world. While we struggle to produce products and services as inexpensively or of the same quality as our foreign competitors, our innovative and creative ideas have few global peers.

What do the most creative and innovative individuals and organizations do to overcome these obstacles? What can be done to encourage creativity in your personal and professional life? How can your department be managed to maximize creative insights from subordinates? To answer these questions, we first examine a set of personality characteristics frequently found in creative individuals. Changing personality characteristics is not an easy task, especially for departmental managers. Thus, we also want to consider the structural ways in which managers, departments and organizations can support creativity.

OVERCOMING THE OBSTACLES

In overcoming these obstacles, it is helpful to categorize factors that facilitate or encourage creativity. Factors to consider include those operating at the individual level and those operating at the departmental level. Every individual has some creative ability, and some individuals are better suited by virtue of personality or temperament to transform that ability into behavior. From the personal perspective, think about the extent to which *you* currently possess any or all the following attributes associated with those who are creative. From a managerial perspective, consider the extent to which your subordinates possess these attributes and the influence possession of such characteristics has had on departmental hiring and advancement decisions. Following are some of the personal attributes that encourage creativity (Figure 6-5).

Go for it! The creative process requires the willingness and ability to approach situations from alternate perspectives and tolerate the frequently critical evaluations of creative proposals. Thus, creative individuals are self-confident, have a strong sense of commitment to their creative ideas, and possess the courage to defend those creative outcomes.

Question it! The motivation to be creative often arises when one is willing to view tradition with a healthy dose of skepticism. Skepticism (not cynicism) is often the first step to evaluating work in more creative ways. Creative individuals are open-minded about new ideas and willingly listen to alternative interpretations of issues. These attributes (skepticism and open-mindedness) relate strongly to a third characteristic of the creative individual, tolerance for ambiguity and uncertainty. Creative individuals do not require complete knowledge and understanding of a situation before taking action. Nor do they need a detailed map of where they are going or how they are going to get there. In fact, many creative individuals actually value ambiguity and uncertainty, because both factors frequently encourage non-traditional reactions to emerging departmental issue. These individuals lack enough information (or certainty) to apply the old ways of doing things, but are comfortable with this information deficit.

Diversify! Creative behavior requires the knowledge of areas of interest (preparation) and the ability to combine elements of this knowledge in new and useful ways (manipulation). To this end, the creative individual is extremely diverse in background, interests, experience, education, job history, etc. These individuals know different people, read different books, do different things. This exposure to a variety of people, places, ideas, and activities encourages the creative manipulation that marks creative behavior. A too-narrow band of knowledge, interests, or expertise can inhibit this necessary manipulation. At your office, what types of books or periodicals do you read? What activities do you engage in off-the-job? How narrow or broad are the interests represented by your answers to these questions?

Accentuate the positive! Finally, creative people are optimistic. They must be, for they constantly confront the hobgoblins of tradition, habit, failure, etc. Pessimists facing such obstacles would find their pessimism reinforced and eventually cease attempts to be creative. Optimism requires self-awareness, or the ability to understand and appreciate one's strengths and weaknesses. Knowledge of personal assets and liabilities allows the individual to accentuate his/her strengths in the creative process, while minimizing the impact of shortcomings.

Each of these imperative statements and their attendant attributes refer to personality characteristics that are difficult (if not impossible) to change. To a large extent, early life experiences and reinforcement from parents, teachers, friends, and ministers or priests shape our personalities. Changing these attributes in an attempt

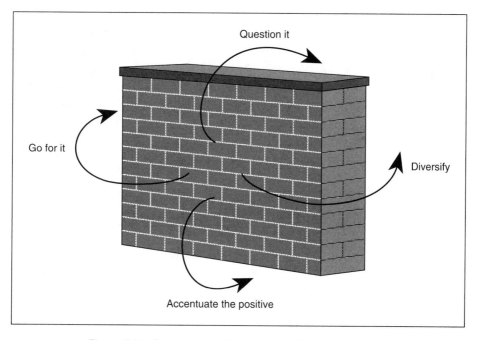

Figure 6-5. Overcoming obstacles to achieving creativity.

to be more creative is probably not a viable strategy short term. It is difficult to wake up one morning and decide to be more confident, more skeptical, or more optimistic. Over longer periods of time (and sometimes with clinical assistance) these attributes might be changed. Short term, it might be wiser to consider skill-based or system-based changes to encourage personal creative efforts or creativity levels of those working for us.

DEPARTMENTAL ATTRIBUTES

We will use the creative process presented earlier as the framework underlying a set of departmental attributes that encourage creative behaviors. This discussion begins by considering those factors that encourage motivation, the first step in the creative process.

Encouraging Motivation

Motivation has been a subject of interest to both researchers and managers for many years. Researchers explain it as a function of attempts to satisfy needs, achieve goals, insure fairness and equity, acquire valued outcomes, and reinforce desired behavior. This chapter is not the place to revisit these basic motivation models. Any number of management or organizational behavior textbooks discuss these models in detail. Instead, these various explanations provide the bases for some suggestions that should encourage creative behavior.

The first suggestion centers on evaluation/reward systems and managerial feedback to employees. One truism found in the study of management and managerial actions is the following: "What gets evaluated/rewarded is what gets done." If you want creative behavior in your department, evaluate and reward such behavior when it occurs. If you don't want creative behavior, then don't evaluate it or reward it. This admonition holds in developing any departmental process.

When writing job descriptions, job standards, and performance plans for example, consider including expectations for creative behaviors in response to departmental issues. Setting such goals for employees will increase the likelihood that they might undertake such actions. Surprisingly, many managers assume that creative responses are an expected part of a subordinate's job without explicitly communicating this to the employee. Employees must be aware that the manager wishes to see creative responses to unit issues. Let them know of these expectations. Set those expectations early in their job tenure.

Performance appraisal/evaluation systems should evaluate not only creative outcomes but also the means taken to reach those outcomes. Evaluation or reward systems that assess or reward successful creative outcomes only will tend to reinforce creativity at the margin. Creativity is inherently risky, and risk brings with it the probability of failure. If success occurs rarely, and rewards are provided solely for successful outcomes (and not for well-intentioned but unsuccessful attempts), then employees will not be reinforced for making creative attempts to deal with department issues. Managers should evaluate and reward subordinates based on their willingness and ability to make the creative effort. Failed attempts at creativity may demand the same rewards as creative outcomes that succeed.

There are many rewards that managers can provide for the appropriate use of the creative process and, as appropriate, for the successful outcomes of that process. In departmental settings, managers may view money as the primary reward. But most employees also have several other important needs or desires they are trying to satisfy in the work place. It is a manager's responsibility to find what those needs and desires might be. Tying creative behaviors to rewards that employees want or value will usually generate substantial improvement in creative outcomes.

A caveat should be added to this discussion of rewards and motivation. Rewards can be either intrinsic (self-rewards, if you will) or extrinsic (rewards provided by others). Our discussion to this point has focused on extrinsic rewards. To get individuals to join our departments and to work in them requires an adequate level of extrinsic rewards. However, Teresa Amabile, a noted researcher on creativity, found that too much extrinsic justification for creativity on the job decreases levels of future creative behavior brought to a position. She recommends designing jobs that provide substantial opportunities for intrinsic rewards, including feelings of responsibility, challenge, achievement, or accomplishment. In settings where creative behaviors generate intrinsic rewards, levels of creativity should be high. In other words, it is difficult to "buy" commitment to creative behavior with the typical extrinsic rewards.

Rewards also can be received vicariously. Thus, successful creative activities should result in the public recognition of these successes. In such instances both the creator and those observing the recognition are reinforced for engaging in creative activities. Whether such recognition occurs at monthly staff meetings or annual retreats, those that successfully increase their creative behavior should be so recognized, that others might learn what success will yield.

While managers should reward creative successes, this does not mean punishing the occasional creative failures. Punishing creative failure is a quick way to eliminate creative behavior in a department. Occasional failures must be viewed as the cost of doing business creatively. Failure, particularly high-risk, creative failure, is to be expected. In fact, the lack of creative failures in a department might suggest that employees are not taking enough creative chances. The unit may have become complacent and rigid in its approach to issues. Quinn et al.'s master managers view failure as simply another way of learning.[20] Identify failure, admit and learn from mistakes, but then forget them. Do not resurrect the failure the next time an employee offers a creative response to a departmental issue.

Evaluation, reward, and feedback have important effects on the motivation to be creative. The same thing can and should be said for the impact of motivation on the remaining stages in the creative process. It takes motivation to prepare for, to manipulate, to incubate, to illuminate, and to evaluate creative activities. Although motivation is not explicitly revisited in the remainder of this discussion, its importance in each stage should be noted.

Encouraging Preparation

The relationship between motivation and creativity is straightforward. As motivation increases so does the likelihood of successful creative behavior. With motivation, the more the merrier. Preparation, on the other hand, has a somewhat more complex relationship to creativity. It may not always be the case that more preparation necessarily leads to more creativity.

Recall in our earlier discussion of the creative process, that preparation required that individuals have the skills, abilities, equipment, and resources necessary to engage in creative behaviors. It could be possible to be overly prepared for creativity. Consider the requirement for necessary skills and abilities. There is some threshold level of creative competence, below which no creative behavior occurs. What happens above that threshold? As individuals gain more expertise in an area, does that reduce the likelihood of creative solutions. In your experience, who is more likely to offer creative ideas, new employees lacking the knowledge that certain things simply are not done in creative ways, or veteran employees set in their ways of dealing with departmental issues. Experience may be a great teacher, but the traditions and habits that experience engenders may reduce the willingness and ability to try new approaches.

Preparation requires the competence to do the immediate job. It also may require opportunities to learn about other work areas. To improve the creative preparation of employees, managers must work to improve communication within the department or between departments. These efforts might include job changes as part of a formal job-rotation policy or an informal "seconding" of employees to other departments for short periods of time. Temporary assignments to task forces, bringing individuals together from other departments in the institution, expose participants to alternative views of reality.

A threshold model of preparation also may exist for resources available within a department. Some minimal level of resources is necessary to engage in any creative activity, but above this threshold what happens? Common sense would suggest that creativity should increase when excess resources are available. Slack gives employees the freedom to experiment with non-traditional approaches without fear of bankrupting the department. But excess resources also can lead to complacency by employees. There is no pressure to develop alternative (and perhaps more creative) ways of dealing with departmental issues. Slack is desirable, sloth is not. We also might expect more creative responses to departmental problems with constrained resources. Necessity may indeed be the mother of invention.

Preparation requires the careful management of resources. Sufficient (but not excessive) financial resources, requisite personal skills and abilities, and provision for the exchange of individuals and their knowledge supports this second stage of the creative process. Careful management at this stage also can enhance employees' abilities to manipulate these many ideas—the third stage in the creative process.

Encouraging Manipulation, Incubation, and Illumination

The earlier discussion of the creative process examined these stages individually. They are grouped here, because similar factors encourage each stage. Manipulation is that stage the lay person frequently associates with creativity. It is the point at which individuals synthesize a variety of existing facts or views to derive something new and useful. To encourage this, the individual and the department can undertake a variety of actions.

From an individual perspective, one can practice a variety of creative thinking tactics that encourage creative ideas. For instance, convergent or vertical thinking seeks the one right answer to a problem. Divergent or lateral thinking encourages the search for second, third, or fourth right answers. Divergent thinking facilitates manipulation.

How does one increase divergent thinking skills? One way is to do more of it; to practice. The brain-teasers found in creativity books are good for practicing lateral thinking. (Many of the references at the end of this chapter contain such activities.) So are mind-stretching activities like the "What-if" Game. Robert von Oech offers one example of this in his entertaining book on creativity, *A Whack on the Side of the Head;* von Oech asks, "What if you suddenly developed seven fingers on each hand? (See Figure 6-6.) List as many implications of this development as you can."

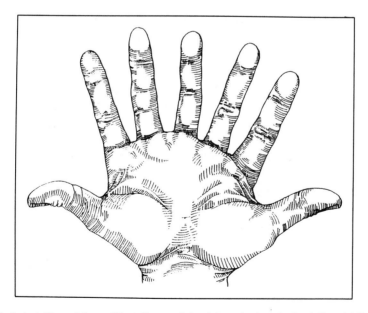

Figure 6-6. A "what if" problem: What if we all had hands that looked like this? Think of five implications if this were true. (From von Oech R. [1983]. *A whack on the side of the head.* Reprinted by permission of Warner Books/New York. © 1983 Roger von Oech.)

Try it! How many did you get? Could you think of impacts in a variety of areas in developing your list? Did you consider the implications for music, sports, hitch-hiking, being a Roman emperor, or carrying plates and drinks at cocktail parties? To the extent you did, you were practicing divergent thinking. These brain-teasers and what-if exercises require that you stop thinking vertically and start thinking laterally.

Successful accomplishment of these stages may require the occasional withdrawal from the frenetic demands of the typical managerial work day. The stages may force the manager to be comfortable with inaction for some period. To actually think on the job. Yet how many organizations give managers the time or encouragement to think?

Do this quick self-analysis. You are in your office with your feet up on your desk. You are not "doing" anything. You are thinking. Your boss walks by your office. What is your typical reaction? Do you immediately sit up in your chair to make it appear as though you are "doing something?" For many managers this is nearly an instinctual response. But didn't your institution hire you to think? Isn't that why you are a manager? Why is it that managers feel so guilty about thinking? This guilt certainly doesn't support creativity.

Creativity often requires undertaking actions and behaviors without complete knowledge of the facts in the matter and without complete knowledge of the possible consequences of these actions. Still, some actions must be taken. Creativity is encouraged to the extent that we trust our intuition or hunches. Managers should be willing to act based on less than complete specifications and analysis of the problem. This is not true only for creative activities. The white-water environment of most departments now requires that many managerial actions, creative or not, be based on intuition and gut feel.

The use of intuition in management is becoming a major area of interest to managers and organizational researchers. Managers have made many important decisions based on intuition or hunches, but were afraid to admit this to colleagues. Managers were taught that their actions should be based on rational analysis. But as the information required for a thorough, rational analysis became overwhelming, managers and management researchers soon realized that intuition could be a most important part of the managerial tool kit. Reading the literature on intuition, intuitive decision-making, and intuitive management reveals many of the same ideas expressed in this chapter. (The interested reader might examine Weston Agor's *Intuition in Organizations*.[3]) Creativity and intuitive decision-making have a great deal in common.

What can departments or institutions do to facilitate manipulation, incubation, and illumination? Some departments encourage (both formally and informally) joint undertakings by individuals and departments with different functional perspectives. As noted above, task forces, project groups, and informal committees take advantage of potential synergies as alternate perspectives consider a seemingly intractable problem. Structural techniques that encourage cross-communication and cross-fertilization of ideas also should encourage creativity. This assumes, of course, that the participants in these activities have the appropriate group process skills to allow the successful exchange of differing viewpoints.

Managers and institutions should consider stretching departmental rules, policies, and procedures that might otherwise hamper creative interactions. If the department has rules regarding work hours, managers might stretch these regulations to allow creative individuals to set their own work hours. For some employees, creative ideas may not surface between 9:00 and 5:00. Sometimes the heat of the creative process demands that employees start early, stay late, or come and go at odd hours. A manager willing to support those actions might see an increase in creativity. Similarly, departments might consider allowing "time-outs" for thinking and incubating. One organization allows no meetings to be scheduled between 8:30 and 9:30. Additionally, only emergency or customer phone calls are connected. For other calls, messages are taken and calls returned later. The open-door policy is suspended. Managers are free to think without fear of interruption or sanction for not "looking busy."

Managers and departments can take many actions to encourage the surfacing of creative ideas. The fragility of these new ideas requires careful handling if they are to survive the final stage in the creative process.

Encouraging Supportive Evaluation/Verification

Most creative ideas perish in the last stage of the creative process. Individuals are quick to criticize that which is new and different for reasons discussed earlier. It is difficult for something as delicate as a new idea to survive this critical onslaught. Creators of new ideas begin to keep their creative thoughts to themselves. What can individuals and departments do to make this final step of the creative process more supportive and less traumatic?

For the creative individual, it is important to realize that criticism of new ideas is not unusual, and in most cases, is not directed at the individual, but the idea. It is important that individuals learn to expect that criticisms will be voiced and to be ready to defend their ideas. This is why self-confidence, commitment, and courage are important to creativity.

If those personality traits do not describe your employees, what can be done to ensure that new and creative proposals receive a fair hearing? What can be done to ensure that creative people are "protected" when proposing new approaches to problems and opportunities?

One option is to establish ground rules in advance for such evaluation sessions. These rules could prohibit criticisms of new ideas until the individual has a chance to explain his/her proposal fully. Someone could be assigned the role of *angel's advocate*, responsible for identifying the valuable aspects of a proposal. A manager in one organization respects the admonition of the Greek philosopher Epictetus when evaluating new ideas: "Make your decisions twice—once sober and once drunk." While it is doubtful that individuals in this organization adjourn to a local bar for their meetings, they do give new ideas a "second chance" for acceptance. Alfred

P. Sloan, long-time CEO of General Motors, asked his top managers to sleep on key decisions and reevaluate them the next morning. Any of these measures serve to reduce criticisms directed at creative ideas and increase the likelihood that some new approaches will be adopted by the organization.

My favorite approach, adapted from a suggestion made by David Campbell,[8] is to stick a "PIN" in creative ideas. If your initial reaction to my idea is that deflating new ideas is exactly the wrong approach to take to foster creativity, you are correct. In this instance, however, I am talking not about a pin in the literal sense, but about the three letters *P-I-N* as an acronym for the words Positive, Interesting, and Negative.

How do you stick this PIN in new ideas? Turn back to the opening of this chapter and review your comments about the new design for a wheelbarrow. How many of those comments were negative? If you are like most of the individuals who have evaluated this new design, most of your remarks are probably critical. These might have included comments like "poorly balanced, hard to dump, too deep, too unwieldy," etc. But why were there so many negative remarks? The instructions simply asked for your comments about the wheelbarrow, not your criticisms or solely negative impressions. Human nature being what it is, the unusual and the different typically engender critical remarks. (If most of your comments were not critical, congratulations!)

To get around this problem, the usually critical evaluators must think about and focus on the positive (P) or interesting (I) aspects of the new approach before entertaining the negative (N) aspects. Thus, in a meeting to evaluate this wheelbarrow for possible development, the astute manager might begin the discussion by asking participants, "Identify three things you like about the design or that you see as interesting." Starting a meeting on such a positive note almost always reduces the number and severity of critical remarks.

Certainly, some new ideas and creative suggestions will be problematic. Anything that is new and different will have some warts. But if only the warts are discussed, then potentially valuable aspects of the new approach may never surface, and creative insights will be lost forever. Take a moment to consider the positive and interesting aspects of the new wheelbarrow design. There are many. How would the members of your department respond?

The next time you are conducting a meeting where you want new ideas to surface and you wish to encourage the creativity levels of your employees, think about sticking a PIN in your discussion. It will work creative wonders.

THE TENSIONS OF MANAGING CREATIVITY

Teresa Amabile[6] argues that managing creativity is not as straightforward as the preceding discussion might suggest. She notes that managing creativity requires "maintaining a delicate balance between the opposites that can either promote or inhibit creativity." To use Quinn's terminology from the introductory discussion, managers must learn to manage the paradoxes associated with creativity. The trade-offs or paradoxes that must be balanced appear in the box on p. 111.

```
┌─────────────────────────────────────────────┐
│              PARADOXES OF                     │
│            MANAGING CREATIVITY                │
│                                               │
│   1. Flexibility versus control               │
│   2. Sufficient versus insufficient resources │
│   3. Focused versus unfocused goals           │
│   4. Overevaluation versus no evaluation      │
│   5. Rewarding ends versus rewarding means    │
│                                               │
│   Adapted from Amabile T. (1988). A model of creativity and │
│   innovation in organizations. Research in Organizational Be- │
│   havior, 10, 123-167.                        │
└─────────────────────────────────────────────┘
```

Flexibility Versus Control

On the one hand, sufficient freedom allows the creative muse to surface; excessive control can stifle creativity. On the other hand, unconstrained creativity may not yield organizationally useful outcomes. There is a fine line between constructive creativity and creative chaos.

Sufficient Versus Insufficient Resources

As discussed earlier, too many resources can lead to contentment and reduce or eliminate the tensions that frequently motivate creativity. Sufficient resources provide the freedom to undertake creative activities without the fear that failure could destroy the department. Too few resources may hamstring the individual attempting to develop creative ideas. Some minimal level of resources may force creative outcomes from individuals as the only opportunity for departmental survival.

This trade-off relates to other pressures confronting individuals in the departmental setting. On the one hand, excessive pressure may result in extremely creative outcomes. On the other, excessive pressure may result in creative paralysis. Too little pressure to be creative minimizes the motivation to act creatively, but it also may provide the time necessary to let the creative process operate fully.

Focused Versus Unfocused Goals

Motivation specialists tell us that setting goals for employees can improve performance as long as those goals are realistic and achievable. Employees will nearly always behave as desired if told what to accomplish. As suggested earlier, creativity can be a goal-related portion of job descriptions and performance plans. The managerial challenge is to provide goals that balance an overly tight focus, inhibiting the manipulation of ideas, and an overly loose focus, resulting in creative ideas that are not useful to the department.

Overevaluation Versus No Evaluation

A performance appraisal system that places too much emphasis on successful, creative outcomes may engender a fear of failure in employees, inhibiting their creative efforts. A lack of evaluation criteria regarding creativity reduces the motivation to be creative (what doesn't get measured doesn't get done). It signals to employees that the department does not think creativity is important.

Rewarding Ends Versus Rewarding Means

We have discussed this apparent paradox earlier. Rewarding successful creative outcomes only may result in marginal improvements in creativity. Rewarding creative means only may result in the development signal that successful outcomes are not important. Reward systems must incorporate measures of both creative activities.

The master manager can simultaneously balance each of these possibly conflicting requirements for creativity. He or she can call on personal and departmental resources to ensure that appropriate levels of creative activities occur within the department.

CONCLUSIONS

Successful management of both personal creativity levels and the creativity of others demands careful attention to and diagnosis of those factors that discourage creativity. Ten of the "big buts" of creativity were reviewed. These inhibiting factors can be minimized, and sometimes eliminated, by introducing policies or procedures that encourage creativity. No matter which of these factors are employed in your department, all managers must recognize and appreciate the delicate balance to be maintained when using these suggestions to manage creativity.

Amabile[6] offers a useful summary categorization of the requirements for successful creativity in organizations and within individuals. She argues that for improved individual creativity and the resulting improvement in levels of organizational innovation, three general areas of concern must be addressed. Each of these requirements addresses one or more of the six stages in the creative process.

First, departments and individuals must nurture the *motivation* to pursue creative outcomes in the first place (Stage 1) and to engage in creative thinking when the time is right (Stage 3). Given our discussion in this chapter, that motivation can be both internally generated (intrinsic motivation) or externally generated (extrinsic motivation). Amabile argues that creative behaviors will occur far more frequently if they are the result of intrinsic motivation relative to the job, than if they are "bought" with extrinsic rewards.

Second, preparation (Stage 2) and validation (Stage 6) require two sets of skills related to the area of creative interest. Amabile calls one set of skills domain-relevant skills. Basic knowledge pertinent to a job or department is mandatory or little in the way of creative behavior will ever rouse.

Similarly, manipulation (Stage 3), incubation (Stage 4), and illumination (Stage 5), require what Amabile calls creativity-relevant skills. Unless individuals have or can develop these abilities, the level of creative activities will be limited.

Finally, some minimal level of resources must be present to enable the skilled and motivated individual to undertake creative behaviors. Insufficient resources in the face of creative motivation and skill will certainly lead to employee frustration.

Amabile represents these three components of creativity with the three circles in Figure 6-7. Each component must be present for creative endeavors to be undertaken and for these to result in useful creative outcomes. If a component is absent no creative outcomes will occur. In Figure 6-7, the area of overlap reflects conditions conducive to creativity. This figure suggests that to encourage creativity managers and organizations must (1) maximize motivation (both intrinsic and extrinsic) through selection, placement, evaluation systems, reward systems, and job design; (2) ensure domain-relevant and creativity-relevant skills through appropriate hiring, placement, training and development, job rotation, feedback, and reinforcement; and (3) provide adequate (but appropriate) resource support. To the extent that these efforts are successful, individual creativity will increase and the department as a whole will be more innovative.

In this era of white-water environments, organizational chaos, and hypertechnological change, creative responses to departmental problems and opportunities may be the only way for institutions to survive. To succeed, managers must unleash the full potential of their subordinates. Maximizing creative opportunities is one way of doing this. Success in this effort ensures that your accomplishments and those of your department and institution will be limitless.

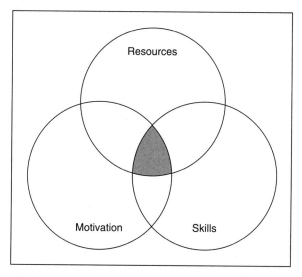

Figure 6-7. The creativity intersection. (From Amabile T. [1988]. A model of creativity and innovation in organizations. *Research in Organizational Behavior, 10,* 123-167.)

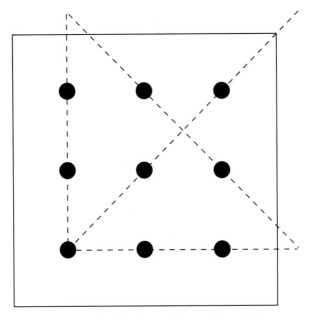

Figure 6-8. Solution to Figure 6-4, p. 100.

BIBLIOGRAPHY

  1. Ackoff RL. (1978). *The art of problem solving.* New York: John Wiley & Sons.
  2. Adams JL. (1979). *Conceptual blockbusting: A guide to better ideas* (2nd ed). New York: WW Norton.
  3. Agor WH. (1989). *Intuition in organizations.* Newbury Park, Calif: Sage Publications.
  4. Albrecht K. (1987). *The creative corporation.* Homewood, Ill: Dow Jones-Irwin.
  5. Amabile T. (1983). *The social psychology of creativity.* New York: Springer-Verlag.
 *6. Amabile T. (1988). A model of creativity and innovation in organizations. *Research in Organizational Behavior, 10,* 123-167.
  7. Amabile T. (1991). *Growing up creative.* New York: Crown.
  8. Campbell D. (1977). *Take the road to creativity and get off your dead end.* Chicago: Argus Communications.
  9. Csikszentmihalyi M. (1990). *Flow: The psychology of optimal experience.* New York: Harper & Row.
 10. Gardner M. (1982). *Aha! Gotcha.* New York: WH Freeman.
 11. Gardner M. (1978). *Aha! Insight.* New York: WH Freeman.
 12. Harman W & Rheingold H. (1984). *Higher creativity.* Los Angeles: Jeremy P Tarcher, Inc.
 *13. Henry J. (1991). *Creative management.* Newbury Park, Calif: Sage.
 14. Kanter RM. (1983). *The change masters.* New York: Simon & Schuster.
 15. Kanter RM. (1988). When a thousand flowers bloom. *Research in Organizational Behavior, 10,* 169-211.
 16. Keil JM. (1985). *The creative mystique: How to manage it, nurture it, and make it pay.* New York: John Wiley & Sons.
 17. Michalko M. (1991). *Thinkertoys.* Berkeley, Calif: Ten Speed Press.

*Asterisk indicates an article or book that is particularly informative and helpful.

18. Miller W. (1987). *The creative edge*. Reading, Mass: Addison-Wesley.
19. Quinn R. (1988). *Beyond rational management*. San Francisco: Jossey-Bass.
20. Quinn R, Faerman S, Thompson M & McGrath M. (1990). *Becoming a master manager*. New York: John Wiley & Sons.
21. Peters T. (1987). *Thriving on chaos*. New York: Harper & Row.
22. Raudsepp E. (1977). *Creative growth games*. New York: Putnam's Sons.
23. Raudsepp E. (1980). *More creative growth games*. New York: Putnam's Sons.
24. Raudsepp E. (1981). *How creative are you?* New York: Putnam's Sons.
25. Ray M & Myers R. (1986). *Creativity in business*. New York: Doubleday.
26. Russel P & Evans R. (1992). *The creative manager*. San Francisco: Jossey-Bass.
27. Thompson C. (1992). *What a great idea*. New York: HarperCollins.
28. Vail P. (1989). *Managing as a performing art*. San Francisco: Jossey-Bass.
29. Van Gundy A. (1982). *Training your creative mind*. Englewood Cliffs, NJ: Prentice-Hall.
30. von Oech R. (1986). *A kick in the seat of the pants*. New York: Harper & Row.
31. von Oech R. (1983). *A whack on the side of the head*. New York: Warner Books.

CHAPTER 7

Fiscal Responsibility

Jill Ridky

— ❧ —

The degree of prosperity depends on the way society uses its resources.

PROFESSOR JORDAN

The first line of Dickens' *A Tale of Two Cities*—"It was the best of times, it was the worst of times"—is quite applicable to managing in the academic environment, because it is the worst and the best of times, a threat and a resource. During these difficult economic times, institutions are coping with meeting budget deficits that could reach in excess of $87 million by 1993, and universities have imposed cuts of up to 13% on administrative and academic expenses to trim budgets by $43 million. Yale University is facing a deficit of more than $8 million in its $799 million budget, with plans to eliminate almost 11% of its faculty positions, merge three engineering departments, combine physics and applied physics, and eliminate linguistics. Most of the country's 3400 colleges and universities are struggling to balance income and spending.

Academics today is in a fiscal crisis, plagued by questions of how to fund academic institutions and programs. Uncertain economic times are causing major budget cuts and adjusted missions. The proposals and debates on budget, program, and organizational reductions have increased. Despite all the debates and lobbying, the underlying question remains: How do we manage scarce fiscal resources? Benefits will not be derived from cuts and a balanced budget unless we develop a clear understanding and hone skills regarding the utilization of fiscal resources.

TODAY'S FISCAL CLIMATE IN ACADEMICS

There are many factors actively at work today that shake the once passive and peaceful existence of academic organizations. Over the last few years there have been cries for cost containment, budget cuts, and questions ranging from "How are the universities managed?" to "What benefits do academic programs provide?" Concerns and demands haunt administrators today, not only as they analyze year-end data but also in day-to-day operations. As the director of the Smithsonian Institute suggested, "We are in an era that is defensive; everyone is suspicious and we are trying to do more with less."[1]

In an era that is defensive, the rise in proposals to limit spending and to cut deficits is not unexpected. However, is it possible for current obsessions and perceptions to be blurred and demands misdirected? Will budget cuts and fiscal balance really reap long-term dividends? What does spending more wisely mean? What does it mean for administrators to be fiscally responsible?

Current economic and political realities demand that academic organizations make wise use of scarce resources. Academic organizations exist and are developed in the economy because they are entrusted with and enjoy the use of private and public dollars put at their disposal. However, the fiscal system in academics has generally been one in which the organization has not been required to reduce costs, to improve programs, or to develop a better delivery system to benefit from the revenue. Accountability is increasingly important; a need exists for academic organizations to be more precise and efficient in the use of fiscal resources as the concern grows for minimizing waste and using donations and fees to benefit the people it serves rather than the institution.

Accountability and Legitimacy

Academic accountability evolved from an original trust that all organizations would be responsible for funds received and disbursed. Over the last decade, however, even the accounting methods have been questioned. Questions arise from the public because of increased concern and awareness that there are limited resources available to academics and a judgment must be made on how to allocate these resources. Decades ago, there was little concern among academics about accounting principles and financial guidelines because of the low financial profile of academic organizations. The business and financial affairs of academic institutions were of little interest outside the organization. For the most part, auditors received inadequate fees for their work. Historically, professional accountants and CPAs focused on the profit sector and developed professional relationships with the academics as part of community work or service, and they would work for the organization as a volunteer, contributing an in-kind service.

Society's acceptance of and the respect for academic institutions are essential to the existence, growth, and continuation of these organizations. The issue of acceptance, or organizational legitimacy, is tied closely to the economic financial activities of the organizations. Universities, especially those that are state supported, are frequently under attack. Many university presidents or other officers have had occasion to hear from legislators that "the very existence of this institution is at stake." As Peter Drucker maintains, administration is a very real responsibility for Academics because the organizations are a vital organ of society.

An academic organization will have a protected status within society as long as its output is considered legitimate. Yet many organizations, often to their surprise, find sectors of the public questioning their services and productivity and actively rallying to restrict or withdraw protected status. The concept of legitimacy is a concern for all academic programs because of the very real possibility that their legitimacy may be questioned or shifted at any time. One of the great challenges facing academic organizations is to establish the legitimacy of their output and of their methods of operation. This is the primary reason you will hear the term *fiscal responsibility* used in speeches, interviews, and reports. This term creates listener satisfaction (a condition to be desired for any organization), an aura that suggests that the organization is sound and legitimate.

Demanders and achievers

Legitimacy is created in the academic environment today with two primary actors: demanders and achievers. The *demanders* exist outside the academic organization; this group includes citizens, donors, contributors, volunteers, and "watchdogs." The *achievers* exist within the organization and include board members, administrators, chairs, division chiefs, directors, and officials. For the achievers, acquiring legitimacy requires convincing the public that they need a service such as education, training, or health care. Leaders and managers in academics have a responsibility to society to ensure the useful and appropriate application of financial resources; these resources should be employed effectively and efficiently to achieve predetermined ends. In reality, both the demanders and the achievers in the academic environment are guided by the same principles and dominated by a single, fundamental goal—success.

Achievers play a significant role in understanding and reviewing the financial position and condition of the organization and focusing on the administrative costs and revenue. Achievers carry with them a high fiduciary duty to carry out their responsibility. Gross mismanagement can leave board members and officers with potential legal liability. Service on the board of a public organization is not a social event, but rather a serious responsibility. Achievers are required to ask penetrating questions about the justification of budget dollars and to question the rationale for certain items being omitted from a budget. They must ensure that federal funds are not misspent, that management is not negligent, and that all have a good grasp on the reality of the financial situation confronting the organization. But, as Anthony and Herzlinger report, "In many organizations the corresponding line of responsibility is often not clear."[2] Board members have an important responsibility to act as one of the achievers when there is trouble. These people must closely watch and appraise the organization. "In order to have a sound basis for such an appraisal, board members need to spend a considerable amount of time learning what is going on in the organization, and they need to have enough expertise to understand the significance of what they learn."[2] Certainly the achievers aspire to responsible involvement with the resources of academics; yet in good conscience they do not know what this responsibility entails. For example, serving as a hospital trustee at one time conferred little more than an honor and an obligation to donate money. Today, however, boards are faced with the demand to cut costs without eliminating services. The board of the Children's Hospital in Detroit was planning a $20 million annex when cuts in government payments forced the trustees to shelve the plan and instead find existing programs to cut. In this case the board decided to keep an inner-city outpatient clinic and to stop supporting a poison information telephone service.[3] Such decisions reflect the dilemma of a trustee's need to be a prudent business manager and the desire to keep services and charitable programs alive.

Demanders can be sympathetic donors, alumni, citizens, foundations that want a service, and public watchdogs. Today the demanders' complaints are more frequent and increasingly critical. The most valuable resource of any academic organization is the willingness of demanders to give—the willingness of contributors, the government, municipalities, corporations, foundations, and granting agencies. If an organization is not considered responsible, willingness to give may erode. Naturally, eroding contributions will cause the revenue base to decline and the value and quality of the organization to deteriorate.

Although demanders are not finger-pointing, with every failed public organization, every fraud, every instance of accounting gimmickry, the demanders cry, "Where were the accountants, the auditors, the officials, the directors, the administrators, the managers?" As Joseph Connor stated in *The Wall Street Journal,* "The public perception is that the accounting profession has fallen short of its responsibilities as a 'public watchdog.' If we cannot have faith in those who are supposed to ensure integrity of the financial information, how can the demanders have faith?"[4] The expectations of the public or the demanders for organizations to be fiscally responsible is a major challenge facing academic organizations. Demanders expect early warnings of possible organizational failure or the disclosure of fraudulent reports. As government and private funding becomes tighter and costs continue to rise, demanders will most likely become even more selective and demanding. For example, a demander might demonstrate selectivity by deciding to contribute only enough funds to cover the expenses of a particular program. Demanders want more than verbal assurance from the organization that they will truly be paying only their fair share: fiscal documentation of the fact is requested. Ratings of organizations, particularly charities, by watchdog demanders have economic consequences. If information is shared with the media, adverse publicity can have a drastic effect. On the other hand, a positive rating by a watchdog group can lead to a significant advantage for one organization over another.

Although the future cannot be forecast for academic organizations, two conclusions can be stated. First, Kastens says, "The affluence enjoyed during the 1960s and early 1970s will not recur in this era; and secondly, the demands for prudent fiscal management and competence will continue to engage our energies and challenge our abilities."[5] The understanding of fiscal responsibility should be pursued not only to increase our understanding of the term, but also to improve academic organizations and the well-being of society. No longer do academic organizations exist in a world in which more and more funds or grants are available to solve every problem. Many colleges, universities, and other academic organizations continue to live by what Charles Levine called the "tooth-fairy syndrome," or the belief that if they muddle along as they have in the past, some benefactors or new conditions will miraculously appear from "under the pillow" to keep them going or to restore better days. The subject of fiscal responsibility has existed in a vacuum; as former Internal Revenue Service Commissioner Sheldon Cohen indicates, "No one has looked at the subject critically since the beginning of time. It cries out for scrutiny."[6]

All organizations compete for resources that are scarce, and most come to terms with the use of the resources within the environment. Today, with the great concern over growing budget deficits, the focus is on budget cuts or placing a ceiling on growth. We exist, improve, and excel in our society because of our resources. Their finite nature marks resources as valuable and precious. Yet what is our approach when utilizing financial resources? What does it mean for academic organizations to be fiscally responsible? How should a manager approach the resources of the academic organization?

The implication is clear: Academic organizations must be responsible for the resources they receive and for the results of the organizational activity. Academic programs, as valuable as they are, must do more in return for the special status they enjoy. Therefore, it is timely and important to discover how fiscal responsibility has been assessed in the past and, in light of recent changes in our economy and society, to consider what fiscal responsibility means today for academic organizations. The general topic of fiscal responsibility has not been extensively studied or conceptualized into practical terms for academic managers, administrators, and board members. Yet the term is important, and its applications are essential to organizations.

Academic institutions need to get a tight grip on operations, since it has become so hard to raise revenues or capital. As Robert H. Atwell, President of the American Council on Education, stated, "My message is, things are not going to get better for a long time." What does it mean for a dean, chair, program director, or division chief managing a $100,000 budget or a multimillion-dollar budget to be fiscally responsible?

THE HISTORIC CONTEXT FOR FISCAL RESPONSIBILITY

A look back into our history reveals the importance and meaning of the term fiscal responsibility for Adam Smith in the 1700s. Smith's writings, such as *The Wealth of Nations,* stressed the importance of utilizing finances to bring about a maximum advantage to a community. Smith believed a community or society would benefit by balancing expenditures and revenues. Smith wrote, "The aim of the statesman is not simply to distribute loss and reduce it to a minimum; it is rather to procure the maximum advantage to the community and to so balance expenditure and revenue as to attain that result."[7] Other economists also wrote about the utilization of resources. In the 1800s, Knut Wicksell, a Swedish economist, is credited with mentioning fiscal responsibility, along with C.F. Bastable, a Scottish economist. In "Our Taxes," Wicksell indicated the need for taxpayers to be guaranteed a certain benefit from their contribution by the suitable employment of state funds. "Each social group, indeed each member of the community if possible, should be able to feel that the annual tribute is not money wasted but is something which will bring real, additional benefit to society."[8] The important element for fiscal responsibility, Wicksell recognized, was that proposals for expenditure be

Your father and I are curious, son.
If they didn't teach you how to balance
budgets to get your degree in economics,
what *did* they teach you?

SOURCE: Wall Street Journal, *Salt and Pepper*

coupled with proposals covering cost. "If a legislator is able to propose expenditure programs without having to make an explicit proposal to cover the cost, fiscal irresponsibility will creep in because the legislator can get away with promising benefits without saying from whom the resources will be taken."[9] Fiscal irresponsibility typically refers to money being raised, and all of it being spent.

WHAT IS FISCAL RESPONSIBILITY?

For AHCs, what does the term fiscal responsibility mean? Does it refer to the balance of revenue and expenditures? Does it refer to proper accounting controls or sound financial reporting? Does it refer to the two-sided nature of budgets? Or does fiscal responsibility mean raising money but not spending all of it?

The most significantly problematic feature of the past and present definition is the tendency to view fiscal responsibility as merely a condition in which revenue is greater than or in balance with expenditures. This definition is too one-dimensional, considering the complexity of our present organizations, and the present structure of academic institutions is too elaborate to predicate a definition of fiscal responsibility solely on the principle of revenue in balance with expenditures.

Is fiscal responsibility a single event, or is it a dynamic process involving many characteristics? Does the simplistic relationship of revenue to expenditure exhaust the definition? Are revenue and expenditure the only fiscally related concepts for academic institutions? Is the definition a product of the age in which it is defined? Does the knowledge of whether expenditures equal revenue indicate that an organization is fiscally responsible? It may indicate whether the organization is financially stable or capable of growth, but, as Kastens states, "The purpose of building a boat is not to see it float but to provide transportation. If it floats it means the construction was successful, but it does not tell us if the venture was successful."[5] Does the "bottom-line" concept mean fiscal responsibility?

From the 1900s to the present, the definition primarily emphasized a disequilibrium of revenue and expenditures. Another problematic issue, then, is whether debt or deficit is responsible or irresponsible. Tollison and Wagner state, "In profit organizations debt is the cheapest form of new capital funds."[9] Although deficits and debt entail a risk to solvency, might there not also be a chance for a long-term advantage? Or does deficit capacity rely on the judgment of the situation or the judgment of management?

There is a fear of deficits, as presented and demonstrated in the historical definition of fiscal responsibility; however, in today's environment is there a place for deficits? Can the proper extension and management of debt perform a vital function and lead an organization to fiscal responsibility, or are organizational deficits fiscally irresponsible? As Regina Herzlinger maintained, "Deficit spending, per se, is not undesirable if it is part of a well-articulated long-run plan. It is the fact that many deficits are surprises that is of concern."[11]

Finally, what about the current definitions that include concepts such as money managing, gathering, holding, and expending? Is this fiscal responsibility? Do efficient accounting and management define fiscal responsibility? Vinter and Kish note, "Excellent use of resources does not equal excellent accounting."[12] Max Singer, author of *The Vitality of Mythical Numbers,* elaborates on the fact that over-reliance on precise numbers alone can lead to misapprehensions by managers. The key point is not the precision or the official status of numbers but the understanding of what lies behind them and what they mean. It is much better to have a crude estimate based on a good understanding than to have a precise statistic or exact calculation, however authoritative, that is conceptually flawed. Again, a program with a meticulous accounting system may not be fiscally responsible. The definitions also do not present the concept of "human will" within organizations. Is there not a degree of human will in fiscal responsibility and the possibility of choosing between different courses, some of which are likely to prove better than others? Although definitions of fiscal responsibility have been developed and adopted, the definitions contain language that limits our understanding. Can we arrive at an adequate definition if we focus only on budgets, revenue, and expenditures? Might we not ignore or misrepresent some aspects that play an important part in this dynamic concept and behavior—concepts such as allocation, resource utilization, management, and reformation?

The Function of Fiscal Responsibility

The function of fiscal responsibility needs to be understood. As Winston Churchill once wrote, "It is much more likely that the process will be improved if we understand its essential function." In exploring the function and the process of fiscal responsibility, we again turn to Wicksell. Knut Wicksell was an ardent believer in economic freedom and, most of all, the means to further general welfare. Uhr notes, "Wicksell believed in economic progress in terms of maximizing the output of goods and services with a given level of economic resources." [13] Wicksell's concepts developed the sensitivity for economic progress, the concepts of maximizing output, furthering general welfare, satisfying human needs with resources, and regard for future generations. These are the concepts administrators struggle with daily but have not been able to develop into a conceptual or systemic understanding. These are the concepts that are so very pertinent to the topic of fiscal responsibility.

How can administrators maximize financial resources? How do administrators convert a dollar into a product or service that will provide the greatest human welfare? The goals of academics rest on the assertion that institutions act and that these actions are purposeful and directed toward a conscious end—to maximize service. As Wicksell believed, "Our goal on earth is to spread the greatest possible happiness to all regardless of class, race, sex, language or religion. The aim [is] . . . the maximization of human welfare." [13]

The generic goal for all academic institutions is to offer quality service, given an amount of funding, or to use as few resources as possible to render a given amount of quality service. Academic medical centers offer as much quality service as possible and provide quality educational opportunities to as many students as possible. These goals match conventional economic theory, which says, "Economic units try to do as well as they can when they make choices, in other words, maximize." [12] This assumption means organizations minimize cost per unit of service—maximizing service and minimizing cost.

Three Phases of Fiscal Responsibility

The three principal phases of strictly equal rank and importance in fiscal responsibility are reformation, allocation, and management (RAM). RAM recognizes the responsibilities rooted in the fact that every academic institution has a potential for achievement that cannot be attained without organizational direction and effort. If the factors are not understood or are neglected and stagnate or malinger, the organization will waste finite resources and opportunities. Inherent in the concept of RAM is the unwritten law that "organizations should endeavor to reach the highest level of existence which they are able to attain in view of their resources and capabilities." [13] As Figure 7-1 demonstrates, public, state, and federal support dollars or revenue resources enter the organization as an input. The finite revenue resources are commissioned to be utilized and maximized. As Knight states, "The problem of life is to utilize resources economically and to make them go as far as possible in the production of desired results." [19] The aim is to produce the maximum advantage to the public or society.

Revenue resources are reformed, allocated, and managed by the organization in an environment of rationality and preference. The RAM factors use resources to produce new value to society or to public welfare. The generic goal to produce a service becomes a consequence of the activities that occurred after the dollars flowed

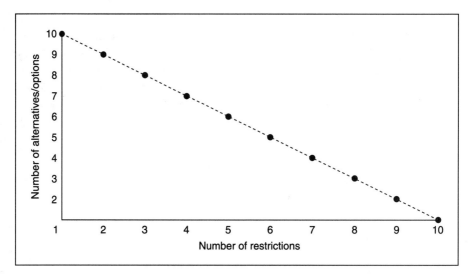

Figure 7-1. The choice function demonstrates the relationship of restrictions to alternatives or options. As restrictions increase, alternatives decrease, creating a diminishing choice curve.

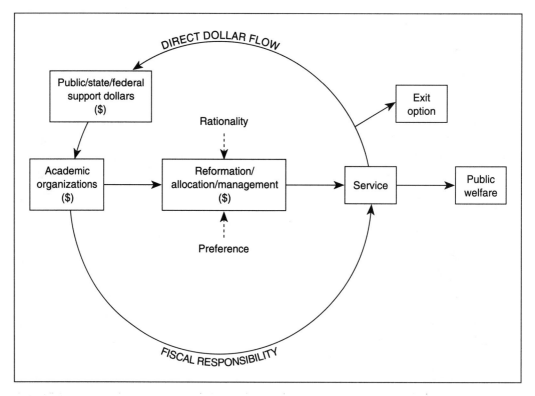

Figure 7-2. Conceptual schematic of fiscal responsibility model incorporating the elements of reformation, allocation, and management (RAM). (Adapted from Ridky J. [1985]. The meaning of fiscal responsibility [dissertation].)

into the organization. The quantity and quality produced with the designated support dollars create a valence, a value, a worth and attractiveness. Contributors or grantors at this phase make the decision either to continue or to exit support. The existing support either dissolves or supports another organization.

Reformation

One phase, then, of fiscal responsibility could be called *transformation,* since transformation refers to a change; you take a dollar and transform it into something else. However, in terms of fiscal responsibility the transition should be more radical than just a change. The emphasis should be on change for the better. The term *reformation* places the emphasis on change for the better, or improvement by changing the form. For example, reformation would tell a university developer holding a resource of 100 acres of prime property with graceful hardwoods not to transform the land (change it into something else) but to change it for the better—that is, change and develop the land only if it can be improved. For an administrator, reformation means taking a dollar and changing its value into something more valuable, something that will further general welfare or will maximize outputs. Reformation is the first phase of fiscal responsibility.

Reformation mandates that the organization make choices and look at alternatives and options for reforming inputs into output (Figure 7-2). Reformation asserts that an organization has a "will" that gives it control over its actions. This implies that the organization can rank alternatives, priorities, options, and constraints and select from the alternatives that rank highest. Choices are then made after selecting the alternative whose consequence ranks highest based on the organizational goals.

No organization knows with certainty what choice is best, but choices are intended to result in providing the best possible service with the available resources. Choices may also be limited, depending on the restrictions placed on funding. For example, an educational institution receiving funding with restrictions on capital equipment purchases will not have a choice of which funding is to be utilized. The more funding restrictions, the fewer the choices, creating the choice function.

Another concept within reformation is the idea of rationality, and a value system. The rationality and value system of the organization ultimately provide the direction for fiscal responsibility within the organization. The concept of rationality is based not only on intelligent behavior but also on behavior motivated by a conscious calculation of advantages, a calculation that in turn is based on an explicit and internally consistent value system. As Allison discusses, in the rigorous model of rational action, "rational choice consists of value maximizing."[14] But Allison sagaciously questions, "What guarantees that value-maximizing behavior within these parameters will in fact maximize the organization values?" Or, what guarantees that an organization that demonstrates rational value-maximizing behavior will, in fact, maximize services and be fiscally responsible? Obviously it would not if the set of alternatives failed to include an option with a consequence ranking higher than any of the stated alternatives.

To maintain the concept of "rational or optimal choice," academic institutions are faced with two possibilities: (1) they can utilize the assumption of comprehensive rationality or (2) utilize the assumption of limited rationality. *Comprehensive rationality* requires the accurate mapping of all consequences in terms of the organization's goals and values. *Limited rationality* restricts the number of consequences the organization would review. Most theories of individual and organizational choice employ a concept of comprehensive rationality, where the organization selects the best alternatives, taking account of the consequences and their probabilities. Comprehensive rationality requires the following:

- Generation of all possible alternatives
- Assessment of the probabilities of all consequences of each alternative
- Evaluation of each set of consequences for all relevant goals

However, organizations must realize the limitation constraint when using comprehensive rationality. The limitation is based on human capacity when dealing with complex organizational problems or choices. In addition to comprehensive and limited rationality, there is a term called *bounded rationality;* this means that humans and organizations have a physical and psychological limit or a limited capacity as an alternative generator, information processor, and problem solver. This limitation constrains the decision-making process and requires simplified models that extract the main features of a problem or a goal without capturing all of its capacity.

Reformation should be approached with the concept of comprehensive rationality. What economic theorist Thorstein Veblen cited about the economy is that it is "not the price system but the value system of the culture in which the economy is embedded." [15] Academic institutions should attempt to find the "best needle in the haystack," thereby maximizing and not satisfying, thereby reforming and not transforming. In the process of comprehensive rationality there must also be an awareness of bounded rationality. Although organizations should attempt to review all alternatives, organizations are limited by human capacity.

Underlying reformation is the concept of preference. *Preference* refers to that which guides the organization's behavior and touches upon the goals, choices, and decisions. Haley notes, "The preference function is a result of influences which affect the value premises of the organization's goals and strategy." [16] The way resources are reformed depends on the concept of preference. "The preference function means the organization understands the means-ends relationships and the organization acts to maximize the output. The decisions are affected heavily by the preferences of the institution/organization." The organizational values, beliefs, and concerns all become in the end the organization's preference function or the impetus for the way resources are reformed or are not reformed.

Allocation

The second phase of fiscal responsibility is *allocation*. Like reformation, the allocation of resources within an academic institution is a critical phase in determining organizational output. Vinter and Kish provide a definition: "To allocate means to set apart, or earmark things for a specific purpose; to allot, to parcel out according to a plan." [12] The extent to which an organization has resources depends on how much was raised, earned, and contributed in the past over and above consumption needs. This in turn depends on how skillfully past resources have been used or reformed to produce new value. Resources are finite and therefore, if they are allocated in one place, they cannot be used somewhere else. The activities receiving resources are elected to live and function within the organization. Yet little has been done to guide the manager of the institution in making resource allocations. Without the proper understanding of reformation, there will always be ambiguity and arbitrariness in the resource allocation process.

Presently, many academic organizations allocate resources on a historical basis, although student choice may occasionally affect the allocation. Budget allocations tend to be made to each unit on the basis of the unit's previous allocation, taking into account changes in the total resources available for allocation. Thus evolves the tendency for the organization to do next year what it is doing this year.

Organizations use a variety of approaches to eliminate this trend. Cyert says, "Sometimes all but a given decrement of 10% of the previous year's budget is allocated to the unit and the chair or the director of the unit must make an argument as to why they should get additional funds."[18] Those making the best argument will get the largest increment. Another device is to require an examination each year of the total amount that the units need by forcing each unit to make an argument each year for its existence.

All of these devices suffer from the fact that no systematic framework exists for the evaluation of the quality of arguments. In an organization, arguments for an increased allocation have to be made in terms of reformation, given the total resources available. As Cyert maintains, "A major problem confronting the university administration is the allocation of resources."[18] To determine the amount of funds that must be allocated to individual units, it is necessary to have completed reformation.

Management

The third phase in fiscal responsibility is *management*. As Kastens states, "The organization is a shell which cannot be managed, but resources can. Whenever the resources are committed to a purposeful end, there must be management."[5] The justification for good management exists irrespective of whether the environment calls for a contraction or expansion or whether we are in the throes of inflation, deflation, or recession. All of us can recall numerous cases of mismanagement, or newspaper headlines which read "Mishandling of Federal Funds," "Officials Knew Funds Were Misspent," "Misused School Funds" or statements that read "There was a kind of climate of not being too fastidious about hewing strictly to the line and following rules and regulations and policies." Espousing the cause of good management is a daily task that requires vigilance. "The function of management is to devise systems to make resources productive. . . . Management will use its resources efficiently only if it acknowledges that it is responsible each day for the decisions of the day."[5] Management keeps the framework running. Kastens says, "Any public and private organization is resource intensive and management of those resources is critical to its economic health."[5]

What Fiscal Responsibility Is Not

Fiscal responsibility is *not:*
- Being frugal
- Being static
- Finding an objective or objectives around which a story value–maximizing choice can be constructed
- Being accountable
- Raising funds, accounting for them, and balancing expenditures and revenue

Fiscal responsibility takes on the following properties:
- It is dynamic
- It is vital
- It is ongoing
- It is a technique, a skill for providing and distributing services with society's resources
- It is an action taken with the purpose or intent of functioning and being cohesively interwoven with components
- It is analytical—that is, not necessarily totally mathematical, but the process of thinking through a problem in a systematic manner, helping organizations to know and recognize the trade-offs that exist among variables

CONCLUSION

Fiscal responsibility encompasses the concept of revenue resources—finite resources that enter the organization and must be reformed, allocated, and managed. Fiscal responsibility requires the organization to take the revenue resources and to reform, allocate, and manage them in such a way that the organization creates something of value that did not exist before. Fiscal responsibility is the process by which public and client support dollars are converted into value, making explicit the critical relationship between reformation, allocation, and management. The foundation of fiscal responsibility is the assumption of rational behavior—not just of intelligent behavior, but of behavior motivated by a conscious calculation of advantages, a calculation that in turn is based on an explicit and internally consistent value and preference system.

Fiscal responsibility shows the goals, values, and preferences the organization is pursuing and how the action is a reasonable choice, given the organization's objective. It is an action capsuled in rationality, value, and preference. Fiscal responsibility is formed by ability, understanding, and effort combined to produce a given level of organizational performance. Fiscal responsibility, then, should yield optimal results in the sense of maximizing quality services. The public sector must be inculcated with the concept that it has been entrusted with certain resources that have been placed at its disposal and that the responsibility exists to reform, allocate, and manage those resources as optimally as possible. *Therefore, fiscal responsibility can be defined as the rational reformation, allocation, and management of finite revenue resources.*

BIBLIOGRAPHY

*1. Hume E. (1986, March 31). Leader of Smithsonian faces budget worries predecessor never had. *The Wall Street Journal,* p 1.

*2. Anthony RN & Herzlinger RE. (1980). *Management control in nonprofit organizations.* Homewood, Ill: Richard D Irwin, Inc, p 47.

*3. Wessel D. (1986, March 18). Hospital trustees bound together as financial and charitable goals clash. *The Wall Street Journal.*

4. Conner J. (1985, December 3). Close accounting confidence gap. *The Wall Street Journal,* p 30.

5. Kastens ML. (1980). *Redefining a manager's job.* New York: American Management Association.

*6. Orr K & Quick B. (1983). Nonprofit groups: Are they worth their tax breaks? *US News and World Report, 94,* 40.

7. Break GF & Rolph ER. (1961). *Public finance.* New York: The Ronald Press Co, p 7.

8. Torsten G. (1958). *The life of Knut Wicksell.* Sweden: Almquist & Wicksells, p 157.

9. Tollison RD & Wagner RE. (1980). *Balanced budgets, fiscal responsibility and the constitution.* San Francisco: The Cato Institute, p 27.

10. Beardsley PL. (1980). *Redefining rigor.* Beverly Hills: Sage Publications, p 15.

11. Herzlinger R. (1978, June 9). *Observations of financial management in public television.*

12. Vinter RD & Kish RK. (1984). *Budgeting for not-for-profit organizations.* New York: The Free Press, p 21.

13. Uhr CG. (1960). *Economic doctrines of Knut Wicksell.* Berkeley: University of California Press, p 27.

14. Allison GT. (1971). *Essence of decision.* Boston: Little Brown, p 31.

15. Bell D & Kristol I, eds. (1980). *The crisis in economic theory.* New York: Basic Books, Inc, p 99.

16. Haley BF, ed. (1952). *A survey of contemporary economics.* Homewood, Ill: Richard D Irwin, p 206.

17. James E. (1983, Spring). How nonprofits grow: A model. *Journal of Policy Analysis and Management,* p 358.

18. Cyert RM. (1975). *The management of nonprofit organizations.* London: Lexington Books, p 18.

19. Knight FH. (1936). Limitations of scientific methods. In *The ethics of competition.* Chicago: University of Illinois Press, p 105.

20. Stone CD. (1975). *From where the law ends.* New York: Harper & Row, p 69.

*Asterisk indicates an article or book that is particularly informative and helpful.

CHAPTER 8

Human and Organizational Resource Development

Carole J. Bland • Jill Ridky

Little change can trigger large consequences—in corporations, schools and hospitals. And this is why, despite everything, people—even individuals—still count.

ALVIN TOFFLER, *The Third Wave*

A vital institution is one that creates and sustains organizational strategies that support the continued investment of energy by faculty and staff both to their own careers and to the realization of the institutional mission.

T.H. MAHER

An old Chinese proverb says, "If you want one year of prosperity, grow grain; if you want 10 years of prosperity, grow trees; and if you want 100 years of prosperity, grow people." Today the highest percentage of an AHC's resources is expended on salaries and benefits for faculty, residents, students, and staff. This represents a substantial investment in human resources. As Figure 8-1 demonstrates, when the expenditure line items for a given fiscal year were analyzed for an academic medical department, 64% of the expenditures was for salaries and benefits. This percentage is typical of most academic units. If people are appointed and then not developed, this will quickly become an investment without a positive return. Thus AHCs are giving increasing attention to "growing" their human resources.

Most departments recognize the importance of hiring good people. Thus they spend countless hours and significant effort and financial resources to support the recruitment of new faculty, staff, and residents. These departments conduct rigorous national searches in which they expend hours developing recruitment packages, recruiting by interviewing, dining, following up on references, and so on. All of these efforts, however, frequently stop once a candidate accepts the appointment. To get the most from this initial investment in recruitment, departments need to move beyond the "fish-and-catch" phase. Whether the appointment is for a faculty, resident, or staff position, lifelong development of the candidate is critical to the long-term success of the new member and of the department or program.

This chapter discusses how to recruit and continually support and develop human resources. Unlike some discussions on development, this chapter is directed not just to faculty development, but to all members of the organization. In today's organizational environment, a successful manager remembers that *human resources* means people—each important and valuable, each with concerns requiring the manager's focused attention.

The purpose of a human resource and organizational development program is to increase productivity by continually assisting and developing staff (new and experienced, administrative and nonadministrative) as well as continually improving the organizational environment in which they work. An effective academic organization relies not only on the continual development of staff and faculty, but productivity and vitality also depend on the development of administrators and on the presence of environmental features that facilitate quality work and work life: equitable personnel policies, effective reward structures, and a supportive climate. Ultimately, to facilitate continuous individual and collective productivity, a department, college, hospital, or academic health center should aim for a comprehensive human resource program that addresses all staff at all career stages. In this chapter we will focus on new faculty and new residents, because these are the academic members most at risk for failure. Programs designed for all faculty, whatever their career stage, are also briefly addressed.

Before we focus on staff and faculty development, we should examine a comprehensive model for developing professional and institutional effectiveness

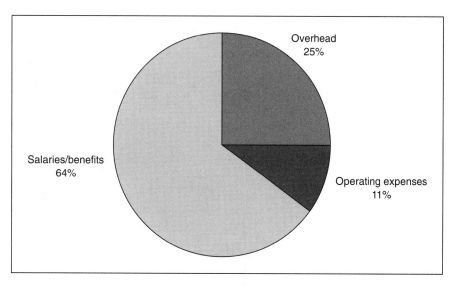

Figure 8-1. Academic medical department's budget for a fiscal year, showing percentages of expenditures.

that can provide an overview of the broader field of human and organizational development. Bergquist, Phillips, and Gruber[1] provide a comprehensive model of human and organizational resource development in their recent book, *Developing Human and Organizational Resources: A Comprehensive Manual.* This model is summarized in the box on p. 133. Drawing on the work of Watson and Johnson,[2] the model states that a successful development effort influences three aspects of an organization: the attitudes of people who perform the work (values, expectations, dreams), the processes used to perform work (teaching, research, writing, patient care), and the structure (lines of authority, procedures, functional units). Anything that has an impact on any one of these aspects eventually affects the other two. Thus the rows in the box on p. 133 are labeled *attitude, process,* and *structure.* (We will discuss the fourth row, *diagnosis/assessment,* later.)

To address these three aspects, over the years three broad development approaches have been used: organizational development, functional development, and personal development. The organizational development approach assumes that people and organizations are improved by focusing on issues larger than the individual person. Thus organizational development strategies include such things as establishing an institutional culture, team building, and adjusting personnel policies or the reward system.

Proponents of the functional development approach concentrate on arming people with the skills, attitudes, and knowledge required to be productive continually in a constantly changing organization. Here the common strategies are technical training, leadership development, and career planning.

The personal development approach assumes that individuals bring to the organization not just their job skills but also personal characteristics and circumstances that affect their professional productivity, such as interpersonal skills, financial status, habits, prejudices, and family situations. Thus advocates of this approach use strategies to address these areas, for example, sensitivity training, personal counseling, interpersonal skill training, and advocating for personal services such as in-house child care.

These three dominant approaches to human and organizational development are shown as the column headings in the box on p. 133. The columns offer examples of the strategies the three dominant approaches use to address the three key aspects of an organization.[1]

The bottom row of the box is labeled *diagnosis/assessment.* Each human and organizational development approach selects which improvement strategy to use after assessing the current level of development of the individual or organization. This row provides examples of the type of assessment methods each development approach uses.

At the present time the training model—or functional development approach—is the one most used by organizations to facilitate the lifelong productivity of their workforce and, collectively, the organization. Functional development (job training) is also the focus of this chapter. However, you should note that to be optimally productive, an organization should work toward a comprehensive approach to human and organizational development as described in the box.

A COMPREHENSIVE MODEL FOR THE DEVELOPMENT OF
HUMAN AND ORGANIZATIONAL RESOURCES

	Organization development	Functional development	Personal development
Attitude	Organizational culture interventions	Employee motivation programs Employee transitions programs	Creativity/sensitivity development workshops Personal counseling
Process	Process consultation Team building	Technical training Management skills development	Interpersonal skills training Self-management workshops
Structure	Sociotechnical Personnel policies/ procedures design	Job planning and design Incentive planning and design	Employee support services
Diagnosis/ assessment	Organizational diagnosis	Performance appraisal	Life/career planning

From Bergquist W, Phillips S & Gruber S. (1992). *Developing human and organizational resources: A comprehensive manual.* San Francisco: Professional School of Psychology.

Next we present an approach to faculty development and resident recruitment and conclude with a brief reminder of the importance of also attending to organization features.

FACULTY DEVELOPMENT

Schuster and Wheeler[3] described eight megatrends that have resulted in increased attention to faculty development. Although they are directed to faculty, these megatrends relate to all members of higher education organizations:

- Working conditions have deteriorated.
- Compensation for faculty has faded.
- The academic labor market has been inhospitable.
- Faculty find themselves caught in a cross-fire of conflicting expectations (e.g., teach more *and* generate more financial support).
- Faculty are growing older and increasingly more tenured.
- Shifting values on campuses leave some faculty feeling undervalued and frustrated.
- Changing conditions have had a negative impact on faculty morale.
- Legislators are calling for greater efficiency and accountability of faculty members.

There is a clear need for supporting faculty and staff now, more than ever, as programs attempt to reach and accomplish admirable goals with tightened budgets in a turbulent higher education environment. Compared with excellent corporations, who claim approximately 10% of their budget goes to human resource development, campuses appear to have accorded faculty development little priority. Critics maintain that even when development programs are present in higher education organizations, they neglect to address development in a comprehensive way. Most campuses do little to help members succeed beyond assistance with some of the basic tasks such as grant preparation, computer training, and teaching.

Thus AHCs need to look at fresh approaches to recruiting and assisting all members, once appointed, to achieve their aspirations and ultimately the program's, department's, school's, and institution's mission. To help campuses wishing to embark on a faculty development effort, Bland and Schmitz[4] reviewed the literature and identified critical features of an effective program:

- Ensure faculty ownership and planning in the vitality program.
- Use a faculty and administrator advisory committee.
- Reward faculty participation in activities.
- Address and reaffirm institutional values and missions as well as academic values and purpose.
- Assess faculty administrator and staff needs before starting a program.
- Estimate the costs of a faculty development program and make it a part of the institutional budget.
- Ensure administrative commitment—it is essential.

The first step, then, in designing an effective program is to involve faculty, staff, and administrators in deciding whether to provide a program or not, and if so, what it should look like. To help you design a program, we will next discuss likely elements of a human resources program for new faculty members: deciding to recruit a new faculty member, recruiting a new faculty member, welcoming strategies, assisting socialization, mentoring, assisting teaching, assisting writing, and assisting research. The areas of socialization, teaching, writing, and research are addressed because studies identify these as areas in which faculty, to be successful, must possess a minimum set of basic skills.[5] Some research also includes administration as an essential skill area for faculty. Strategies for addressing the needs of established faculty members are also discussed. The elements of a program for all faculty are career planning, editing, instructional assistance, and special programs.

A PROGRAM FOR NEW FACULTY MEMBERS
Deciding to Recruit a New Member

Recruitment is best conducted in the context of and as a means of achieving a program's or department's goals and objectives. Every year and as a part of the program's planning activity the level of staffing, staffing needs, and expansion areas should be reviewed. When areas are considered lacking or in need of growth, or when new programs are developed that current staff cannot accommodate, then recruitment of new faculty needs to be considered.

The chair or program director, ideally in conjunction with a faculty development committee and/or senior staff, should carefully review the productivity and goals of individual faculty members, looking for opportunities to promote and develop individuals. They should also review the career stages of existing faculty, the number expected to retire, their health status, and any other trends that might signal future vacancies. This analysis will allow existing personnel to grow in the organization and prevent the need for "crisis recruitment" activities, avoid members stagnating or developing in ways inconsistent with program objectives, and lead to a more stable, durable, and effective organization.

Chairs or program directors must also be alert to the need to review and communicate staffing needs to those responsible for approving new position requests at the institution. In times of state and private funding cuts, vacant positions may not be automatically approved for recruitment. The needs and justification for filling a vacant position should be clearly communicated to the dean of the center or school.

Deciding How to Recruit Faculty Members

A professional level of recruitment activities is needed to attract faculty who are highly qualified and the best fit for a department or program. Matier notes, "By one estimate, between 1990 and 2004, departments will need to recruit 335,000 new faculty . . . and do so in an intensely competitive seller's market."[6] Thus it is important that managers in academics develop rigorous recruitment programs that attract quality candidates. Bowen and Schuster[7] further point out that by the year 2009, the number of new appointments will likely equal two thirds of the entire 1985 faculty. "Thus the caliber of the faculty as a whole will be largely determined by the appointments made between 1986 and 2010." How do managers in academics successfully develop a recruitment program?

Every institution seems to have its own individual style of recruitment as well as specific advertising, recruitment, and hiring procedures. Thus it is important to check with your institution's office of personnel, human resources, or equal opportunity to be certain of these procedures. These offices will often have handbooks or kits to guide the search committee through their process. If your institution does not have such a guidebook, you may find it helpful to look at resources from other institutions or national associations, for example, from the University of Minnesota, *Guidelines for Academic Searches*[8]; the American Association for Higher Education's *The Search Committee Handbook: A Guide to Recruiting Administrators*[9]; from the Association of American Colleges, *It's All in What You Ask: Questions for Search Committees to Use*[10]; or *Looking for More Than a Few Good Women in Traditionally Male Fields.*[11]

Although a variety of recruitment approaches are used, there are some commonalities among successful recruitment plans. The plan is usually prepared by the appointing official, who also decides whether to recruit at a senior or junior level. A strong junior-level appointee offers the advantage of having his or her early professional growth occur in alignment with the needs of the organization. Some also believe that junior candidates bring more energy and malleability to the hiring institution than do candidates who became established in another institution. On the other hand, an advantage to recruiting a senior-level faculty member is the immediate depth and national network he or she can bring to a department. Of course, a senior appointee will cost more to hire than a junior one—but a senior appointee can often *generate* more income as well, via grants, consultations, special procedures, and so on.

The first step in a systematic search is to prepare a description of the position. The careful preparation of the position description is critical. It will guide the search committee, be the first introduction of the job to potential candidates, and serve as the basis for deciding who to hire. It should describe the major job functions and the criteria for the evaluation of applicants. The box on p. 137 offers more detail on the job description.

Next the appointing official selects a search committee and appoints the chair, who should be highly regarded, an experienced professional with a significant professional network, respected by diverse constituencies, skilled in conducting meetings, and experienced in conducting recruitment searches of qualified individuals, especially women and minorities.

The committee will be responsible for identifying qualified candidates, evaluating curricula vitae (CVs), following up with references, interviewing candidates, and recommending top candidates to the appointing official, such as the director, chair, or dean.

Search committees vary in size, but usually consist of three to eight members. The committee should include women and minority members where possible, and if the position is for an interdepartment position, each department should be represented. It may also be appropriate and valuable to ask a non-insider to assist in the search. For example, if searching for a university or hospital attorney, ask a local highly regarded attorney to be on the committee; if the search is for a residency director, ask a director of a successful program elsewhere to be a member; or if searching for a clinician or researcher with unique skills, ask a similar person in another department to be a member.

At the first meeting of the committee the appointing official should go over the job description and formally give the committee their charge. We suggest the charge also be provided in writing to the committee and should include:

- The date by which the names of final candidates should be forwarded to him or her
- The minimum and maximum number of candidates expected
- Equal opportunity/affirmative action requirements and expectations; the affirmative action officer may make a brief presentation
- Union requirements (if appropriate)
- Financial and staff support available (e.g., phone calls, advertising budget, meals, candidate expenses—meals, housing, travel)
- Required records—some institutions require minutes of meetings and records on any contacts with nominees, applicants, and references
- Special aspects of this position or this search

DEVELOPING QUALIFICATIONS AND CRITERIA

Developing essential qualifications
Qualifications must be job related.
They must be demonstrable and/or measurable.
Qualifications must be already developed and position training not considered.
Qualifications represent the tools necessary to perform the job well.
If qualifications become too specialized, the candidate pool is reduced.

Developing selection criteria
Establish the criteria before recruitment begins.
Criteria should be job related.
Selection criteria should be ranked by importance.
Criteria must be free of bias.
Criteria must be measurable or demonstrable.

Adapted from University of Minnesota Guidelines for Academic Searches (1992) Minneapolis.

Next the committee begins its search. It is important to remember that this is a *search* committee; their most important function is to identify at least three and sometimes as many as five serious final candidates. In addition to attracting candidates by journal advertisements and networking at national meetings, recommendations by other managers, chairs, or program directors, faculty, and staff should be aggressively solicited. National organizations can also be good resources. Advertising in nontraditional organizations or publications may be appropriate such as the National Indian Education Association, Association of Mexican American Educators, and the American Association of University Women. In compliance with most institutions' affirmative action policies and to acquire the benefits of a diverse organization, women, African Americans, disabled, and other minorities should be actively sought during the recruitment process. Women and minorities have had so little success in academe that many institutions have developed special programs to which a search committee can turn for assistance in recruiting and promoting these candidates. For example, the University of Minnesota has pamphlets to help search committees, such as "Active Recruitment of Women and Minorities" and a "Multicultural Guide to the Twin Cities," which can be included in information packets sent to candidates. It is suggested that search committees query all candidates on their understanding of and approach to diversity and interest in working in an inclusive organization. Considerable creative effort should be expended by each member of the committee to build as rich a pool of applicants as possible. After all, the final candidate may well be their colleague for a lifetime. It has been said it is easier to divorce a spouse than to change one's colleagues in a "tenured-in" department.

The committee will find the task of reviewing CVs easier if a review protocol and a means of weighting information drawn from the CVs is established. If there are many applicants, such a system can allow subsets of CVs to be reviewed by different members of the committee. At this stage a special effort should be made to broadly consider unique experiences, training, and backgrounds. Women and minorities often do not fit the typical career ladder or academic profile.

Candidates whose CV information receives high weightings should next be screened by seeking information from their references. Requesting general letters of reference on these candidates is a start, but it may be more efficient, depending on the job, to ask the individuals providing references to address specific areas. You may also want to talk personally with reference persons and with others who have worked closely with the applicants. It is important to get multiple perspectives. Remember, few people are highly regarded by everyone, so one negative conversation should not rule out a candidate. On the other hand, completely positive references collected only from the people named by the applicant probably will not reveal the complete picture.

Once credentials, experience, and references are reviewed and an initial list of top candidates is prepared, the top candidates should be invited for an initial interview. Before the interview, a core set of questions and areas to be covered should be developed and given to the candidate and to interviewers. A system should be established for summarizing and using the information gathered during the interview. In addition, the committee chair should review some principles of effective interviewing with committee members:

- Listen carefully.
- Provide a good impression—treat the individual as a scarce resource.
- Stay on schedule.
- Ask productive questions regarding interests, accomplishments, and future plans.
- Be slow to judge.
- During the interview process, don't leave the candidate alone to fend for herself or himself.

Besides the specific questions regarding the job for which the person is needed, the committee members should also attempt to assess the following:

- The candidate's energy and achievement level
- The candidate's general strengths/weaknesses in relation to job responsibilities (e.g., teaching, research, patient care, administration, and qualifications such as degrees, experience, products)
- The candidate's concerns, enthusiasm, interest level
- The candidate's attitude
- Is the candidate known by existing faculty?

Of course, the interview works both ways, so the committee should be clear about how and what the candidate will be able to learn about the job, organization, colleagues, and city. The boxes on pp. 139 and 140 illustrate sample agendas for a first- and second-visit candidate. These agendas differ in that for the first visit the agenda should be general: an overview of the institution, department, and program should be provided, with a limited meeting time with some of the important institutional members. The candidate should receive the agenda before the interview date, as well as other logistical information, such as flight times or lodging arrangements.

SAMPLE AGENDA FOR FIRST-VISIT CANDIDATE

ITINERARY
Scott Martin, M.D.
Professor of Urology
Smith Brothers University

Monday, September 21

2:15 PM   Arrival at Airport, flight number 278. Reservations at Inn. Dr. Rick Able, Resident in Surgery, will meet, take to Inn, and bring to Medical Center

3:45   Dr. Anthony Simms, Professor of Surgery and Director, Critical Care Services, 164 Health Center

4:30   Dr. William Shea, Professor of Medicine (Nephrology), 300 Clinic Building

7:30   Dinner—Club 700: Drs. Anthony Simms, H.C. Johnson, Ed Jones, James Mark, Peter Cardwell

Tuesday, September 22

7:30 AM   Breakfast at Inn with Dr. George Emerson, Chairman; Dr. Emerson will bring to Medical Center

9:00   Dr. Mark Kahn, Professor and Chief of Urology, 420 Clinic Building

10:00   Sharon Allen, Executive Director, University Hospital, 912 Wing E

10:30   Dean Julian Evans, 160 Health Science Center

11:00   Dr. Mark Fearringron, Professor of Surgery (General/Transplant), 212 Clinic Building

11:30   Dr. William Faber, Professor of Surgery, 15 Clinic Building

12:00 noon   Ms. Joan Armor, R.N., Director, Surgical Services, 789 Wing D

12:30 PM   Lunch—Urology Residents

2:00   Dr. George Moss, Professor and Vice Chairman, Department of Surgery, 312 Clinic Building

2:30   Susan Murphy, Director of Administration, Department of Surgery, 163 Administration Building

3:00   Dr. Tim McCabe, Associate Professor of Surgery, Urology, 380 Clinic Building

4:00   Dr. H.C. Johnson, Professor of Surgery, 680 Clinic Building

4:30   Mr. James Mark, Assistant Professor of Surgery, Urology, 320 Clinic Building

7:30   Dinner—Collegiate Club: Drs. George Emerson, Tim McCabe, George Moss, Sharon Allen

SAMPLE AGENDA FOR SECOND-VISIT CANDIDATE

ITINERARY
Scott Martin, M.D.
Professor of Urology
Smith Brothers University

Thursday, November 5

8:00 PM   Arrival at Airport, flight number 1537. Reservations at Inn. Dr. Emerson will meet Dr. and Mrs. Martin.

Friday, November 6

7:00 AM   Breakfast at Inn with Dr. Michael Wilde—Professor of Surgery, Associate Dean, and Chief of Staff. Dr. Wilde will bring to Medical Center.

8:00   Dean Julian Evans, 160 Health Science Center

9:00   Dr. David Lam, Professor of Pediatrics, 320 Health Science Research Wing

9:45   Dr. Eugene Kramer, Vice Chairman, Research, Department of Radiology, 200 Clinic Building

10:30   Dr. Robert Jordan, Professor of Medicine and Director, Cancer Center, 110 Cancer Research

11:15   Dr. Paul Kale, Associate Professor of Pathology, 404 Clinic Building

12:00 noon   Lunch with Division Chiefs, Clinic Conference Room

1:00 PM   Mr. Phillip Strader, Director of Operations, University Hospital, 915 Wing E

1:30   Dr. John Stone, Assistant Professor of Medicine, Cancer Research Building

2:00   Dr. George Moss, Professor and Vice Chairman, Department of Surgery, 312 Clinic Building

2:45   Dr. James Mark, Assistant Professor of Surgery, Urology, 320 Clinic Building

4:00   Free to see area/community with Mrs. Martin; meet in front of Clinic Building.

7:00   Dinner—Collegiate Club—Board Room: Dr. and Mrs. Scott (Elizabeth) Martin, Dr. and Mrs. George (Mary) Emerson, Dr. Loraine and (Bruce) Vance, Mr. and Mrs. Phillip (Lisa) Strader, Dr. and Mrs. Anthony (Nancy) Simms

Saturday, November 7

7:30 AM   Breakfast at Inn: Dr. Tim Ross, Assistant Professor of Surgery (Urology); Dr. Sarah Tuttle, Professor of Surgery (General/Oncology)

9:00   Dr. George Emerson will meet at Inn.

10:30   Free—Optional time with local realtor

It is also important to understand that during the interview process candidates need to be escorted to the various interview locations or should be centrally placed in an office, with the interviewers brought to them. The common courtesy of this approach to candidates unfamiliar with the environment is often overlooked, and failure to do so may be counterproductive. Institutional brochures, such as annual reports on the community/state, and benefits program materials, are also useful to send before the first visit so the candidate can become familiar with the area.

For candidates invited for a second interview, a more specific agenda should be developed, providing the candidate with more concentrated time during the meetings. Typically a spouse or significant other and sometimes children are invited to join the candidate on a second visit. The family's special interests or acquaintances in the area should be considered before the visit. Special consideration should be made for spouses, or significant others, especially if joint employment is an issue. Incorporating these interests into the agenda for the candidate and his or her family will provide for a comfortable and rewarding visit.

Discussions of resources, salaries, benefits, and other topics with a new recruit are best initiated by the chair. Usually these are areas that can cause discomfort for the candidate, and unfortunate misunderstandings may occur if these topics are not fully discussed. It is good practice to give printouts of various levels of compensation (see the box below). It is also essential to let the individual know which of their needs can be addressed immediately and which ones cannot. Some needs or requests can be provided as the program grows.

SAMPLE BENEFITS SUMMARY

Salary	$100,000.00
Supplemental retirement plan	2,660.00
State retirement	9,630.00
Disability insurance	950.00
Health insurance—employee	1,735.00
Health insurance—family	2,594.00
Vision care	50.00
Supplemental medical insurance	1,127.00
Dental insurance	876.00
Life insurance	1,279.00
Accidental death and dismemberment	288.00
Professional liability	8,470.00
Social security	5,329.00
TOTAL BENEFITS	$ 34,988.00
TOTAL SALARY AND BENEFITS	$134,988.00

Throughout the process, all applicants should receive an acknowledgment of their application, and all should be apprised of their status as the search proceeds. All of the candidates interviewed should have the telephone number of the committee chair, who they should be encouraged to contact with any questions. The committee chair should personally keep all interviewed candidates apprised of the search process, since searches can seem interminably long for the candidates.

After a candidate has been selected, the department or program should move with speed on the recruitment. Top candidates are recruited quickly, and departments or programs can easily lose their prime candidates to administrative delays. The next phase is the appointment offer. It is always recommended to call the selected candidate first and to express sincere interest in offering the position. At this point the selected candidate will either indicate that he or she is no longer interested, or is interested and will summarize what type of package is required to accept the appointment. Then the manager should stand ready to prepare and send a position offer to the candidate.

Be prepared to be creative in your offer to get the candidate you want. Especially consider important nonsalary features, such as space, equipment, graduate assistants, travel, titles, benefits, and mortgage packages. This is not the time to quibble over nickels and dimes. The selected candidate should feel you want to provide him or her with all that you can to make this the right job. Again, there are many letter

---

RESIDENT RECRUITMENT

Although we are focusing on program development for new faculty members, we would be remiss not to address briefly the recruitment of residents. Academic health centers can spend a tremendous amount of time and energy on resident recruiting; some academic medical departments have annually more than 44 residency positions to fill. The recruitment for residents begins early in the year, when medical students begin inquiring about residency programs and requesting information. Typically a department will employ a residency program coordinator who is assigned, as one of his or her responsibilities, residency recruitment. The coordinator is to make certain that inquiries, whether via letter or telephone call, receive immediate and professional responses. Most departments provide a professional brochure on residency that describes the programs, activities, faculty, and faculty interest areas, along with a salary level index and benefits plan. Residency interview dates should be established early in the fiscal year and faculty members involved in the interview process scheduled with interview dates and times. The chair should make certain that faculty and current residents are involved in the process as much as possible. Customarily the chair or program director will present an overview of the program, and then during the day the candidates will have an opportunity to meet with faculty and residents. Break and lunch sessions can be an excellent forum for faculty, residents, and staff to meet informally with the candidates.

References on residency candidates should be thoroughly reviewed. Faculty involvement at this level can be very important and useful, since a diverse faculty will have established collegiate contacts at other AHCs. Residency program directors must make certain candidates possess all the credentials stated on their application.

styles; the box below presents an example of one type of offer letter. Managers should check their university's hiring policy and procedures, since the wording of appointment letters will vary from institution to institution.

Once the candidate accepts the faculty or staff position, everyone is jubilant that the search process is over and life in the organization can get back to normal. In reality, this is just the beginning for the academic manager. As the obstetrician walking out of the birthing room said to the new parents, "Good job—but your work is only beginning," this is also true for new appointments. What follows will be time and effort devoted to socialization, orientation, training, development, and years of mentoring.

SAMPLE OFFER LETTER

Paul N. Thomas, M.D.
Department of Medicine
Jefferson University
803 Oak Street, S.E.
Charlotte, Virginia 58923

Dear Paul:

On behalf of the Department, I want to thank you and Carol for visiting us. We hope that the visit was useful in allowing you to see the personal and professional opportunities of a faculty position in this institution. Our evolving geriatric program would greatly benefit from an individual with your background and skills. We also believe your contributions to these activities would provide the basis for an enriched career in medicine.

We are pleased to recommend your appointment as an Assistant Professor of Medicine in the tenure track and would like to set forth the terms and conditions. The appointment carries with it the title of Assistant Director of Geriatric Care, with your primary responsibility for the Geriatric Service.

We recommend a salary level of $90,000 a year. The salary comes with a full fringe benefit package, an outline of which is attached to this letter. The salary/benefits and retirement dimensions are quite good and make the entire package offer substantially greater than the base salary. We will also fund relocation expenses up to $5000 and one house-hunting trip for you and Carol.

As with all University appointments, final approval resides with the Board of Trustees of the University.

On a final note, I feel strongly that the position will be mutually beneficial. I would be delighted to have you join the department.

Sincerely,

George A. Emerson, M.D.
Chairman

GAE:nb
enclosure

Welcoming Strategies

One of the most important initial steps is to make the new member feel welcomed and appreciated. Some welcoming strategies include hosting a reception for the new member and inviting other department or program members, especially those who will be collaborating with the new member. Another option is to take the member on a personal tour of the campus, pointing out the important, historical, and fun aspects of his or her new academic home. The new member should meet with all the important academic and hospital members (hospital director, practice plan director, dean, and so on). Another welcoming strategy is to print and mail faculty appointment announcement cards (Figure 8-2) and to place the announcement in the university, local, or community newspaper or a national journal. The announcement typically indicates the new member's educational background and specialty interests. Announcement cards work well for special groups, such as referring physicians.

Another important welcome is to arrange for and to put into place all of the items and materials a new faculty member will need *before* his or her arrival. *Before* is emphasized, since there is never a more lonely experience for a new member than to arrive at an empty office with no support or knowledge of how and where to get things accomplished.

There are many logistical details that require attention to make a new faculty member comfortable in his or her new environment. One of the details that can be taken care of before a new member arrives is having new office or research furniture or equipment purchased and installed. The new member should be consulted about the purchases regarding preferred manufacturer, style, color, and other specifics. Since many institutions can encounter lengthy purchase and/or bid processes, if the

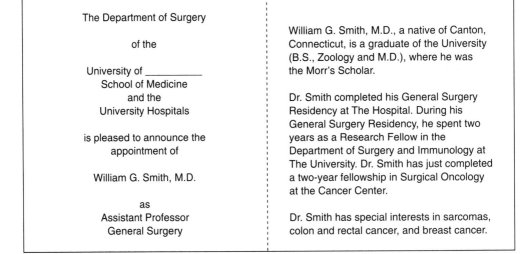

Figure 8-2. Sample announcement card.

manager waits until the new member arrives, he or she may have to endure substantial frustration and anxiety in getting new objectives launched. This is not a productive way to begin the new member's appointment. Other logistical items are listed in the new member checklist below. This includes the need for clinic coats to be ordered and name embroidered, business cards printed, stationery updated and available, support staff hired, and pager, equipment, and supplies ordered, delivered, and in place. Although some of the items on the checklist may seem like mundane minutia, together they are all important factors in the member's orientation, sense of belonging, development, and image of his or her new academic home.

NEW MEMBER CHECKLIST

Name _____

Division _____

Title _____

Assigned office number _____

Assigned laboratory _____

Telephone number(s) _____

Fax number _____

Secretarial support _____

Parking decal: _____ Yes _____ No   Lot _____

Pager: _____ Yes _____ No   Number _____

Clinic coat: _____ Yes _____ No   Size _____ Style _____

Office equipment:

    Typewriter: _____ Yes _____ No

    Dictation equipment: _____ Yes _____ No

    Computer(s): _____ Yes _____ No

    Type _____

    Software _____

Office furniture _____

_____

Laboratory equipment _____

_____

Benefits appointment _____

Photo appointment _____

Medical license provider number _____

Business cards _____

Memo pads _____

Rx pads _____

Stationery _____

ASSISTING SOCIALIZATION*

The usual advice given to new faculty members trying to adjust to life in academics is to maintain their content or clinical skills and to develop skills in teaching and research. Occasionally administrative skills (e.g., time management, project administration) are added. This is good advice, but it is insufficient. It is now clear that the successful academician, particularly the researcher, has also acquired certain values, networks, and behaviors that are not addressed in the usual training of faculty members.

All professions are characterized by a unique set of unwritten norms, rules, and practices. Effective attorneys, scientists, priests, and physicians know more than law, science, religion, or medicine. They have learned many unwritten rules, concepts, and behaviors that allow them to "act like an attorney" or "think like a scientist." They have acquired the professional attitudes and social skills of their chosen occupation. These skills include a "... somewhat special language, an ideology that helps the critical aspects of the work that is being accomplished, matter-of-fact prejudices, models for social etiquette and demeanor, certain customs and rituals suggestive of how members are to relate to colleagues, subordinates, superiors, and outsiders. . . ."[12]

Virtually all studies on successful faculty conclude that socialization is critical for effective performance. Conway and Glass state, in *Socialization for Survival in the Academic World,* "If the faculty of a given school want to see that school ranked among the acknowledged best in the university, the socialization of each new faculty must become a concern of the corporate body."[13] In study after study, socialization factors were both the critical feature and the eventual characteristic that differentiated highly productive from less productive faculty.[14,15] In most studies where "highly productive" is defined more broadly, however, socialization appears to predict which faculty members will be achievers and which will not.

In his recent book, *The New Faculty Member,* Boice[16] reported on his study and work at three types of universities with several cohorts of faculty members that he carefully followed for the first 4 years of their academic careers. A consistent and compelling finding was that to succeed, above all else, these new faculty needed a network of stimulating colleagues, an understanding of the unwritten rules and norms of their organization and their discipline, psychological and substantive support in tackling their new tasks and roles, and a sense of belonging and contributing to their academic community. In short, they needed to be socialized to, and adapted into, their organization and field. Unfortunately, what most new faculty reported they experienced in their new setting was no orientation, no ongoing mentoring, few collegial activities, heavy teaching responsibilities, and often resentment from older colleagues of their up-to-date skills. This experience left them

---

*Parts of this section were adapted, with permission, from Bland CJ, Schmitz CC, Stritter FT, Henry RC & Aluise JJ. (1990). *Successful faculty in academic medicine: Essential skills and how to acquire them.* New York: Springer Publishing. Used by permission.

poorly armed to succeed in their new roles and also caused them to feel lonely, isolated, overwhelmed, and disillusioned.

Boice found this consistent finding reported by both new faculty who entered directly from graduate school and by those who entered after several years of professional practice. It is also important to note that Boice's studies, and other studies which focus on women and minorities in academics, find that these two groups particularly do not receive the socialization and acceptance necessary to succeed in universities.[17]

Of course, some new faculty do manage to get socialized on their own or find a mentor and have successful lifelong careers. But rather than use this expensive "social Darwinism" approach to faculty survival, many departments are now systematically socializing new faculty through planned mentorship programs and programs on networking, collaborating, institution and disciplinary values and procedures, and so on. The following orientation and mentoring programs are designed to assist new faculty in becoming socialized to their new roles and organizations.

Orientation

Each year academic institutions appoint about 30,000 or 40,000 new full-time faculty members. In addition, they also hire between 11,000 and 20,000 new people as part-time or adjunct faculty each year.[7] Most of these faculty members begin their responsibilities without an orientation to their job or to their environments. However, recent studies have found that substantial orientation programs for new faculty can provide major benefits for newcomers and their institutions.[18] Given the responsibilities, stress, and the resultant dispirited condition of many new faculty members as described by Boice,[11] it is not surprising that an orientation has significant benefits for new faculty. Such orientations help not only new faculty but all organizational members to begin to develop networks, to identify with and feel a sense of belonging with their organization, to approach basic professional responsibilities such as teaching, service, and research with a better information base, and thus provide new faculty members with a "head start" in their careers. These benefits also explain why in a recent study, when faculty members were asked at the end of their first year to identify the most important recommendation they would make to chairs, they said, "provide better information at the start of the year."[18]

There are also benefits to the institution from providing an orientation. These programs enable newcomers to become fully functioning members of the organization more quickly. They also increase the likelihood that new members will identify with the organization and feel a commitment to contribute to it. Universities with orientation programs report that such programs help them in faculty recruitment and retention; these programs are perceived by candidates as evidence of real institutional concern and support for faculty success.[19]

Orientation programs for AHCs should be offered for new organizational members throughout the year. A year-long format allows members to acquire contacts by meeting with colleagues over an extended period. In addition, it allows a significant amount of information to be addressed without overloading new

---

ORIENTATION PROGRAM OUTLINE

I. Introduction
   A. Background of program
   B. Size of department
   C. Relationship to the medical school and university
   D. Training and development
   E. You are appreciated
   F. Introduce attendees

II. Slide presentation
   A. Where we have been—history
   B. Where we are
   C. Who's who in the department, medical school, hospitals, and university
   D. Where we are going

III. Review of the orientation manual

IV. Facility tour
   A. Clinics
   B. Copy center
   C. Day-op
   D. Clinic auditorium
   E. Library
   F. Administrative offices
   G. Medical illustration department
   H. Medical school
   I. University

DEPARTMENT OF SURGERY
ORIENTATION MANUAL CONTENTS

1. Who's who in administration
2. Organizational chart of university
3. Organizational chart of hospital(s)
4. Organizational chart of department
5. Organizational chart of administration
6. Faculty listing
7. Listing of faculty and resident pager numbers
8. Telephone policy and procedure
9. How to schedule outpatient appointments
10. Scheduling conference rooms
11. Mail distribution
12. Fax service
13. Copying/printing
14. Purchasing policy
15. Personnel policy
16. Adverse weather conditions
17. Travel policy
18. Confidentiality
19. Training and development opportunity
20. Parking
21. Laundry
22. Maps

members at the beginning of the year when they are already overwhelmed with new information and responsibilities.

The purpose of an orientation program would be to introduce new members to major organizational structures, governance policies, and procedures of the AHC and the university and to begin to socialize them to the underlying values and principles that guide behavior in an academic setting and in a scientific community.

There are many options to developing an effective orientation program. One approach is to develop a program with various stages. The first stage would be an orientation to the university, which would consist of an overview of the history of the institution, history and overview of the school, present-day activities, and a concise discussion of important policy and procedure guidelines. Handouts and detailed manuals are also useful. A department orientation program could contain the department's history and culture, along with a slide presentation of "who's who" in the department and institution. Reviewing the organizational structure and everyone's main responsibility areas is helpful. Finally, a walking tour of the facility is in order to point out the health science library, copy center, graphic illustration department, administrative offices, clinics, auditoriums, conference rooms, and day-op facilities. The box at the top of p. 148 offers an example of the content of an orientation program. The box at the bottom of p. 148 is a sample table of contents for an orientation manual for staff members.

The program would include an orientation of the practice plan, focusing on the reimbursement process, clinical reporting, fee setting, collection rates, and so on. A research orientation is also beneficial, since it can present an enormous amount of pertinent information on the institution's internal processing procedures, overhead rates, budget provisions, and other important facts. This type of orientation will eliminate some of the high anxiety associated with a new member's first preparation and submission of a grant proposal at a new institution.

Mentoring

Mentoring is an important component of human resource development. Research on successful faculty—particularly research-productive faculty—has shown that the presence of a mentor during training in early years as a faculty member and later significantly and positively affects a faculty member's success. The box on p. 150 lists potential outcomes of a mentoring program.

Despite the proven value of mentors for new faculty members, there is little research on an ideal design for an effective mentor program. A recent study by Boice, however, does provide some guidance on prompting effective mentoring relationships. Several helpful findings emerged from this study[16]:

1. *Keep meeting.* Mentor pairs that met the most frequently had the most consistent improvement in the protégé's productivity, feelings of satisfaction, and feelings of security and confidence about his or her career.
2. *Small talk.* If mentors and protégés focused only on professional tasks and did not learn the art of small talk, they did not establish the relationship necessary for the mentor to be able to offer moral support and critical feedback and to serve as a sounding board.

3. *Use of career plans.* This is one of the most effective mentoring strategies. The career plan includes a brief account of the faculty member's past accomplishments, ongoing projects, and planned projects. These plans served as concrete reminders of what the new faculty member hoped to accomplish and helped the mentor move the new faculty member along more efficiently.

4. *Training session.* Even seasoned faculty thought they were better mentors after formally reading and learning about the process.

5. *External mentor.* Mentors selected from outside the department were the most effective. Protégés that had mentors from other departments received a perspective that they were not receiving daily from senior faculty in their own department, thus increasing their understanding of faculty life.

OUTCOMES OF THE MENTORING PROGRAM

Professional socialization
Understanding the academic environment
Broadening perspectives
Providing access to key people and resources
Developing role clarity

Role modeling
Intellectual stimulation
Involving the junior person in one of the mentor's projects
Teaching by example

Nurturing
Generating enthusiasm and confidence
Serving as a sounding board
Career planning
Collegiality
Reality testing encouraging the dream
Counseling
Offering moral support

Teaching
Developing specific knowledge or skills
Constructive feedback
Coaching
Taskmaster

Advocacy
Association with a track record that fosters the credibility
    of the junior person
Protecting time
Sponsorship

From Strange IC & Hekelman F. (1990). Mentoring needs and family medicine faculty. *Family Medicine, 22,* 183–185.

Assisting Teaching

Although the educational process in managing in academics is discussed in greater detail in Chapter 13, it is important to consider teaching as a critical component of faculty development. (For a complete guide to developing faculty members' teaching skills, see Bland et al.[5]) Studies of new faculty find that they discover teaching to be a far greater challenge and consumer of time than they ever anticipated. New faculty tend to underestimate the skill and time it takes to plan courses, prepare lectures, advise students, prepare the rounds, serve as preceptor in a clinic, lead seminars, and evaluate students, courses, programs, and themselves.

Teaching effectiveness is an important component of faculty development. If new faculty members perform their teaching activities in a positive, reinforcing, and satisfying way, it reinforces their satisfaction with their career decision of being faculty members. If they teach in a time-efficient way, it allows them more energy and time to commit to their other roles. Effective teaching will also help to avoid the possible painful consequences of poor teaching (low student ratings or verbal and nonverbal expression of disappointment with a faculty member's performance by colleagues and supervisors).

A workshop on "Getting Started in Teaching" is recommended for the first year to new faculty members. This type of workshop addresses the overall curriculum of the school and department in which they teach and emphasizes that their role is part of the complete role that they are to play as an educator—not just teaching students, but also establishing a rapport with students, getting to know them, and socializing them into the profession for which they are being trained; how to access resources available in their college and in the university; how to use colleagues to help them understand students; how to identify teaching materials and discuss their teaching; and the place of teaching in the context of their other faculty roles of writing, administering, developing networks, and so on.

New faculty members should also be encouraged to participate in a seminar that addresses basic teaching skills. Some of these skill workshops would include:

1. Understanding characteristics of effective teaching strategies and techniques
2. Using microteaching techniques (e.g., feedback, questioning)
3. Effective lecturing
4. Facilitating effective small group discussions
5. Computer-assisted instructional approaches
6. Understanding characteristics of effective clinical teaching

The purpose of these workshops is not to make instant master teachers out of new faculty members, but to enable the new faculty members to address their new teaching roles competently, efficiently, and with positive results. The ultimate goal is to help new faculty members have a balance in their roles where teaching, writing, research, service, and collegiality all get attention. Rather than being competing forces in a faculty member's life, these roles feed into and enrich each other.

Assisting Writing

The ability to write well is a valued asset in academics, largely because it leads to valued products, such as training or research grants, scholarly documents, and so on. Academic writing requires mastery of basic and complex writing skills. Well-written pieces communicate, inform, educate, inspire, synthesize the literature, or move entire committees to action; poorly written ones do not. Because of the importance of the ability to communicate in writing, this area should be addressed both in programs for new faculty and in programs for all faculty members.

Writing is a critical component to faculty development. The obvious costs of not writing are failures to gain promotions, grants, and other rewards. However, there are other less obvious costs of nonwriting. Failing to write denies a faculty member visibility, mobility, and satisfaction. Not expressing oneself in writing denies the faculty member the self-education and clarity of thinking from putting thoughts into printed words. Writing places a faculty member into the network of professionals that comes from reading each other's writings. To fail to produce one's writings is a powerful form of disenfranchisement for a new faculty member.

One way to assist writing is through two workshops, on getting started and on basic writing skills. Many faculty do not write simply because they just never get started. According to Boice,[16] getting started seems to involve acquiring several important habits of writing: automaticity, hard work and borrowing rather than waiting for inspiration, constructive self-talk, arranging schedules of regular time to write (contrasted with waiting for inspiration or huge blocks of time), establishing social networks with other writers and people who influence writers, such as editors and reviewers, and developing coping strategies for dealing with rejection and criticism. The second workshop would concentrate on the basic skills of writing, such as writing for particular audiences, organizing content, writing within publication styles and formats, and writing with a word processor.

Assisting Research

A large portion of clinical faculty members have no formal training in research. The Association of American Medical College's faculty roster reports 44% of clinical faculty have less than 6 (usually zero) months of formal research training. This percentage is higher for women and minorities.

In AHCs members of the organization will eventually have varying responsibilities for research. However, all members, regardless of appointment type, need a foundation in some research competencies. Basic research abilities will allow the member to evaluate research grant funding, conduct quality research, promote collaboration, and be a role model for students, residents, and staff.

Research development is discussed in more detail in Chapter 18. Bland et al. provide a detailed guide for developing research skills.[5] Some development activities and programs to be considered include developing a grant and contract handbook or manual. The manual would be specific for an institution and would include the research proposal procedures, protocol, forms, sample of a completed proposal, budget development with fringe benefits, overhead rates, and so on. Also, a diagram outlining where the proposal is routed at the institution and how much time is required at each location should be included.

In addition to offering research workshops on applying for NIH grants and developing contractual agreements, some departments have found the utilization of a research seminar to be very beneficial. Typically, a faculty member is assigned the responsibility of coordinating a research seminar. The seminar is held weekly in a convenient conference room and refreshments are served. At each seminar, one or two researchers present a project or findings from their laboratory. Often all researchers, fellows, and others from across the institution are welcome to attend. Such a seminar serves many useful functions. For example, knowledge of new techniques gained and knowledge and skills are improved. In addition, shared equipment labs can result as well as an increase in research collaboration and an improved understanding of investigators' research interests and specialty areas.

It is important to note, however, that faculty with no formal training in research seldom acquire sufficient skills to make meaningful contributions to knowledge via in-department short-term courses or seminars. Thus faculty members who have no formal training in research should be supported to attend basic research methods courses.

PROGRAMS FOR ALL FACULTY MEMBERS
Career Planning

Faculty members who have been on board for years, previously completed Ph.D. programs or fellowships, or who complete the above "new faculty member series" will each need individual development programs to help them, over a lifetime, continue to improve and accomplish their individual goals.

Nearly all writers in faculty development talk about the need for multiple strategies to meet the highly varied needs of established faculty members in different disciplines, at different stages of careers, and having different personal circumstances. How can a program be comprehensive and still manageable? One way is to focus the program on helping faculty examine their circumstances and needs. Thus the organization does not offer all types of development programs, but rather assists faculty in identifying their yearly career goals and what is needed to meet these goals, and then serves as a locator or clearinghouse to other resources to meet the identified need. Exceptions to this would be development activities the program runs because it meets a need identified by many faculty or because there are no other resources that meet that need.

This strategy works best when departments and divisions have organizational goals within which faculty members write yearly work plans. But the faculty member setting goals alone, even when it is not an organizational strategy, by itself increases productivity and provides the information needed for a faculty development effort to provide assistance. Ideally, faculty members would be asked to write goals in a somewhat measurable form for each year. These goals should be related to the broad college goals, to the mission of the department, and to the divisions in which the faculty members teach. Also, at least one goal should be aimed at improving one's faculty abilities. Before these goals are submitted to the division head, each person could formally discuss his or her goals, how they will be accomplished, how they will be assessed, and resources or training needed to accomplish them with two other departmental faculty members. This discussion is recommended because of the Andrews studies on productive research organizations.[21] He found that the most productive ones had a system in which more than one person contributed to a scientist's work plan, although, of course, the scientist had the final say. This step also ensures that faculty colleagues will know about what others are doing; thus they can serve as immediate reminders of goals established and serve as informed celebrants of accomplishments. This also relieves the division head of being the only "heavy" expecting reasonable goals and accomplishments. On the other hand, it provides the faculty member support for his or her plan in negotiations with the division head.

In return for developing yearly career plans, the faculty member gets a commitment from the division head on essential resources or training needed to accomplish the plan and, when appropriate, help from the faculty development program to find resources for his or her plan. These plans and the year-end review of how well goals have been met provide the framework for an automatic but individualized faculty development and evaluation system.

Thus for all faculty, including new faculty, an annual workshop should be held on how to set annual goals, identify resources, and evaluate goals.

Editing

As we discussed under programs for new faculty members, success in writing is very important to the overall success of the faculty member. Thus we suggest that there be editorial assistance to help on any major documents, whether it is an article, a grant, or a teaching package. An editor may find that there are areas in which many faculty members consistently need help. In these areas, it may be appropriate to offer workshops or to locate workshops that faculty members can attend. There are also several editing hotlines in the country and at individual institutions. That is, if you are sitting at your desk and need immediate help on whether to use "who" or "whom" or if you need advice on the *Chicago Manual* style for a particular phrase, you can call a number, for example, in your English department during certain hours. A department may not need to have its own editor but can use the editing services of the institution.

Instructional Assistance

Instructional assistance is one of the most commonly provided services of most institutions' faculty development offices. The department should make faculty aware of their institutions' faculty development office. An instructional assistance section in the faculty development office can help faculty members who in their annual goals decide to make major changes in their courses, teaching materials, or teaching abilities. This section of the office would also help faculty wishing to improve their approach to evaluation. In addition, this section can help faculty who are working on grants that require educational strategies or evaluation components.

Special Programs

Departments, colleges, and centers may need special programs for groups that are particularly at risk for not succeeding in academics, such as new faculty, new administrators, women, minorities, and faculty in new disciplines. Many of the strategies for helping these "at-risk" faculty members are included in the programs just described, such as programs for orientation, mentoring, and writing. It will be important to take particular care that at-risk faculty participate in these programs. Some special programs may be appropriate; women and minorities would benefit from programs directed specifically at their needs, led by successful minority and women faculty members. Such programs not only provide models from across the university, but also provide participants a view of themselves and their potential, mirrored in the eyes of others like them. They may not get this in their own department, where "majority people" have provided the reflection that shaped their understanding of who they are and what they can be.

Other special programs are likely to emerge from faculty members' annual goals statements. For example, the Harvard program of career development has found that one of the pressing barriers to success of women and dual-career faculty members is the lack of day care for children and elderly parents. Thus to help these faculty members succeed, Harvard took on the project of identifying day care and elder care convenient to the university. Also, as more faculty members near retirement, it is likely that many of them will have goals that include phasing out of an academic career and into retirement. If there are a number of these faculty members in your organization, you may find it useful to organize special programs to help them meet their retirement goals.

There will be a few faculty members who find themselves in especially unproductive situations because they no longer enjoy academics, or the paradigm, or emphasis in their department has shifted, leaving them no longer wanted or valued, or they have had unresolvable conflicts with senior colleagues or their unit leader such that they no longer are assigned or included in meaningful work. These conditions are detrimental not only to the faculty member but to all members of the unit, including the leader. For example, the University of Minnesota studied the participants (respondents and complainants) of all the University Senate Judicial cases since 1946.[22] Unfortunately, the colleges in the health sciences were one of the most frequent sites of these cases. The enduring and widespread negative impact of these cases was shocking, no matter who "won," but especially if the faculty member "won" and remained in the same unit.

Department, college, and institution leaders should help reassign, retrain, or outplace faculty members or administrators who can no longer thrive in their current situation. Loyola, for example, has had success with a program for faculty and administrators wishing to try out a nonacademic life. They help their personnel acquire 1-year positions elsewhere and pay half of their salary, with the new organization paying the other half. Loyola reports that about half of the individuals placed have chosen to leave the university permanently. Those that stayed returned with new perspectives and commitment to the University.[23] Another example: during times of retrenchment, the University of Wisconsin system has used a three-pronged program of reassignment, relocation, and retraining to avert as many actual layoffs as possible. Of the three, retraining was the most frequently used.[23]

ORGANIZATIONAL VITALITY

Organizational factors, more than individual faculty characteristics and abilities, are now thought to influence vitality and productivity. For the past 30 years Blackburn[24] has studied faculty in all types of higher education institutions, including health professional schools. He concludes that "the institution determines to a high degree a faculty member's productivity—faculty at some institutions produce appreciatively more than faculty at other institutions. The differential rate is independent of place of preparation, ability, work-load, and prior places of work." Blackburn states, "Nearly every positively correlated factor of productivity resides in administrative hands and hence can be fostered by the organization."[24] Similarly, Bland and Schmitz,[14] in their review of characteristics of productive researchers, conclude, "Institutional and organizational characteristics affect, perhaps even control, the faculty member's productivity." These findings are consistent with the corporate literature, particularly in the total quality management area, that 85% of all problems with worker effectiveness and product quality are the result of organizational processes, and only 15% are failures of people. Thus, as described at the start of this chapter, the concept of human resource development has evolved beyond staff training. However, the purpose remains the same. Like the recruitment activities and orientation and training described earlier, the purpose is simply to produce a vital department, program, or organization. What is a vital and effective department or program? To paraphrase Maher,[25] a vital department is one that creates and sustains organizational strategies that support the continued investment of energy by faculty and staff both to their own careers and to the realization of the institutional mission.

CONCLUSION

Managers in academics must become sensitive and proactive in developing their human and organizational resources. As illustrated in the box on p. 133, recruitment, mentoring, orientation, training, career planning, and special programs are only some of the foundational areas of a comprehensive development program. Further, an effective program requires consistent monitoring, evaluating, and revising. With some academic health departments easily exceeding 100 members, organizational and human resource development requires significant time and effort—but the rewards are substantial.

BIBLIOGRAPHY

*1. Bergquist W, Phillips S & Gruber S. (1992). *Developing human and organizational resources: A comprehensive manual.* San Francisco: Professional School of Psychology.

2. Watson G & Johnson D. (1972). *A social psychology: Issues and insights* (2nd ed). Philadelphia: JB Lippincott.

*3. Schuster JH & Wheeler D. (1990). *Enhancing faculty careers: Strategies for development and renewal.* San Francisco: Jossey-Bass.

4. Bland CJ & Schmitz CC. (1990). An overview of research on faculty and institutional vitality. In Schuster JH & Wheeler DW, eds. *Enhancing faculty careers: Strategies for development and renewal.* San Francisco: Jossey-Bass.

*5. Bland CJ, Schmitz CC, Stritter FT, Henry RC & Aluise JJ. (1990). *Successful faculty in academic medicine: Essential skills and how to acquire them.* New York: Springer Publishing.

*6. Creswell JW, Wheeler DW, Seagren AT, et al. (1990). *The academic chairperson's handbook.* Lincoln: University of Nebraska Press.

7. Bowen HR & Schuster JH. (1986). *American professors: A national resource implied.* Oxford: Oxford University Press.

8. *University of Minnesota guidelines for academic searches.* (1992). Minneapolis: Human Resources Department.

9. Marchese TJ & Lawrence JF. (1989, April). *The search committee handbook: A guide to recruiting administrators.* Washington, DC: Association for Higher Education.

10. Sandler BR, Hughes O & DeMouy M. (1988, February). *It's all in what you ask: Questions for search committees to use.* Washington, DC: Project on the Status and Education of Women, Association of American Colleges.

11. Ehrhart JK & Sandler BR. (1987, January). *Looking for more than a few good women in traditionally male fields.* Washington, DC: Project on the Status and Education of Women, Association of American Colleges.

12. Van Maanen J & Schein EH. (1979). Toward a theory of organizational socialization. *Research Organizational Behavior, 1,* 209-264.

13. Conway ME & Glass LK. (1978). Socialization for survival in the academic world. *Nursing Outlook, 26*(7), 424-429.

14. Bland CJ & Schmitz CC. (1986). Characteristics of the successful researcher and implications for faculty development. *Journal of Medical Education, 61,* 22-31.

15. Creswell J. (1985). Faculty research performance: Lessons from the sciences and the social sciences. *ASHE/ERIC Higher Education Research Report No. 4.* Washington, DC: Association for the Study of Higher Education.

16. Boice R. (1992). *The new faculty member: Supporting and fostering professional development.* San Francisco: Jossey-Bass.

*17. Zuckerman H, Cole JR & Bruer JT. (1991). *The outer circle: Women in the scientific community.* New York: WW Norton.

18. Fink LD. (1992). Orientation programs for new faculty. In Sorcenelli MD & Austin AE (eds.): *Developing New and Junior Faculty, New Directions for teaching and learning,* No. 50. San Francisco: Jossey-Bass.

19. Evans C. Director of Harvard Medical School Office for Academic Careers (personal communication, 1992).

20. Strange IC & Hekelman F. (1990). Mentoring needs and family medicine faculty. *Family Medicine, 22,* 183-185.

21. Andrews FM, ed. (1979). *Scientific productivity.* Cambridge, England: Cambridge University Press.

22. Bland CJ, Deinard A & Park R. (1988, May). *Study of the senate judical process at the University of Minnesota.* In-House Report. Minneapolis: University of Minnesota.

*Asterisk indicates an article or book that is particularly informative and helpful.

23. Baldwin R, Brakeman L, Edgerton R, et al. (1981). *Expanding faculty options*. Washington, DC: American Association of Higher Education.
24. Blackburn RT. (1979). Academic careers: Patterns and possibilities. *Current Issues in Higher Education, 2,* 25-27.
25. Maher TH. (1982, June). *Institutional vitality in higher education. AAHE-ERIC/Higher Education Research Currents,* Ed.216668, 3-6.

ADDITIONAL RESOURCES

Bergquist W & Phillips SR. (1975). *The handbook for faculty development*. Washington, DC: Council for the Advancement of Small Colleges.

Boice R. (1990). Mentoring new faculty: A program for implementation. *Journal of Staff Program and Organizational Development, 8,* L43-L60.

Fink LD. (1992). Orientation programs for new faculty. In Sorcenelli MD & Austin AE, eds: *Developing new and junior faculty, new directions for teaching and learning,* No. 50. San Francisco: Jossey-Bass.

Hitchcock MA, Stritter FT & Bland CJ. (1992). Faculty development in the health professions: Conclusions and recommendations. *Medical Teacher* (accepted for publication).

Lanks KW. (1990). *Academic environment, a handbook for evaluating faculty employment opportunities.* Brooklyn: Faculty Press.

Matier MW. (1990). Retaining faculty: A tale of two campuses. *Research in Higher Education, 31,* 39-60.

North J. (1991). Faculty vitality: 1990 and beyond. In Zahorski KJ, ed: *To improve the academy: Resources for student, faculty, and institutional development.* The Professional and Organizational Development Network in Higher Education. Stillwater, Okla: New Forums Press.

Schoenfeld C & Magnan R. (1992). Mentor in a manual. *Climbing the academic ladder to tenure.* Madison, Wisc: Magna Publications.

Strange IC & Hekelman F. (1990). Mentoring needs and family medicine faculty. *Family Medicine, 22,* 183-185.

Toffler A. (1980). *The third wave.* New York: Bantam/William Morrow.

Van Maanen J & Schein EH. (1979). Toward a theory of organizational socialization. *Research Organizational Behavior, 1,* 209-264.

Zuckerman H, Cole JR & Bruer JT. (1991). *The outer circle: Women in the scientific community.* New York: WW Norton.

CHAPTER 9

Facility Planning and Management

Jules I. Levine

Architecture is my delight, and putting up and pulling down, one of my favorite amusements.

THOMAS JEFFERSON, to a visitor at Monticello

ELEMENTS OF FACILITY PLANNING AND MANAGEMENT

Managers in academics today typically find themselves responsible for planning and managing either a substantial amount of square footage with diverse applications (office, research, and clinic) or an entire academic health center facility.

There are significant issues and elements related to the effective management and planning of academic health care facilities. For example, what is the difference between planning and management, where can assistance be obtained, what are space standards? How do you plan, how do you work with architects and engineers? These issues will all be addressed in this chapter.

Although it may seem obvious, it is essential to remember that a facility is not an end unto itself but a place in which things happen—that is, the programs related to the mission of the department or group occur in a given space. Activities of the facility may be clinically oriented, part of a research program, an element of the educational process, or an important service element. First and foremost, a facility must be recognized as a resource, much like people, money, and equipment, that is used to support the programs devoted to a particular mission or objective. When people lose sight of this basic concept, facilities are developed as testaments to individuals or as part of some grandiose scheme. Remember: Facilities exist simply to support relevant programs.

In talking about facility planning and management, we should recognize the two disparate elements. *Planning* is a continuous activity dedicated to the creation or renovation of facilities, whereas *management* is a continuing process oriented toward maintenance and utilization. Facility planning should not be confused with strategic planning, program planning, or other kinds of planning that often lead to the need for facility planning. At the departmental level, there is a certain continuity to facility planning, but often it is done at discrete times to resolve a particular problem.

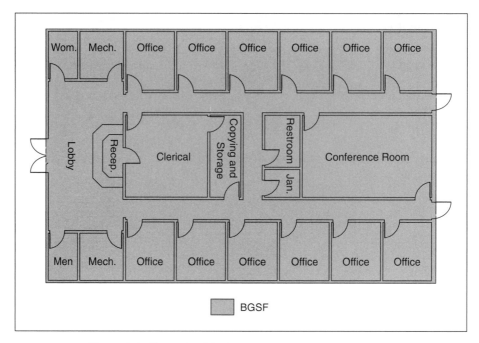

Figure 9-1. Example of building gross square feet (BGSF).

Management of facilities is the day-to-day activity that permits continued utilization of the facility for its intended purpose. That is often the function of a Department of Physical Plant or a Department of Facilities Management. Such management relates to the provision of utilities, janitorial service, repairs, and general maintenance. Basically, facilities planning helps to create a space, whereas facilities management is oriented to maintaining it in a condition for appropriate use.

As with any technical area, definitions are essential to good communication and understanding. Agreement on definitions in facility planning and management is imperative to avoid misunderstandings, cost overruns, and failure to achieve completion of high-quality facilities, on time and within agreed-upon budgets.

Vital terminology begins with how space is measured. There are significant differences in the various units of measurement, such as square feet, net assignable square feet, departmental gross square feet, and building gross square feet, with respect to the same space; it is essential in a discussion of space that the appropriate units of measurement be used. One of the better sources of definitions of building areas is the Federal Construction Council Technical Report No. 50 (Publ. 1235), *Classification of Building Areas,* National Academy of Sciences, Building Research Advisory Board. The box on p. 162 presents some basic terminology and definitions adapted from that publication. The terms are also demonstrated in Figures 9-1 through 9-3. For example, the difference between net assignable square feet (NASF) and building gross square feet (BGSF) must be fully understood before you can effectively nego-

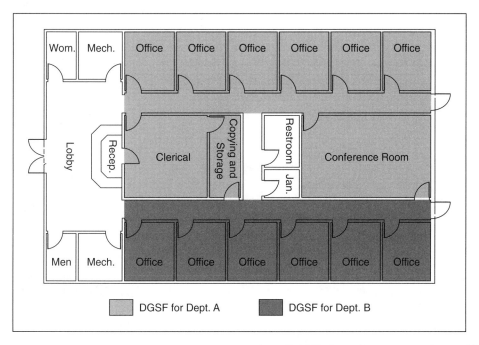

Figure 9-2. Example of department gross square feet (DGSF). Two departments shown. Note common-use spaces such as lobby, restrooms, and janitorial/mechanical facilities.

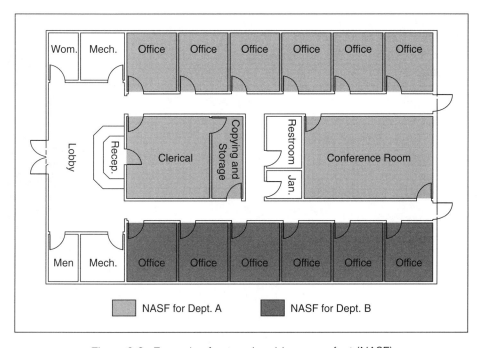

Figure 9-3. Example of net assignable square feet (NASF).

FACILITY PLANNING AND MANAGEMENT TERMINOLOGY

net assignable square feet (NASF) The sum of all areas assigned to, or available for assignment to an occupant, but not including circulation corridors, toilet rooms, janitor closets, stairs and elevators, and mechanical/electrical areas. Includes:
- Actual usable area within a space as measured from the inside faces of walls that form the boundaries of the space

departmental gross square feet (DGSF) The sum of all areas available for assignment to an occupant, including circulation space within the area designated for assignment to the occupant. In addition, DGSF includes all partitions, columns, and mechanical chases within the designated area. Includes:
- Actual usable area within a space
- Corridors that make the usable areas functional
- All interior partitions enclosing the usable areas
- All columns or chases within the designated area

building gross square feet (BGSF) The sum of all areas within the exterior face of the walls of a building. This measure is inclusive of all mechanical/electrical spaces that support building systems, all corridors in addition to those accounted for in the DGSF, all public toilet rooms, all stairs and elevators, and any public areas (lobby, etc.) not included in the DGSF. Includes:
- Actual usable area within a space
- Corridors that make the usable area functional
- All interior partitions enclosing the usable areas
- All columns or chases within the designated area
- Building circulation system
- Public toilets
- Elevators
- Stairs
- Mechanical spaces (heating, ventilation, air conditioning)
- Electrical equipment spaces
- Mechanical chases/shafts
- Exterior building walls

---

tiate or discuss any facility allocations or formulate plans. Examples of utilizing these most common facility management terms on a facility floor plan are demonstrated in Figures 9-1 through 9-3.

WHO IS RESPONSIBLE?

In the typical academic health center, the lines of organization are unclear regarding facility planning and management. The lines of responsibility and authority are blurred, and it is important to clarify them before commitments are made that cannot be met. For example, the dean of the school of medicine and/or the department chair may have overall responsibility for faculty office space, while clinical space may come under the authority of the hospital director. Research space is generally the domain of the school of medicine. However, educational space may be split, since allied health programs are often hospital based and nursing and medicine programs are more oriented toward schools of medicine and schools of nursing. It must first be determined exactly which organizational unit has authority for the space being discussed and which administrative officer has responsibility and authority for providing space for a particular function. Erroneous assumptions in this area can often be divisive, time consuming, and costly. It is best to clarify organizational relationships with respect to control of the space, responsibility for provision of space for a particular program, and identification of the organization responsible for assisting and providing for the planning and construction activities related to preparing a space for use.

WHO CAN HELP?

There are many ways to obtain help in facilities planning and management. Often the university's Department of Physical Plant or Facilities Management can be of some assistance. Academic health centers often have an architect responsible for activities there. Such national organizations as the Association of Academic Health Centers and the Group on Institutional Planning of the Association of American Medical Colleges can help in planning facilities. The American Hospital Association has a sub-group, the American Society for Hospital Engineering; the Society for College and University Planning may also be of help.

WHAT ARE THE SPACE STANDARDS?

Although there are standards for general academic space used by universities, there are no agreed-on standards in schools of medicine. Some consensus is developing in the area of research, but beyond that, the book has yet to be written. This is probably appropriate, because there are as many ways to organize as there are ways to count square feet. Organizational activities as well as the actual function of space determine the space requirements. There is little commonality in many areas, except, perhaps, with respect to office size. Nevertheless, there are some useful principles for research, clinical, and educational space that I will delineate here.

Although establishing space standards eliminates some flexibility for the department chair, developing such standards for faculty office space, clerical support space, and library and conference areas is very beneficial. An agreed-on set of standards at the department or school level is very useful as a guideline for determining individual departments' space requirements, requests, and allocations.

Research Standards

Typical biomedical research space can generally be considered in one of three categories: laboratories, support space, and clerical/office space. Laboratories are usually considered to be those spaces containing benches, hoods, research equipment, and so on. Support activity areas include glass-washing facilities, vivarium space, hazardous material storage facilities (if separate from the actual laboratories), common use cold rooms, and so on. Office space is allotted for investigators and clerical support persons. Technician and graduate student space can be contained either in the laboratory or clerical support space.

The debate on standards for research space in schools of medicine has been going on for at least 15 years. The Association of American Medical Colleges Group on Institutional Planning has discussed standards at many of their annual meetings. Most of the master plans developed for various research facilities and schools of medicine contain information on the allocation of research space. Nevertheless, no generally agreed-on standards exist. It is generally best to think of research space as individual modules to be assigned on one of two bases: (1) "seed" space for new undertakings or in support of new faculty, and (2) space in direct support of ongoing funded research. While it is relatively straightforward to assign office and academic space based on head counts, this is not easily done for research space. One allocation basis typically used is peer-reviewed research grants, and the specific measure is dollars per square foot. This can typically be used as a measure of productivity along with some quality judgment and can be used over time as a method for allocating space. It must be remembered that he who "giveth" can also "taketh away," and it is imperative that such an approach be employed if space is to be used well. Other methods have been attempted, but with less success. A typical order of magnitude for research space planning may be 1000 NASF per funded principal investigator. This is an average that is useful in sizing facilities for an entire research program rather than as a tool to make individual assignments. The senior investigator may need 1500 to 2000 NASF, whereas the new junior faculty member may require only a single laboratory of 350 NASF.

Basic decisions in determining the allocation of research space should include the question of support activities and whether those support activities ought to be contained in specific departmental allocations or located centrally in the facility for use by all departments. If it can be made to work, it is most efficient to have glass-washing facilities, operating rooms for animal work, and so forth available to an entire building or department and not allocate such space to individual investigators. An optimal approach is to establish standards, a basis for allocation of space, and a basis for taking space from one researcher and assigning it to another. Such an approach is difficult but necessary if space is to be effectively and efficiently used and justified at the biomedical research facilities in academic health centers.

Clinical Standards

Clinical space is more easily judged, because a more direct quantitative analysis is possible. For inpatient facilities, we can look at average daily census, admissions, length of stay, and other factors to determine the need for a particular number of beds dedicated to a particular service. Beds are much more easily shifted from one service to another in most modern hospitals, although physical constraints may make it difficult in particular areas. Generally, the assignment of beds is a function of hospital administrative policy and is generally negotiated by the hospital with individual clinical chairs.

Ambulatory care space is somewhat different. It is imperative in these days of rising health care costs and increased public and payor scrutiny that ambulatory care space be used effectively and efficiently. Measures such as annual visits per square foot and visits per examination room per day can be used to properly size an ambulatory care facility. Again, it is important to know what types of square feet are being discussed and whether the space is being used in a *private* or an *academic* mode. Generally, ambulatory care space in which significant teaching activities take place requires either a greater number of or larger examination rooms. This will be determined by the particular institution's approach to teaching. For example, if medical students and/or residents do a complete workup on a patient before the patient is seen by the attending physician, there is generally a need for more examination rooms than would otherwise be the case, since each patient will spend more time in the examination room. On the other hand, if the medical student and/or resident accompanies the attending physician, larger rooms are needed rather than a greater quantity of rooms. Programs dictate space, and this is another example in which the general approach to medical education should influence the configuration of ambulatory care space.

Educational Standards

Generally accepted standards exist for most educational programs but are not necessarily applicable in the medical school environment. There is generally a need for lecture halls, classrooms, small-group study areas, laboratories, computer rooms, and so on. All of these should be considered educational space and all necessary for a quality educational program. The number of spaces is a relatively straightforward function of the curriculum, and the size of these spaces is a function of the size of the medical school class. If the basic sciences are taught for other health disciplines, space size adjustments must be made.

Allotment of space for small-group use should not be overlooked. The direction of medical education is such that physical diagnosis, interview processes, and so forth require small groups and small spaces; thus a large number of such spaces is generally needed. They may also be used for small-group conferences and group study space, if properly designed.

PLANNING PHILOSOPHY

In addition to the need to develop facility standards, another important consideration is the planning philosophy of the institution and the need to understand how an institution thinks about the facility.

One cannot overestimate the time, money, and difficulties that may be eliminated by proper thinking about facilities. A portion of this concept was outlined earlier, in that facilities should be considered resources (much like people, money, and equipment) that exist to house programs. Facilities must be functionally correct and aesthetically pleasing. Form must follow function, and the general "feel" of facilities should not be overlooked. A facility says a great deal about the institution, the department, and the individuals working there. Facilities convey a sense of the quality of care a patient is about to receive, the importance of the research being undertaken there, and just how good a school the space houses. One can argue about the appropriateness or rationality of such thinking, but such perceptions abound and should be taken into account in planning facilities.

Many elements of facilities should be considered as they are being purchased, designed, rehabilitated, or simply redecorated. Such terms as *flexibility, maintainability,* and *durability* should be part of your vocabulary. It is not enough to simply say that more space is needed or that a different configuration is required. Remember that the architects, engineers, and planners will walk away from the facilities they design and develop, but the faculty and staff will call it home for many years. Thus it is imperative, while recognizing extremely demanding schedules, that faculty, staff, and administrators get involved in the process of thinking about and planning facilities.

Institutional needs should also be incorporated into the planning philosophy. These needs can be regarded as facilities that provide general utility to a group of departments or programs, such as dining rooms, libraries, conference centers, and other general-use spaces. In times of limited resources (and those times always seem to be upon us), institutional needs must be properly balanced with departmental needs, and vice versa. However, particularly in academic health centers, there are times when individual departmental needs supersede the importance of institutional needs. Obviously, the reverse is also true, and a proper balance must be maintained. It is essential that individual departments be well represented in institutional decision making, particularly with respect to facilities. It is equally important for large departments to encourage participation by division heads as well as individual faculty members. The importance of the participation by individual departments, with faculty and staff members being given the opportunity to be involved, cannot be overemphasized. In many instances faculty and staff have expertise and knowledge of specifics that should be shared with administrators, planners, and architects *before* costly decisions are implemented. They may not avail themselves of the opportunity, but it is imperative that they be given that opportunity.

There is always an interest in minimizing institutional needs in favor of departmental needs. In many institutions, department chairs have no problem in recommending the elimination of bathrooms, janitors' closets, communication and electrical closets, mechanical space, and all other facilities that are not directly occupied by members of the department. While these issues can and should be discussed, elimination of such spaces cannot be realistically implemented without affecting the entire institution. We recommend balance in the creation of useful, quality space, which does require some of the building amenities and spaces for utility and other systems.

ARCHITECTS, ENGINEERS, AND INTERIOR DESIGNERS

If you manage an academic health center, you will undoubtedly have the opportunity at some point to work with architects and engineers and to be involved with interior design. Several issues to consider when working with architects and engineers are selection, design, and the review process. The selection of architects and engineers for a specific project should never be left solely to the institution's architects, engineers, and planners. As the ultimate owners/users of the facilities, the department chair and faculty should participate in the selection to ensure that you will be able to communicate with the selected design team and that your needs and desires will be listened to and accommodated to the extent possible. Architects and engineers should be selected as much on personality, interpersonal skills, and a sincere interest in accommodating the needs and desires of the ultimate users as on their technical ability and architectural/engineering experience. An excellent reference for good architects and engineers for a health-related facility can be obtained through discussions with physicians and staff at facilities they designed that are now in operation. Reference-checking is a role that chairs, faculty, and staff can play; they not only should volunteer to do so, but should emphatically ensure that discussions with colleagues at other institutions play a role in the final selection. It is akin to what is said about government: If you don't vote, you haven't exercised your voice, and you have less right to complain.

THE DESIGN PROCESS

There are many examples of successful and unsuccessful design projects for academic health centers, including research facilities, ambulatory care buildings, teaching hospitals, and faculty office buildings. Successful projects tend to follow a well-defined process during design, a process in which the users must participate. The phases of the design process are summarized in the box below.

Preplanning/Program Development

Participation by the users is particularly critical through the schematic design period. During the preplanning or program development phase the owner and its team define just what is needed: what programs will be contained in a particular facility, its relationship to other facilities, accessibility, and circulation patterns. A general concept of how the facility will work is also discussed. A comprehensive site plan for the particular building or buildings is developed, and general *footprints* (outlines and locations) of the buildings are considered.

PHASES OF THE DESIGN PROCESS

Preplanning and program development
Functional space program development/block diagrams
Schematic design
Preliminary design or design development
Working drawings or construction documents

Functional Program Development

Functional programming then takes the program needs and translates them into the individual spaces necessary to provide for those needs. The general size and quantity of individual spaces are also defined. For example, a particular department might identify six single faculty offices of 110 NASF each, three double faculty offices of 140 NASF each, a clerical area to house four secretaries, file cabinets, and a reception area of 400 NASF, and so forth. Some comments on particular characteristics of importance for each space are gathered at this time. On the basis of a functional space program and the other work done in the preplanning and program development phase, buildings can be sized and general cost estimates developed. An important part of this segment of the design process may be the development of *preschematics,* which are rather rudimentary sketches of how spaces may fit together, using their approximate sizes. They contain essentially no detail with respect to specific usage within individual spaces, where windows and doors may be, or other details of that nature. They simply block out spaces to show their relative relationships and provide an idea of how designs may be accommodated within particular footprints or spaces available. These activities are among the most important in the design process, since they in fact develop the general concept and size of the building, as well as the relationship between spaces. Everything from this point forward is refinement and detail. During the preplanning and program development activities and the creation of the functional space program and preschematics, it is vital that faculty and staff participate.

Schematic Design

The development of *schematics* is a more formal process in which fairly precise shapes and sizes of spaces are determined, windows and doors are placed in context, and the specific relationship between rooms, corridors, mechanical spaces, elevators, and stairs is detailed. If any changes are to be made in the overall concept, this is the time to make them. Beyond the schematic stage it is expensive, both in terms of dollars and time, to make changes. This is the time for final thinking and a critical review.

Preliminary Design

The next level of detail in the process is generally called design development or preliminary design. The set of drawings created by the architects or engineers at this stage is based on the schematic drawings discussed earlier. These really establish the size and design detail of the facility. This set of drawings deals not only with the architectural aspects of the project, but also integrates the structural and utility systems with information already developed. Between development of schematic drawings and the design development drawings, it is important that the architects meet again with the ultimate users of each room to determine all of the important characteristics for that particular space. This should include a clear understanding of the equipment and furniture required, needs for particular types of lighting and electrical and telecommunication services, specific plumbing and medical gas requirements, the desirability of built-in casework (such as counters and bookshelves), and other important elements of the room. That information, in conjunction with the approved schematic drawing, forms the basis for creating the design package.

Working Drawings

The final element of the process is the creation of the construction documents, sometimes called working drawings. This is the final plan that is used to direct the construction team, and it is used as the basis for bidding. It includes detailed drawings as well as written specifications, the combination of which precisely defines the project. Each phase of design should be based on a specific approval of the preceding phase, and it is important that the users of the space participate in each of those approvals. Again it must be emphasized that changes that you make at any point in the process are costly but are always more costly the farther along the project has developed.

Review

For the review process, even if the institution's project manager does not require reviews by the ultimate users of space, the ultimate users should take the initiative and demand the opportunity for review. This is imperative at each stage of development but is most important at the schematic design stage. The reviews should be detailed and a member of the design team should be included in the group to answer questions and ensure a clear understanding of what is being reviewed. Typically, individuals not well versed in reading architectural drawings have difficulty understanding what is being presented. Therefore, the best approach is a general review with someone with an excellent architectural or engineering background, or in fact, a member of the design team, to ensure that everyone understands exactly what the final product or facility will be. When given the opportunity, PARTICIPATE.

To summarize the design process:

- Select the right team.
- Define the facility through the programs to be housed there.
- Participate in the development of functional space programs, site plans, and schematics.
- Do not delegate responsibilities for these activities too far down in the organization.
- Make sure you understand what is transpiring, and see that your faculty and staff have the opportunity to provide input.
- Talk to colleagues at other institutions. Visit facilities housing similar programs to glean ideas and ensure that the design is one that you fully understand and approve.

Your new facility will have a significant impact on your ability to operate programs of interest, recruit faculty, retain staff, and generally have a functional and pleasant environment. The key word is participation.

THE INTERIOR DESIGN PROCESS

The interior design process is generally left to interior designers and architects, but again, participation by the ultimate users of the space is critical to the selection of appropriate finishes, furniture, furnishings, standards, and cost.

Finishes refers to what materials will be used on surfaces (floors, ceilings, and walls) as well as their colors and/or patterns. The selection of carpet or vinyl composition tile for a particular application is a finish decision. Wallpaper, vinyl wall covering, or paint, with or without chair rails and crown molding, is another finish decision. Such decisions have a significant impact on the general feel of the space as well as on long-term maintenance costs. A related issue is the quality of the finishes. Not all carpet is the same. There are important characteristics of the carpet that will determine how easily it can be cleaned and repaired and how it will function in a particular setting. Make sure that you understand this to the degree that it is important to you and ensure that the impact of these various characteristics is well understood.

Selection of *furniture* is not something that should be left exclusively to the designers. Institutional and/or departmental decisions should be made with an awareness of the need to establish standards and the degree of autonomy that individuals can have in selecting furniture for their areas. The establishment of standards permits buying larger quantities, and thus reducing costs, while permitting a great deal of flexibility and interchangeability without replacing items for compatibility. On the other hand, furniture preference is very individual, and many faculty and staff members may feel strongly that they should have a significant say in selection of the furnishings for their particular office or operating area. This applies to the general type of furniture, finishes, and materials used for upholsteries.

Furnishings are generally understood to include draperies, blinds, plants, pictures, and decorative items. These should be considered when general budgets are being developed, yet they represent an area often overlooked. While it is true that this is probably the lowest cost area of any major facilities project, furnishings can make a significant difference in the overall feel of the space when it is completed and fully furnished.

RENOVATION AND CONSTRUCTION

In addition to working with architects and engineers during a design process, managers will also be involved with renovation and construction activities. Renovation and construction will require involvement with the process, time schedules, and quality and change issues. When the entire project has been defined by the creation of construction documents, including interior design and furnishings, the institution is in a position to obtain costs from various contractors and to award a contract for execution of the project. Projects of significant size are typically made available to be bid by licensed general contractors. The requirements, in state institutions in particular, are generally that the contractor be licensed in the state in which the project takes place and be in a position to obtain a bond to guarantee completion of the project. The bond is necessary so that if the general contractor finds that he cannot complete the project for financial reasons (bankruptcy, for example), the bonding company is obligated to step in and have the project completed at the agreed-on cost. The bidding process takes place, a contract is awarded, and a schedule is then agreed on.

Scheduling

Time schedules are an important issue. It is not only important to ensure that cost estimates are complete, but it is equally important that schedules reflect the actual total completion of the project. Often terms such as *substantial completion* are used, and it is important that the user understand the meaning of such terminology. "Substantial completion" generally means that there are still small things to be done, but that the space can be occupied and used for its intended purpose. This may not be satisfactory for certain activities, however, and the actual detailed schedule should be clarified by the project manager and clearly explained to the user. It is also important to understand the responsibilities of the owner with respect to maintaining the schedule. There may be activities required of the owner that affect the schedule, and those too must be carefully monitored. Should the owner not take timely steps to meet its commitments, it may affect not only the time for completion by the general contractor, but also the general contractor may indicate that the extended time is costly to him and make a claim for additional compensation.

Quality

The quality of a building project is in many cases a subjective issue difficult to define. Nevertheless, it is important to consider three characteristics of all projects: time, cost, and quality. It is quite easy to provide any two of those three as long as the third one can be varied. It is simple to meet time and quality requirements for a project if cost is not an issue. Similarly, I can almost always complete a project in a particular amount of time and at a specific cost if I need not be concerned with quality. Owners of facilities should always insist on *all three characteristics*. With proper planning and management, all three are achievable. Whenever you discuss one of those elements, you should recognize and fully understand the impact on the other two characteristics.

Changes = Money

Although it has been stated before, it is most important during the construction period to remember that change is equivalent to money. Changes are expensive during the construction process for a whole range of reasons. There is no competitive reason for the general contractor to be particularly cost effective in quoting costs for changes. He already has the project and can use this as an opportunity to adjust for areas where he may not have estimated costs high enough. Every attempt should be made to minimize or eliminate changes during the construction process. In some cases, paradoxically, it is less expensive to come back and make changes after the contractor leaves the site than to ask him to use more time at high costs to make changes during construction. Costs should be monitored carefully and the overall budget reviewed frequently.

FACILITY MAINTENANCE

Managers should understand three basic types of facility maintenance: routine, emergency, and preventive. Often the financial responsibility for the different types of facility maintenance rests with different organizations or individuals. That responsibility should be clearly determined early on and should also be well understood at the time the development of a new facility is being contemplated. These are cost elements that typically come out of operating budgets rather than capital budgets.

Routine maintenance may include everything from janitorial services through periodic painting of facilities. It includes changing washers on sinks, repairing a broken door hinge, and changing light bulbs. A response time should be established for a particular facility, and it is reasonable to expect that routine maintenance be taken care of within that time. Routine maintenance is often budgeted on a central basis for an entire building but still must be the concern of the individual departments.

Emergency maintenance is the repair of problems that simply cannot wait. Emergency maintenance might deal with repair of the central air conditioning system for a surgical suite, whereas repair of a window air conditioning unit in a student study area might be considered more routine. A well-defined system for emergency facility maintenance on a 24-hour per day basis should always be in place, and instant responses should be expected when necessary. On the other hand, faculty and staff must be realistic and not claim the need for emergency service when a repair can be handled routinely.

Preventive maintenance generally relates to equipment. It includes periodic lubrication of bearings, cleaning filters, periodic checks of emergency generators, and so on. A preventive maintenance program must be in place to minimize the need for expensive emergency repairs. The Facilities Management Department should have a detailed schedule, and faculty and staff should be aware of that schedule of preventive maintenance for equipment and spaces under their purview.

CONCLUSION

Facility planning and management is an area generally foreign to faculty and staff in academic environments, yet daily they are directly affected by these matters. Thus it is important that they gain a basic grounding in the process and understand the related terminology. They must participate in the design and development phases and be aware of the characteristics of the construction process as well as maintenance procedures. The key word is *participation*. Time must be made available to ensure that the facilities needed are developed and maintained in a high-quality and cost-effective manner.

BIBLIOGRAPHY

1. Berriman W, Essick T Jr, William J & Bentivegna P. (1976). *Capital projects for health care facilities.* Rockville, Md: Aspen Systems Corp.
2. Cushman RF & Perry SR. (1983). *Planning, financing, and constructing health care facilities.* Rockville, Md: Aspen Systems Corp.
*3. Froom JD, ed. (1991). Group on Institutional Planning and Group on Business Affairs. *Space planning and management in academic medical centers: Issues, models and resources.* Washington, DC: Association of American Medical Colleges.
4. Hardy OB & Lammers LP. (1986). *Hospitals: The planning and design process.* Rockville, Md: Aspen Publishers, Inc.
5. Harrell GT. (1974). *Planning medical center facilities for education, research, and public service.* University Park, Pa: The Pennsylvania State University Press.
6. Porter DR. (1982). *Hospital architecture: Guidelines for design and renovation.* Ann Arbor: Health Administration Press.

*Asterisk indicates an article or book that is particularly informative and helpful.

CHAPTER 10

Building Success

Jill Ridky

&

Only in the dictionary does success come before work.

MARK TWAIN

Every chair, director, and division chief strives to build a successful program or department. "Building success" can be accomplished more readily if you incorporate some basic—even intuitive—traits or skills into your leadership style and mode of operation in the department. Whether a department is just beginning to build success or has already achieved it, the concepts presented in this chapter will assist you in achieving your department's potential. Since success derives from a masterful blend of skills, abilities, and traits, this chapter presents summary discussions and different techniques and strategies that will help develop academic organizations.

COMMUNICATION

Academic managers quickly learn that communication is a key to operating a successful department or program. Communication must be developed and nurtured as a top priority. The communication flow should be not only from the managers to the department or program, but also from the departmental members to the chair. As highlighted in Chapter 3, fostering communication benefits individual performance levels and productivity. Knowledge, ideas, and suggestions must be shared within the communication flow. As Allan Tucker says in *Chairing the Academic Department,* "A department that is kept in relative ignorance about budget, programs, and personnel development is a department mismanaged and unable to defend itself against decisions made about its destiny by those outside it."[1]

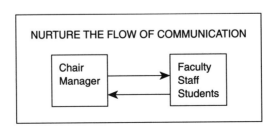

NURTURE THE FLOW OF COMMUNICATION

Chair Manager → Faculty Staff Students

THE ART OF LISTENING

An old management truism is that if you want to learn about an organization—how it functions, who is in charge, and what the problems are—speak to the janitor. Why the janitor? The janitor quickly goes about his function daily, never saying much, but listening to people in "corridor conversations" every day. Because of his listening skills, he may have some real insights into the organization. In *Thriving on Chaos,* Tom Peters states it more directly[2]: As a chair or director, you have to listen carefully and constantly, review and evaluate, share ideas, suggestions, and information, and recognize achievement. Peters emphasizes *listening,* whether you are engaged in a corridor conversation or a formal advisory or division chief's meeting.

For some, active listening is not an easy skill to acquire; many directors have not mastered the art of listening. Listening is much more difficult than talking; it requires total concentration and a focused and engaged mind. Many chairs will passively listen while distractedly considering another problem or crisis they are facing that day. Over time, a chair may develop listening skills to a level at which interjecting questions for clarification is not required as much; this will help the chair to understand colleagues' goals, concerns, and motivations.

A good listener can grasp not only the meaning of the conversation, but also overtones, subtle nuances, body language, and context. This sometimes requires asking questions to clarify the speaker's meaning, or listening intuitively—with your "antennae" up. It is important to withhold evaluation or judgment until after the speaker has finished. Listening requires patience, a skill most chairs develop over time.

To improve your listening skills, practice the following:
- Don't let your mind wander.
- Let others talk first.
- Don't interrupt; be patient.
- Focus on substance, not style.
- Ask questions to clarify a point.
- Empathize.
- Withhold judgment or evaluation.
- Give yourself time to think before you react.

NEGOTIATION

There is not a manager in academics who does not attain improved negotiation skills by the end of the first term of appointment. Chairs and managers utilize negotiation skills almost daily to obtain renewed contracts and in salary discussions, recruitment activity, and other tasks. Roger Fisher and William Ury, in *Getting To Yes,*[3] advocate negotiating based on merit and not butting heads or entering into a conflict or battle. Successful agreement is more likely if negotiation is based on merit.

Many times chairs and directors will find they are not negotiating on a "level playing field," a term used frequently in academic medicine, especially when departments are negotiating with larger entities (such as larger academic departments, the dean's office, hospitals, and so on). What do you do when the other side has better political connections or is better funded, larger, or in a more powerful position? Although the differences in the "playing field" cannot be changed, you can protect yourself and your department by being prepared. This means taking time in advance of negotiations to fully comprehend the issues and problems, having your data or trends ready to present, developing the least favorable outcome you will accept and adhering to it, and establishing your bottom line. You should also have a contingency plan to implement if the negotiations reach a stalemate. If opposition is expressed, sometimes the best response is silence—or no response. This will sometimes move the other side to break the stalemate and present or consider another option or offer.

A key to successful negotiation is to be able to communicate. This does not mean that you must, or should, talk continuously during the negotiation time. During communication, you must listen carefully and think before you speak. Be selective in what you say; use the time productively by presenting only the pertinent information. Do not communicate useless information or verbiage.

Another key in negotiations is not to make the other party defensive or to launch an attack. For example, if you are negotiating an affiliated hospital contract with an administrator to support a residency rotation and the hospital is not considered a very contemporary facility, do not criticize the facility. Even with direct ownership, most employees have a sense of pride in their facility and will become defensive to any criticism. Instead, indicate you want to develop a residency rotation at this fine, established facility but that you will require the following support for your residents.

Before any negotiation, take the time necessary to decide what it is your department or center needs to attain, what you can function with, and what your operation cannot give up. Although rehearsing the negotiation is recommended, another approach is to visualize the negotiation in your mind, walking through the negotiation mentally. Some negotiators will conduct the entire meeting in their mind, from the time they enter the room to the final handshake. This technique

---

SUCCESSFUL NEGOTIATION

1. Understand interests—yours and the other party's. Give the other side positive support. Look for shared interests.
2. Develop win-win options to achieve a mutual gain.
3. Take time to prepare yourself in advance and evaluate options.
4. Listen and attempt to build a solid working relationship. Try to understand the other party's perspective.
5. Get your ducks in a row. Have your data, handouts, and facts available to support your argument.
6. Rehearse or practice the negotiation either with a nonparticipating party or on your own, or spend time visualizing the negotiation.

entails far more than just thinking about the meeting; by visualizing small details and anticipating questions and responses, you automatically prepare to meet the unexpected with assurance. It also means that when you do walk into the meeting room, you are not really doing it for the first time. Jack Nadel, a very experienced negotiator who wrote *Cracking the Global Market,*[4] recommends this approach. He has said his visualization of the meeting is typically 60% to 70% accurate. He notes that this gives you an enormous advantage. He also recommends starting negotiations by understanding what the other party wants. Finally, especially in academics, negotiators should not be out to obtain, like the Merchant of Venice, a "pound of flesh." This can create rifts in departmental or university-wide relationships that over time will not be beneficial. If there is not a fair resolution for both parties, move to other options.

In negotiation, as with many management techniques, keep it simple.[5] If the issue in negotiation is very complex, try to break it down into more understandable components and let each component build on the last. The box on p. 176 summarizes the keys to successful negotiation.

PRODUCTIVE MEETINGS

Academic health organizations tend to develop seemingly unending numbers of committees, subcommittees, and blue-ribbon task forces. The purpose of a meeting must be worthwhile and fruitful from a cost-benefit standpoint, since many of the organization's top-salaried members participate in the meetings, and it is not unusual for meetings, particularly in academic medicine, to extend on for several hours. As

Before we adjourn, let's decide on the agenda, so we can put something in the minutes.

SOURCE: The Chronicle of Higher Education

CHAIRING A PRODUCTIVE MEETING

1. First, question whether a meeting is necessary or if another medium can be used.

2. Determine the purpose of each meeting and communicate it clearly in advance to the participants.

3. Have a clearly stated goal and a written agenda.

4. Keep the meeting short.

5. Start on time; end on time.

6. Keep minutes of all meetings.

7. Encourage participation. Listen and respect all ideas.

8. Develop a team spirit; emphasize shared goals.

9. Focus on the agenda; if the discussion diverges from it, return the group's attention to the specifics of the topic.

10. Summarize progress succinctly, and do not let peripheral issues sidetrack progress.

11. At the meeting's close, reiterate agreed-on solutions to any problems discussed so that each person leaves the meeting with the same understanding of what was decided.

---

discussed in Chapter 5, meetings are costly; for example, a meeting of eight members, lasting several hours, can in reality consume half a work week of time. Meetings are a useful function, but they must be worthwhile and productive to all the participants. The box above offers a concise summary of how to make meetings productive.

The first step is determining the purpose of the meeting, and whether this purpose requires an actual meeting or if the topic could be handled by a conference call, computer mail, fax, or some other means. Committee members should be selected carefully. Meetings or discussions are not usually productive with more than six participants. Prepare an agenda and make sure all participants receive it at least 5 days before the meeting. A draft agenda is sometimes recommended if the committee members are to be active participants in the process. The agenda should include the date, time, place of meeting, list of participants, and functions. Select a chair for the meeting. The chair will be responsible for seeing the meeting starts and ends on time, checking attendance, and arranging for meeting summaries. The chair should introduce all participants.

PLANNING AND GOAL ATTAINMENT

Developing goals in an academic institution requires developing a focus. As noted in Chapter 3, productive research groups have clear organizational goals. Where does the department want to go, where does the department want to be positioned in the next 5 years? Especially for chairs or people in positions that are in 5-year track appointments, the question should be, Where do I want to take the department or program in the next 5 years? What is my vision? Setting goals will direct the department, establish priorities, and help to determine the strengths, achievements, and weaknesses of the department at the end of the period of time. The goals can be specific to the functions in the department. For example, what are our financial goals? Program goals? Administrative goals?

Goals should be written down and a plan for attaining the goals developed. It is important to keep the goals specific. Some chairs develop a list that they carry with them; the list can be numbered in the order of importance. As goals or steps to goals are achieved, each item can be checked or crossed off. Some of the keys for developing goals should be as follows:

- They must be attainable.
- They must be challenging.

In setting goals, you must assess the realities of your department: What is the environment in which the department functions? What is the competition? What are our strengths and weaknesses? What are our preferences, priorities, commitments, and values?

Many times admirable goals are not achieved because they are not placed into a realistic timeframe, with a sincere commitment to their achievement.

In the planning process, the leader's role is critical. Leadership functions to initiate the process, articulate strategy, commit cooperation, and manage problems. Without leadership and commitment, the goal can never be attained.

During the process of goal achievement, periodic updates should be prepared by managers and presented to organizational members. Questions to be asked are:

- Are the steps to the goal occurring within the anticipated period?
- What progress has been made?
- If a budget is attached to the goal, is the project functioning within budget or over budget?

Periodic reviews are key, because they provide flexibility to adjust the plan as problems are encountered. The plan should not lose flexibility and responsiveness to opportunities in changing the academic department. Managers or chairs should consider adjustments to the plan appropriate.

Objectives, which can be defined as the general statements of what the organization must do to accomplish the goal, are then formulated from the goals. Once the objectives are formulated, the next phase is to develop strategies. Strategies, or the action phase of the plan, become the means through which objectives are accomplished. The strategies should relate directly to the desired objective. To achieve an objective, several strategies might be used rather than a single one.

Departments in today's volatile and competitive environment cannot survive without a plan to focus the energies of the department. Through the planning process, departments recognize that they can and will change over time and that the potential for new opportunities abounds.

Planning will greatly assist practices in the decision making process. In a successful department, planning is an ongoing process for goal development, appraisal, and evaluation.

PUBLIC INFORMATION

Traditionally, the concept of public information or marketing was primarily utilized in the "profit sector" of the organization. Times have changed, however, and marketing or public information is no longer looked upon as anathema to the academic environment. Academic programs are well served in today's environment when some time and effort are spent on this area.

Public information in academic departments can take a variety of forms. The first form is the information release. Managers must develop an understanding of the institutional process for releasing information to the public. This can sometimes be an arduous process because of the complicated organizational structure of medical schools and health centers. For example, should the information be released by the affiliated hospital or by the medical school or the university news bureau? It is important for the manager to become knowledgeable about the appropriate protocol and to know the names of the public affairs staff members. For example, at some academic medical centers there are staff members assigned to report only research-related releases and others only clinical-related releases. Understanding the personnel involved and the appropriate procedures is important.

Once the news release structure and protocol are understood, managers must organize a departmental system for reporting the newsworthy event (such as a grant award, new clinical accomplishment or program, major gift/contribution, or faculty award). Some departments designate one staff member to receive and coordinate newsworthy items. The staff member is then responsible for relaying the information to the appropriate institutional public information specialists.

Other forms of public information are brochures and reports. At one time only the profit sector employed annual reports, but today more and more academic institutions are using the concept. Whether it is published in-house or by an external agency, the concept of an annual report is a good one, because it ties together and summarizes all the activities, achievements, and awards for the department for a given year. Once developed, annual reports can be used for a multitude of purposes. For example, an academic medical department utilizes its reports for recruitment of faculty and residents, for developing the referring physician base, university relations, and private and public program support, and also as a recording document for the department's historical archives. Reports may be tedious to produce initially, but once a format is established and the capability developed to produce the report with in-house with PCs, desktop publishing software, and laser printers, the project will become routine as well as cost effective.

Another form of reporting is a quarterly newsletter. This information reporting device summarizes activities regularly and is used to keep alumni, other departmental associates, and board members informed of growth and program activities.

Public information can also be disseminated by faculty announcements. It is a nice gesture to develop a formal announcement for the arrival of a new faculty member (see Chapter 8). The announcement can be a simple single card format that gives the faculty the name of the new faculty member, appointment, a brief background on educational degrees and achievements, and special interests. The announcements can be mailed across campus, targeted to associates the new faculty member will be collaborating with on and off campus.

TIME MANAGEMENT

In academics it is very easy to get lost in the daily surge of paperwork, meetings, and interruptions. Typically, with so many events occurring each day, it seems impossible for a beleaguered manager to make any strides or to feel a sense of accomplishment at the end of the day. In this intense environment it is very easy to spend the day with relatively unimportant phone calls, reading routine mail, or working on a crisis that could be better delegated to a member of the staff.

To begin achieving, a first step is to take a few minutes either at the end of the work day or in the morning before the work day begins to review the upcoming day, taking a few minutes before the start of the next day to set priorities and to make a short list of tasks to accomplish (see the box below). Some academicians elect to do this not only daily, but also weekly and monthly. This type of structure will help to keep you focused and will help you to see what you have accomplished at the end of a time period. As other projects or "to do's" come along, it is also easier to integrate them into your already organized plan. Discover when your productive times are. When are your research, teaching, administrative, or clinical days? Block these times out, since this will not be productive time for many of your to do's. Also, consider whether you are a morning, afternoon, or evening person; when can you be most productive? Can you modify your schedule to accommodate your most effective periods for administrative tasks?

"Learning to say no" and screening calls and visitors are useful skills, but are also difficult to implement at a chair level. Interruptions can be a major impediment to managing time; taking telephone calls or a colleague or staff member who drops in and asks "do you have a minute?" are essential interruptions, but they can be

---

MANAGING TIME

1. Develop priorities. Review them periodically.
2. Maintain a "to do" list, use and update it, and encourage others to use one.
3. Educate the staff on many details so you can delegate and they can make informed responses.
4. Use the technology available: computers, modems, teleconferencing, voice mail, fax.
5. Schedule only important meetings.
6. Delegate as appropriate.
7. Be realistic—do not overextend yourself.

ruinous to a time scheduled for other tasks. Typically, chairs want an open-door policy to demonstrate their responsiveness to the organization. A delicate balance of being responsive and also being able to have time for those to do's must be achieved. Administrative staff members can help to create this balance by being knowledgeable about the organization, how it functions, and the political climate. With this knowledge they will be more effective in screening calls, assisting, and problem solving independently. This level of support is critical for a successful time management plan.

USING GRAPHICS

Academic medical departments are inundated daily with reports, such as operating room statistics, outpatient visits, the number of day-op procedures, hospital census, and patient discharge. There are reports on finances, collection rates, research activities, student enrollment, residency operative experience, and many other matters.

These reports are all quite necessary and useful, but typically they are not in a format for quick analysis and interpretation. The use of graphs can often help such analysis and interpretation (see the box below). The use of line diagrams, pie charts, and bar graphs helps to communicate the data and can reform very complex and lengthy reports into a one-page report that is informative, beneficial, and easily interpreted.

For example, academic medical departments receive lengthy reports on referral data. This is a very time-consuming report to review. However, all of these data can be combined into a graphic display of the state, blocking referral density by county (Figure 10-1). Once this is accomplished, the chair or program director can easily interpret the level of density per county and answer important questions, such as where do the majority of department referrals come from?

Other types of graphic displays are illustrated in Figure 10-2. The net receipt trend shown in Figure 10-2, *A,* illustrates 11 years of data and clearly demonstrates a trend of dramatic increase in outpatient receipts. Figure 10-2, *B,* demonstrates the amount of annual budget attributed to supporting the administrative unit of the department. This information could also be shown in a tabular data report; however,

---

GRAPHIC DISPLAYS

1. Graphics represent a beneficial technical format for complex, lengthy academic reports.
2. Multiple pages of data can be presented in a one-page format; a picture *can* be worth a thousand words.
3. Various data can be compared on a single page.
4. Graphics illustrate the subject with clarity.
5. Display should be kept simple; avoid the junk.

by summarizing a multitude of number columns, the pie chart quickly and visually demonstrates the percentage of administrative expenditures compared with the department's total budget.

Financial managers find historical trends beneficial in projecting clinical revenue. Figure 10-2, *C,* illustrates 3 years of monthly clinical revenue. This visually consolidates 3 years of detailed monthly revenue reports and will assist with departmental projections and may also lead to questions regarding collection performance or level of productivity.

Just as profit organizations are eliminating middle management positions, academic institutions are reviewing how top-heavy their organizations are. Once again, there are many personnel reports that can assemble data on the numbers of faculty members by rank. However, a graphic display such as Figure 10-2, *D,* illustrates the percentage of faculty members by rank in an academic department for a given year. This type of graphic can also be done in a trend format to demonstrate the trend of faculty ranks over a period of time. Graphic displays can also include raw data. Graphics can be coupled with a table of the data, which might benefit those who are more quantitatively oriented.

Quality graphic displays can really benefit a chair or program director in improving the knowledge base and understanding of others regarding the reality of the department or departmental needs. Graphic displays should not be used as visual decorations but to clarify, to aid analysis of complex reports, improve understanding, and to assist managers and staff in decision making. Tufte notes, "Data graphics should draw the viewer's attention to the sense and substance of the data, not to something else. The graphic display should help members of the organization to reason about quantitative information."[6]

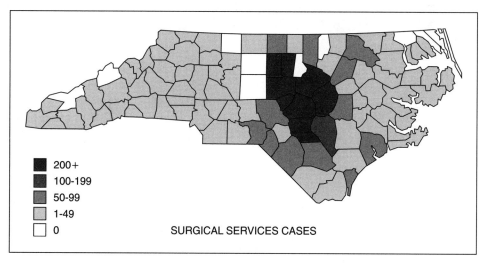

Figure 10-1. Department chairs and faculty are daily inundated with complex data and reports; therefore, it is wise to present data graphically, as in this state-shaped summary, to make information instantly accessible and easy to interpret.

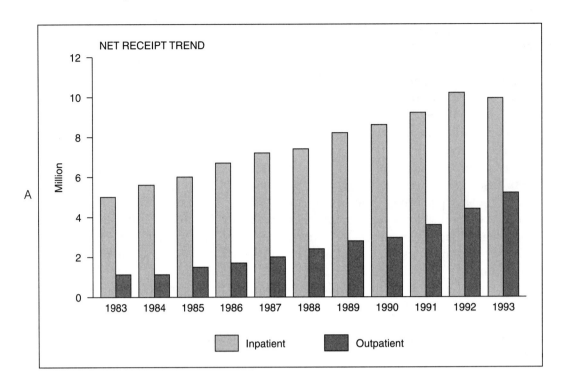

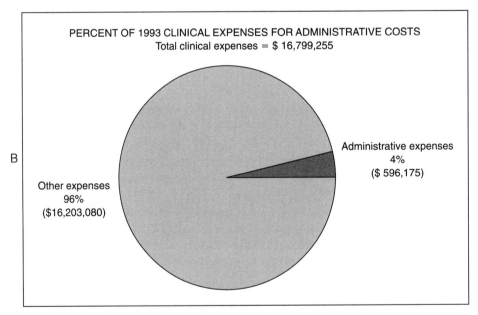

Figure 10-2. Some examples of how presenting data through graphics can be an effective and readily understood method of communicating information. Note how bar graphs **A** and **C** and pie charts **B** and **D** are most appropriate for the kinds of data they present.

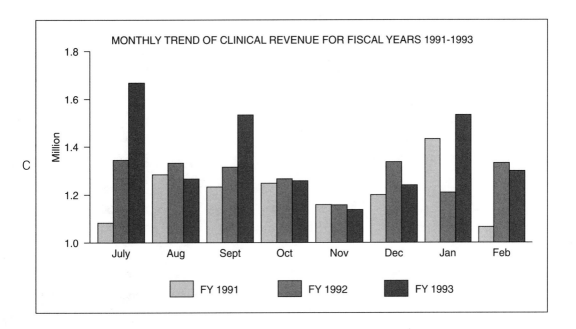

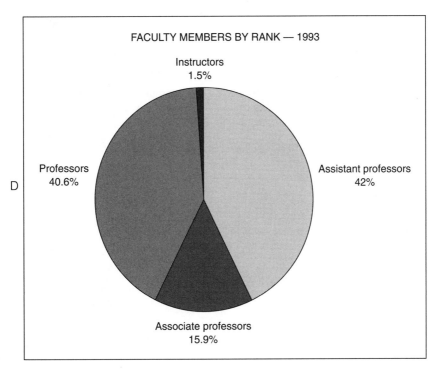

Figure 10-2, cont'd. For legend see opposite page.

SAMPLE AGENDA FORMAT
(Name of Site Visit)
(Date of Site Visit)

You will be met by Ms. Marsha Owen, Conference Coordinator

Time	Activity	Location	Staff Attending	Time Allocated
8:00 AM	Welcome	Conference Room	Jacobs Smith Dunn	30 minutes
8:30-10:00	Institutional support	Conference Room	Provost Dean Chair Director	1 hour, 30 minutes
10:00-10:30	Coffee break	Room 710		30 minutes
10:30-11:30	Review of proposal	Conference Room	Rutter Harris Johnson Thomas	1 hour
11:30-12:30	Lunch break	Room 710		1 hour
12:30- 2:30	Tour of facility	Meet in Room 710	Harris Johnson	2 hours
2:30- 3:30	Summary of proposal	Conference Room	Thomas Rutter	1 hour
3:30- 4:00	Question and answer period	Conference Room	Harris Johnson Thomas Rutter	30 minutes
4:00 PM	Departure			

SITE VISIT ATTENDEES

Date: _____   _____   _____

Name	Title/Location	Attend pre-site meeting	Attend site meeting	Available at office
J. Smith	Professor, Surgery	X	X	
J. Talbert	Laboratory Director, Vascular			X
R. Peters	Assistant Professor, Medicine	X		X
P. Walters	Dean, Medical School	X	X	
C. Jacobs	Chair, Surgery	X	X	
J. Lacey	Assistant Professor, Nutrition	X	X	

SITE VISITS

Site visits are often made to academic medical organizations. Typically a site visit is related to research projects or residency accreditation.

Whatever the reason or cause for a site visit, you should carefully prepare and plan for it (see the boxes on p. 186). The following list of procedures will assist your preparation for the visit:

1. Assign a staff member to coordinate the visit.
2. Develop a list that includes visitor names, titles, and addresses, and request a copy of a CV or excerpt on background.
3. List attendees' names, titles, and division/department (include applicable university members, such as chancellors, deans, hospital directors, chairs, and administrators).
4. Prepare name tags for visitors and attendees.
5. Send a supplemental package to visitors with information on:
   The organization
   Tour areas
   Applicable research
   Applicable information/news
   Applicable brochures/reports
   The agenda for the visit, with the name of the staff member who will greet visitors
   Applicable CVs of staff members involved in the site visit
   Include name tags for visitors in the supplemental package
   Develop parking/transportation/board arrangements
6. Reserve conference rooms, arrange for slide projector/overhead/VCR, and make arrangements for coffee breaks, lunch or dinner, and/or departure.
7. Assign a staff member to meet visitors on their arrival and to assist in departure.
8. Arrange for a rehearsal meeting before the site visit to review the agenda.
9. Contact each attendee by memo and telephone, providing the date of the meetings and the CVs of visitors, as appropriate. A well-timed reminder of the upcoming site visit is also helpful.

FACILITY TOUR

AHCs often need to provide a facility tour to visiting colleagues, guest lecturers, and so on. You may find it useful to have a prearranged tour plan that can be easily implemented. The following is a sample facility tour agenda:

1. The visitor will be met by a tour guide at Dr. Smith's office, 136 Howell Building.
2. Have senior or distinguished visitors sign the guest register outside Dr. Smith's office.

3. The tour will begin with several laboratories in the Howell Building. For most of these the activities in the laboratory are posted on the outside, but the guide should pause to point out that these are research facilities and that the department occupies 30% of the building.

4. The group can then be taken to the Smith Building to see the dean's office and the health sciences library.

5. The group should visit the division office area to see the resident's library, the computer center where literature searches are made, and the chief residents' offices.

6. From there the guide should escort the group to the operating room area. There the conference room, day-op center, and entrances to the operating rooms should be pointed out. The number of operating rooms available should be explained during this part of the tour.

7. The clinic area should be viewed, followed by the intensive care unit. Visitors can be introduced to Dr. Meyer, who serves as medical director for all the intensive care units.

8. The group should then take the elevator to the fifth floor and cross the corridor to the pediatric unit. As this is done, the guide can highlight a typical new hospital bed facility.

9. Before going to the pediatric unit, the unit should be called so they will expect visitors. If a multiple-tour day occurs, they should be notified in advance. It is an appropriate courtesy to call even at short notice. This is also true of the operating room and the intensive care units.

10. The tour should then proceed to the bed tower area, highlighting the newly renovated area and providing some current hospital data (number of beds, national standing, and so on).

11. From the bed tower, the tour should go to the emergency room, where the remodeling is still in progress. From there the group can walk to the front entrance of the hospital on the first floor to point out the helicopter landing pad, which usually will have a helicopter on it.

12. From that location, the cancer center and rehabilitation center can be pointed out.

13. Next the research complex should be highlighted, noting research data (number of NIH grants, total research dollars, number of researchers, national ranking, and so on).

14. To conclude the tour, the guide should escort the visitors to the Howell Building or to another appropriate location.

BIBLIOGRAPHY

1. Tucker A. (1992). *Chairing the academic department: Leadership among peers* (3rd ed). New York: Macmillan.
2. Peters T. (1987). *Thriving on chaos*. New York: Alfred A Knopf.
*3. Fisher R & Ury W. (1991). *Getting to yes: Negotiating agreement without giving in* (2nd ed). New York: Penguin Books.
4. Nadel J. (1987). *Cracking the global market: How to do business around the corner and around the world.* Rockville Centre, NY: Farnsworth Publishing Co.
*5. Seltz DP & Modica AJ. (1980). *Negotiate your way to success*. Chicago: Farnsworth/Dearborn Financial Publishing Co.
*6. Tufte ER. (1993). *The visual display*. Cheshire, Conn: Graphics Press, p 91.
*7. Schermerhorn JR Jr. (1986). *Management for productivity* (2nd ed). New York: John Wiley & Sons.

*Asterisk indicates an article or book that is particularly informative and helpful.

❧ Part Three ❧

PROCESSES

A government without good management is a house built on sand.

FRANKLIN D. ROOSEVELT, 1937

CHAPTER 11

Internal Controls: Policies and Procedures

Edwin A. Capel, Jr.

━━━━━━━━━━━━━━━ ﹩ ━━━━━━━━━━━━━━━

Internal controls are management controls and they are not for auditors only. Academic managers usually react negatively to the mention of internal controls. "Internal controls!" they exclaim. "The external and internal auditors are always complaining that 'internal controls' are not in place or need to be improved. What are they, and why do we need them, anyway?" I have heard this numerous times from managers at many different levels, but the questions are good ones. What *are* internal controls and why do organizations need them?

WHAT ARE INTERNAL CONTROLS?

Whether you realize it or not, you deal with internal controls in the daily routines of your job and life. Sometimes these internal controls will not appear as such and will be, in your opinion, obstacles to completing a task or obtaining services. Often internal controls are described as "organizational bureaucracy," forcing you to get approval at various levels in an organization or requiring a certain form for a certain transaction.

Most organizations either have too many internal controls that have been haphazardly developed over the years, or they have not yet developed any internal control structure. Many controls in organizations are found either to be out-of-date or contradictory; many have never been written down. As a result, the consequences can be disruptive, detrimental, and costly to the operational efficiency and effectiveness of the organization.

Managers in organizations lacking internal controls tend to act hesitantly, indecisively, and spend inordinate time searching for answers and problem solving. In general, internal controls serve four primary functions: they safeguard assets, check accuracy and reliability of accounting data, promote operational efficiency, and encourage adherence to prescribed managerial policies. Some experts refer to internal controls as proceedings that summarize operational transactions of an organization and become part of its character. To develop internal controls requires the art of organizing a framework for the flow of business activities, operations, and transactions.

Most controls are developed because management wants to reduce operational problems and increase the efficiency, clarity, effectiveness, and accountability of the organization. In addition, other important considerations call for well-developed internal controls:

- Staff members may achieve greater efficiency by having a clearly defined framework for procedures.
- Controls will signal to management whether any one person is handling too many transactions.
- The transactions will be executed as authorized, thereby facilitating organizational effectiveness.
- Controls provide safeguards from unintentional errors.
- Controls organize data, provide better reporting to auditors or boards, and provide easier access to data for financial statements and reports.
- Internal controls play an important role in the overall credibility of the organization.

In addition, controls will increase the likelihood that an organization will provide its community with effective service and will reduce the possibility that an organization will incur a loss of public trust. In the long term, well-developed procedures will minimize anxiety and problems caused by no controls or inappropriate controls. As Timothy J. Facek of Arthur Anderson stated, "Management should turn the responsibility of accountability into an advantage; accountability will enhance the chances for organizational survival and growth."[1]

Let's examine the technical aspects of internal controls and their application within an organization and then look at some practical reasons why management should be aware of internal controls.

The American Institute of Certified Public Accountants (AICPA) defines internal controls as follows:

> Internal control comprises the plan of organization and all of the coordinated methods and measures adopted within a business to safeguard its assets, check the accuracy and reliability of its accounting data, promote operational efficiency and encourage adherence to prescribed managerial policies.

The AICPA requires external auditors to examine an organization's internal controls and then render an opinion in the auditors' report as to whether internal controls exist. The Institute of Internal Auditors (IIA), in setting standards of professional practice, requires internal auditors to examine the organization's internal controls and report to management whether such controls exist. IIA's definition of internal control is basically the same as AICPA's.

Internal and external auditors make recommendations to managers on ways to improve the organization's operating policies and procedures. Most auditors prefer to have all processes documented by management so an assessment can be made comparing what should have been done with what actually is being done. The documentation of processes introduces management to the necessity of having control points along various transaction cycles. These control points for review, for approval, for acceptance, and so on are really internal controls and were designed or established by management. Thus the concept of "management controls" or "administrative controls" was created. Management and administrative controls are in fact internal controls.

SEPARATION OF DUTIES

Managers, if they have dealt with auditors, have heard the phrase *separation of duties*—a simple principle that, if adhered to in management practice, can go a long way in eliminating some management concerns and problems, as well as making auditors happy. Although separating duties is actually a simple concept, it is sometimes hard or almost impossible to implement. It is most difficult for a small organization with very few employees. Larger organizations have an easier time accomplishing the separation of duties but are not exempt from some of the problems.

What is separation of duties and how does it relate to internal controls? The flow of an ordinary transaction might begin by someone's requesting a good or service to be rendered to the organization or to an individual. The order is placed, received, accepted, and paid for. The organization or individual is satisfied, and the cycle repeats as other goods and services are needed. This example reveals several control points that should be separated so the organization or individual can be assured that only what was requested was received and at the cost at which it was requested. Suppose the order was for 10 items. A staff person was instructed to place the order; that person also received it and okayed the payment. As long as the 10 items that were ordered were received by the organization, everything is okay, correct? Maybe not—without another person's being involved in the ordering and receiving process, what prevents the staff member from ordering 20 items and keeping 10 for himself? Maybe this seems unrealistic, but without separation of certain duties, or checks at

---

EXAMPLES OF DUTIES THAT SHOULD BE SEPARATED

Revenue Transactions
Receiving—Writing prenumbered receipts
Depositing—Preparing deposits and transporting to bank
Verifying—Balancing bank accounts or monthly financial reports

Disbursing Transactions
Ordering—Determining vendor, product, etc.
Receiving—Accepting delivery
Approving—Authorizing transaction
Paying—Authorizing payment to vendor/supplier

Payroll/Personnel Transactions
Entering employees on payroll
Distributing payroll checks
Approving overtime
Approving vacation and sick leave
Terminating employees from payroll

various control points in a transaction cycle, management cannot be absolutely sure the transaction was completed in accordance with its wishes or policies and procedures.

The separation of duties is an internal control. Not allowing one person to do everything in a transaction cycle is a management control. The box on p. 195 gives some examples of duties that should be separated if possible. Because of staff size or other limitations, it is not always possible to have a good separation of duties. In those cases, the manager should be aware of potential problems and should ask questions, review transaction documentation, and review financial information and reports. If something seems amiss, the manager should investigate immediately and personally until satisfied with the answers.

WHY DO WE NEED INTERNAL CONTROLS?

Internal controls can act as a deterrent to inappropriate employee activities. Employees may or may not understand the concept of internal controls, but they do understand, assuming internal controls are in place, that when something occurs outside of the routine, either someone will question the actions or a system will not proceed with the transaction.

❧ Case Example

The Southeastern Medical Center requires all of its receipting transactions (payments on an account, donations, and so forth) to be recorded on a prenumbered receipt form, either manually prepared or machine generated. The organization's procedures require that all receipts, including voids, be turned in. Each day Bob Willis turns in the day's transactions to the cashier, Linda Smith, who will verify numerical sequence of the prenumbered receipts and the monies indicated as received. One day Bob makes a mistake on a receipt and destroys the receipt, continues the daily activity, and turns the receipts and money over to Linda. While verifying the receipts, Linda detects a missing number and immediately questions this. At this point, an internal control has signaled a discrepancy of procedures that needs to be checked out. This does not necessarily indicate that a problem exists, but that an explanation of what happened is needed. When Linda requests an explanation from Bob, that indicates to him that a verification of work mechanism does occur; actually, it is an internal control at work. If no one questions the missing receipt number, the receipting person may or may not attempt to breach the internal controls within the receipting process.

Having internal controls designed in a transactions process and then not having them used is worse, in my opinion, than not having them at all. Generally, employees are honest and do not set out to steal or embezzle from their employers, but some employees, given the opportunity when they think the controls do not work or do not exist, will test the system to see whether anyone notices.

Evaluating Existing Systems

A manager may want to assess the internal controls in the department or in the institution to see whether they work or do not work for whatever reason. If the manager is not certain what internal controls are or if they exist in the organization, he or she may need some assistance from someone who does understand. Later in the chapter there are some suggestions on where and how a manager might get some assistance with internal controls.

Let's assume the manager does have a limited understanding of the concept of internal controls and wants to see whether there are any potential problem areas in the department. Where do we start and how do we know when we're finished?

The first thing is to determine what types of transactions are routine within the department. Some examples are cash receiving, accounts receivable, disbursements, and payroll. The manager should review the flow of transactions to see where a transaction takes a different course on its journey to completion. At each change of course, receiving approval to order something, for example, the manager should examine who is involved and why. If the same person is doing a number of tasks along this transaction journey (remember our separation of duties concept), that may be a weakness in the system that should be noted and followed up after the manager's review is complete. This type of analysis should be repeated for each type of departmental transaction, providing the manager with a list of possible concerns that need further examination. One method for obtaining a detailed explanation of how transactions flow is to have each employee maintain a job log that records what is done at each stage of the transaction. This log should be maintained for at least 1 or 2 months so that it will capture a full monthly cycle of transactions. A job log also provides a manager with documentation of the employee's effort, which can be compared with the organization's formal job description to see whether any changes are necessary.

Once the review of each transaction cycle is completed, the next step is to overlay the transaction cycles and determine whether an employee may be doing too many tasks that are repetitive. As a manager you should not expect to become an internal-control expert overnight, but with time and opportunity your skills will improve.

The review of internal controls is really never finished. External auditors review internal controls with each annual audit. Internal auditors generally review internal controls each time an audit is done in a department. Thus the manager should always be concerned with internal controls. This does not mean you should work on internal controls daily, but you should employ some form of periodic review or testing to see whether internal controls are still in place and working. You could assist in preparing a daily deposit or count a change or petty cash fund on a surprise basis. Do not make your management reviews or tests too routine, such as counting cash on the second Tuesday of each month; instead, make them randomly and intermittently.

One word of caution: even when a department or organization has internal controls in place that are periodically tested by external and internal sources and seem to be working, problems can still exist. You should not allow yourself too large a comfort zone; be alert, ask questions, and try to understand what is going on in your department and always follow up on any complaint the department receives regarding its services or employees.

How Do I Design and Implement an Internal Control System?

Designing and implementing a system of internal controls is not an exciting project for most managers. A sample internal control manual is illustrated on pp. 203–209. It takes some knowledge of all the various transactions that occur within a department on a routine and nonroutine basis. Managers generally do not have the skills to create flowcharts of transactions and to identify key control points needed within a transaction cycle, nor do they have the time and resources to accomplish these tasks. Since we have established the need for internal controls within an organization, where can a manager turn for assistance if there is no such resource in the department? Most universities have internal auditors who can assist the department to establish and evaluate new or existing internal controls. If your institution does not have an internal auditor, there are several possible resources on campus that may be willing to assist you. If you have a business department or school, there should be faculty members who would help in designing or establishing an internal control system. Help may be obtained from your institution's data processing department. Some systems analysts may have experience or background in evaluating controls. Every university has external auditors—either a public accounting firm or state auditors. These external auditors, like internal auditors, can assist departments in establishing and evaluating internal controls.

Like a lot of managerial responsibilities, maintaining or improving internal controls in an organization or department requires some effort. Reviewing these controls is a task that is easily postponed in favor of other job responsibilities. Nevertheless, managers should not take internal controls lightly or believe they are just the concern of auditors. Actually, internal controls and their maintenance are organizational responsibilities. As discussed earlier, external funding from government entities requires maintenance of internal controls, as do corporate and private donors. They want some assurances that their monies will be spent according to their wishes.

The following are some case studies of organizations within the university in need of internal controls.

❧ Case Example: Medical School

Ed Griffin, an ob/gyn department employee, was given the authority and responsibility of ordering and receiving the department's supplies and equipment based on requests from the faculty and other staff members. It was determined from past experiences that certain supply and equipment items should be stocked for routine as well as emergency needs. Ed began accumulating the supplies and equipment as instructed and began maintaining inventory records of items purchased, issued, and on hand. He had been instructed by his supervisor to maintain such inventory records, which would be reviewed and verified periodically. One of the inventory items used or requested almost daily was video tape cassettes. These tapes were used by the faculty to film human subjects in various classroom or laboratory situations. Frequently staff members assisting the faculty would go to the stockroom to request a tape or tapes. Ed failed to record some of the tape issues on the inventory record, thus creating a shortage in the inventory. When the time came for his supervisor, Judy Crawford, to review the inventory and count the items on hand, Ed explained he had failed to record some of the tape issues to departmental employees for various reasons. Judy accepted his explanation without question; she told him to make certain this did not happen again. Yet it did happen again: not only did Ed issue tapes to departmental employees without properly recording the issues, he also began taking some of the tapes for his personal use. In addition, he took some tapes and sold them, keeping the money for himself. At inventory time Judy again reviewed the depleted stock and incomplete records. Ed again cited problems with departmental employees taking supplies from the stockroom without his knowledge, or that he just failed to record the inventory being issued. Ed resigned, leaving the department with a large amount of supply and equipment items not accounted for. After an investigation of the matter, criminal charges were filed and Ed Griffin was convicted.

Discussion. What could have been done by the department to prevent such an occurrence? Since Ed Griffin had the authority to order, receive, and issue the supplies and equipment and also had the responsibility of maintaining the stock inventory, he had control over numerous duties he should not have had. If the duties of ordering and receiving the stockroom items had been separated, the possibility of this problem would have been diminished. The responsibility of maintaining the inventory compounded the problem. Ed should have been responsible for maintaining the predetermined levels of stock, notifying another departmental employee when items were needed. Inventory levels should have been verified by some other employee on a routine schedule such as monthly, semiannually, or annually. Physical counts (test counts) should be taken each time the inventory is done. Any shortages need immediate attention to determine the cause. If shortages do occur, more frequent inventories should be considered until the cause of the problem is determined or the problem ceases.

Case Example: Dental School

As a result of staff reduction and reassignment, the duties of Betty Williams, an employee of Midwestern Dental School, were combined to include receiving cash and maintaining the clinic patients' accounts receivable records. Maintenance of the patient accounts included posting charges, payments, and account adjustments for fee reductions made at the request of the attending dentists. After a period of time, Betty volunteered to assist Nancy Reed, who mailed the patients their bills. Nancy welcomed this assistance, since she also had a number of other job responsibilities. Patients would routinely mail their payments to the department in the form of a check or money order made payable to the department. During this period, for various reasons, the department was not participating in the dental school's centralized billing system. None of these reasons, as it turned out, was valid, but still the department's option not to participate was granted by the school.

A complaint from a patient was received by the chairman's office. The patient, Brett Holt, stated he had made a payment during his last visit a month earlier and that payment was not reflected on his accounts. The chairman's office staff sent the complaint to Betty Williams and asked her to research the problem and communicate with Mr. Holt about the cause of the problem and how it would be resolved. However, Betty *was* the problem. Since the duties of receiving patients' payments and posting patients' charges were not separated, there were no control points in the transaction cycle. Mr. Holt had made a $100 cash payment. Betty wrote a receipt, gave him a copy, and later took the money and voided the receipt. She forgot to complete the fraudulent transaction by posting the payment to his account. When she was asked to research the transaction, she adjusted the patient's account, indicating a courtesy fee reduction based on the type of service rendered, and called Mr. Holt, indicating an error had been made and that his bill had been taken care of.

Luckily, another employee, Leasha Mann, knowing of the complaint, asked Betty how she had resolved it. Betty explained it, but Leasha was not satisfied with the explanation, and she pressed for more information about the courtesy fee reduction. Soon after Leasha's request for more information, Betty abruptly resigned and subsequently left the area.

Leasha requested an investigation of the transactions relating to the patient's complaint. Investigation revealed that Betty had taken the $100 payment and had falsified Brett Holt's account, along with other unusual transactions on many of the other patient accounts. Betty had so successfully sabotaged the patient accounts that it was difficult to determine whether any other fraudulent transactions had occurred.

Discussion. In this situation Betty Williams had too much control over the transaction cycle. No one person should have the responsibility for receiving the payments and posting charges to accounts receivable, as well as participating in mailing the statements. Furthermore, giving her the opportunity to research a complaint of her own work was not a smart management decision. As a result of this incident, the department transferred their patient accounts receivable to the school's centralized billing system. Criminal charges were not brought against Betty Williams, because she had left the area and could not be found.

≈ Case Example: Service Department

Tony Adams, manager of the medical illustration department of Western Health Sciences Center, was assigned the responsibility of hiring employees to work in his department. He prepared the personnel forms that initiated employment, that changed the employee's employment status, and that terminated employment. He was also responsible for picking up and distributing the payroll checks each payday. Since his department had frequent turnovers in positions, it was not unusual for him to be preparing personnel forms weekly. Employees would flow in and out of the department, quit and return after a short time away.

As a manager Tony was liked by most of his employees. On some paydays he would take his employees to a local bank so they could cash their payroll checks. Sometimes he took some endorsed checks to the bank for his employees and returned to work with their cash.

At one point Max Coleman quit and Tony failed to process the personnel forms in time to remove Max from the next payroll. On payday Max had a check from the department's payroll. Tony held the check, thinking someone from the payroll department would call and request that the check be returned. Several weeks passed and no one requested the check be returned, so Tony endorsed the check, forging Max's name, and carried it to the bank and got it cashed. Tony again tested the payroll system after Rusty Brown quit; he left Rusty on the payroll one extra pay period. When Tony picked up the payroll checks, a check for Rusty was included. Again Tony waited a few weeks to see if anyone would call and question the transaction. As before, no one inquired about the check, so Tony repeated his earlier scheme. Tony began leaving employees on the payroll one extra pay period, taking the checks, forging the endorsement, cashing the check, and spending the cash. This went undetected for almost 1 year.

Fred Sneed, a former employee, upon receiving his earnings statement (W–2 form), called the Center's payroll department to complain that his earnings were overstated. He had compared his last paycheck stub, which reflected cumulative earnings, with his W–2 form and identified a discrepancy. An investigation revealed Tony's scheme. He was fired and later criminal charges were filed against him. He was convicted and repaid the money to the university.

Discussion. Again, this example illustrates what can happen when one employee has responsibilities that involve all of or most of the transaction cycle. If the personnel/payroll duties of the department had been segregated, the likelihood of this embezzlement would have been remote.

❧ Case Example: Health Affairs

Smith University's biomedical department provided consulting services to the general public as part of its systems engineering program. Graduate students would receive payment for the services in the form of checks and sometimes cash. The department also allowed its faculty, staff, and students to use its copy machine for personal and professional copies, reimbursing the department at a set price per copy. The department had established internal controls over the cash-receiving process following an internal audit that recommended such controls. The internal controls included writing prenumbered receipts for each transaction and turning all daily activity over to the department's administrative manager, Jason Cooke, for processing. Jason explained the controls and why they were necessary to all staff. Several months passed, Jason's workload increased, and sometimes the daily receipts were not processed with the university's cashier (who functioned as the "bank" for the department). Verification of the numerical sequence of the receipts was not always checked for breaks, since that took some time to verify. Amanda Page, who was responsible for receiving cash, knew Jason was always busy and one day did not turn in all of the monies collected that day. Jason did not detect the missing receipt Amanda had withheld that day and prepared the deposit and transmitted it to the university cashier. Amanda on several occasions withheld receipts, with no action taken by Jason. Once Amanda determined that Jason was not verifying her work daily, she began embezzling on a regular basis. When employees or others paid for services in cash, she would write a receipt or tell them she was busy and that she would send it to them later. Sometimes the employees paying for copying would not request or desire a receipt for a small amount. Amanda began what auditors call *lapping receipts*. Here's how lapping receipts works: One day Pam Cole pays $50 in cash for services rendered. She wants and receives a receipt, number 101. Next Fran George pays $50 for services by check and receives receipt number 102. Then Alice Ball pays $30 for services by check and receives receipt number 103. At this point $130 in cash and checks has been receipted. Amanda takes the $50 cash and just turns in receipt numbers 102 and 103, along with $80 in checks. The next day Gary Lewis pays $50 for services by check and gets receipt number 104. Beth Hausfeld pays $30 in cash for services and gets receipt 105. Then Bill Moore pays $50 by check, Kay Smythe pays $30 by check, and they are issued receipts numbers 106 and 107, respectively. Amanda turns in receipt 101, which was Pam's receipt for cash, with Gary's $50 check. At this point, the first day's receipts balance, but now the second day is short $50. Amanda must keep this lapping going day after day. In the example described the customers were being billed, so when they made payment, their account would reflect the payment. Since Amanda did not have access to the customers' accounts (a good internal control), she had to continue her lapping scheme so a customer would not complain regarding a paid account. This scheme went undetected for almost 1 year until the manager began questioning why the revenue in the copy machine account was not sufficient to cover the operating costs. Jason questioned Amanda regarding the copying payments, and she admitted "borrowing" some money for lunch out of the copy payments. Jason requested an internal audit of the situation, which uncovered the lapping scheme along with verifying the shortage in the copy machine account. Amanda Page was dismissed, charged with embezzlement, and found guilty. She paid the money back.

Discussion. In this illustration, Jason understood that internal controls were necessary and had seen that the controls were in place after the original internal audit. He allowed them to break down primarily because of his increased workload. He should have requested that the internal auditors assist him in rearranging duties within the department so the internal controls in critical areas would not be breached.

The Single Audit Act of 1984 was passed by Congress to establish uniform audit requirements for federal financially assisted programs, which are found in most colleges and universities. The U.S. Office of Management and Budget (OMB) has issued various circulars (A-128 and A-110) providing auditors instructions on examining internal controls and other financial concerns at organizations receiving federal financial assistance. These actions brought additional concern to organizations that they must have a system of internal controls in place and verified by an external auditor or face having federal funds cut off or reduced.

Internal controls are necessary and required in most cases. They are not just for auditors to review and comment on but are designed to assist management in accomplishing its goals and objectives. If used effectively, internal controls can become a beneficial tool for a successful manager. You should become familiar with your organization's internal control structure, seek out assistance if necessary, and review the internal controls periodically to verify that they are still in place and working.

BIBLIOGRAPHY
1. Connors TD. (1980). *The non-profit organization handbook.* New York: Author, pp 6-49.

APPENDIX

SAMPLE INTERNAL CONTROL MANUAL

INTERNAL CONTROLS
POLICY AND PROCEDURES

Department of Clinical Science
Academic Health Center

Table of Contents

Accounts Receivable Accounting

1. Invoices are designated in a three-part prenumbered format. The invoices are used in numerical sequence.
2. The first and second parts of the invoice are issued to the payer. The third part is maintained in the Unpaid Alphabetical Invoice file. The payer is requested to return the second part of the form with the payment.
3. When the payment is made, the second part of the form is attached to the third part (located in the Unpaid file). Before the invoice is placed in the Paid Alphabetical Invoice file, the invoice is stamped paid and the following information is recorded:

PAID

Amount   _____

Date   _____

Deposit No. _____

Check No.   _____

Account No. _____

4. Terms of payments are net upon receipt.
5. Invoiced amount for all services and agreements conform to the contractual agreements or rate schedule.
6. Invoices are mailed at the 15th of the month for services provided for the following month (i.e., January 15 invoices are mailed for the services provided the month of February).
7. Invoice numbers are always referenced in the Cash Receipt Journal.

Authorized Signatures

The authorized signatures approved by the University are as follows:

George R. Smith, M.D.
Robert F. Morgan, M.D.
Joan Erickson, M.H.A.

Cash Disbursements

1. All checks will be prepared and issued by the University Accounts Payable Office.
2. All invoices are authorized for payment first by the Divisional Manager/Division Chief and then the Director of Administration/Chairman. The invoice is then forwarded directly to Accounts Payable for payment.

Cash Receipts

1. When checks are received they should be scanned to ensure that they are:
   a. Made payable to the organization
   b. Endorsed
2. The following endorsement should be applied to the back of all money orders or checks:

   > For deposit only
   > Department of Clinical Science

3. All cash, money orders, and checks will be recorded in the Cash Receipt Journal and deposited in a timely manner.
4. A copy of the Cash Receipt Journal should be attached to each deposit form as a supporting document. A copy of all deposit forms should be retained in the Administrative Office.
5. Deposits should be sequenced numerically, starting with *1* at the beginning of each fiscal year.
6. A prenumbered receipt for each deposit is prepared by the Cashier's Office. The receipt number and receipt date should be indicated on the Cash Receipt Journal and amount confirmed. The receipt should then be attached to the deposit form maintained in the Administrative Office.
7. Checks for grants are forwarded directly to Contracts and Grants for deposit. A copy of the check should be retained for the files.

CASH RECEIPTS JOURNAL

Check Information				Reference Information		Deposit Information				
Date Rec'd	Amount	Check No.	Name	Invoice No.	Account No.	Dep #	Dep Total	Dep Date	Dep Recpt #	Recpt Date

Chart of Accounts

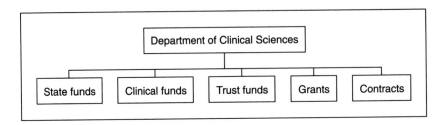

1. State Funds

Acct. No.	Acct. Title

2. Clinical Funds

Acct. No.	Acct. Title

3. Trust Funds

Acct. No.	Acct. Title	Division	School/Med. Fdn.	Balance

4. Grants/Contracts

Acct. No.	Acct. Title

Equipment

1. Equipment is defined as all items with a unit cost of $500 or more and a useful life of more than 1 year.
2. All equipment acquired directly through University procurement should automatically be decalled.
3. It is the responsibility of each area to notify Administration of any equipment received as a gift or donation. Administration will maintain a value statement, item description(s), and serial number(s).
4. Annually, Equipment Control will issue an equipment inventory listing.
5. A notice of disposal or change in location should be completed at the time the location or status of equipment changes.
6. Off-campus use of equipment must be approved with the Off-Campus Use Agreement and Authorization Form and approved by the Department Chairman.

Overtime Policy

1. All overtime must be approved in advance by the employee's supervisor.
2. There is to be no overtime unless there is an emergency.
3. There shall be no falsification of an employee's time records.
4. All time records are to be an accurate and correct representation of the hours worked. It is against the wage-hour policy to falsify time sheets. Each signed and certified time record should be an accurate representation of hours worked.

Payroll Records

All payroll records include the following:
- Payroll reports
- Applications
- Faculty appointments/promotions
- Leave records
- Deductions
- Employment history
- Curricula vitae
- Letters of recommendation
- Performance evaluations

These are maintained by the Department's Personnel Coordinator.

Petty Cash

The Department of Clinical Science's policy, for all Divisions, is to not maintain a petty cash account for the following reasons: (1) the difficulty of maintaining security the petty cash, and (2) the need for assigning the responsibility of the fund to a custodian (staff member). However, if there is a special need to establish a petty cash account, the Department recommends that the level of petty cash be kept at an absolute minimum. The Department currently has the following Petty Cash Accounts:

_____

_____

_____

_____

_____

The guidelines for these accounts are as follows:
1. *Authorization:* All funds should be authorized by the Division Chief, Chairman, and University Accounting Department. Funds may not be set up from undeposited receipts.
2. *Security:* The funds should be secured in a locked safe or file cabinet accessible only to the person(s) responsible for custody. An individual should be selected for custodial responsibility.
3. *Use of funds:* The funds should be used only for making change and for the cash purchase of minor items. No employee loans should be made from the funds, and no personal checks should be cashed from the funds.
4. *Documentation for expenditures/refunds:* Items purchased by cash require the original sales document, which should be marked paid, and which should include a description of the item purchased. In the case of refunds, the person receiving the refund should sign a Receipt for Payments Made by Petty Cash.

RECEIPT FOR PAYMENT MADE BY PETTY CASH

Division _____   Custodian _____

Authorized amount of fund: $ _____

Date	Paid to	Description	Amount	Acct Bal.

5. *Balancing:* The custodian should balance the fund at least once each month to verify that the total funds expended and receipts on hand equal the authorized amount of the fund.
6. *Frequency of reimbursement:* The account should be replenished once a month (depending on usage) and by the end of each fiscal year.
7. *Reconciliation:* The custodian of the account should match the petty cash reimbursement request forms to the monthly financial reports.
8. *Fund shortages:* Fund shortages should be reported to the Director of Administration, Campus Security, the Property Department, and the Internal Audit to identify control weakness and filing for insurance reimbursements.

Space Inventory

Departmental facility plans/floor plans are housed in the Administrative Office. In addition to the floor plan and space assignment, a report on the space utilization is also maintained.

All new and revised space assignments must be approved in writing by the Chairman.

Telephone Policy

The Department's policy is for no personal telephone calls to be made on any departmental telephones. This includes telephones housed in the departmental/divisional Offices, research and/or clinical areas, and cellular phones.

The Department recognizes that occasionally a personal call must be made. If the call is local, it may be initiated on office phones. If the call is long distance or billable, the user should initiate a collect call or charge the call to a personal telephone credit card. All personal calls initiated on cellular phones should be charged to a credit card or personal telephone.

CHAPTER 12

Computer Systems

Robert Rutledge

— ❧ —

The modern age has a false sense of superiority because of the great mass of data at its disposal. But the valid criterion of distinction is rather the extent to which man knows how to form and master the material at his command.

JOHANN WOLFGANG VON GOETHE

❧ Case Example

Dr. Roberts, chair of the university's department of medicine, was concerned about the level of research activity in his department. He asked his grants manager for some data on the level of grant activity over the last 5 years. Some of the grant data, he learned, however, was kept by the various divisions of medicine, and it was very hard to receive a comprehensive report. Dr. Roberts was tenacious, however, and now is able to receive periodic comprehensive reports on the research activity in his department, along with schoolwide comparison research data.

Dr. Roberts was able to achieve this new reporting level by entering the computer age. A conventional data base program was developed for the department that tracks, by researcher, the number of grants submitted, awarded, the award period, award level, funding agency, and so on, along with school and institutional comparison information.

Academic managers are using basic personal computers (PCs) with conventional software at an increasing rate. For some managers, their computer systems are linked to the university's or institution's mainframe. Managers typically do not use the computer systems as much as support staff do, but when decisions need to be made and data are required, managers must have the data readily accessible. A manager's role is to look at the data rather than to produce the data.

This chapter will discuss the management and impact of *medical informatic systems* or computer systems in academic health centers. The AHC has goals that it must meet to function successfully. These include clinical activities in patient care; education of students, residents, faculty, staff, and society; and research. The AHC administration struggles to manage the information it generates, and the success or failure of a department can be related to its ability to manage information. Managing information is fundamental to the full spectrum of the department's day-to-day

210

operations. An administrator cannot make sound, informed decisions with incomplete or inadequate information.

A well-executed plan for implementing a computer system can have a major impact on departmental functioning. This process requires a significant amount of analysis and planning so the chair or administrator can make the correct decisions in its implementation.

DECIDING TO IMPLEMENT A COMPUTER SYSTEM

The question of whether to implement some sort of computer system in an academic department has become less and less common; computers have made their way into virtually every department in some form or other. There are still many departments, however, that have not implemented computer systems or whose computers have been acquired piecemeal over a period of time and that do not fully meet the department's requirements. To understand the potential value of computers, you must classify the goals of your department and then analyze the impact each computer purchase and installation would have on achieving these goals.

Although some functions performed by computers can be performed without them, computers can aid the department by increasing productivity. An obvious example of this is typing letters, clinic notes, or manuscripts. A manuscript can be typed easily on a typewriter, but a computer provides improved capabilities such as spell-checking and controlling the style and format of the document, and it is particularly valuable when changes or corrections to the document need to be made. Computers also have the potential to decrease paperwork. Many years ago the concept of the paperless office was developed. The idea was that no paper would be used and all information would be transmitted over computers. Experience in implementing computer systems in various academic organizations has shown that although this is not impossible, such a system is a long way in the future. On the other hand, use of computers can mean more efficient use of paper and decreased costs for forms, memoranda, and reporting.

Computers can automate repetitive tasks, such as calculations for budgets, and maintain accuracy. They are able to track a variety of types of information, particularly large volumes of information, through data base techniques. Today's graphics programs may provide individuals who have little or no training in graphic design with the ability to produce their own graphs, charts, and slides, thus decreasing departmental graphics and illustration costs.

If you are reviewing the possibility of instituting computers in your department, you should keep a list of various informational jobs that might be addressed by the computer system in the department.

Making Use of a Consultant

Often the advice for the implementation of a computer system within a department is "homegrown." Individuals or groups are identified as computer literate, and they form a committee to provide advice for the implementation of a computer system. However, whether or not an in-house individual or group with the appropriate expertise level is available, a consultant should be used. A consultant's expertise can be invaluable in selecting the best computers and software for the areas required by the department. Consultants can be found through other departments, trade groups or publications, or user groups. The consultant's qualifications should be carefully evaluated. The review should include a comparison of candidates. Previous clients should be contacted and an interview with the prospective consultant conducted. In general, it is appropriate to contract with the consultant for a specific outcome; this payment may be based on an hourly rate or for a full project. In general, a report from the consultant and/or committee is appropriate during the development of the system. The report should include advice and recommendations for implementation.

Goals for a Computer Purchase: The Return on Investment

Computer systems can range in cost from a few thousand to hundreds of thousands of dollars. One of the advantages of computers is that you may limit the initial investment to a few thousand dollars for a small project area to determine whether the computer is successful for your application. The number of computers can be gradually increased as funding becomes available.

Investment in a computer system requires a clear understanding of what the goals are for the specific computer system. These goals may be either tangible or intangible. Tangible results include those which can be quantified and measured, as in dollars and cents. For example, instead of professionally typesetting a report, the "typesetting" may be produced either in part or in whole on a PC. Potential costs can be identified and reduced by instituting a computerized typesetting process in-house. An intangible result is an improved working environment: staff morale can be improved as they feel supported by the implementation of computer systems.

Before purchasing a computer system, a manager needs to consider the return on investment. Although one of the objectives to automating in academics is to reduce costs, costs can increase as a result of information systems: initial equipment purchases, hiring the consultant, buying software, and other implementation costs can represent significant capital expenditures. Managers may then feel that the investment has not led them closer to achieving their objectives. How can this be prevented? Typically the basic failure is not with the hardware as much as in selection and implementation of the optimal system for the department—the best "fit" for the tasks at hand.

Steps Toward Computer Implementation

To successfully implement a computer system, you need to understand precisely what you are purchasing and receiving. Although computer technology has made great advances, success will not be achieved unless you purchase a system that will meet the goals and objectives of your academic program.

Needs and budget analysis

For computer implementation, the first step is involvement by management and a needs analysis. This includes an understanding of what the department or program wants to accomplish. Some departments have found it useful to appoint a committee to gather information on what needs to be automated, build consensus for the system, and document the actual requirements for the system. If a consultant has been hired, he or she can assist in this process. A needs analysis includes a statement that identifies the problems and information flow within the department, delineates the specific goals of the computer implementation, and sets forth the degree to which each goal must be accomplished for the system to be declared successful. Does the department need to improve word processing, financial management, clinical reporting? Once needs are identified, a review should be conducted of current manual processes to see which are inefficient and ineffective. If a system is deemed ineffective, it should be revised before computerization of the system.

Employees are a good source for information on the project, and all staff should be consulted. This builds commitment to the process. The department or program director should be involved from the beginning of the assessment process; he or she will have to live with the results of the computer system selected and installed. A variety of problems can be addressed, and an information flow diagram may occasionally be useful. How does information come into the department? Where does information go out of the department? What kind of information needs to be kept and how is it moved through letters, documents, and newsletters, and how are these managed?

You can also involve employees as you select the appropriate *ergonomic* furniture. For staff members using computer terminals, the correct chairs and desk heights can help prevent back and eye strain. The contrast color of monitors and the amount of low-level emissions from terminals are also employee issues.

After needs have been analyzed and hardware and software systems reviewed, a final step is to prepare a budget to purchase equipment and support the implementation. A rough budget estimate for supporting a computer system is 35% for hardware, 15% for software, 15% for outside services, 15% for training, 10% for printing, and a 10% reserve for unexpected contingencies (Figure 12-1).

Selecting the computer system

Computers may be generally classified into mainframes, minicomputers, and personal computers. Some of the basic terms related to computer systems are given in the box on p. 215. A computer system can be IBM, one of the IBM-compatible systems by a variety of manufacturers, Apple, Macintosh, or NeXT. You will need to completely review the advantages and disadvantages of each computer system and make a selection based on need, budget, and support. Before the development of PCs, mainframes and minicomputers were the principle choices for departmental computer systems. The problem with these systems was that they were large and

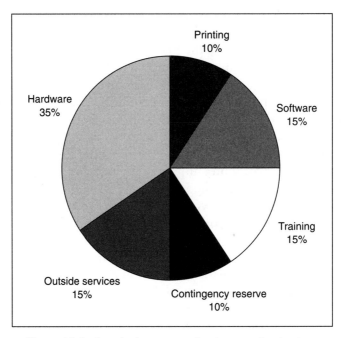

Figure 12-1. A typical computer implementation budget.

expensive, application development was difficult, and they had limited, imperfect, and "user-unfriendly" software. Through developments in central processing unit (CPU) technology, PCs have been revolutionized. Personal computers have become user-friendly, with a tremendous explosion in the availability of different types of software programs. Prices have decreased substantially. In addition, a growing number of computer tasks previously performed on mainframes and minicomputers can now be performed on PCs. These tasks include word processing, spreadsheets, graphics, data bases, and other applications.

The history of the computer industry has been a steady migration of projects and tasks from mainframe and minicomputers to the PC and PC local area networks (LAN). Even the largest of data base projects with several hundred thousand records are now handled by PC LAN–based systems. High-level statistics, large data base projects, or intensive graphics operations can now be implemented on PC-based systems for a significant cost savings, usually with a significant improvement for the user. Future expectations for computer systems include a continuation of the steady gain of capabilities over time. Single-user computers and their multiuser version using LAN appear to be supplanting mainframe and minicomputers. Most experts expect this trend to continue. Presently, for a small investment and a better expectation of continually improving system capabilities, the single-user computer, whether DOS base or Mac base, is one of the better investments.

COMPUTER TERMINOLOGY

bar code A pattern of printed lines on an object identifying it and containing information about it that can be read into the computer by a scanner.

bit A binary digit, a "0" or a "1."

clock speed Refers to how fast a computer works. Computers do their work in clicks of a clock. This is rated in megahertz. The higher the number, the faster the machine.

conventional or base memory Memory size of up to 640K (RAM).

CPU or chip A device containing many transistors and other components formed on the surface of a piece of silicon. Generations of CPUs have been made: 80386 and 80480. Computers using the 80386 run 15 to 20 times faster than the 80286, and the 80486 runs faster still.

disk Two types, floppy and hard. Floppy are 3½- or 5¼-inch circles of plastic that are enclosed. Hard disks are sealed in the computer and hold 20 or more times the amount of information as do floppy disks.

DOS (disk operating system) The basic function of DOS is to tell the computer how to store information on disks, and how to find it.

extended memory Memory above 640K.

external memory Usually consists of a magnetic tape or disk on which binary information is stored and "called up" by the computer as required.

file An organized collection of information.

interactive A way of operating in which the user is in direct and continual two-way communication with the computer, perhaps answering its questions and reviewing its reactions to the answers.

internal memory Usually consists of silicon chips within the body of the computer.

LAN Local area network.

megabyte Computers process *bits;* it takes eight bits to make a single character; eight bits together form a *byte.* There are 1000 kilobytes to a megabyte; a gigabyte equals 1,073,741,824 bytes.

minicomputer Midway between a "micro" and a "mainframe" computer.

modem Peripheral device for PCs that attaches either inside or outside the computer and then to a telephone line. A modem allows one computer to be connected over telephone lines to another computer.

monitor The picture tube for the PC. Several types are: CGA—ok for games; EGA—good for text and numbers; and VGA—for fine graphics work.

network A system in which a number of computers, terminals, and other components (printers and disk drives) can be linked together.

OS/2 Operating System/2, developed by Microsoft. OS/2 offers multitasking, that is, you can run two or more programs at once.

ports Typically classified as serial and parallel. Serial ports carry data over a single line and are typically used for modems or a mouse. Parallel ports can bring eight bits of data simultaneously over eight separate wires. Most of today's printers use parallel ports.

RAM (random access memory) Memory into which information can be put (written), and from which it can instantly be copied (read) no matter where it is in the memory.

ROM (read only memory) A memory circuit in which the information stored is built into the chip when it is made and cannot subsequently be changed by the user.

Choosing hardware and software

Once the types of hardware and software are reviewed and the types of support for hardware and software from the institution are known, purchase decisions will need to be made. Hardware decisions should be driven by a problem, and software solutions should be selected to solve that problem (Figure 12-2). Typically, for a small department or program with limited information needs and only a few members, all located in the same geographic area, a single computer or small group of computers running some basic software (such as word processing, spreadsheet, graphics) may be needed. Obviously, a larger department with multiple locations throughout the same or different building, or even different cities, with many organizational members, requiring a data base of several hundred thousand records and managing a substantial budget, will require a larger system. A key decision in this case will be whether to select individual or network computers. One of the important advantages of personal computers over mainframes or minicomputers is that one may decide to purchase a few individual computers initially and then subsequently add or convert to a network as the initial computers prove their worth and as the need for a network becomes more obvious.

PURCHASING, INSTALLING, AND TESTING THE COMPUTER SYSTEM

In academic departments, purchasing computer systems is often based on annual institutional contract negotiations. Department managers need to take into account any existing institutional contracts, and purchase decisions need to be made on this basis. Universities typically negotiate substantial educational discounts with companies such as IBM, Apple, Hewlett-Packard, and others. One of the advantages of IBM-type computing is the availability of IBM clones or compatibles. These systems can provide significant cost savings as well as an attractively priced service contract.

The final stage after the system is purchased is setting up and testing the system. Typically, support for the final stage may come directly from the vendor or from the institution's computer support center. In purchasing a computer system, support is one of the more important considerations. Who will support the hardware and what is the cost? Is there an annual fee, or is it a fee for service or an annual rate that includes labor and parts? Managers should review the support that the institution can provide. Typically, this support is at a more reasonable price level.

IDENTIFYING COMPUTER SOFTWARE APPLICATIONS

Identifying computer solutions to problems requires a familiarity with computers and especially software capabilities. Some of the most common classes of software applications include word processing, spreadsheets, graphics, data bases, telecommunications, desktop publishing, project management, and statistical analysis (Figure 12-3).

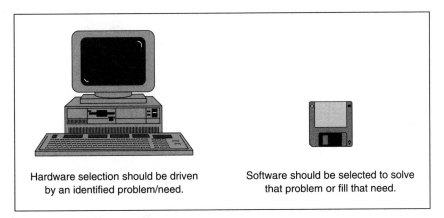

Hardware selection should be driven by an identified problem/need.

Software should be selected to solve that problem or fill that need.

Figure 12-2. Making the appropriate purchasing decision for a department computer system requires a needs analysis to identify areas where efficiency and productivity can best be increased.

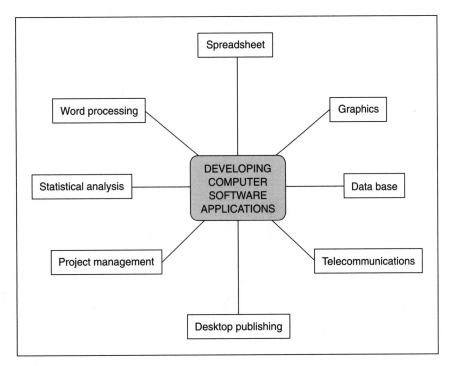

Figure 12-3. An array of software applications is available. The capabilities you choose for your system should be carefully matched to the needs of your department.

Word Processing

By far the most common use of computers, and probably the most immediately useful and beneficial application, is word processing. Indeed, the return on the investment of the computer can often be recouped through word processing programs alone. Word processors can reduce the time, effort, and tedium involved in writing, editing, and printing documents of all types, including forms, correspondence, and book-length manuscripts. A variety of programs are available, ranging from simple and easy to use to high-level and full-featured programs with desktop publishing capabilities. An important decision is what type of program to initially purchase. At present there are several popular and worthy word processing software programs for IBM- and Mac-based computers.

Before selecting a word processing program, you should review programs supported at the institution. *Support* means not only in terms of special discount offers, but also in terms of installation and training support. Special features of word processing software should include global spell-checking, setting up of style sheets to produce similar styles and repeated documents, global search-and-replace capabilities, and high-level character formatting. Other capabilities include the ability to produce outlines, develop glossaries, facilitate mass mailings, and produce *macros,* or sets of program commands that can be stored and executed with a single keystroke so that saving, retrieving, and printing of documents can occur easily.

In summary, word processing on computers has been the lead application that has allowed computers to penetrate business and educational activities throughout the world. The enhanced capabilities and improvement in productivity that are possible for a secretary using a word processor compared with using a typewriter are remarkable, and these often will provide a clear payback, especially if frequently used form letters are needed, or recurring reports are generated. The hardware requirements for word processing are generally fairly limited. If budget constraints

Hey, this is *software* work!

SOURCE: Wall Street Journal, *Salt and Pepper.*

are the pivotal issue, a small investment can be made for a basic computer. As the benefits of the project are demonstrated, further investments can be initiated, upgrading the computer's hardware and software capabilities.

Spreadsheets

A spreadsheet program is an application invented by Dan Bricklan when he was a Harvard School of Business MBA student. He found that the calculations for performing his activities were too complicated, so he developed an electronic spreadsheet program and named it Visacal. Subsequent development of Lotus 1-2-3 and Excel led to a marked increase in productivity with ledger-type problems. Spreadsheet software produces a screen that resembles an accountant's pad, with columns and rows. These columns and rows allow entry of data for instant calculation of sums, averages, totals, and so on. The spreadsheet has proved to be very useful in academic health centers for setting up budgets and producing financial reports, trend reports, productivity profiles, and other applications (see Chapter 14, Understanding the Numbers). Spreadsheet software can also be used for developing and preparing research budgets and calculating student grades.

Graphics

Today most computer manufacturers offer full graphic software programs that allow production of images in multiple colors on the monitor (Figure 12-4). Graphic capability has grown dramatically and now includes relatively straightforward "painting" and "drawing" applications for creating diagrams and illustrations. PCs are now capable of producing multicolor graphs and charts that can be printed on high-resolution laser printers or on an in-house film recorder or through a commercial slide service. These provide superb capabilities for utilization in preparing documents or presentations and can provide professional-quality hard copies or slides or transparencies.

Data Base Management Programs

Data base management systems are tools for creating a large set of data that can be sorted, retrieved, printed, and analyzed. Large *data sets* typically consist of numerous individual data records that contain information in a designated field. An example would be a patient's name, age, race, sex, and hospital number. Each patient would have data that completed a record, and each part of the record would be a field, such as first name, last name, date of birth, and so forth. This group of records then creates a file, and multiple files form a data base. In an academic health center a variety of lists of information, such as number of procedures, patient numbers, and procedure types may need to be tracked. Unfortunately, this information may be difficult to retrieve because of its volume. A computerized data management system permits sorting, shuffling, and analysis of hundreds, thousands, even hundreds of thousands of records on a PC within a short period. A data base system has a mechanism to query

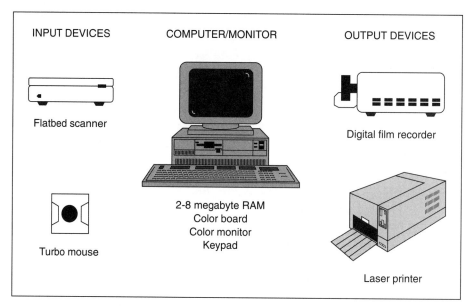

INPUT DEVICES   COMPUTER/MONITOR   OUTPUT DEVICES

Flatbed scanner

Digital film recorder

2-8 megabyte RAM
Color board
Color monitor
Keypad

Turbo mouse

Laser printer

Figure 12-4. With the appropriate software, today's computers are capable of producing multicolor high-resolution images for creating charts, diagrams, or even slides.

the data base—that is, to ask questions of itself so that information can be retrieved, such as identifying all patients who have had a given operation or complication within the last 2 years. This allows retrieval of the information from the data set. In addition, the information may also be graphed to demonstrate cost and changes over time or changes in the number of procedures. Clinical, research, and educational information may be used and stored on a data base system. This remains an area of rapid flux, and new PC programs continue to be produced and improved. Once again, it is important to find out what data base programs are supported by the institution. Data bases are typically divided into fields, which separate the variables into a certain order. For example, the second field may contain spaces for the patient's name, the fifth field for his zip code, and so on. *Relational data base programs* allow a relation or linkage between different files so that if one file contains information on a patient and another file contains information on physicians, they may be linked through the data base to provide information on the physicians for different types of operations or patients.

Obsolescence

There is no way that AHCs can protect themselves from software becoming obsolete. We live in a world of rapidly changing technology. Fortunately, software prices have declined significantly over the years, and today most packages can be purchased for a few hundred dollars or less. This is a fairly insignificant investment, considering the benefits to be derived from the software, and thus it is likely the programs will pay for themselves before they become obsolete. Many major software companies also offer version updates to software for less than $50. Additionally, academic institutions sometimes purchase a licensing agreement with major software companies that will allow purchase of software at a significantly reduced cost. Some academic computer support centers offer software libraries from which the department may "check out" software on a trial basis before purchasing it.

Telecommunications

The personal computer was initially designed to function as a standalone unit. The first step in linking the computer to other computers has been through on-line telephone access to a variety of different types of data bases. For the AHC, the most prominent example of this is the National Library of Medicine (NLM) MEDLINE. With a telecommunications program such as Procomm and a modem, you can access the NLM. This access allows retrieval of literature, including medical textbooks, journals, or other publications and specific data bases such as cancer or AIDS. The entire world of medical literature in abstract form is available through MEDLINE, and other capabilities are available from NLM over the telephone line through the modem. The emergence of CD-ROM technology now allows the data base to be located at the computer itself, eliminating the need for a modem and per-minute charges for connecting with remote computers. This is a relatively easy application to master and provides a significant return for a very small investment. Such an investment can have a tremendous impact on a department's research, presentation, publication, and educational activities in an academic health center.

Another telecommunications ability is sending facsimile (fax) transactions through the computer; this linkage improves transmission and can save costs of overnight mailings. Fax capabilities are now also available on small portable notebook-sized computers that use a fax board and any phone line. The fax board is placed into a free expansion slot.

A computer will usually require 400K of free memory, a hard disk, and a graphic adaptor, which allows the computer to receive and store information as graphics, rather than as text and numbers.

Desktop Publishing

A burgeoning area in computer applications is desktop publishing. Desktop programs permit PC typesetting and layout of individual pages and documents for reports, manuals, newsletters, or entire books. With a personal computer and a laser printer, you can produce high-quality, professional-looking reports and graphics, which can also greatly decrease the costs associated with document production. Forms can also be produced cost-effectively and efficiently on the PC, particularly if a scanner is available. Any type of form can be scanned into the computer, edited or revised on-screen, and then produced. This eliminates the need for purchasing new forms and the services of specialized printers.

Managers of AHCs are faced with delegating or assigning responsibility for a project or a phase of a project to an organizational member. Project management software will track the delegation, the assignment of responsibilities, schedule, deadlines, and so on for the manager. Project management software is beneficial for time management as well as tracking of multiple projects.

Project Management

Complex and even simple projects are better handled if they are well organized, well thought out, and well planned. A useful tool is project management software. Entire reference books or a national library's publications can be housed on one CD-ROM. The major disadvantage of the CD-ROM is that you can only read from it; you cannot add data as you could with a floppy disk or a hard drive.

Statistical Analysis

Beyond initial visualization of information derived from the department's activities, such as looking at a trend in the number of patients cared for or the increase in charges, you may require more complex statistical analysis. This is particularly true in research. When T testing, chi square analysis, multivariate analysis, regression analysis, and life tables studies need to be done, mainframe statistical packages are being supplanted by PC-based packages. Packages such as the statistical analysis systems (SAS), SYSTAT, and others have demonstrated that there are few limitations to handling high-level statistics on the PC. These software programs capabilities are now available and, depending on the needs of the department, can be purchased relatively inexpensively. PC-based statistical programs have markedly decreased the need for a mainframe and related costs. The software has reduced the need for consultants as well.

DEVELOPING IN-HOUSE SOFTWARE

Essentially, because of the declining cost of "off the shelf" software, most AHCs first review all existing packaged software before developing their own software. The development of major departmental data bases or other types of new software programs is often a significant undertaking requiring extensive programming expertise and specialized skills. This may make it necessary to contract for custom software development support. You should not, however, overlook skills available in-house among employees of the institution. Often the expertise in the department's primary activities can be leveraged with some minor training in the development of a significant data base development project. Developing an in-house custom software data base also requires skill from the experienced staff members who use the data base and understand its day-to-day operation. An experienced programmer and often an experienced technical writer are required to explain the utilization and to provide documentation of the software to the staff.

SELECTING A PC

A variety of PCs are available: IBM, IBM-compatible, Apple and a small number of other types. The Apple computer system interface is based on the Park Place Operating System developed by Xerox. It uses a desktop metaphor, a mouse, and a number of visual cues that improve the rapidity with which an inexperienced user can gain computer skills. This advantage has led many inexperienced new users and those interested in a graphical user interface to select the Apple computer. A disadvantage of the Apple computer, however, has been its cost, which ranges from 30% to 50% more than a comparable IBM-compatible system. In addition, Apple computers generally have fewer capabilities as far as connection to mainframes, and less capacity for high-level networking. IBM and IBM-compatible PCs have clearly dominated the marketplace in personal computers since their introduction several years ago. The IBM personal computer has an installed base of over 50 to 60 million personal computers while Apple has one fifth to one tenth that number. The market share for IBM-compatible computers continues to remain strong. Over time, the proliferation of the IBM-compatible computers, or *clones,* has forced the cost of IBM-type computers down, making systems available at a much more competitive price than a comparable Apple system. In addition, the graphic user interface that was first recognized in the Macintosh world is now being ported to the IBM systems via the Microsoft OS/2 Presentation Manager and Windows System. The new graphic interface for IBM-based systems take advantage of Xerox's development of the Park Place Operating System and utilizes their own graphic user interface similar to that used in the Apple. In reviewing networking, the system by AppleTalk is superior to networking provided in the PC. However, sophisticated networking, as evidenced by the market leader of NETWARE, Novell's software system, is clearly the network operating system of choice for departments considering networking for the high performance required for large files of over several megabytes.

STANDALONE VERSUS NETWORK

There are certain advantages to standalone or single-user systems. For example, with a single-user system, the only activities generated are those initiated by its own user. The system is not slowed down by the accounting department running their reports during the day or other simultaneous logging-on by other users. In a network or multi-user system, programs and data files are stored, for example, on a single designated device and can be shared among all those connected to the network. The most common arrangement for networking is one in which storage of the software and data file occurs on a central file server. Each individual computer then requests this file and its application. The application is sent over the network line to the individual PC, and there processing occurs locally. This is called a *local area network* (LAN); it has achieved extensive popularity and is projected to have explosive growth over the next several years. Central file storage is accomplished on a computer that is configured as a file or network server. An advantage of a network is simultaneous access to a data base; in particular, several individuals can be reviewing a single data base at the same time. A network is consolidated, so there is no need to duplicate that data base on multiple computer systems. The network also allows for new versions of software or new software programs to be installed only once, rather than installing updates or new programs on each standalone system.

In addition, *electronic mail* allows contact among all the participants in the local network and, typically, the institution's network. With such a system, many individuals may work on a single project, such as an annual report, to produce different sections of it without moving the file around to different computers. Other advantages of LAN include improved data security with password control, improved data integrity and consistency, and decreased software expense from not having to buy individual copies of software for each standalone unit.

"Networking" has become a popular institutional buzzword, but before investing funds into this project, the organization must carefully consider what the network is to be used for and what the cost advantages would be. Some organizations have found, when comparing the cost of the network with the applications of networking, that it was not cost effective for them, as shown in the following example.

❧ Case Example

Dr. Deborah Lane, chair of the ophthalmology department, and her director of administration, Dr. Senna Yoffe, wanted to be able to review their clinical budget on the computer system. The department decided to look into networking, with the Practice Plan, which maintained and updated the clinical budgets. An estimate was given for several thousand dollars to network the department's PC to the practice plan for clinical budget information. Since the network was not to be interactive and Dr. Lane and her administrator would be able only to access and read the budget, the investment from the department was not considered cost effective. Other options were explored, and the most cost-effective approach was for the practice plan's accountant to prepare a disk-copy of the department's budget (a task taking a few minutes) and send it via the plan's courier, who was already making two scheduled daily runs. This approach allowed the department to receive the needed budget information, and the only cost was to purchase a box of disks. However, when the plan was able to provide an interactive network, allowing entry and access to such information as purchasing, fee schedules, collection rates, and undocumented charges, this type of network was considered a worthy investment and was implemented.

COMPUTER HARDWARE

A variety of computer hardware exists today that will benefit the functionality and flexibility of computer systems. Because computer applications vary widely, there is a great deal of variability in what may or may not be included in the computer itself. All computers are built around a central processing unit or microprocessor. The computer microprocessor is the so-called brain of the computer that performs all the instructions directed to the computer. There has been a rapid development in capabilities and power of central processing units (CPUs) for computers. This increase in power is expected to continue to grow. In fact, many of the CPUs in personal computers today have power units similar to the mainframes of only a few years ago.

Random Access Memory

The random access memory (RAM) of the computer is the *transient* electronic storage place of the memory of the computer. The RAM keeps track of the program presently in use and proportions the data currently being utilized. RAM is volatile or temporary; once the power is turned off, any information stored in RAM is lost unless it has been written to a more permanent medium, such as a hard disk, a floppy disk, a tape, or other permanent storage medium. In the past, for IBM DOS-based computers, 640,000 bytes (or 640K) was the maximum available. For future developments, particularly the use of such software as Windows and OS2, 4 to 8 megabytes (4 to 8 million bytes) of RAM will be necessary to maintain adequate performance. The CPU communicates with the outside world through a variety of methods; this is called the basic *I/O input and output system*. Input may occur through a mouse, the keyboard, scanners, from a diskette, from a hard disk, and so on, and output may occur to the screen, printer, hard disk, or telephone line.

Ports

Ports are available to plug in various peripheral devices, and these are generally referred to as *parallel* or *serial ports*. Parallel ports are called parallel because they can bring eight bits of data simultaneously over eight separate wires, each carrying one bit of data at a time. Serial ports carry the data over a single line, one bit after the other. Most of today's printers are parallel, while serial ports are used for other devices, such as a modem or mouse.

Disk Drives

Because RAM is volatile and transient, a method of permanent storage is essential. Disk drives, also called floppy disk drives, are available in a variety of sizes, the common standard being 5¼ -inch or 3½ -inch diskettes. In addition, hard disks can store large amounts of data; disk sizes range from 20 megabytes to 1.2 gigabytes. This provides massive amounts of storage for large data bases and optical applications. Optical drives are modified audio compact disks (CDs) that allow storage of up to 800 megabytes per rewritable optical disk; these have a variety of capabilities. Tape drives are utilized to backup the hard disk in case of damage to the hard disk and are crucial for large data base applications. In general, tape backup should be available in some format for all personal computer systems.

Sufficient RAM data capacity and hard-drive memory are vital to the effective long-term use of any computer system. A general rule of thumb is to spend as much as the budget will allow in this area to avoid obsolescence of your system as demand increases in the department.

Monitors

Monitors, the "picture tubes" for computers, range from a black and white or green and black screen to a multicolored screen. There are several types of monitors: the OGA monitor's resolution is acceptable for games, the EGA's is good for text and numbers, and the VGA is excellent for graphics or desktop publishing.

Printers

Once the computer has completed a document for printing, it transmits the data to a printer. A variety of printers are available. Dot matrix printers are least expensive, producing the somewhat ragged-looking type that has commonly been associated with computer-generated reports. The daisy wheel printer produces completely formed characters like a typewriter, and had been the standard until the development of reasonably inexpensive laser printers. Laser printers are now available for under $1000, and can print high-level graphics and crisp "letter quality" type. Laser printers have generally become the standard in AHC offices. Many laser printers can also accommodate the printing of multiple labels or large quantities of envelopes. Ink jet printers have also become popular. They cost less than laser printers and produce higher quality output than matrix printers do.

Bar Code

For tracking, identifying, or entering information into a personal computer system, bar coding can be one of the easiest and most efficient and cost-effective methods, compared with other data entry systems.

A bar code consists of a series of bars and spaces printed in defined ratios that are readable by a machine. We have become accustomed to seeing them on products in bookstores and supermarkets. The code is reproduced in bit-streams of zeros and ones, like the internal logic of the digital computer. The dark bars are analogous to the 0s and the 1s on magnetic media. A scanner sees a bar code and converts the visual image into an electrical signal.

Bar code scanning is very fast compared with data input via a keyboard. Data can be entered with minimal training and produces accurate results. Whenever the same data are used repeatedly, bar coding is an efficient method. A bar code data collection system can offer not only higher productivity, but also increased accuracy, cost effectiveness, better managerial control, and great operational efficiency. Bar code systems can be "user friendly" and economical to implement.

Modems

Modems are devices that change information from digital information produced by the computer so that it can be transmitted over telephone lines and then translated back into computer language to be received by a computer at the other end of the line. This is useful for communications between remote systems.

Modems have also made it possible for on-line databases to be feasible for academic health centers.

Film Recorders

Technology has brought a new wave of film-recording devices to AHCs. The equipment and process have also become substantially less expensive and are now in a cost-effective price range. Film recorders enable slides to be made directly from a computer graphic program. Considering the cost of slide production by medical illustration units or external graphic agencies, an in-house system can pay for itself in less than a year. Film recorders are connected to a computer by a cable. The recorder contains a 35 mm camera. The exposed film is removed from the film recorder and processed at any film processing location.

Telecommunications

Over the past decade incredible advancements have been made not only in personal computers but also in telecommunications. Managers in academic health centers must stay informed of this ever-changing technology and consider applying this new technology to their operations. For example, electronic mail and voice message systems have greatly reduced the annoyance and considerable staff time of "telephone tag" or message taking. These new tools can contribute significantly to an organization's effectiveness and efficiency.

Telecommuting

New computer technology presents new opportunities for how and where organizational members can conduct their work. Managers must always be thinking of how this technology can better serve their program or operation. For example, using E-mail, faxes, and so on, it is now possible for some members of the organization to work at home or at remote locations while still maintaining continuous access to important information and daily involvement with the organization. As managers in academics are faced with space and parking constraints and shortages, utilization of these technologies may well prove to be a major institutional benefit.

Projections are now being made that by 1995 we will experience shortages in labor in both the private and public sectors. *Business Week* notes, "With the 'Baby Bust' generation entering the job market, the United States is going to have a real labor crunch around 1995. Telecommuting is going to become a very important alternative."[10] To prepare for that potential shortage, *telecommuting* can be a real alternative. Why can't the preparation of clinic notes, transcriptions, manuscripts, data entry, be conducted from the home or other locations? Alex Malcolm, Director of Software Services for John Hancock Mutual Life Insurance Co., says, "Employers are clinging to an industrial-age view that people will not work unless you watch them."[1] Managers who have used new telecommuting technology report good results. The key, however, is in giving more quantifiable, results-oriented direction. As telecommuting consultant David Fleming says, "You start by managing by results, not surveillance."

Input Options

Input options include the standard keyboard, the mouse, and scanners. The mouse has been popularized through the Macintosh computer and is now readily available on DOS systems. However, scanner technology is improving rapidly and can be a very cost-effective tool. Scanners provide efficient methods for "reading" and inputting characters in text or graphics into a computer format.

Film-capture input devices are also available in which a camera connected to the computer can photograph individual frames of videotape. This can be useful clinically for reproducing intraoperative color films for text publication, or, as in plastic surgery, for producing preoperative stills that can be enhanced by computer graphics to demonstrate expected postoperative results. These images can then be printed for patient records or publication.

Surge Protector

The surge protector is another important feature. Again, the computer and its software are quite delicate and vulnerable. Even a small surge in power or static electricity has the potential to damage the hardware or software. Therefore, it is wise to invest in a surge protector for each electronic component of the computer system.

STANDALONE FACSIMILE TRANSMISSION

Standalone facsimile (fax) machines have rapidly proliferated. The fax can send any paper image to anyone else with a fax machine and is now available also through a variety of personal computer systems. Electronic mail services such as MCI and CompuServe accept any ASCII text file and can route it to a fax destination. Therefore, use of fax with the computer system is a wise, efficient, and inexpensive choice.

CONCLUSION

The advances in computer hardware and software over the years have led to many advances in word processing, data bases, spreadsheets, graphic, and statistical programs. These advances can provide cost-effective and efficient outputs for managers in academic health centers. The key to any computer system, however, is high-quality original data. Quality information/computer systems are critical to managers in academics. The system can provide a full range of information from financial, clinical, research data, trend reports, and graphic-related reports. However, these systems are only as good as the data being entered into them. The computer expression for this is GIGO: garbage in, garbage out.

Quality data can be achieved in many ways. For some academic health center programs that require quality data for accreditation and other needs, it means having one organizational member or a committee overseeing the data entry and reviewing periodic reports to make sure that the appropriate and correct data are getting entered into the proper fields and that any calculations are accurate. Having readily accessible quality data should be the top priority for any AHC computer system.

BIBLIOGRAPHY

*1. Frisse ME. (1992). Informatics in academic health science centers. *Academic Medicine: Journal of the Association of American Medical Colleges, 67*, 238-241.

2. Masys DR. (1989). Medical informatics: Glimpses of the promised land. *Academic Medicine, 64*, 13-14.

3. Beltow K. (1992, Summer). Voice-activated patient reporting systems and medical practice management. *Journal of Medical Practice Management, 8*, 38-45.

4. Holbrook J & Aghababian R. (1990). A computerized audit of 15,000 emergency department records. *Annals of Emergency Medicine, 19*, 139-144.

*5. Greenes RA & Shortliffe EH. (1990). Medical informatics: An emerging academic discipline and institutional priority. *Journal of the American Medical Association, 263*, 1114-1120.

6. Keane DR, Norman GR & Vickers J. (1991). The inadequacy of recent research on computer-assisted instruction. *Academic Medicine, 66*, 444-448.

*7. Blois MS & Shortliffe EH. (1990). The computer meets medicine: Emergence of a discipline. In Shortliffe EH et al., eds. *Medical informatics: Computer applications in health care.* Reading, Mass: Addison-Wesley, p 20.

*8. Forthman LC. (1990). Achieving competitive advantage through information management. *Computers in Health Care, 1*, 38-43.

9. William R. (1992). Development and evaluation of information technology in medicine. *Journal of the American Medical Association, 267*, 267.

10. The portable executive. (1988, October 10). *Business Week*, p 105.

11. Templeton M. (1990). Team software: 1990s project management. *Computing Canada, 16*, p 32.

12. Girard RE. (1989). Productivity and information systems. *Computers in Healthcare, 10*, 26-30.

13. Hurwicz M. (1989). Network management tools: Tool divisions reflect work patterns. *Computerworld, 23*, 85-90.

14. Austin CJ. (1989). Information technology and the future of health services delivery. *Hospital and Health Services Administration, 34*, 157-165.

*15. Sachs MA. (1989). Healthcare information needs in the 90's. *Computers in Healthcare, 10*, 43-44.

16. Forthman LC. (1990). Achieving competitive advantage through information management. *Computers in Healthcare, 11*, 38-43.

17. DeMello S & Gardner BH. (1990). Systems thinking: A powerful tool for healthcare management. *Healthcare Forum, 33*, 27-31.

18. McWilliams P. (1990). *The personal computer book.* Los Angeles: Prelude Press.

*Asterisk indicates an article or book that is particularly informative and helpful.

CHAPTER 13

Managing the Educational Process

Frank T. Stritter

The successful teacher is no longer on a height, pumping knowledge at high pressure into passive receptacles. . . . He is a senior student anxious to help his juniors.

SIR WILLIAM OSLER

A department in an academic health center has four components to its mission: education of the learners assigned to or electing it, research of questions important to the profession and to society, care of patients, and professional service. This chapter focuses on the first—education. Education has historically been the primary reason for the existence of a university; the other components are primarily twentieth century additions. Yet education is often the most illusive because of the changing nature of what must be taught and the variety of types of learners who are the focus of all educational programs sponsored by a department.

Any educational program has three basic components. First is the curriculum, which according to its Latin derivation, is "a course to be raced." Many learners would most likely agree with the original meaning of the word, as they must often feel that they are engaged in a continuous race. The curriculum can be conceptualized as either all the educational offerings of a department or each separate program, such as the residency program or the third year clerkship. The curriculum appears in the form of a written document developed by a subgroup of the faculty and approved by the body politic of the faculty. It can be as simple as the educational intentions of the program in question stated in the form of instructional goals and objectives. It can include the intentions, instructional experiences planned for the learners, instructional resources to be used by learners, and the evaluation protocol to be implemented. The curricular document serves as a guide for the individual instructor who interprets it and then delivers the material that it represents to the learners. The second basic component of the educational program, then, is instruction. This stimulates the third basic component, learning, which results from each individual learner's interpretation of the instruction. The remainder of this chapter will discuss both curriculum and instruction in hopes that these can bring about the most important product of an educational program—learning.

CURRICULUM

A curricular document will contain the following elements: (1) identification of the need or rationale for the curriculum, (2) identification of resources and constraints to support the curriculum, (3) a meaningful grouping and sequencing of the major concepts to be addressed, (4) the establishment of more specific expectations for learning with regard to each of the major concepts, (5) the development of measures for assessing learner performance, (6) the selection of instructional strategies and media, (7) the creation of learning activities and responsibilities for learners, and (8) the design of a program evaluation protocol. Whatever one's thinking about the specificity of the elements, each curriculum should be committed to paper before being considered, debated, and approved formally by the faculty whose responsibility it will be to deliver it. Once it is approved, a small committee of faculty should be appointed or elected to guide, monitor, and evaluate the implementation of the curriculum.

The members of the curriculum committee should be appointed because of their overall educational interest, not because they represent specific vested interests. All members should be able to rise above any specific interests they might have for the benefit of the overall educational program and the learners. They should be appointed because of their interest in organizing and facilitating learning, as opposed to an interest in protecting contact hours or exposure time of certain topical emphases. They should be appointed for specific periods of time, allowing systematic rotation and replacement. The committee should be expected to function dynamically and proactively, ensuring that curricular change is evolutionary, not revolutionary. It should be empowered to make many programmatic decisions without seeking the consensus of the full faculty. It might be a small standing committee with a specific charge empowered to appoint small ad hoc task forces from the faculty at large to address specific curricular questions and to make concrete proposals to the committee. Such a task force can then be discharged and its recommendations considered.

INSTRUCTION

The written curricular document should be communicated to individual faculty members who either accept or are assigned responsibility for instructing a particular component. Instruction can be divided into two different aspects: formats that include organization of the activity in which the learners participate, and media through which information, skills, and attitudes are communicated to the learners. Each member of the faculty will have specific instructional strengths and weaknesses. Because learning and recruiting to the profession or specialty are of paramount importance to the department, every attempt should be made to determine those strengths and weaknesses and to allocate the instructors and their resources carefully. Not only will learning be facilitated if learners have the best that a department can offer for the particular teaching task at hand, but also learners will be attracted to a particular profession or specialty based on the role models with whom they come into contact. The following instructional formats can comprise a curriculum and can, singly or in combination, be considered based on the strengths of each individual instructor:

- Large groups
- Small groups
- Clinical teaching
- Tutorial
- Individualized instruction
- Advising

Large Group

A lecture/discussion, used with large groups of 15 or more, is the choice for good public speakers. The instructor, using a variety of media, is the primary source of information normally addressing the learners in a one-way manner at a specific time and place. Some learners may have an opportunity to answer questions by the lecturer, but interaction is generally limited. Lectures can establish structures and are efficient in communicating facts, some of which can generally be recalled by learners when tested. Lectures serve a modeling function, giving learners an opportunity to observe practitioners and scientists dealing with the concepts of their specialties. Lectures cannot, however, accommodate the needs of individual learners, give learners an active role in their own learning, or effectively facilitate the development of decision making or clinical reasoning skills or attitudes.

Small Group

Small groups are generally composed of less than 15 learners. If the group is learner centered, that is, has no instructor/leader, the size should be no more than eight. If the group is instructor centered, that is, an instructor leads and controls the pace, it is called a seminar and can include up to 15. The learner-centered group promotes extensive peer interaction, addresses a specific task developed by the instructor, and uses the instructor only as a consultant or resource. Learner-centered groups tend to generate more and better information from the group, with members more inclined to accept the information when they have discussed it and developed solutions for any problems posed. Participants in such groups are more likely to apply concepts, increase their motivation to learn, develop positive attitudes, and improve their collaborative skills. Seminars are also based on group learning and active participation, but a session must be led and facilitated by a patient instructor. The instructor defines the task by selecting the stimulus that energizes the group and outlining the goals and procedural rules. The instructor, while making decisions a matter of group discussion, establishes a model for behavior of the participants, facilitates interaction with well-timed and well-articulated questions, and serves as an expert by giving short presentations when appropriate. The good seminar leader is skilled at obtaining the participation of all learners, listening to the group, and leading the group to its own conclusion. In using small groups, the instructor tends to lose some control of the learners; group interaction can add to the total time required for instruction, and generally, insufficient numbers of instructors are available to facilitate every group.

Clinical Teaching

Clinical instruction is the interaction between an instructor/practitioner (either a member of the faculty or a resident) and a learner about a patient or a patient's problem. In a contemporary clinical department, residents are responsible for a significant amount of clinical instruction received by medical students and younger residents and should therefore be an important part of any instructional planning undertaken by a department. The goal of such an interaction is generally improved knowledge and/or skill regarding the particular patient's health status. Learners generally assume some portion of the physician's role, endeavoring to determine the relevance and application of material learned in more abstract situations. The patient can be an individual in an operating room, a hospital bed, or an ambulatory clinic. The number of learners is generally no more than five, since the instructor's ability to observe and access each learner sharply decreases when the number of learners exceeds five. Learning may occur in an inpatient setting, or more commonly, in an outpatient setting, where the patient appears before the physician episodically. Time constraints are always an issue, but generally much more so in the latter setting. The teaching strategies of inpatient medicine, such as an operating room demonstration or an attending round, share a specific pattern, although a variety of individual styles are apparent. Strategies useful in the outpatient setting are not nearly as well understood, although interacting with more than one learner at a time seems extremely difficult. As more and more outpatient clinical teaching is developed, it will begin to characterize the medical education of the future. Clinical departments might well focus on developing strategies for the outpatient setting that can facilitate more effective learning for both residents and students.

Tutorial

An individual interaction between a learner and the instructor is generally the format for a tutorial. The learner prepares for the scheduled discussion with a practical experience, such as a project or patient care and/or directed reading. The instructor then uses socratic dialog to question the learner's comprehension, formulating new questions asked based on the learner's responses to earlier questions. The instructor provides brief comments, or feedback, to help the learner better understand the concept being discussed. The tutorial approach is extremely helpful for the learner, although it can also be intimidating. Medical students and residents alike can benefit from interacting individually with an instructor on a regular basis. It can be personally satisfying for the instructor as well, although it can also be time consuming.

Individualized Instruction

In this format the instructor prepares instructional materials from which the student can learn individually, usually at an individual learning rate. Often the materials are portable, so learners can use them in libraries, specially designated rooms within the department offices, or at home. They can include monographs, manuals, or syllabuses, augmented by 35 mm slides; videotaped programs that can be used on a personal videotape playback unit and monitor; or computer-assisted instructional (CAI) software and simulations to be used interactively on specific types of hardware. Development of materials to support individualized instruction is time consuming for the instructor but helpful to the learner.

Advising

Advising is a format of instruction that fills a critical void for learners, but one that is often overlooked when documenting teaching time. Both medical students and residents need someone with whom they can meet individually to discuss a variety of academic or personal situations. Advising can serve many functions as varied as counseling, encouraging, mentoring, challenging, and even reprimanding. The adviser's functions can be scheduled and systematic or unscheduled and haphazard. They can be either frequent or infrequent, depending on each learner's individual needs. The presence of an adviser at a particularly stressful time or at a particularly happy moment can be extremely important in the professional development of any learner. Advising is a function often not listed in an instructor's job description. Some instructors are far more proficient advisers than others. Those instructors who can and do make a contribution as advisers should be adequately rewarded.

No one best strategy exists for all instructors to use with all learners in all situations. Sometimes a lucid analysis of an important concept is needed; sometimes a well-articulated question that forces the learner to offer his or her own solutions is best. At other times modeling a particular procedure or approach to a patient is necessary. The best instructor is one who can analyze the situation and provide what is needed, but not every instructor can respond in that way. Most have particular instructional strengths. A wise chair knows the strengths and weaknesses of each instructor in the department, allocates resources to instructional tasks according to those characteristics, and rewards faculty for being proficient in whatever type of instruction they are assigned.

EVALUATION OF CURRICULUM AND INSTRUCTION

Evaluation involves the collection and analysis of information to inform a decision concerning the value or worth of an educational program and/or a teaching responsibility. Several issues must be addressed in making a decision to evaluate: (1) the purpose of the evaluation, (2) the concept of education and teaching that will serve as criteria for evaluating departmental teaching, (3) the specific behaviors that will be evaluated, (4) methods used to evaluate, (5) the use of the information obtained in the evaluation process, and (6) departmental considerations that foster sound and effective evaluation.

Evaluation can be undertaken for one or more reasons. First, faculty and other educational resources must be allocated logically and effectively. Assignments should be determined so that the best instructors can be used in the most critical situations, where they can make their most effective contributions. Second, a departmental values system regarding education should be articulated and an awareness to the intricacies and rewards of good teaching developed. Third, instruction and education can be improved when the analysis of information is communicated to those responsible and coupled with a counseling and/or improvement program. Fourth, instruction and education can be evaluated so that those responsible can be rewarded through teaching awards, merit salary increases, and faculty promotion and so that new educational programs can be evaluated. Finally, educational research can be undertaken so that contributions can be made to new knowledge about teaching and learning and a department can sponsor the most effective educational programs for their learners.

As indicated in the previous section, identifying the best instructional or curricular format for all learners in all situations is virtually impossible. A dogmatic chair or senior faculty member could prescribe that instruction be organized and delivered according to any one of the following concepts: (1) that it be rationally planned according to specific characteristics, highly systematic, and routinized; (2) that it be delivered using specific techniques but be implemented without detailed direction; (3) that it be delivered according to general guidelines, while permitting considerable judgment and latitude as to when and how a particular technique is applied; or (4) that it be unconventional and unpredictable, allowing the teacher complete autonomy in teaching. In practice a teacher in a medical school implements some combination of all of these types, and the chair will generally not want to prescribe a specific type to which each member of the faculty should adhere. Even though unspoken departmental norms for behavior are often set and the chair and the senior faculty will often model certain teaching behaviors, it is wise practice to allow individual faculty members considerable latitude in the type and style of instruction they employ. It is also wise to evaluate individual faculty on any or all of the specific formats that they may choose to employ. This can and should be negotiated with each individual.

Irby[1] has described a process of collecting information about curriculum and instruction that is adaptable to any medical school department. Darling-Hammond, Wise, and Pease[2] have reviewed the research on several methods that can be helpful in developing a valid, reliable, and generalizable process. A brief review of those methods, summarized in Figure 13-1, is as follows.

Learner Ratings

Assessments by learners are inexpensive to collect and generally quite reliable. Learners can provide information both in the short run and over time. They are the only individuals in the educational process who can tell whether a program or a particular instructor is really communicating information, concepts, and skills effectively. Information can be obtained from learners by written questionnaires, in focus-group discussions, or in individual interviews.

Peer Review

Peers can provide the best review of validity, indicating whether the substance of teaching is accurate, current, and reasonably representative of the domain from which the material is selected. They can review the documents of teaching such as outlines, syllabuses, bibliographies, and examinations. Peers cannot evaluate teaching performance reliably, because generally they do not see enough of teaching to do so. In addition to evaluating substance, peers can profitably be asked to form a committee, as suggested by Irby,[1] to monitor a department's overall performance of educational efforts. This committee can review information obtained through a variety of evaluational methods, consider proposals for program revision, suggest modifications, make recommendations for faculty teaching assignments, and provide valuable information to the chair regarding educational effectiveness of individual instructors and programs offered by the department. A committee of this type can be assigned responsibility for one program only or for several programs.

Observation

Administrators and educational consultants, such as medical educators, can review a teaching performance or the specifics of a curriculum and indicate whether the style and presentation are appropriate. Such individuals will generally not be able to observe enough of an individual's teaching to provide reliable data over time, and they will often not have the expertise to provide valid judgments concerning the

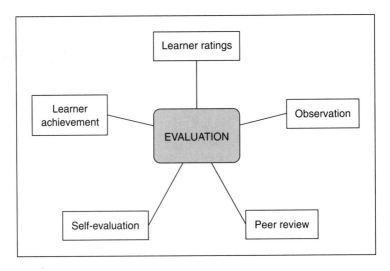

Figure 13-1. Methods for evaluating curriculum and instruction.

substance of instruction. The information that they can provide on style, however, can often be extremely helpful in improving various aspects of the educational program in question.

Self-Evaluation

Individuals, whether they are responsible only for delivering segments of instruction or for coordinating entire educational programs, can provide descriptive documentation of their own educational efforts, as well as of their efforts to improve their own educational skills. Such information can be an important source of information to the chair and to a faculty monitoring committee and serve as a source of motivation to individuals themselves. More importantly, perhaps, it can help individuals better understand their own skills and abilities and plan strategies for improvement. Individuals can be asked to provide an essay or respond to specific questions. An approach cited by Rothman et al.[3] and Wolf,[4] which combines several similar methods, is the educational dossier or portfolio. This is a chronological record maintained by the individual that documents educational efforts by the instructor. It is a container for storing and displaying evidence of an instructor's knowledge and skills. It is based on multiple sources of evidence collected over a specific period of time by the individual. It should include the raw materials of one's teaching, an interpretation of those materials, a reflective self-analysis about the strengths and weaknesses of one's teaching, and an indication of what the individual plans to do to improve skills or knowledge. This can help individuals determine exactly how they perceive their instruction and what they have to do to be the best instructors that they can be.

Learner Achievement

The ultimate reason that educational programs exist is to assist learners in obtaining certain prescribed educational achievements—knowledge, skills, and/or attitudes. It would seem that some measure of achievement would be appropriate in evaluating the success of a faculty member's instruction and the department's curriculum. A chair could ask the faculty to develop a departmental criterion for effectiveness. It could be completion of previously agreed upon educational objectives, expert opinion, gain over time, or comparison to a national norm of some type. It could be the accomplishments of specific learners completing instruction or a curriculum. However, some difficulties exist in evaluating individual instructors in academic health centers according to their learners' achievements. First, individual instructors are rarely assigned responsibility for a specific curriculum; a group is more often assigned the responsibility, and thus it may be nearly impossible to determine an individual instructor's contribution to the total result. Second, the same instructor often produces different results in different situations, with an accompanying low reliability of data obtained. Achievement, such as item analyses on program, departmental, and national examinations and the aggregate of ratings on particular learner characteristics, can and should be used to provide information on specific educational programs. Such data should, however, be used in perspective and in consort with other types of evaluational information.

In the final analysis, no single best method for collecting information about instruction exists. Educational research has not identified one method that is always successful. The chair or the committee that the chair appoints should first consider the type of information needed to make a particular decision and then adopt a multidimensional protocol. The criteria of validity, reliability, generalizability, and utility should always be primary considerations. One chair recently made significant changes to a particular course upon hearing the complaints of 10% of the enrolled learners, not realizing that the remaining 90% were quite satisfied. If the criterion of generalizability had been observed, additional information would have been collected from a more representative sample of learners, and the change would likely have received much more discussion before it was implemented.

The following departmental characteristics, which the administration and faculty can implement or at least facilitate, can help to ensure the success of an evaluation system (Figure 13-2). First, the chair and the faculty should have a congruent and shared understanding of the goals, criteria, and standards for performance of the curriculum and instruction. No misunderstanding regarding the definition of successful performance can exist. Second, the faculty should have meaningful input into decisions about the criteria and standards for evaluation, and the criteria should be diverse. Faculty should have some say as to what they will be evaluated on and how they will be evaluated. Third, personal interaction and communication between the chair and the faculty concerning various aspects of instruction and curriculum should be frequent and meaningful to both parties. Fourth, the prescription regard-

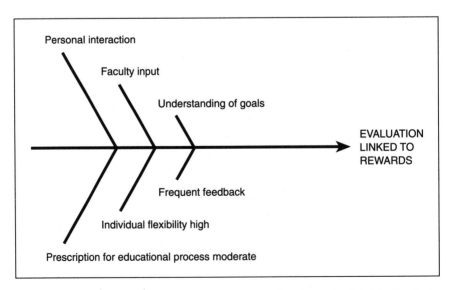

Figure 13-2. Departmental characteristics implemented by faculty and administration that can help to ensure a successful evaluation system.

ing the nature of the tasks to be undertaken in the educational process should be moderate and the level of individual flexibility high. A definite balance of departmental prescription and individual choice should exist, but the faculty should be allowed considerable latitude in how they perform their instructional and curricular assignments. Fifth, feedback to the faculty concerning the quantity and quality of educational assignments should be frequent. Finally, the faculty must perceive that the evaluation system has been systematically and soundly developed and that it is linked to rewards that they receive. Attention to these points may not guarantee a completely effective evaluation system, but it will definitely facilitate faculty enthusiasm and will provide impetus for all instructors to reflect on their beliefs about instruction and curriculum and their behavior.

FACULTY DEVELOPMENT

Educational institutions, and universities in particular, are in the business of human development. Included are not only the young people who are being prepared to assume various professional roles in society, but also those who are responsible for that preparation—the faculty.

As discussed in greater detail in Chapter 8, Human and Organizational Resource Development, universities, and academic health centers in particular, have a responsibility to evaluate, develop, reward, and renew their own faculty. Chairs should therefore assist their faculty in developing and improving those skills, both clinical and otherwise, that are necessary to undertake their responsibilities in the best possible manner. Otherwise those faculty will likely lose some portion of their vitality and become less effective in and enthusiastic about the preparation of these professionals. Bland and Schmitz[5] define faculty development as facilitating the acquisition of those competencies important to succeeding as a faculty member and those essential, yet intangible, positive qualities of individuals and institutions that enable purposeful production. Production refers both to education of learners and to new knowledge.

Writings about faculty development during the 1960s and 1970s promoted faculty development to address individual faculty problems, such as instructor burnout, outmoded teaching skills, and inadequate research productivity. The literature of the 1980s and 1990s views faculty development more as addressing institutional problems such as tenured-in departments, different types of students, outmoded curriculum, lack of adequate professional opportunities for faculty, decline in real earnings and support for research, and deteriorating departmental climate for productivity. Blackburn[6] noted that nearly every factor that can be positively correlated with faculty productivity resides in a chair's hands and can therefore be dealt with administratively. Among those factors are material resources, common goals, departmental climate, communication processes, decision-making processes, and leadership. He concluded that faculty are much more likely to be vital and productive if a strong, positive relationship exists between departmental goals and individual faculty goals and desires. Bland and Schmitz[7] defined the chair's role as ensuring the connection between the institutional mission, the personnel policies, and the department's faculty development strategies that are adopted. They believe further that the chair must take personal ownership and ensure that the faculty feel the same ownership of any faculty development program that is implemented. In addition, the faculty should be expected to allocate specific time to participate in the program. The characteristics of a successful program are that it be considered by all to be an integral component of the department, be comprehensive, include a variety of strategies, address the organizational context in which the faculty function, define the faculty's professional responsibilities and various personal needs of the faculty, and include skills needed by faculty at each distinct stage of their careers.

A program to address the educational skills of a departmental faculty should be based on skills required by the faculty of a particular department. Stritter, Bland, and Youngblood[8] described a method for ascertaining the educational skills and concepts useful to faculty in fulfilling their responsibilities. Bland et al.[9] reported the complete results of their study in a book describing several faculty development strategies, referring to the skills as *competencies*. The educational competencies fall into the following broad categories: program development, needs assessment, instructional goals and objectives, large-group teaching, small-group teaching, individualized teaching, clinical teaching, development and use of instructional media, evaluation of learning and performance, and evaluation of programs and instruction. Once the initial step of determining the competencies to be developed is completed, the strategies can be selected and developed.

Stritter[10] categorized faculty development in the health professions into three broad categories—*technical assistance, high faculty involvement,* and *assessment*—and commented on the efficacy of each.

Technical Assistance

Technical assistance includes those activities in which an educational consultant works with an individual faculty member in planning and/or implementing an instructional responsibility of the faculty member or solving a faculty member's instructional problem. Technical assistance includes both individual consultation or collaborative educational research. The goal of the faculty member and the consultant is to study or improve some aspect of the instructional process. The consultant, for example, can either be from a school of education, from an office of medical education at the level of the dean of the school of medicine, or attached to the department. Although using an educational consultant at the dean's office level may be more efficient financially, one at the departmental level may give more valid and effective input for the specific department's purposes. Many grant programs sponsored by the U.S. Department of Health and Human Services, such as the NHLBI Preventive Cardiology Academic Award, the NIAAA/NIDA Faculty Development initiative, and the Bureau of Health Professions Primary Care Residency grant, include educational components to which an educational consultant of this type can make a significant contribution.

Faculty Involvement

High faculty involvement activities involve those activities in which faculty colleagues learn with and from each other about instructional issues such as teaching methods, performance evaluation, use of computer instruction, and advising. Extended approaches have the greatest potential for effecting positive change; these may include fellowships and formal study for a degree in education. Fellowships can be either part time or full time. Participants report significant impact, but few can afford the time necessary to participate. One cautionary note: Chairs and participants must make every effort to ensure that such programs are relevant to the participants' departmental needs and context. Short programs are the most common, appearing in the form of workshops, short courses, and seminars sponsored by professional associations, such as the Association of Professors of Gynecology and Obstetrics, or schools and departments.

More specifically, such programs include longer residential offerings of 5 days to 2 weeks in which the goals to be accomplished are broad, shorter residential programs of 2 to 4 days where the objectives to be accomplished are focused and specific, half-day or 1-day programs conducted in departmental facilities for which the objectives are specific and brief, and programs of 1 to 2 hours focusing on a limited objective and conducted in departmental facilities. Faculty can travel to an off-campus location to attend a residential program or invite a consultant to present a shorter program in departmental facilities. Participants' knowledge in such shorter term programs can be increased and they can be sensitized to certain potential issues and concepts, but actual behavior change is unlikely unless an organized follow-up activity is provided within the department and the participants are rewarded in some way for implementing the learned changed. If the chair can integrate support for participation, evaluation of new effort, and success and reward for change into the fabric of the department, the faculty will more likely devote energy to improving their own curricular and instructional efforts. Embedded in the "high involve-ment" category are the programs that can be provided for residents to develop and improve their clinical teaching skills. Edwards and Marier[11] discuss considerations and describe several possibilities for organizing and implementing a program of this type. Many workable types exist, but perhaps the most important point to be made is that the chair and the faculty make a statement to the residents about the impor-tance of their teaching roles. Ways must also be devised to keep the residents in-volved in continued discussion about teaching after the initial workshop or seminar has been completed. They could participate in periodic "learner of the month" dis-cussions led by chief residents or interested faculty where difficult teaching situa-tions and problem students are discussed. Residents could also have their clinical teaching evaluated individually and receive consultations from the chief resident or from experienced faculty. A variety of strategies could be used to remind them about the roles they have in the development of learners participating in the department's educational program.

Assessment

Assessment occurs when an instructor's teaching is evaluated by some combination of learners, peers, administrators, and consultants and the individual in a self analysis. Interestingly, Boice[12] indicated that new instructors begin their teaching responsibilities and persist with disappointingly narrow styles. Further, he suggested that they be initially safeguarded from all but private and formative evaluations of their performance. Such precautions may reduce their reliance on only the methods that they experienced as learners and help them to appreciate and experiment with alternatives. The specific techniques for evaluating are described and summarized on pp. 234 through 239. Cohen[13] concluded that instructors will change little, if any, from feedback based on learner data alone. Instructors will change some if an expert or experienced peer interprets the feedback based on learner data, and are likely to change the most if there is some type of ongoing consultation with departmental faculty and a developmental program is provided by the expert or peer in consort with the learner feedback. The final option is far more productive in effecting positive change in instructors' teaching behaviors.

Bland and Stritter[14] and Hitchcock, Stritter, and Bland[15] offer the following suggestions to be considered in planning and implementing a faculty development program:

1. Faculty development will be enhanced if first a specific mission is developed in general and for each specific program.
2. Give the total effort a visible location in the departmental organization.
3. Consult experienced experts at your own or another institution in designing and implementing the program.
4. Involve departmental faculty in planning the program and make clear why participation in the program is advantageous to them and to the department.
5. Give responsibility for designing and implementing the program to a leader with interest and background, designated time, administrative support, and resources.
6. Consider an instructional evaluation procedure as a first step to help faculty become aware of their individual and group deficiencies.
7. Consider approaches that will change the department environment, such as group educational projects and rewards for participation and for good teaching.
8. Share resources with other departments and with other institutions by establishing regional centers that facilitate the accumulation of resources.
9. Evaluate the effectiveness of the program to ascertain whether the program has achieved its objectives and whether the faculty has found it be useful and enjoyable.

This chapter has summarized the many educational responsibilities and activities that can characterize an academic department in an academic health center. First, all curricular programs offered by a department must be documented and monitored. Second, all the different instructional formats that are possible should be reviewed, discussed and reinforced so that all faculty members are able to teach in the format they find the most comfortable and are the most skilled in implementing. Third, all curricular programs offered by the department and the instructional practices of each member of the faculty should be systematically evaluated so that the best possible programs accomplishing the greatest amount of learning will occur. Finally, every faculty member should be helped to become the best instructor that he or she can be by participating in regular and effective faculty development programs.

BIBLIOGRAPHY

1. Irby DM. (1983). Evaluating instruction in medical education. *Journal of Medical Education, 58,* 844-849.
2. Darling-Hammond L, Wise AE & Pease SR. (1983). Teacher evaluation in organizational context: A review of the literature. *Review of Educational Research, 53,* 285-328.
3. Rothman AI, Poldre P, Cohen R. (1989). Evaluating clinical teachers for promotion. *Academic Medicine, 64*(12), 774-775.
4. Wolf K. (1991, October). The schoolteacher's portfolio: Issues in design, implementation and evaluation. *Phi Delta Kappan,* 129-136.
*5. Bland CJ & Schmitz CC. (1990). An overview of faculty and institutional vitality. In JH Schuster & DW Wheeler, eds. *Enhancing faculty careers.* San Francisco: Jossey-Bass.
*6. Blackburn RT. (1979). Academic careers: Patterns and responsibilities. *Current Issues in Higher Education.* Washington, DC: American Association for Higher Education.
7. Bland CJ & Schmitz CC. (1986). Characteristics of the effective researcher and implications for faculty development. *Journal of Medical Education, 61,* 22-31.
*8. Stritter FT, Bland CJ & Youngblood PL. (1991). Determining essential faculty competencies. *Teaching and Learning in Medicine, 3*(4), 232-238.
*9. Bland CJ, Schmitz CC, Henry RH, Stritter FT & Aluise JJ. (1990). *Success in academic medicine: Essential faculty skills and learning experiences.* New York: Springer Publishing Co.
10. Stritter FT. (1983). Faculty evaluation and development. In C McGuire et al., eds. *Handbook of health professions education.* San Francisco: Jossey-Bass.
11. Edwards JC & Marier RL, eds. (1987). *Resident teaching: rules, techniques, and programs.* New York: Springer.
12. Boice R. (1992). *The new faculty member.* San Francisco: Jossey-Bass.
13. Cohen PA. (1980). Effectiveness of student rating feedback for improving college instruction. *Research on Higher Education, 13,* 321-341.
14. Bland CJ & Stritter FT. (1988). Characteristics of effective family medicine faculty development programs. *Family Medicine, 20,* 282-288.
*15. Hitchcock M, Stritter FT & Bland CJ. Faculty development in the health professions: Conclusions and recommendations. *Medical Teacher* (in press).

*Asterisk indicates an article or book that is particularly informative and helpful.

CHAPTER 14

Understanding the Numbers:
A Look Beyond the Financial Statements

Jill Ridky

ॐ

For which of you, intending to build a tower, sitteth not down first and counteth the cost, whether he have sufficient to finish it?

LUKE 14:28

Understanding the numbers can serve as a strong, essential weapon in your management arsenal. A manager must depend on intuition to lead, but you also need to support your position and direction with a body of well-researched and accurate data. Understanding the financial facts assists not only in guiding the course of actions, but also in supporting recommendations with facts and figures. Every chair is expected to develop solutions to problems and to understand the funding implications or financial impact of the developed solutions. The dean or the vice-chancellor will also need to understand the financial implications to reach the solution. Chairs can strengthen their position when they are able to present sound solutions to problems and consider financial implications: Will the solution develop new funding? Is it cost effective? Will it reduce expenditures? Will the solution have an impact on the number of referrals or the number of patients seen by the institution? An understanding of the numbers can greatly enhance support for the chair's position.

Major challenges for academic health centers today include managing with fewer resources, maintaining quality, and managing new technology. Revenue and funding pressures continue to mount as departments grapple with cost control and budgetary constraints while finding means and methods to continue to support daily operating expenses as well as future expansion and development. Concerns about cost control, program productivity, and utilization of staff time are commonplace as pressure continues from the federal and state governments to lower costs and reduce budgets. Academic departments are challenged to find new sources of revenue and to manage their current funding structure carefully. In this era of decreasing federal and state funding, the importance of everyone's understanding the finances has greatly

increased. What do the numbers mean, and how do they help us get from point A to point B in our program plan?

This chapter will discuss several financial topics. First is a brief discussion on fiscal literacy. How does the department relay financial information, and how well informed are organizational members? The second topic is understanding the costs of operation. Financial statements and accounting systems are necessary and beneficial, but managers must be able to comprehend and interpret this information. The third topic is overhead allocation. What is overhead and how is it assigned or allocated? Finally, budgets will be considered. How can budgets be developed in a simple and meaningful process and employed to benefit departmental and program goals?

FISCAL LITERACY

The evolving theme over the years has been this: Information is power. This point is nowhere more true than in financial matters. Organizations are developing and assisting with the support to develop data bases that will allow them access to the continuous analysis of information. Reports, graphics, and other instruments proliferate as organizations continue to increase their knowledge level. The box on p. 246 offers some terms that are important to developing fiscal literacy.

Disseminating knowledge throughout the organization is now believed to be beneficial. In years past, when organizations functioned within a purely hierarchical mode, the "brain power" or knowledge was at the top of the organizational structure. The difference between the mail clerk and the executive director involved not only the level of decision making, but the amount of information to which each was privy. Today, however, the idea that all workers should be better informed about the organization's operation is believed to be one of the keys to better job productivity and performance. Communication and decision making are viewed on a level playing field. If the staff assistant has the same information as the program director does, he or she will be better able to make informed decisions.

KEY TERMS

assets Items owned by an organization that have a monetary value.

balance sheet Statement of assets and liabilities at the close of a financial period.

budget The financial blueprint for the department; the converting of operational plans into financial terms.

capital budget A 3- to 10-year budget, depending on the organization, with a typical focus on a building or equipment needs.

cash budget Anticipated cash receipts.

cash flow Total revenue less actual expenditures.

cost allocation To measure out or apportion costs according to a plan.

cost/benefit analysis A method for evaluating the costs of a project to the benefits expected.

cost effective When the benefits exceed the costs.

deficit When expenditures exceed revenue.

depreciation Decrease in value over a given period of time.

direct costs Costs that are directly attributable to a single cost objective (supplies, postage, travel, etc.).

fiscal year A 12-month period of time, typically from July to June, January to December, or October to September.

fixed expenses Expenses that do not vary with the level of output.

indirect costs Costs outside your control that are charged to your department; these are sometimes also referred to as *overhead.* Overhead, however, is an imprecise term. If your department or area is charged an overhead cost, make certain you have a clear understanding of what costs make up the overhead cost. Does it include space, utilities, social services, housekeeping, security?

investment Commitment of funds for the purpose of future gains.

mixed expenses Expenses incurred predominantly for one program, and charged to that program even though a minor part of the expense is incurred for other programs. (A sacrifice of purity for the sake of simplicity.)

operating budget 1-year specific activities for the department.

operating reserve The positive gain in an organization's account after expenditures are subtracted from revenue. Organizations typically should develop a reserve equal to 3 to 6 months of annual expenditures.

program costs The full cost of a program, which includes direct and indirect costs.

reserve Sometimes also referred to as *operating reserve,* the difference of expenditures from revenue at fiscal year-end.

responsibility centers Work unit formally charged with budgetary responsibility for carrying out an activity.

variable expenses Expenses that fluctuate in direct relationship to production (supplies, postage, travel, etc.).

Within this perspective it is believed that all staff members and faculty in the academic environment should possess *fiscal literacy,* or the understanding of the fiscal dimensions of the organization. To develop fiscal literacy, the staff and directors must work together. In a two-pronged approach, employees in the academic environment must take it upon themselves to ask questions related to the finances of program or departmental funding. In turn, the directors, chairpersons, and deans must relay financial information so that all members of the organization can understand the reality, the needs, and concerns the department faces. The organizational leaders must educate all members so they can continue to work toward the betterment of the organization. All members must know what is coming so they can prepare and position for budget reductions, loss of funding, or (on the brighter side) funding development. Developing fiscal literacy will also assist in preventing organizational surprises, as illustrated in the case example.

Fiscal literacy creates a positive, collegial, "group-think" problem-solving environment. When special concerns and issues arise, if members are alerted to the problem and can review trends and projections, a group cohesiveness develops that will strengthen the academic organization. Organizational members will support an academic organization's leaders when they are willing to educate and present the data and information in advance. Fiscal literacy also creates credibility for the department's leaders. Management's philosophy should be to share it all. A "rose-colored glasses" approach benefits neither the organizational members nor the department. Organizational members also need to understand that organizational advancement and accomplishments can be cyclical. Setbacks can occur, as can reductions in budget lines and workforce, but managers should use these times for developing solidarity and a consensual climate. When the department's members learn to trust that their input will be sought and valued, they can direct their energies and initiative to creative fiscal problem solving at all levels.

❧ Case Example

For almost a decade the performance of the Hudson Rehabilitation Center was bleak. The center ended every fiscal year with an operational loss. This ongoing loss was substantial, and Dr. George Emerson, the chair, was eventually faced with a choice of closing the center down completely or attaining a positive balance. Most observers believed attaining a positive budget would not only be an arduous endeavor but would also require a touch of magic. How was the organization going to reverse years of budget shortfalls?

For years Hudson Rehabilitation Center's management had made the executive decision not to alarm the staff about the chronic shortfall, and as a matter of managerial choice withheld details about the poor performance of the center. Under redesign, new management was brought in to reverse the operational shortfalls. The staff were immediately assembled and told just how poorly the center was doing and what levels of referrals and productivity were required to reverse the poor performance. There is no nice way to tell organizational members that for the organization to survive, objectives, goals, productivity, and overall performance measures must change. For the Hudson Rehabilitation Center, change meant down-sizing the organizational structure, implementing an improved billing and collection system, developing a new accounting system, increasing referrals, revising clinical schedules, reducing overhead, postponing raises, and other cost containment measures.

The decision was made to try to turn the center around, and all of these strategies were implemented. Management's decision to promote full disclosure and establish periodic fiscal literacy meetings was one of the leading components, which led to fiscal stability for the organization within 2 years.

UNDERSTANDING THE COSTS

Most academic organizations today have developed an established, sophisticated accounting system capable of generating impressive accounting and financial statements. Financial and accounting statements alone, however, frequently do not allow for interpretation or understanding of the numbers, or what the program or projects costs are, or how to go about cutting or reducing expenses. A department manager must not be lulled by impressively displayed compilations of computer-generated financial data unless he or she has a thorough grounding in analyzing the implications of such data.

Academic institutions can generate periodic financial reports calculating revenues and expenses, assets and liabilities. However, department chairs and managers cannot run their operation by the financial statements without a fundamental understanding of what these numbers mean and how they relate to the day-to-day operation and development of their department. Financial statements alone are not the most reliable source of information. Over the years many academic departments have suffered not from financial failure as much as from management failure—a failure of academic leaders and managers to recognize how important excellent data and information are in managing and leading an academic department.

CPAs and controllers all have a vital role in an organization's effective operation. The CPA approach is vital for financial accountability certification, audits, accreditation, board members, and so forth. Financial statements are prepared in accordance with established accounting policy, but they cannot tell administrators what it costs to produce a program or to help evaluate performance and productivity of units or programs. Nor do they assist in the development of funds or identify areas to reduce or lower costs. This is a critical shortcoming.

Organizations must be able to review departmental and divisional costs along with program effectiveness by measuring productivity and identifying inefficiencies in the operation. The scope of so many organizations' mission creates a very complex organizational and managerial structure. This complex structure must be consistently monitored and analyzed as human and monetary resources fulfill organizational expectations. Every aspect of a project or program should come under review. Did the function, objective, or goal justify the cost? Was there a less expensive way to accomplish the same goal? If a potential savings were to cause a lower quality or standard, would the savings be worth the lower quality? As programs and projects are developed, constant monitoring of costs ensures that there will be no surprises. Keeping a close watch also allows managers to make adjustments before financial issues become insurmountable problems.

Presently, no standard evaluation instrument to understand the numbers prevails. As a pilot study, a division within an academic medical department set out to address this question and to initiate the development of a profile and trend reporting system.[1] The primary purpose of the instrument was to control cost, understand program cost, and to develop a road to dialog with the "underachievers" and "over-achievers." The study's objective was to create and develop a financial framework that would analyze productivity and costs. The objectives of the instrument included the ability to:

- Assist with program planning and decision making
- Analyze expenditures related to program and divisional activity
- Analyze trends
- Spot strong and weak activity areas
- Assist in annual budget development
- Analyze time and effort

The system is composed of a set of "building blocks" that each relate to the activities and trends of a single program unit or faculty member. The system contains both historical and current information placed into an interactive data base for ease of analysis. For example, the salary document has been useful for analyzing salary trends for all faculty members over a 6-year period (see below). These departmental trend data are compared with current national salary levels at the 50th and 80th percentiles obtained from the *Report on Medical School Faculty Salaries,* a publication of the Association of Academic Medical Colleges (AAMC).[1]

			Salary Increase Document						
Name	Division	Rank	FY 90 Salary	FY 91 % Increase	FY 92 Salary	FY 93 % Increase	FY 94 Salary	93-94 50%	AAMC 80%

Another component of the system positions faculty members in an analysis center for programs or units (see the box). This component provides information essential to decision making and provides a cost comparison basis that can be used to compare results of similar programs. The primary objective of the analysis center has been to achieve an agreed-upon relationship between revenues and expenses. Each faculty member is regarded as a separate analysis center within a program or unit.

- Fixed and variable expenses for faculty members are assigned individually. Fixed expenses are defined as those that do not vary with the level of output, such as personnel and staffing cost, insurance, membership dues, rent, and service contracts. Almost 60% of nonphysician personnel costs are included in this category.
- Variable expenses, defined as costs that fluctuate in direct relationship to production, include such items as office and laboratory supplies, medical supplies, postage, billing and collection, travel expenses, and so on. Because each faculty member in the program incurs expenses in proportion to the level

of activity, the variable charges are allocated directly to the faculty or in relation to the percentage of faculty activity.

• Expenses related to the level of clinical activity, such as the dean's deduction and practice plan deduction, are assigned according to the deduction policy (see below). In some cases, if a faculty member insists on retaining a special nurse, research technician, or secretary, the solution is to apply this expense directly to the faculty member.

					Expenditure Profile				
Name	Salary	Benefits	Travel	Dues	Practice Plan	Dean Deduction	Clinic Cost	Secretary	Total

Within the system, each faculty member is accountable for expenses, and therefore each has a different overhead percentage. Some costs, such as research and development, are based on the program's overall cost and are allocated proportionally. Therefore, a faculty member sharing a secretary has a lower direct expense for clerical support than a faculty member with one or two secretaries. Based on the financial framework, the faculty member would be encouraged to either increase activity or decrease cost. Every faculty member has control over containing direct costs in terms of travel, membership in societies, office and research expenses, and other costs.

In addition to the financially related profiles, another dimension has been added by developing an activities profile (see the box below). Along with clinical activity levels, the profile includes other activities associated with the program's mission. In

---

ACTIVITIES PROFILE

Name _____

Inpatient procedures   _____
Outpatient procedures   _____
  Operations   _____
  Referrals   _____
  Patient visits   _____
  Funded research projects   _____
  Research projects submitted _____
  Educational courses   _____
  Presentations   _____
  Administrative committees   _____
  Publications   _____

an academic clinical program, the integration of patient care, research, and education are three essentials. The profile incorporates these by focusing on the activity levels in each area. Clinical activity includes data on the number of procedures, operations, referrals, and patient visits. Research activity includes the number of research projects (submitted and funded). Educational activity integrates the number of presentations and publications as well as activity in administrative committees and educational courses.

A final component includes an operational summary analysis, which combines data from the other reports into a summary format. The operational analysis (see the box below) provides additional data, including collection rate gross charges, net receipts, expenditures, other funding, and year-end balance. This report forms a collective account that relates to the other components. Periodic printouts are made available that summarize the analysis. In addition, year-end projections have been developed along with comparisons of prior-year results.

OPERATIONAL SUMMARY ANALYSIS—FISCAL YEAR-END

	Total Program	Dr. Smith	Dr. Hall	Dr. Mason	Dr. Harvey
1. No. of patient visits					
2. No. of procedures					
3. Gross charges/year					
4. Net receipts/year					
5. Collection rate					
6. Percentage of net receipts					
7. Fixed costs (equally)*					
8. Variable costs (pro rata)					
9. Direct costs					
10. Total expenditure (7 + 8 + 9)					
11. Balance (4 − 10)					
12. Research funding					
13. Other funding					
14. Adjusted balance (12 + 13 − 11)					
15. Faculty salary					
16. Faculty benefits†					
17. Year-end balance (15 + 16 − 14)					

*Excludes faculty salary and benefits.
† Includes retirement, liability insurance, disability, heath care, FICA, etc.

The study has required numerous changes and revisions from the onset, but the format has been accepted by management. There is no doubt that management must know the true costs, including where expenses occur and funding is developed. Knowing the costs and funding development means being able to factually answer the following questions:

- What are the fixed and variable costs for the department and divisions?
- Can activity be increased before costs move up?
- How do costs change with volume?
- What are the effects if activity declines?
- How do cost structure and activity and historical trends compare with those of other organizations?

Without answers to these questions, it is difficult to make informed decisions. The system has allowed most faculty members to develop a better understanding of the funding and cost structure. The analytical framework enables departments to draw together numerous components to understand the level and intensity of activity of faculty members and the level of resources that are required for development. The system serves not only as an important information source but also as a communication vehicle. Timely feedback to faculty members regarding productivity and activity has further strengthened the organization by improving the finances and allowing reserves to grow for new program development.

OVERHEAD ALLOCATION

As academic health organizations continue to be faced with funding limitations and cutbacks, managers face the important and challenging responsibility of managing and leading with diminished resources. They must be knowledgeable of expenses—variable, fixed, direct, or indirect—and the method or methods used to allocate indirect or overhead costs.

Overhead or indirect costs for academic institutions are sometimes referred to as "voodoo" numbers, because they are not understood. For AHCs overhead is considered to be the costs for lights, heat, air conditioning, building maintenance, security, support of administrators, and so on. Overhead costs can also include data processing expenses and costs associated with operating areas such as purchasing, contracts and grants, central supply or warehouse, and libraries. The point is to alert managers to the various items that can be included under the "umbrella" of overhead and indirect costs. Managers need to be aware of this and to understand all of the costs associated with their overhead or indirect costs. Since AHCs are such complex organizational structures, typically there can be many overhead or indirect costs that a department or program supports. Customarily, overhead costs related to operating a practice plan, dean's office, or a department or ambulatory care facility are allocated by some formula back to a department or program.

Overhead for academic institutions can represent an enormous expense. In addition to understanding the expense items included in overhead, managers must also understand the formula or method for how the overhead items are allocated back to programs or departments. Are overhead costs allocated in a methodical and equitable way, or is the cost allocation allocated in a whimsical, arbitrary way? There are numerous ways to allocate cost. In the case of institutional overhead, the criterion most often used in allocating overhead is the direct expense. This means that if a program uses 20% of the direct costs, 20% of the total overhead expenses are assigned to the program whether the program uses overhead resources or not. Other criteria sometimes used in academic health centers to distribute overhead receipts will be based on a percentage of net receipts, or the square footage occupied, or clinical utilization, and so on.

In developing an overhead allocation method, it is essential to develop an allocation that is accurate, easy to understand, straightforward, meaningful, and cost effective.

Case Example

The Midwestern Physician Practice Plan was established in 1985 at Rockville University Hospitals as the central billing and collecting arm for the clinical departments. In addition, the plan is also responsible for managing the benefits program for clinical faculty members. The plan has traditionally supported their overhead by placing a "tax" on clinical departments' net receipts (including inpatient and outpatient) at a rate of 11% to 12%. Additionally however, clinical departments have also taken on some support for practice plan overhead by directly supporting training and development of practice plan coders and the support for financial counselors in the ambulatory care facility. There are several issues requiring managerial review. First, is the allocation method cost effective and equitable? Straightforward taxing methods are typically cost effective, since they require little manpower to oversee and implement. The second question is, however, is it equitable? In the case of an academic surgery department, professional fees and volume can typically be higher than other clinical departments. With an overhead cost allocation based upon a percentage of net receipts, the department then becomes the primary supporter of the plan's overhead. Does the plan, however, expend the majority of its budget for activities related to the surgery department? Are the majority of bills and collection activity associated with the department of surgery or other departments? In addition, the department now also supports some direct expenses, such as the training cost for coders and 50% of salary support for financial counselors in the clinics. The plan, therefore, over the years, has evolved to an overhead allocation method that includes a percentage of net receipts plus some direct expenses.

It is imperative that first, department managers understand what overhead they are supporting and second, how the overhead is being allocated. To develop an overhead allocation measure, one must base it on a simple, reasonable, and equitable unit. Some units, as mentioned before, may be the number of examination rooms, number of patient visits, and/or number of faculty members. The allocation should not be dysfunctional, meaning the allocation should not hinder the motivation of clinical departments to be productive. Allocation methods that utilize productivity factors (such as receipts, number of patient visits) can deter faculty and program managers from building and expanding services or programs.

BUDGETING

Dr. Glenn Shaffer, a department chair, decided to purchase a ten-speed bicycle for his daughter, Jennifer. He intended to purchase an assembled bicycle, but the salesman gave some disappointing news; the store had no assembled bikes in stock. As the box was loaded into the car, Glenn worried about assembling such a complex machine. By evening, all the parts and pieces were laid out on the rug, and Glenn knew this would be a considerable challenge. There were nuts and bolts, cabling, pads, and all types of metal tubing. How would Glenn ever re-form these pieces into the ten-speed bicycle Jennifer dreamed of? Through many tedious hours, Glenn demonstrated his tenacity as he struggled to attach part #1001AB to part #1221AZ. In a search for yet another part, he found an all-important "missing link" that would help him in the assembly process—the "schematic."

Just as the schematic is a critical link to re-forming parts and pieces into a workable bicycle, a budget is a "master blueprint" or "financial schematic" for re-forming dollars into services. The budget is a series of goals with price tags attached. Since funds in academic institutions are limited and require careful allocation, the budget process becomes a very important and critical mechanism. The budget is the department's tool or instrument for controlling and developing activities; it is the financial plan of action for the coming months and fiscal year. In AHCs budgets allocate and commit resources across multiple (sometimes competing) uses and help to clarify and reinforce action priorities, maintain coordination and facilitate evaluation and control of results. The budget should be the blueprint for transforming dollars into effective and needed services. Vinter and Kish state that the budget is "the planned and integrated use of resources."[2] The current crisis between organizational needs and budgetary constraints calls for the fundamental expression of defining the organizational objectives. The objectives or goals have to be clearly expressed. The aim of the organization is to give clear, concise information on objectives and areas of achievement and to clearly associate dollars and fund requirements. Weak objectives will lead to weak funding and budgets. A goal that cannot be clearly connected or integrated with the department's financial resources reduces the means of implementing and achieving the goal.

Few academic department managers would dispute that well-planned, well-executed budgeting is vital to fiscal health. However, the task of developing and implementing budgets can be a very unsettling experience. Although managers agree on the importance of budgets, a lack of confidence in their budgetary skills can reduce the motivation to use the tool. To be useful, a budget must be a planning device that everyone takes seriously and have a format that is easily understood.

❧ Case Example

The department of medicine at Sierra Chula Health Sciences Center conducted an annual retreat for planning. The entire staff met with one major mission—to begin budget development. The first session included a review of the mission statement (the purpose and objectives of the organization) and a review of the annual accomplishments, the current position, and the direction of the organization. The process was helpful in identifying the key areas of concentration and program development. Additional discussions included global, national, and regional concerns of the industry. The retreat allowed members of Sierra Chula to develop and recognize goals before plotting numbers on a spreadsheet. Without goals, realistic and meaningful financing development is very difficult. Far too often the process is completed in reverse, with budgets developed and then unplanned expenditures arising later. To be effective, a budget must be developed through a joint effort of members of the organization. The budget must be a meaningful, working document that forms the plan.

Once a meaningful budget is developed, it must be actively monitored throughout the fiscal year. Many budgets fail because managers fail to take aggressive and timely corrective action. According to Vinter and Kish, academic medical departments should be "budget driven, since the funding support level sets critical constraints on the scope and quality of services to be offered."[2] The budget serves little purpose if the organization is unwilling to monitor costs and then take action when it becomes apparent that expenses exceed the budget or that income has not been as high as expected. Bonini noted, "If times are good and the organization has been doing well, then a relaxation of cost consciousness may occur and a simultaneous upward trend in department budgets may also occur."[3] In monitoring the budget, the department must be able to determine what expenditures were anticipated for last month, what was actually spent last month, and how and when the organization is irrevocably committed to spend in the future. The department must be prepared to take action to modify the plan if it becomes apparent the budget cannot be met. If the organization has substantial resources to fall back on, some deviations may be acceptable without serious financial consequences.

Budget reports are also essential for monthly and yearly cumulative comparisons. Fortunately, most academic institutions have accounting departments that will generate monthly financial reports to departments. Since most academic medical departments cannot afford much deviation from the budget, a monthly review of the statements is critical. There are serious consequences when actual revenue falls short of projections. The organization must know where it stands on a timely basis. Academic departments should review reports once they are received, which is typically within 15 to 20 days of the end of the prior month. As Aron Wildausky stated, "The budget is the lifeblood of the organization, the financial reflection of what the organization intends to do. . . . There can be no doubt that lack of comprehensiveness in budgeting means that in making a specific decision important values affected by that decision are neglected at that time."[4]

The preparation of annual budgets and budget projections forces organizations to look ahead and constructively plan, clarify objectives and *responsibility centers,* identify results, and develop an awareness of expenditures and revenue (see the box at the top of p. 256). As Vinter and Kish observed, "Budget development for a succeeding fiscal year must be done during a current year to service uninterrupted continuing support."[2] For example, an academic medical department's fiscal year is from July to June. With the budget due each year at the end of March, the director of administration initiates the budget process for the following fiscal year by the first of the calendar year. A spreadsheet is prepared in advance of the meetings indicating actual expenses for the first 6 months of the fiscal year and a projection of final figures for the fiscal year. The director and division chiefs then meet. There are

STEPS IN DEVELOPING A BUDGET

1. Prepare a list of goals or objectives for the coming year.
2. Reevaluate the priority given to existing programs.
3. Estimate the cost of goals. Last year's actual expenses and last year's budget will be a starting point. For new programs, a substantial amount of work may be necessary to accurately estimate the costs involved.
4. Estimate expected income of the organization with careful consideration given to the economic climate in the profession. Programs could be expanded if they were financially viable or contracted if they were not.
5. Compare estimated income with estimated expenditures.
6. Submit budget for approval.

SPREADSHEET FOR PREPARING A CLINICAL FISCAL YEAR BUDGET

| | Actual Current Year | | | | | | Budget For New Year | | | Increase or Decrease (%) |
| | To Date (First 6 mo) | | | Projected Year-End | | | | | | |
	IP	OP	Total	IP	OP	Total	IP	OP	Total	
Revenue										
Gross charges										
Net receipts										
Collection rate										
Total revenue										
Expenses										
Salaries										
Benefits										
Supplies										
Communication										
Printing										
Travel										
Fixed charges										
Equipment										
Total expenses										
Difference										

IP = inpatient; OP = outpatient.

two planned budget meetings—preliminary and final. The preliminary meeting is to review the budget data and to begin program planning. The final budget meeting reviews all the program needs, required recruitment/staff, equipment, and so on, along with projections on receipt levels based on approval by the chair. During this time the department also reviews fee schedules, contracts, and other matters for any adjustments or additions. The box at the bottom of p. 256 shows the spreadsheet used to begin the budget process. Revenue is grouped first, then expenses. Since a budget spreadsheet is done for each division and cost center, the chair, administrator, and division chief can review and quickly analyze the activities and fiscal condition of each program.

৯ Case Example

Dr. John Lacey became the new chair of the department of medicine at Chandler Health Center. He knew that within 6 months of his appointment he would be in the midst of preparing budgets for the following fiscal year. Dr. Lacey wanted to control costs. He wanted to make sure, in a funding period of resource cutbacks, unknown new reimbursement plans, and volatile clinical activity, that the budget was conservative yet could also include some of his visions for new program development. Dr. Lacey reviewed the department's trust fund and financial reports and quickly learned that his largest budgeted line items were for faculty, staff, and benefits. Yet he could not find a report that listed all names and position titles of the faculty and staff he was funding, nor what division of medicine (such as Cardiology, Pulmonary, Geriatrics) they belonged in. Dr. Lacey's first step was to sit down with his administrator, Luca Bennett, and develop a report that would place all faculty and staff into appropriate cost centers with current funding sources and position titles (see the box below).

ORGANIZATIONAL MEMBER LISTING AND FUNDING BY COST CENTER

Administration Cost Center		Funding Sources					
Employee	Title	State	Grants	Trust	Practice Plan	Contracts	Totals
Lacey	Chair	54,900	15,000		62,000		131,900
Bennett	Administrator	24,000			42,000		66,000
Fiorino	Associate professor	32,500	24,000	11,000	44,000	5,000	116,500
Alabboud	Assistant professor	28,400	5,000		47,000		80,400
Total faculty		139,800	44,000	11,000	195,000	5,000	394,800
Hinajosa	Secretary				22,000		22,000
Miller	Editorial assistant				27,400		27,400
Tapp	Accountant		5,000		26,000		31,000
Stepanek	Administrative assistant	6,000			20,000		26,000
Robinson	Data base coordinator	9,000			20,000		29,000
Gupta	Research technician		11,000		12,000		23,000
Total staff		15,000	16,000	0	127,400	0	158,400
Total Cost Center		169,800	76,000	11,000	449,800	5,000	711,600

Luca Bennett prepared these reports in the form of spreadsheets, and together they sat down to review them. Dr. Lacey was shocked to find a number of faculty and staff, funded by his administrative cost center, of whom he had no knowledge of their purpose or function. In tedious detail they reviewed each report by cost center and identified the individuals and functions and the funding sources. They then conducted another tedious review to determine whether it was appropriate for these organizational members to receive support by administration or whether they would be more appropriately funded by another cost center. On the initial review of his administrative cost center budget, Dr. Lacey found that he was funding personnel line items at a total of more than $400,000. After reviewing the budget and identifying positions and responsibility areas, Dr. Lacey was able to reduce the personnel line items by more than $185,000.

Budgets should be considered a *fiscal hub* for academic health centers—the financial center for incoming revenue and outgoing expenditures (Figure 14-1). The fiscal hub represents in financial terms the *result* of organizational goals and objectives. If organizations prepare budgets only to present board members with a financial document or only to review them annually, such budgets are a waste of time.

The role of budgets as fiscal hubs or intermediaries focuses not only on budget development but also on the management of financial activities throughout the fiscal year. For the budget to function as the hub, several areas must be consolidated and integrated (see the box on p. 259). The first area is the development of objectives and goals that have been agreed on by the chair and/or board. Second, since the budget will be used as a management tool, the budget needs to be formatted into increments to transfer into the financial statements. Third, the financial statements must be reviewed by management periodically and compared with the budget. Finally, the organization must be prepared to take corrective action when necessary.

Once total expected income and revenue are examined, projected income is compared with projected expenses. Usually, expenses exceed income. When this occurs, management must conduct a careful review and make some critical decisions. What are the really important programs? Can any line items within the budget be reduced first before an entire program or service is eliminated? Can a given program still function with a budget cut? What costs can be reduced? The legitimacy of expenditures is also carefully reviewed? For example, if a travel budget line item for a program is based on $7000 per member, will a $2000 reduction per member substantially affect the program? Careful consideration must be given to the reliability of the data on estimated income and expenditures; overestimates or underestimates could cause serious difficulties. Especially if the organization has small cash reserves or has little likelihood of getting additional funds quickly, a realistic safety margin should be built into the budget.

Most accounting guidelines suggest that reports should be produced and reviewed monthly or at least quarterly, within 15 to 20 days of the end of the period. Reports produced at a later time are outdated and therefore not meaningful. The management team or staff members should be prepared to meet after reports are generated so they can act on deviations while there is still time. The reports should show

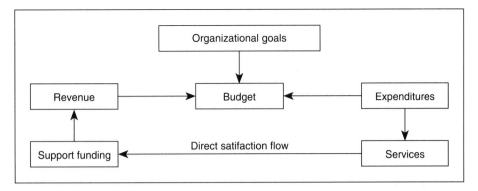

Figure 14-1. The budget as a fiscal hub.

DEVELOPING A MEANINGFUL BUDGET

1. Administrators should not be overly optimistic in estimating income. Overestimates can be the department's downfall if there is no margin for error.
2. Realistic figures must be used, or the budget will have little meaning.
3. Overestimate expenditures and underestimate revenue.
4. Total expected income should be compared with the expense of achieving the objectives/ goals.
5. The budget must be well conceived, and approved by the board.
6. The department administrator must be prepared to take action when the actual financial activity exceeds the budgeted revenue and expenditures.

---

budgeted and actual data. For example, a report for the first 3 months of the fiscal year should compare the budget with the actual revenue and expenditures for the first 3 months.

Budgets should be formally presented to the board and other organizational members, not just because of bylaws or as a matter of protocol, but for the higher purpose of creating a sense of unity and commitment among the group to the resulting plan of action.

THE ROLE OF DEBT

Traditionally, debt has been feared by academic institutions, especially at the departmental level, and has been considered fiscally irresponsible. The fear has been based on the ideas of reckless spending and its being a burden to future chairs, directors, and deans. However, as Peterson notes, " The fear of deficits or debt is wrong, not because there are no seeds of truth with the general concern about debt, but because so much of the sermon is devoted to aspects which are not true."[5] We include a discussion of debt in this chapter not to promote or encourage the idea of debt to managers in academics, but to consider the positive role debt can and does play under certain circumstances and in light of certain criteria.

Before an AHC manager can analyze potential indebtedness, two major criteria should be reviewed. First, is the borrowing essential or nonessential? Robinson says, "Debt should be a constructive measure that recognizes the vital role of debt in organizations. The task is to make future generations glad a debt was taken on by the organization."[6] Second, what size deficit or debt is being considered? The size of the debt must be viewed in relation to the effects of debt and the point at which the level of deficit becomes unbearable for the organization; that is, you cannot say that debt is too high except in relation to the effects of the debt on the organization. You must also determine whether borrowing is feasible. "Borrowing from a commercial institution may be forbidden or payment of interest charges may not be permitted," Vinter and Kish observe. If borrowing is possible, the organization should have a superb accounting system in place and keep clear records of authorizations and repayment transactions."[2]

Deficits can enable AHCs with financing for a major undertaking. But what criteria need to be reviewed before an academic institution enters into debt? First, *capacity to pay:* All AHCs must review their ability to pay the debt before they commit the organization to a deficit. Capacity to pay includes not only the ability of the organization to pay, but also the *potential* possession of resources—that is, resources both developed and latent. Second, *economic background:* How does the organization fit into the environment at the time debt is being considered, and what will the probable economic conditions be during the period of the debt and up to maturity? Third, *the size of the organization:* What is the size of the organization in relation to other organizations in the same field? What are the prospects for organizational expansion in future years? "Although not necessarily so, there is a fair relationship between the size of the organization and the level of resources," Winakor notes.[7] Fourth, *history of the organization:* What is the organization's reputation, past performance, character of management, and innovative ability? Fifth, *operating reserve levels:* The operating reserve level reflects accumulated funds from prior years. The composition of the operating reserve level must be reviewed, since the mere presence of an operating reserve does not indicate a superior financial position. For instance, have these funds been earmarked for a specific planned purpose? What are the sources for and nature of the funds in the operating reserve? Although the level may be misleading, the other consideration is that the reserve may be used temporarily for meeting maturing obligations. Says Winakor, "Debts maturing in the period when these funds are not required for their final purpose are likely to be repaid because funds thus temporarily free can be diverted if necessary."[7] Sixth, *review of assets and liabilities:* A review of balance and income statements, the long-range forecast and plan, the direction of the funds into the organization, and obligations on those funds is beneficial. For example, is it possible to divert some of the incoming funds to purposes such as debt repayment? The amount of "free funds" may be an important determining factor in whether an organization should go into debt.

The points listed are just a few of the determining factors that an organization should review before entering into debt. There are many others, and no single factor can be classified as *the* factor. To be fiscally responsible, debt management requires a careful weighing of the concepts presented in this section. An analysis of the mission and policies of the organization and related economic and financial data is necessary to resolve the debt question. The nature of the organization and of its properties, its type of operation, its resources, and similar features should all be weighed and considered. A careful appraisal of all of the above factors bearing on the present and future should permit a final decision for the organization.

COST/BENEFIT ANALYSIS

One of the first applications of cost/benefit analysis can be traced to 1902, when the River and Harbor Act directed the Army Corps of Engineers to assess the costs and benefits of all river and harbor projects. Today the applications of cost/benefit analyses include justifying various types of public investments and expenditures ranging from defense projects to health programs.

AHCs must at each step along the way question costs and how much additional benefits cost. As Anthony and Herzlinger state, "There is a need to look at proposals, at least in a general way, in terms of whether the benefits are probably worth more than the costs. The relationship may not be quantifiable, but this way of looking at problems tends to distinguish the factors that are relevant from those that are not relevant."[8] Cost/benefit analysis suggests the best alternative way of reaching a goal. Usually, all things being equal, the lower cost is selected.

Cost/benefit analysis cannot make decisions, but it does help management to focus on the consequences that can be estimated in quantitative terms and aids in selecting alternatives. Cost/benefit analysis is an analytical method that enumerates the advantages and disadvantages of alternative actions. It provides a specific organizing framework and a set of procedures to summarize information and display the tradeoffs associated with these actions—generally in monetary terms. The analysis judges action based on an efficiency criterion and requires resources to be allocated to their highest valued use. The role of the analysis is in the policy and management of the organization. When the capital equipment budget committee for the operating room meets, for example, the analysis can evaluate the plausibility of the cost over measurable benefits. The analysis is not the final decision-maker, but it is a useful tool in leading management to the ultimate decision. For any organization, decision-making is a gamble, with the manager attempting to achieve the "best deal" for the organization, yet with incomplete knowledge. Benefits assessments assist in the complex process by reducing the uncertainty about facts and formalizing the judgment about values.

Understanding cost data is important not only for considering benefits but also for cost allocation and to associate output costs with output charges or, in a health care setting, charges paid for services versus costs of service. Every AHC today must be informed about costs and benefits; they handle millions of dollars of funding each year while walking a precarious path between rising costs and inadequate revenue. Academic health centers cannot survive without the best possible cost analysis. The funding gap between need and available resources is deep and promises to grow deeper. From measuring performance and productivity, debt capacity, equipment proposals, and fund-raising activities, cost/benefit analysis continues to play an active role as a component of fiscal responsibility.

CONCLUSION

Understanding the numbers requires much more than a look at the financial statements. It is a master blend of fiscal literacy, knowledge of cost allocation, use of budgeting skills and techniques, beneficial and useful financial reporting, and an understanding of the role of debt and cost/benefit analysis. In today's economic environment, understanding the numbers is a crucial challenge to managers in academics.

Ultimately, understanding the numbers ensures the effective and efficient use of resources and will assist in positioning organizations for the future. No amount of long-term planning will lead to an outstanding department if the basic financial aspects are not understood, budgeted, and allocated appropriately.

BIBLIOGRAPHY

*1. Ridky J, Johnson G Jr, Sheldon G. (1991). Understanding the numbers in academic medical centers: Looking beyond the financial statements. *Journal of Medical Practice Management, 6,* 182-185.
*2. Vinter RD & Kish RK. (1989). *Budgeting for not-for-profit organizations.* New York: The Free Press.
3. Bonini CP. (1963). *Simulation of information and decision systems in the firm.* Englewood Cliffs, NJ: Prentice-Hall, p 19.
4. Wildausky A. (1964). *The politics of the budgetary process.* Boston: Little, Brown & Co, p 128.
5. Peterson RA. (1964). *Debt in a new environment.* New York: New York University, p 3.
6. Robinson MA. (1959). *Debt and the american economy.* Washington, DC: Brookings Institute, p 10.
7. Winakor AH. (1936). *Capacity to pay current debts.* Urbana: University of Illinois, p 20.
8. Anthony RN & Herzlinger RE. (1980). *Management control in nonprofit organizations.* Homewood, Ill: Richard D Irwin, p 288.

*Asterisk indicates an article or book that is particularly informative and helpful.

CHAPTER 15

Current Legal Issues:
Discrimination and Affirmative Action

Laura N. Gasaway

We are going to pass the civil rights bill. Nothing has happened to deter us from that course. The demands of justice and decency make that necessary. . . . I believe America stands for full and equal rights of all its citizens, for the realization of freedom and justice for all its people, for equality of treatment, and equality of opportunity for all its citizens in every sphere of national life. — April 9, 1964

This entire approach to equal opportunity in employment is as full of commonsense as it is of equity. We cannot afford the luxury of depriving the nation of manpower or brainpower. — April 21, 1964

PRESIDENT LYNDON B. JOHNSON

The legal environment in which the administrator of an academic department must function has changed dramatically in recent years. The body of law pertaining to personnel practices has expanded greatly, and a manager's freedom has been constrained in matters such as employee selection, salary termination, conditions of employment, and benefits. On the other hand, the current legislative framework was necessary because voluntary measures had not been successful in improving the working conditions of the average university employee. The laws relating to personnel practices have been instrumental in providing workers with a physically safe work environment, greater job security, privacy protection, and other employee rights and benefits. Such laws also help ensure that every individual, regardless of age, race, gender, religion, national origin, or disability, has an equal right to any job for which he or she is qualified.

This chapter focuses on law relating to personnel administration. It does not cover some of the more complex legal issues, such as medical ethics and patient care, that academic department managers encounter; these are beyond the scope of this chapter.

EMPLOYMENT DISCRIMINATION

Equal employment legislation in the United States is of fairly recent vintage. Although there were antecedents before the 1960s, the first comprehensive antidiscrimination in employment statute was Title VII of the Civil Rights Act of 1964.[1] Commonly referred to as *Title VII,* the primary aim of the statute was to make overt discrimination illegal in all phases of private employment. The act does not guarantee that women and minorities will be hired for vacant positions or promoted within an educational institution; rather, it requires that they be fairly considered and neither excluded nor hindered because of race, sex, religion, or national origin.[2] Employees who bring successful Title VII actions are entitled to back pay, and the court may order reinstatement or hiring and award attorneys' fees and costs for employees who prevail in litigation.[3]

Title VII covers employers with 15 or more employees engaged in interstate commerce; colleges and universities have been covered since a 1972 amendment.[4] Title VII embraces all aspects of the employment process from recruitment, advertising, and hiring to salary, terminations, layoffs, and retirement. The act created the Equal Employment Opportunity Commission (EEOC) to enforce its provisions.[5] Along with other agencies, the EEOC helped develop the 1978 Uniform Guidelines on Employee Selection Procedures.[6] The Uniform Guidelines assist employers in understanding the provisions of the act and guide enforcement agencies. Generally, an administrator must look at an individual's qualifications and avoid making hiring decisions on the basis of racial, ethnic, or sexual stereotypes. In promotions, an employer should establish neutral criteria for eligibility for promotion and should not disqualify individuals because of their gender, religion, race, or ethnicity.

The Civil Rights Act of 1991 was enacted in response to a series of U.S. Supreme Court decisions that limited the enforcement of Title VII and created a heavier burden for plaintiffs in employment discrimination suits. Among other important matters, the act expanded the damages provisions available under Title VII. Before 1991, compensatory damages were not available under Title VII. Now victims of *intentional* discrimination may receive compensatory damages for future pecuniary losses, emotional pain, suffering, mental anguish, loss of enjoyment of life and other nonpecuniary losses.[7] The act also provides for punitive damages, but they are available only against private employers and not federal, state, or local government employers.[8] There are caps on compensatory and punitive damages for all Title VII actions except race discrimination, based not on the seriousness of the discrimination but on the size of the employer's workforce. For academic departments, it is the size of the university's total workforce that determines the damage cap[9]:

No. of Employees	Damage Awards
15-100	$ 50,000
101-200	$100,000
201-500	$200,000
500 or more	$300,000

The higher damage award potential, coupled with the new right to jury trial for employers seeking compensatory or punitive damages,[10] will probably mean an increase in the number of employment discrimination suits brought.

Academic administrators responsible for personnel management must be aware of the antidiscrimination requirements of Title VII and must comply with its mandate. This is even more critical today because of the increased damages available to claimants. Fortunately for managers, the college or university will have established procedures in place to ensure compliance and fairness in dealing with employees and applicants for positions. The manager's responsibility thus is to comply with the institution's procedures and to function within the spirit of the law.

Title VII
Covers employers with 15 or more employees
All aspects of employment
EEOC enforcement
Back pay and compensatory damages

Religion

Two of the protected categories require additional explanation: religion and sex. Under Title VII, an employer is required to make reasonable accommodation for the religious practices and beliefs of employees. This has been held to include the wearing of religious dress and working on religious holidays.[11] The area is not static; courts continue to clarify what constitutes "reasonable accommodation." Clearly, an employer may not accommodate one worker's religious preference to refrain from work on certain holidays observed by his or her religion if such accommodation unduly burdens other employees who must fill in for the celebrant.[12] Because of the relatively large workforces of academic institutions, religious accommodation has not proved difficult for most.

Sex Discrimination

In the area of sex discrimination, there are some unique issues: pregnancy and maternity, sexual harassment, and compensation because of a statute that applies only to gender. Each is treated below.

Pregnancy and maternity

Since only women become pregnant, any discrimination on the basis of pregnancy constitutes sex discrimination.[13] Congress specifically amended Title VII to make it absolutely clear that discrimination on the basis of pregnancy is sex discrimination. Thus an employer may not refuse to hire a woman because she is pregnant. Likewise, if the employer provides health or disability insurance for employees, it may not exclude only pregnancy from coverage.[14] If an employer's health insurance provides benefits for pregnant employees, and if all medical conditions are covered for the spouses of female employees, then the insurance must include pregnancy benefits for the spouses of male employees.[15] Further, an employer may neither terminate the employment of a pregnant employee nor require or mandate a specified maternity leave period for employees.[16] On the other hand, some states offer increased benefits for pregnancy and maternity, such as paid maternity leaves and a guarantee that an employee on maternity leave may return to her job. The U.S. Supreme Court has upheld the recognition of the uniqueness of pregnancy and maternity and thus allowed special treatment for maternity; it would not permit a special disadvantage for pregnant workers that would frustrate the goals of Title VII.

In *California Federal Savings & Loan Association v. Guerra,*[17] the Court upheld a state statute that provided greater benefits for pregnant employees than were mandated by the 1978 amendments. The state of California provided that an employer must hold a job available for 1 year for any employee on maternity leave. The provision was challenged as discriminatory against men and nonpregnant persons, whose job were not held for them for a year if they were on disability leave.[18] The Court reasoned that a state was not prohibited from going further than the federal law in passing laws that guaranteed that a pregnant woman would not be penalized by losing her job for taking maternity leave.[19] To give women equal opportunity in employment, the Court recognized that it might be necessary to treat pregnancy as a unique condition and provide such benefits as guaranteed return to enable women to participate in the workforce equally with men.[20]

Another important employment issue involving pregnant women and women of child-bearing years is whether an employer may implement a fetal protection policy and exclude women from work areas where exposure to hazardous chemicals is a condition of employment. Typically, jobs that require exposure to various types of hazards are recognized as dangerous and are compensated at a higher rate than are other jobs. Employers have voiced concern about their potential liability for damage to a fetus for exposure to x-ray equipment,[21] and more recently, to the presence of lead in the workplace environment. The problems posed by lead exposure have the potential of even greater damage, because the danger is not only to pregnant women but also to women who later become pregnant. Since the residual effects of lead exposure may be found in the blood of the worker for up to 2 years after she ceases to be exposed to lead, all women of child-bearing age could be at risk.[22] In 1991 the U.S. Supreme Court held in *United Auto Workers v. Johnson Controls, Inc.*[23] that an employer may not exclude women from the higher-paying jobs that require work in a lead-contaminated work environment. The Court found that the antidiscrimination provisions of Title VII could not be thwarted by an employer's desire to avoid liability for fetal damage, which pitted women's employment rights against those of an unborn fetus. Title VII extends to workers and not to their potential offspring.[24]

There have been studies on abnormally high miscarriage rates among workers exposed to computer video display terminals for extended periods, but the evidence is contradictory at present.[25] Suffice it to say that an employer could excuse a

Reprinted by permission of the Center for Creative Leadership, *Issues and Observations*, © 1992.

pregnant worker from the aspects of her job that required working at a computer terminal if she so requested. According to the *Johnson Controls* decision, however, the employer could not do so on its own initiative. If computer terminals are later found to cause miscarriages, an employer should warn pregnant employees of the potential danger but let them decide whether to request an altered job assignment.

Pregnant Employees
Covered by Title VII as sex discrimination
An employer:
    May not refuse to hire or promote
    May not exclude from insurance
    Could offer greater benefits than mandated

Sexual harassment

While most people recognize that an employee should not be subjected to demands for sexual favors on the job, only recently has the Supreme Court recognized sexual harassment as sex discrimination. It is precisely because of the person's sex that he or she is subjected to such treatment.[26] The key issue in a sexual harassment complaint is whether an employer is liable to the employee for the harassing conduct on the part of supervisors, co-workers, or clients. Conduct that qualifies as sexual harassment may range from offensive sexual innuendos to physical assault, and courts tend to consider a victim's response to such conduct in determining whether the conduct is sexual harassment. In other words, some employees enjoy and participate in sexual jokes, whereas other workers would consider them harassment. Although not dispositive of the issue, whether the victim has participated in such workplace banter may be relevant to a court in determining whether particular conduct constitutes sexual harassment in a given situation.

The EEOC promulgated guidelines that define sexual harassment as unwelcome sexual advances, requests for sexual favors, and other verbal or physical conduct of a sexual nature that occur under any of three conditions: (1) where submission is either explicitly or implicitly a term or condition of employment, (2) where submission or rejection of the conduct forms the basis for an employment action, or (3) where the conduct has either the purpose or effect of substantially interfering with the individual's work performance or creating an intimidating, hostile, or offensive working environment.[27] Thus any retaliatory action by a supervisor such as firing or denial of a promotion or raise because of a refusal to submit to sexual demands creates liability for the employer. This is the so-called quid pro quo type of harassment, and the early case dealt with situations in which the employee usually had been fired or forced to resign because she rejected the supervisor's advances. Courts have had no difficulty in finding employer liability for quid pro quo cases.

In *Meritor Savings Bank v. Vinson,*[28] the Supreme Court endorsed the definitional portion of the EEOC guidelines, including the "offensive or hostile work environment" part of the definition.[29] In hostile work environment cases, the woman suffers no adverse employment action by her refusal to comply with her supervisor's sexual demands; rather, enduring the jokes, innuendos, requests for sexual favors, and the like becomes a condition of employment. She must either put up with the conduct or leave her job. Clearly, in most situations, an employer is liable for the actions of supervisory personnel. The EEOC guidelines impose strict liability on the employer regardless of whether the employer specifically prohibited harassing conduct or even knew about it but failed to take immediate and appropriate corrective action.[30] The *Meritor* opinion does not go so far as to impose strict liability on employers for hostile work environment situations, but the Court does indicate that, in general, principles of agency law would apply in determining liability.[31] Liability for harassment of an employee by fellow employees was not addressed in *Meritor;* however, the EEOC guidelines state that the employer is liable for failure to take immediate and appropriate action if the employer knew or should have known of the co-worker's conduct.[32] In other words, the employer is responsible for maintaining a work environment that is free from harassment.

A recent case involving co-worker harassment is likely to have considerable impact in this area, not only because it deals with co-worker behavior, but also because it adopts a new standard to determine whether certain conduct constitutes sexual harassment. In *Ellison v. Brady*[33] a woman was repeatedly asked for dates by a co-worker who appeared to be fixated on her. He wrote "love notes," maintaining that they had some type of relationship, which they did not. She complained of this behavior and he was transferred to another office for a time, during which he continued to send her love letters. Although the woman was frantic over his behavior, neither the employer nor the trial court found this conduct to be harassing. Instead, it was characterized as isolated and trivial.[34]

The conservative Ninth Circuit U.S. Court of Appeals reversed the trial court and determined that the correct standard for judging harassing conduct was the *reasonable woman standard*. The court held that the proper perspective was that of the victim, especially since women disproportionately suffer rapes and sexual assaults. Therefore, when a woman is subjected to milder forms of sexual harassment, she probably worries whether the harasser's conduct is merely a prelude to a more violent sexual assault.[35] Further, the court made it clear that the *reasonable person standard* was not the appropriate standard, since it tends to be male biased and systematically ignores the reality of women's experiences.[36] Should this become the standard in other circuits, hostile work environment cases will be considerably easier for victims to prove, since courts would have to apply the reasonable woman standard.

The EEOC guidelines focus on voluntary action by the employer to publicize the seriousness with which the employer views sexual harassment. Employers are encouraged to make employees aware of the law and to develop complaint and investigatory procedures for harassment complaints. Further, employers should educate management personnel about sexual harassment and its prevention.[37] The Supreme Court recognized the importance of such employer-initiated programs and indicated that employer liability might be lessened if affirmative steps to stop sexual harassment were undertaken.[38] At a minimum, academic administrators must take complaints seriously, investigate them fairly, and, if such complaints are found to be accurate, take corrective action. The worst thing an administrator can do is to assume that the complaint is groundless. Departmental administrators who have found themselves at the center of a widely publicized sexual harassment claim usually failed to take the complaint seriously at the initial stage and conduct a proper investigation. The investigator must maintain confidentiality throughout the investigation stage. Some writers even recommend that an independent investigator be appointed by the administrator.[39] Not only to comply with the *Vinson* Court's reasoning, but also because it is sound business practice, most educational institutions have developed mechanisms for handling harassment complaints from students, staff, and faculty. Educating supervisors and all employees about the fact that sexual harassment is illegal and that the department will take corrective disciplinary action goes a long way toward eliminating harassment in an academic department.[39a]

In 1992 the U.S. Supreme Court decided an extremely important sexual harassment case, *Franklin v. Gwinett*.[40] The victim in this case was not an employee but was a high school student who sued under Title IX of the Education Amendments of 1972.[41] The student claimed she had suffered quid pro quo harassment by a male teacher, and the school closed the investigation when he resigned his employment. The Court recognized that this was intentional discrimination and that the school could be forced to pay monetary damages.[42] Although this case did not involve employment, it may be applicable to situations in which the victim is both a student and an employee, such as a laboratory or research assistant. The potential damage award should make educational institutions take particular precautions to protect student employees from sexual harassment.

Steps to Prevent Harassment

1. Develop an antiharassment policy:
   Disseminate it to all employees.
   Post it in a prominent place.
2. Train supervisors to:
   Know about harassment and the policy.
   Be alert to inappropriate workplace behavior.
   Recognize their own responsibility if they tolerate such conduct from others.
3. Follow up with employees:
   Remind employees about the policy frequently.
   Conduct harassment policy sessions at least annually.
4. Listen and take rumors seriously.
5. Investigate complaints.
6. Take disciplinary action when appropriate.

Compensation

Title VII covers salary and benefits, but there are several issues regarding compensation that uniquely pertain to gender-based discrimination. Even before the 1964 Civil Rights Act, Congress passed the Equal Pay Act of 1963,[43] which guaranteed to women equal pay for equal work. Subsequent cases and administrative interpretation determined that equal work meant substantial equality as opposed to absolute equality of work.[44] To determine substantial equality, jobs are compared on the basis of equal skill, equal effort, and equal responsibility, performed under similar working conditions.[45] The actual job duties are examined to evaluate equality of work instead of simply comparing written job descriptions.[46] In any event, to recover under the Equal Pay Act (EPA), a claimant must prove that an employee of the opposite sex is performing substantially equal work and receiving higher wages or benefits. Further, the reason for the pay differential must not be one of the statutory exceptions: a bona fide seniority system, a bona fide merit system, a piece-work or quantity system, or any factor other than sex.[47]

The EPA has been used successfully to eliminate pay bias in factory jobs, but it has been used less successfully for professional and managerial jobs. There are, however, some cases involving faculty members that have been decided in favor of the lower-paid female faculty member under the EPA.[48] These cases frequently couple Title VII and EPA compensation claims.

Recognizing the failure of the EPA to eliminate salary inequities, university workers in recent years have pushed for pay parity. In American society, jobs that are predominantly occupied by females tend to receive lower pay and have less status than jobs that are traditionally held by males. An examination of this problem has led many states to conduct comparable worth or salary parity studies that attempt to evaluate jobs on the basis of their value or worth to the employer. Although it eliminated a potential technical stumbling block to such cases under Title VII,[49] the U.S. Supreme Court has yet to hear a comparable worth or pay parity case. Some state governments have moved forward to implement pay parity for public employees, but other states have not done so.[50]

Equal Pay Act
Two or more employees
Performing substantially equal work
Covers salary and benefits

Glass Ceiling

Within the past 2 years, the U.S. Department of Labor has recognized that although women and minorities have been hired in record numbers, they have not moved into upper management as these numbers would predict. In fact, evidence from research conducted by a variety of groups ranging from universities to corporations document a dearth of minorities and women in management—the so-called glass ceiling, above which individuals in these groups do not rise.[51] The Department of Labor began a pilot study of the glass ceiling in nine Fortune 500 companies and then introduced initiatives to eliminate the glass ceiling.[52] A follow-up study was released in 1992,[53] and the Secretary of Labor has begun to work with the Small Business Administration to eliminate barriers to the promotion of women and minorities in upper management positions.

Although efforts to date have been directed at the private sector, they well could be extended to the public sector, where similar barriers exist. At a minimum, academic department administrators should be aware these barriers exist and work to ensure that women and minorities are promoted into management positions.

Age Discrimination

Another class of employees is protected from employment discrimination under the Age Discrimination in Employment Act (ADEA).[54] Although this is a separate statute, the prohibitions are quite similar to those found in Title VII. Basically, all employers with 20 or more employees are covered and all employment actions are included. Persons who have reached the age of 40 may not be discriminated against in hiring, promotion, termination, retirement, and so on. Until recently, persons older than age 70 were excluded, but Congress now has removed the upper age limit.[55] The primary effect of this recent amendment is that there no longer is a mandatory retirement age, although under a special exemption, institutions of higher education may retain compulsory retirement at age 70 for tenured faculty until 1994.[56]

Most of the ADEA cases deal with terminations or forced early retirement, as opposed to failure to hire. ADEA claimants tend to be more successful than other employment discrimination claimants. There are several possible reasons: (1) a recognition of how difficult it will be for a terminated older worker to find another job; (2) the right to jury trials,[57] which was not available under Title VII until 1991, made attorneys more willing to represent ADEA plaintiffs; (3) the availability of liquidated damages, which can double the back pay award[58]; and (4) jury sympathy. Jurors, as well as everyone else, realize that they will get older and may be faced with age discrimination; they may not be able to imagine what it is to be a member of a minority group or female.

Academic institutions will face considerable difficulty over the next few years with the elimination of mandatory retirement for tenured faculty, and schools probably will develop various enticements to encourage retirements. Although there are many instances in which excellent and productive faculty members had to retire at age 70, there also are instances in which universities have been able to terminate ineffective tenured teachers only when they reached age 70. After 1994, the only way an institution will be able to compel a tenured faculty member to retire is to demonstrate incompetence, which will be both difficult to prove and emotionally difficult for the academic administrator and the individual faculty member. Even schools that offer enticements to retire early still are likely to have to face the unpleasant task of challenging the competency of some older tenured faculty members. A corollary problem is that with the elimination of compulsory retirement at age 70, coupled with static growth in academic programs, fewer tenure slots will be available to newer faculty members. Managing a department's faculty resources and tenure-track slots will be even more challenging after 1994.

Age Discrimination in Employment Act

20 or more employees
Covers people age 40 and older
Covers all aspects of employment
No mandatory retirement after 1994

Discrimination Against Persons With Disabilities

In July 1992, the employment provisions of Americans With Disabilities Act (ADA) became effective.[59] Both private and public employers are included. The basic provisions of the act cover employers with 25 or more employees until July 26, 1994, and for 15 or more employees after that date, but the act excludes the federal government as an employer. It prohibits discrimination against individuals with disabilities by a variety of entitles including those which provide employment. Some of its provisions are coextensive with the earlier Vocational Rehabilitation Act of 1973,[60] which applies to government contractors, agencies of the federal government and other programs or activities that receive federal funds.[61] For example, the three-pronged definition of *disability* is consistent with the earlier statute. An individual is deemed to have a disability if he or she (1) has a physical or mental impairment that substantially limits one or more of life's major activities, (2) has a record of such an impairment, or (3) is regarded as having such an impairment.[62] The central directive of the employment portion of the ADA is to prohibit discrimination against a person because of the person's disability in regard to job application procedures, hiring, advancement or discharge, compensation, training and other terms, conditions, and privileges of employment.[63] At the same time, the act contains a near blanket prohibition against any preemployment inquiry into the medical condition of a job applicant. This includes not being able to ask about the extent or severity of even an apparent disability, either on an application form or in an interview. Further, employers may not require applicants to submit to a medical examination to determine whether and to what extent the applicant is disabled.[64]

Although the act is recent and its accompanying regulations are new, it is clear that only those individuals with disabilities who are also *qualified* for the job will receive protection under the act. A court certainly will consider the employer's assessment of what functions are essential to a particular job, but an employer is prohibited from evaluating a disabled individual's qualifications for the job based on the ability to perform marginal tasks. The starting point is to evaluate which job functions the applicant or employee would actually have to perform.[65]

An employer may establish physical or psychological standards for a particular job but may not withdraw an offer of employment based on a disabled applicant's failure to meet that standard unless the standard is both "job related" and "consistent with business necessity." A job-related standard is one that measures a legitimate qualification for a particular position.[66] An example of a job-related standard is typing ability for a clerical job. "Consistent with business necessity" means that the standard is related to the ability to perform an essential function of the job. An example for a firefighter's job might be the ability to carry more than 100 pounds, because it is necessary for firefighters to be able to carry an unconscious person from a burning building.[67] Further, an individual may remain qualified for the position even if he or she requires reasonable accommodation in order to perform those functions.

Reasonable accommodation is the key concept under the ADA; it is triggered by a request from an employee or applicant. Such reasonable accommodation might include making existing facilities accessible, the restructuring of jobs, modification of work schedules, modification or acquisition of equipment, and providing of readers and interpretators.[68] Unlike other antidiscrimination statutes, which require employers to ignore certain characteristics such as race or gender, the ADA imposes on employers an affirmative obligation to assist disabled applicants or employees to overcome barriers to equal employment. The employer should work with the person to determine whether a reasonable accommodation could be achieved that would permit the applicant or employee to preform the job.[69] It could include reassigning a disabled employee to a vacant position if all other attempts at accommodation have failed.[70] The only way an employer can avoid making reasonable accommodation is if it causes undue hardship. *Undue hardship* is to be judged by enumerated criteria, which include the nature and cost of the accommodation, the overall financial resources of the facility, the number of persons employed, the effect on expenses and resources, and the type of operations of the entity.[71] These factors indicate that the pivotal consideration in determining whether a requested accommodation causes undue hardship is not its cost in the abstract but whether this particular employer is able to bear the costs.[72] There is no bright line test to determine whether a requested accommodation causes an undue hardship. Rather, it embraces a relative standard and will be judged on a case-by-case basis. Even when the accommodation requested by the applicant or employee would not impose an undue hardship, the employer is not obligated to provide that particular accommodation if it is not necessary to the performance of that particular employee or if the employer would rather provide some other equally effective yet reasonable accommodation.[73]

The ADA is the most important antidiscrimination legislation in a decade. The act is important not only because it expands protection for disabled persons, but also because it helps clarify existing laws that relate to hiring handicapped individuals.[74]

Americans With Disabilities Act

15 or more employees
Disabled applicants or employees
Reasonable accommodation to perform essential job functions

Antidiscrimination Executive Orders

Most of the antidiscrimination statutes do not apply to federal government employees. Instead, federal employees are covered under the provisions of various executive orders that apply similar prohibitions against discrimination directed at federal employees. The primary one is E.O. 11478, under which federal agencies are required to maintain affirmative action plans.[75]

The most relevant executive order for academic institutions is E.O. 11246, which applies to federal government contractors and, as a part of the contract, requires an agreement not to discriminate on the basis of race, color, religion, sex, or national origin.[76] It covers contractors with a specified number of employees and contracts that exceed certain dollar limits. The primary remedies for discrimination under this order are the revocation or denial of further government contracts. Individual employment discrimination complaints are forwarded to the EEOC for resolution. An important requirement of E.O. 11246 is that contractors maintain affirmative action plans.[77] Academic departments, as components of governmental units, have federal contracts that require nondiscrimination and the maintenance of affirmative action plans. Departments usually contribute to preparation of such plans but seldom have sole responsibility for their preparation and submission.

AFFIRMATIVE ACTION

Affirmative action is a term that too often evokes an emotional response by managers. This is unfortunate and is perhaps the result of a misunderstanding of the various meanings of the term. Regarding employment discrimination, affirmative action describes three separate types of actions. First, affirmative action is used to define a remedial action that a court may order an employer to take if it finds discrimination has occurred. In other words, whenever an employer has been found to be violating various antidiscrimination statutes, the court may order the employer to take affirmative action to correct the problem.[78] The court might order recruitment, hiring, and promotion of minorities and women as affirmative action. It is perfectly proper for a court to order specific hiring or promotion quotas as a part of this remedial action, because the employer has already been found to be in violation of the employment discrimination laws.

Second, affirmative action describes a voluntary program undertaken by an employer to achieve a more racially and sexually balanced workforce to provide equal employment opportunity for women and minorities. Such voluntary affirmative action programs have been supported by the courts when challenged by disgruntled white male employees.[79] The third type of affirmative action refers to the mandated maintenance of written affirmative action plans as required under certain executive orders. While quotas are appropriate in the court-mandated remedy, they are inappropriate in the other types of affirmative action.

Voluntary and mandated written plans are the most relevant types of affirmative action in the academic setting today. In its broadest sense, affirmative action refers to a plan in which certain specific personnel steps, including recruiting, hiring, and promotions, are taken for the purpose of eliminating the present effects of past discrimination. There is no requirement of a previous judicial finding of discrimination or an inference that an employer that maintains either a voluntary or mandated affirmative action plan is guilty of discrimination. The most common reasons for an employer's maintenance of a plan stems from E.O. 11246,[80] which was issued by President Johnson in 1965 and amended by E.O. 11375.[81] The order requires government contractors to have a written plan of affirmative action to remedy the effects of past discrimination and guard against any future discrimination. The Office of Federal Contract Compliance Programs (OFCCP) administers the order.[82] Regulations under the order have been amended from time to time; presently, any organization that has at least 50 employees and has a nonconstruction contract of at least $50,000 is required to put its affirmative action plan in writing.[83] Thus most large employers in the private sphere as well as most academic institutions are legally mandated to maintain written affirmative action plans.

The OFCCP defines affirmative action programs as[84]:

> . . . a set of specific and result-oriented procedures to which a contractor commits himself to apply every good faith effort. The objective of those procedures plus such efforts is equal employment opportunity. Procedures without effort to make them work are meaningless, and effort, undirected by specific and meaningful procedures, is

inadequate. An acceptable affirmative action program must include an analysis of areas within which the contractor is deficient in the utilization of minority groups and women, and further, goals and timetables to which the contractor's good faith efforts must be directed to correct the deficiencies, and thus, to increase materially the utilization of minorities and women, at all levels and in all segments of his work force where deficiencies exist.

Perhaps one of the least understood aspects of affirmative action programs is the establishment of hiring goals. Under the executive order, covered contractors are required to make a good faith effort to achieve a self-imposed goal that falls within the ranges acceptable to the government. Hiring goals are not the same as court-imposed quotas. Affirmative action clearly does not require the academic department to hire unqualified individuals.

The EEOC issued affirmative action guidelines in 1979, and other affirmative action guidelines have been issued by the OFCCP and the Office of Personnel Management.[85] These guidelines, along with information from the campus affirmative action officer, can assist the department administrator responsible for compliance with an affirmative action program.

Most people expected that the Reagan administration's antiregulation bias, continued by the Bush administration, might seriously damage affirmative action; indeed, the Department of Justice made a series of attempts to erode affirmative action requirements. In two recent decisions, however, the U.S. Supreme Court provided significant reinforcement to the concept of affirmative action. Considered in conjunction with related decisions rendered a few years earlier, the Court sent a message to employers about their responsibilities to free the workplace from the present effects of past discrimination.

In *Johnson v. Transportation Agency, Santa Clara County*[86] and *U.S. v. Paradise*,[87] the Supreme Court was confronted with three questions left unanswered by previous decisions in this area: the legality of sex-conscious plans under Title VII, the factual basis necessary to support voluntary affirmative actions under Title VII, and the constitutionality of court-ordered numerical relief to remedy promotion discrimination.[88] It should be noted that these cases dealt with both voluntary affirmative action plans and court-ordered quotas.

In *Johnson,* The Court upheld the use of voluntary affirmative action plans that consider the sex of an applicant as one of a series of factors to be weighed in promotion cases. The Court affirmed that sex-conscious voluntary plans are entitled to the same protection under Title VII as are race-conscious plans.[89] In *Paradise*, the use of court-ordered numerical quotas for the promotion of members of minority groups was upheld after the trial court found a Title VII violation.[90] These decisions have narrowed the terms of any future debate on affirmative action; however, it must be remembered that in each of these cases the majority ruling in favor was small.[91] Changes in the composition of the Supreme Court may well weaken judicial support for affirmative action programs, so the area should be monitored by academic departmental personnel.

Affirmative Action

Denotes three types of actions:
    Court-ordered, after a finding of discrimination
    Voluntary plan
    Government contractor mandated
Good faith, results-oriented procedures
Hiring goals to achieve a balanced workforce

PERSONNEL RECORDS
Privacy of Records

Over the years, interest in protecting the privacy of individuals has increased in all aspects of society. The constitutional right of privacy has been expanded in several ways; it has been important in the realm of personnel administration at least for the past decade. Privacy in the workplace includes a variety of issues, ranging from the use of polygraph examinations to the collection of personal and work-related data on employees, and the disclosure of such information.[92] Additionally, mandatory alcohol and drug testing and screening for the AIDS virus are important, current, privacy-related employment topics.

Employers maintain various types of personnel records on current and former employees for a myriad of reasons. These records contain such information as positions held, past employment data, salary, performance reviews, disciplinary actions, medical records, and so on. Until recent years, there was little restraint on the types of information an employer might retain on individual employees, nor was there any guarantee that the employee would have access to the data in the file. In fact, a supervisor's performance reviews might be written, while the employee remains totally unaware of the content of the review or even that such a review of his or her work existed. Further, release of the data from the files was unrestricted, whether the inquiry came from a future potential employer or from a credit-granting agency.

In 1974 the federal Privacy Act was enacted.[93] The act protects the privacy rights of federal government employees and focuses on the right of employees to control access to the data contained in their personnel records. Employees are guaranteed the right to review the contents of their files and an opportunity to correct erroneous factual information. Disclosure by the employer of information contained in the personnel records may constitute an invasion of the employee's right of privacy. Additionally, the act restricts the types of information that may be kept to that which is relevant and necessary.[94] Private employers are not covered by the Privacy Act, although there have been proposals for a new federal law that would include private as well as public employers.[95]

Several states enacted statutes similar to the Privacy Act to protect state, county, and municipal employees under similar circumstances[96]; thus employees in most state-supported institutions are covered. Critical to these statutes is the right of the employee to control access to the data and to respond to erroneous or unfair information contained in the files. Some states' statutes cover private employers as well as state and local government employers. An example of such a law is the Illinois Personnel Records Statute,[97] which became effective in 1974. It covers all employers with five or more employees and closely follows the federal Privacy Act.[98]

Other federal statutes have applicability to this area, such as the federal Fair Credit Reporting Act.[99] Although the act primarily regulates activities of credit-granting agencies, employers and applicants for employment are covered by the act. An employer using a consumer investigative report as a screening device must notify the applicant that such a report is to be made, and, upon request by the prospective employee, disclose the results of the report.[100] Another example of a federal statute with some applicability to employee privacy is the Omnibus Crime Control and Safe Streets Act, which prohibits wiretapping and other interceptions of oral communications.[101] Thus employers may violate the act if they listen to an employee's personal telephone conversations.

With the conversion of personnel records to machine-readable form, many people fear an increased likelihood that confidential records may be available to unauthorized persons.[102] The trend to automate personnel records is the impetus behind many of the state laws governing the confidentiality of personnel records. Another concern for employers is that the release of unauthorized data from a personnel file could subject the employer to liability for defamation.

Privacy of Records

Federal employees are covered by Privacy Act
Many states have parallel laws that cover employees
Release of performance data is limited

Mandatory Testing

The institution of mandatory drug and alcohol testing of employees by corporations and other organizations has generated much debate and attracted media attention. Concerns range from invasion of privacy to the degree of control an employer should be able to exercise over an employee's private life. Based on public safety concerns, however, it is likely that such mandatory drug and alcohol testing may be allowed in some industries, such as public transportation. It is possible that the drivers of vehicles transporting goods or people for an academic institution might come under similar restraints because of the public safety aspect of that particular job. Departments might consider whether nurses, technicians, and others involved in direct patient care might also be subject to such testing because of similar public safety concerns.

In academic departments, where controlled substances may be used for research, employees have greater access to drugs than in a general employment situation. An administrator might determine that certain employees should be tested for drugs because of this availability. The legal and constitutional problems are myriad, and department administrators should approach this issue carefully. Consultation with the university's legal counsel is critical before implementing any employee drug testing program.

Mandatory testing for the AIDS virus is extremely controversial, especially since it appears unlikely that the virus is spread by casual contact. As fear of the spread of the disease rages, however, some employers have discussed mandatory screening to protect themselves and other employees and to limit insurance coverage. Not only is the screening probably unconstitutional, but any adverse employment action taken because of a positive result on an AIDS test is probably subject to challenge under either the federal or state handicapped discrimination statutes. Confidentiality of results of AIDS testing presents yet another serious privacy issue. Neither drug nor AIDS testing is a settled area, however, and academic employers should continue to monitor legal developments.

Illegal Aliens

The Immigration Reform and Control Act of 1986[103] makes it unlawful for a person or other entity to hire, recruit, or refer for a fee any illegal alien for employment in the United States. The act permits employers to employ properly identified citizens of the United States as well as noncitizens who can document that they are lawfully authorized to work in this country. All employers are covered, including colleges and universities. Prior to hiring, employers must view and may copy original documents that establish the job applicant's identity and employment status. Upon request from the employer, applicants must submit copies of one of the following documents: U.S. passport, certificate of U.S. citizenship, certificate of naturalization, unexpired foreign passport, alien registration receipt card, temporary resident card, employment registration card, or Native American tribal document.[104]

If none of these documents is available, certain combinations of other enumerated documents may be submitted by the applicant. Forms to be completed are supplied by the U.S. Department of Justice, Immigration and Naturalization Service; forms must be retained by the employer as specified. Penalties are imposed on employers that violate the act; such employers may be fined not less than $250 nor more than $2000 for each individual with respect to whom such a violation occurred. Employers with a pattern and practice of violating the act may be fined not more than $10,000 for each unauthorized alien for whom such violation occurs.[105]

To date, the primary effect on universities has been an increase in the number of preemployment forms to be completed on job applicants. The burden is exacerbated by the fact that student employees also are covered by the act; thus the amount of paperwork related to hiring has increased dramatically.

CONCLUSION

Any attempt to define the legal environment of academic administration must fall short of being complete. Although major employment laws are discussed, the body of law relating to various minor employment issues is enormous. Additionally, statutes governing both public and private employment are amended frequently; thus one should make every attempt to keep up-to-date with the laws and regulations discussed, since any chapter on legal issues is outdated before it can be published.

Administrators of academic departments should rely on parent organizations for procedures and forms that have been developed to ensure organizational compliance with various federal, state and local employment laws. While such compliance may seem cumbersome, the security of knowing that one will not run afoul of the law is worth the increased effort and additional paperwork.

Details of any employment problem make generalizations about the law of limited value in settling particular issues. Thus academic managers should consult with the university's legal counsel on all questions of departmental compliance with statutory or regulatory mandates. In any event, good record keeping facilitates proof of compliance with laws and regulations and may be considered "preventive maintenance" in personnel management. Personnel records should be added to the array of important records that receive attention. Contemporaneous written justifications for employment actions provide the documentation necessary to demonstrate that the department complies with both the letter and spirit of antidiscrimination laws.

BIBLIOGRAPHY / ENDNOTES

1. 42 USC § 2000e–h-6 (1988).
2. *Id* § 2000e-2(a)(1).
3. *Id* § 2000e-5(g).
4. 42 USC § 2000e, as amended (Supp II 1972 & Supp II 1978).
5. *Id* § 2000e-4(a).
6. 29 CFR § 1607 (1979).
7. Civil Rights Act of 1991, Pub L No. 102-166 105 Stat 1071 (1991).
8. 42 USC § 1981a (Law Co-op Supp 1992).
9. *Id* There is no cap on racial discrimination damages because its victims have another statute under which they may bring suit, 42 USC § 1981 (1988).
10. 42 USC § 1981a (Law Co-op Supp 1992).
11. EEOC Guidelines on Discrimination Because of Religion, as revised, 29 CFR § 1605. 1-3 (1980).
12. *Id* § 1605.2.
13. 42 USC § 2000e(k) (Supp II 1978).
14. *Id*.
15. Newport News Shipbuilding & Dry Dock Co v EEOC, 462 US 669 (1983).
16. Guidelines on Discrimination Because of Sex, 29 CFR § 1604.10 (1979).
17. 479 US 262 (1987).
18. *Id* at 275-76.
19. *Id* at 292.
20. *Id* at 289.
21. *See* Hayes v Shelby Memorial Hospital, 726 F2d 1543 (11th Cir 1984).
22. United Auto Workers v Johnson Controls, 886 F2d 871, 890 (7th Cir 1989).
23. 111 S Ct 1196 (1991).
24. *Id* 1208-09.
25. *See* Julie Gannon Shoop, *VDTs Do Not Increase Miscarriage Risk, Study Says,* 27 Trial, May 1991, at 17.

26. Meritor Savings Bank v Vinson, 477 US 57 (1986).
27. 29 CFR § 1604.11 (1980).
28. 477 US 57 (1986).
29. *Id* at 65-66.
30. 29 CFR § 1604.11(c) (1980).
31. 477 US 57, 71-72.
32. 29 CFR 1604.11(d) (1980).
33. 924 F.2d 872 (9th Cir 1991).
34. *Id* at 874-76.
35. *Id* at 879.
36. *Id* at 879-80.
37. *Id* at 1604.11(f).
38. 477 US 57, 72-73 (1986).
39. *See* Cheryl Blackwell Bryson, *The Internal Sexual Harassment Investigation: Self Evaluation Without Self Incrimination,* 15 Employee Rel LJ 551 (1990) and James J Oh, *Internal Sexual Harassment Complaints: Investigating to Win,* 18 Employee Rel LJ 227 (1992).
39a. *See* Sharon Begley. Hands Off, Mr. Chips! Newsweek, May 3, 1993, at 58.
40. 112 S Ct 1028 (1992).
41. 20 USC § 1681-88 (1988).
42. 112 S Ct 1028, 1037-38 (1992).
43. 29 USC § 206(d) (1988).
44. 20 CFR § 800.122 (1966).
45. *Id* § 800.125-32.
46. *Id* § 800.121.1.
47. 29 USC § 206(d) (1988).
48. For example, *see* Board of Regents of University of Nebraska v Dawes, 522 F2d 380 (8th Cir 1975), *cert. denied* 424 US 914 (1976) and Ende v Board of Regents of Regency Universities, 757 F.2d 176 (7th Cir 1985).
49. *See* County of Washington v Gunther, 452 US 161 (1981).
50. The states of Minnesota, Wisconsin, and Iowa have implemented pay equity following statewide studies. After appropriating money for a pay parity study, the North Carolina legislature apparently had second thoughts and withdrew the funding early in 1985.
51. US Department of Labor, *A Report on the Glass Ceiling Initiative,* 1 (1991).
52. *Id.*
53. US Department of Labor, *Pipelines of Progress* (1992).
54. 29 USC § 621-34 (1988).
55. *Id* § 631(a)-(d) (Supp I 1989).
56. *Id* § 631(d) (1988).
57. *Id* § 626(c) (1988).
58. *Id* § 626(b) (1988).
59. 42 USCS § 12101-12213 (Law Co-op Supp 1991).
60. 29 USC § 701-796i (1988).
61. *Id.*
62. 42 USCS § 12102(2)(A)-(C) (Law Co-op Supp 1991).
63. 42 USCS § 12112(a) (Law Co-op Supp 1991).
64. Philip L Gordon, *The Job Application Process After the Americans with Disabilities Act,* 18, Employer Rel LJ, 185, 188 (1992) [hereinafter Gordon].
65. 42 USC § 12111(8) (Law Co-op Supp 1991).
66. Gordon, *supra* note 64, at 190.
67. *Id.*
68. 42 USC § 12111(9) (Law Co-op Supp 1991).
69. Gordon, *supra* note 64, at 199.
70. Renee L Cyr, *The Americans with Disabilities Act: Implications for Job Reassignment and the Job Treatment of Hypersensitive Individuals,* 57 Brooklyn L Rev 1237, 1247-48 (1992) [hereafter Cyr].

71. 42 USC § 12111(10) (Law Co-op Supp 1991).
72. Robert B Fitzpatrick and E Anne Benaroya, *Americans with Disabilities Act and AIDS,* 8 Lab Law 249, 261 (1992).
73. Gordon, *supra* note 64, at 201.
74. Cyr, *supra* note 70, at 1275.
75. Exec Order No 11478, 3 CFR § 803 (1966-70).
76. Exec Order No 11246, 3 CFR § 339 (1964-65).
77. *Id.*
78. 42 USC § 2000e(g) (1988).
79. *See* United Steelworkers of Am v Weber, 443 US 193 (1979).
80. Exec Order No 11246, 3 CFR § 339 (1964-65).
81. Exec Order No 11375, 3 CFR § 803 (1966-70).
82. Exec Order No 11246, 3 CFR § 339 (1964-65).
83. 41 CFR § 60-140 (1986).
84. *Id* § 60-2.10 (1978).
85. *See generally,* EEOC Guidelines 29 CFR § 1608 (1979); OFCCP Guidelines, 41 CFR § 60-4 (1978); OPM Guidelines, 5 CFR § 720 (1979).
86. 480 US 616 (1987).
87. 480 US 149 (1987).
88. Marsha Levick, *Affirmative Action Cases Benefit Working Women,* 9 Nat'l LJ, Aug 17, 1987, at S4 [hereinafter cited Levick].
89. 107 S Ct 1442, 1447 (1987).
90. 490 US 149, 184-85.
91. Levick, *supra* note 88 at S4-5.
92. Jan Duffy et al. *Big Brother in the Workplace: Privacy Rights Versus Employer Needs,* 9 Indust Rel LJ 30, 31 (1987).
93. 5 USC § 522a (1988).
94. *Id.*
95. Karl J Duff & Eric T Johnson, *A Renewed Employee Right to Privacy,* 34 Lab LJ 747, 760-62 (1983).
96. *See generally,* NC Gen Stat § 126-22-30 (1986); § 153A-98 (1983); § 160A-168 (1983).
97. Ill Rev Stat ch 48, ¶ 2001-12 (1986 & West Supp 1991).
98. *Id.*
99. 15 USC § 1681-1681t (1988).
100. *Id* at § 1681(b); 1681(k).
101. 18 USC § 2510-20 (1988).
102. *See* James Ledvinka, *Privacy Regulations and Employee Record Keeping,* 7 J Libr Admin, Winter, 1986, at 25.
103. 8 USC § 1324(a) (1988).
104. *Id* § 1324(b) (Law Co-op Supp 1992).
105. *Id* § 1324(e)(4).

RESOURCES
Affirmative Action

Greene KW. (1989). *Affirmative action and principles of justice.* New York: Greenwood Press.
Niel R. (1991). *Racial preference and racial justice: The new affirmative action controversy.* Washington, DC: Ethics and Public Policy Center.
Urofsky MI. (1991). *A conflict of rights: The Supreme Court and affirmative action.* New York: Scribner's Sons.

Disabilities

The Americans with Disabilities Act: A practical and legal guide to impact, enforcement, and compliance. (1990). Washington, DC: Bureau of National Affairs.

West J. (1991). *The Americans with Disabilities Act: From policy to practice*. New York: Milband Memorial Fund.

Employment

Batterman D. (1984). *Manager's desk book on employment law: Practical guidelines for preventing discrimination on the job*. New York: Executive Enterprises Publications.

Equal employment opportunity manual for managers and supervisors: A publication of the Society for Human Resource Management and Commerce Clearing House, Inc. (1991). Chicago: Commerce Clearing House.

Fretz BD. (1987). *The law of age discrimination: A reference manual*. Chicago: National Clearinghouse for Legal Services.

Grasso JC. (1984). *Pregnancy & work*. New York: Avon.

Larson LK. (1992). *Civil Rights Act of 1991*. New York: Matthew Bender.

Levine ML. (1988). *Age discrimination and the mandatory retirement controversy*. Baltimore: Johns Hopkins University Press.

Player MA. (1992). *Federal law of employment discrimination in a nutshell*. St. Paul, Minn: West Publishing Co.

Religious accommodation in the workplace: A legal & practical handbook. (1987). Washington, DC: Bureau of National Affairs.

Riccucci N. (1990). *Women, minorities, and unions in the public sector*. New York: Greenwood Press.

Ritz S. (1992). *The Civil Rights Act of 1991: Its impact on employment discrimination litigation*. New York: Practising Law Institute.

Sullivan CA, Zimmer MJ & Richards RF. (1988). *Employment discrimination*. Boston: Little, Brown.

Travis D. (1991). *Racism, American style: A corporate gift*. Chicago: Urban Research Press.

Trotter R & Zacur SR. (1986). *Government regulation of employment discrimination: A sourcebook for managers*. Lanham, Md: University Publications of America.

Miscellaneous

Bible JD. (1990). *Privacy in the workplace: A guide for human resource managers*. New York: Quorum Books.

Campbell D & Graham M. (1988). *Drugs and alcohol in the workplace: A guide for managers*. New York: Facts on File Publications.

Cornish CM. (1988). *Drugs and alcohol in the workplace: Testing and privacy*. Wilmette, Ill: Callaghan.

Rubenfeld AR. (1987). *AIDS legal guide*, New York: Lambda Legal Defense and Education Fund.

Sexual Harassment

Gutek BA. (1985). *Sex and the workplace*. San Francisco: Jossey-Bass.

Omilian SM. (1987). *Sexual harassment in employment*. Wilmette, Ill: Callaghan.

Sexual harassment manual for managers and supervisors: How to prevent and resolve sexual harassment complaints in the workplace. (1991). Chicago: Commerce Clearing House.

CHAPTER 16

Quality Management

Fusun Erkel

ଈ

We need knowledge. We need instruments for adaptation and change.
We need theory. What we do is too important to let our pride keep us from lessons
that have been taught and learned outside medicine about how quality can be
planned, controlled, and improved.

D. BERWICK, B. GODFREY, and J. ROESSNER

ଈ Case Example

The department's vice-chair for clinical affairs, was furious when the chief resident related the story of a referral patient who had walked out of the hospital after a 10-hour wait for admission. An oncology patient, she was told to come to the admitting office at 9 AM to be admitted. She was told kindly that she had to wait for a bed to open. At 7 PM she finally lost faith in getting admitted and left with her husband's help, extremely fatigued and frustrated.

In anger, the vice-chair called the directors of admitting and of bed control, as well as other hospital administrators. There were some explanations about the tight bed situation, patients awaiting discharge, the possibility of borrowing a bed from another department, and so on, but nothing could erase the damage done to the patient and to the reputation of the academic medical center.

The vice-chair felt helpless. This incident was not the first of its kind. "What kind of quality patient care can we promise if we can't even guarantee a painless admission?" he asked himself. "And how can we expect our referral base to grow if we can't provide a satisfying experience for both patient and the referring physician?"

The preceding events occurred at the University of North Carolina (UNC) medical center. Application of an analytical systematic approach to the problem achieved dramatic results. A team of 25 people was selected from the academic department and from the 11 hospital departments whose procedures affected the process of admission and discharge. Among the key team members were attending and resident physicians, nurses, unit clerks, laboratory and radiology personnel, pharmacists, and housekeepers.

284

The team used quality management tools and techniques as *diagnostic tools* to analyze the admission and discharge process and to discover the root causes of long admission waits—just as one might use x-ray films for diagnosing a lesion. The team developed flow charts that revealed the unnecessary complexity of the discharge process (Figure 16-1). Data revealed multiple causes for discharge delays and slow bed turnaround. One point became very apparent: all the departments and functional groups involved in the process were highly interdependent, and unless these groups could work together to streamline the process, patients would continue to fall victim to barriers and bottlenecks in the system.

Over an 8-month period, scientific methods, teamwork, and "data-driven decision making" led to dramatic improvements. Response times for ancillary and support services and timeliness of discharge orders all improved. Figure 16-2 demonstrates the significant improvement in laboratory results reporting time for medical patients due to be discharged. The peak discharge time for medical patients dropped 4 hours, from 3:30 PM to 11:30 AM. Average admission wait times went down to 24 minutes—an improvement of more than 50% (Figure 16-3). These improvements were achieved without the addition of new beds or personnel, and as direct results of process realignment around customer needs.

BACKGROUND

Designing or realigning systems around customer needs is the essence of *quality management*. This innovative management methodology was masterminded by American experts W. Edwards Deming and Joseph M. Juran back in the 1950s. Japanese manufacturing companies, unlike their American counterparts, were very receptive to the teachings of Drs. Deming and Juran, because they saw it as a major opportunity to achieve high quality and competitiveness. Quality management or continuous quality improvement techniques have enabled the Japanese to erase the perception that "made in Japan" meant "junk" and to build their reputation as producers of high-quality consumer goods at competitive prices. This strategy ensured customer satisfaction and yielded Japanese dominance in the world markets.

After losing their market share to Japanese firms, some industrial companies in the United States started adopting quality management techniques during the 1980s. For many, it was a matter of survival. The results of quality management in these companies have been remarkable. Companies such as Motorola, Westinghouse, and Xerox Corporation have reported impressive measurable improvements in the quality of their products while maintaining competitive prices. They all recaptured and further increased their market shares, realizing record profits. Some companies from the service industry, such as Federal Express and Florida Power and Light, quickly followed the new quality movement, and their successes have achieved national acclaim.

In this chapter, academic medical centers or health centers (AHCs) will be discussed as part of the U.S. health care and education systems. The applicability of quality management theory to these unique institutions will be explored.

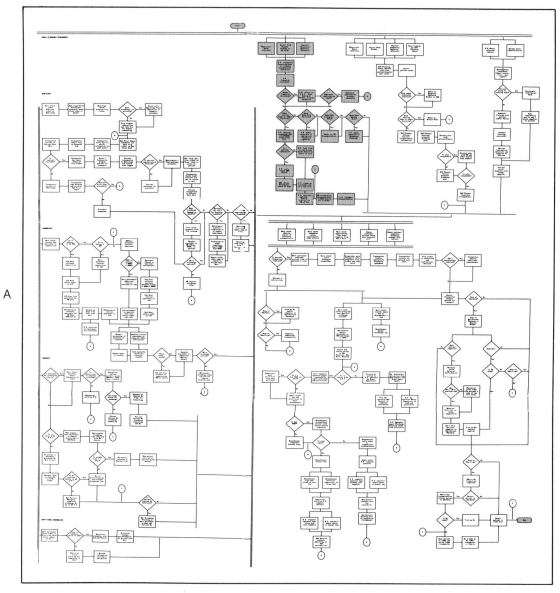

Figure 16-1. A, A team selected to analyze the causes for delays in patient admissions and discharges at UNC medical center developed this flow chart that revealed the unnecessary complexity of the discharge process. (Courtesy UNC Hospitals.)

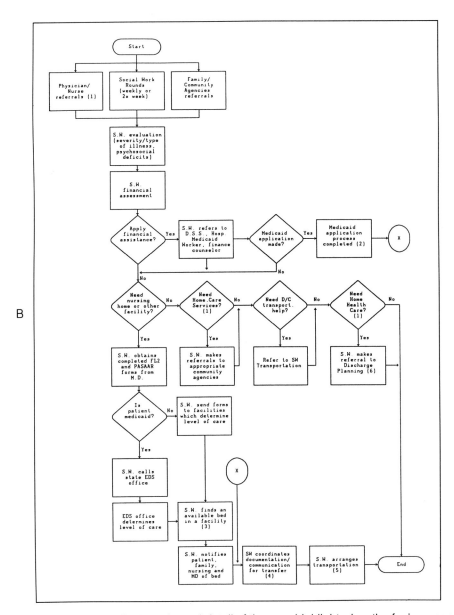

Figure 16-1, cont'd. B, An enlarged detail of the area highlighted on the facing page.

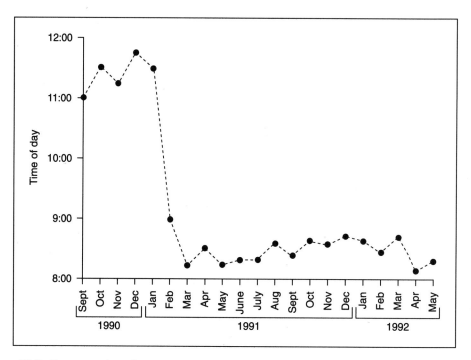

Figure 16-2. Response times for support services improved dramatically at the UNC medical center after the review of systems by the quality improvement team.

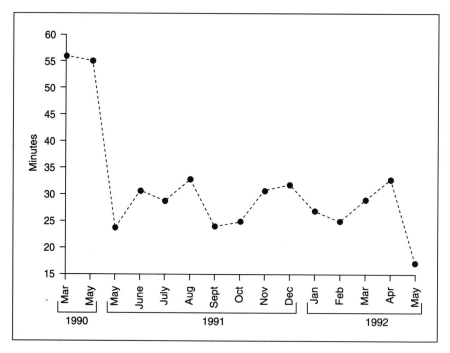

Figure 16-3. UNC's improved admission and discharge procedures resulted in 50% improvement in elective admission wait times.

THE AMERICAN HEALTH CARE SYSTEM UNDER ATTACK

In modern history, no other area of endeavor has contributed as much to the human condition as has health care and academic medicine. The revolutionary pace of scientific achievements through medical research and medical engineering has wiped out many deadly diseases, has prolonged human life, and reduced human suffering. Yet today's health care system in the United States is under attack. A 1990 survey shows that the American public is least satisfied with the present health care system in comparison to nine other leading industrialized nations.[5] Only 10% of the American respondents agreed with the statement, "Our health system works pretty well and needs only minor adjustments." Ninety percent of the American public asked for either "fundamental changes" (60%) or "complete rebuilding" (30%) of the health care system. What is the basis for this discontent? The criticism focuses on issues of access, utilization, cost, and quality.

Access to Health Care

Since the number of uninsured persons in the United States has reached 37 million, and the number is still growing, access becomes a concern not only for the uninsured, but also for health care providers and for all Americans. The entire nation senses the implications of national health policy options that are being considered to fix the problem. The Clinton administration wishes to insure every American while considering a national cap on all U.S. health care expenditures. Preliminary plans appear to encourage managed competition while controlling the rate of growth in the health care industry. Proposed reforms do not empathize with the inherent inefficiencies of academic health centers and other teaching institutions.

Utilization of Health Services

Recently, researchers have described dramatic variation in utilization of health services that cannot be explained by demographic factors or health status of different communities.[1,21,22] High variation exists in utilization of many expensive medical procedures, in the indication of interventions, and in hospitalization rates and rates of outcomes. This research provoked the debate on appropriateness of care and the interrelationship with the cost and quality of care.

Cost of Health Care

Although almost everyone in our society has concern about rising health care costs, cost implications differ among various sectors. The nation's health policy makers are nervous, since the United States currently spends 12% of the gross national product (GNP) on health care. When they see projections that 15% of the U.S. GNP will be devoted to health care by the year 2000 and about 19% by 2010, they ask: "Can we afford to spend this much of the GNP on health care?"[16]

In addition, corporate America identifies its health care costs (to insure its workforce) as the major impediment to its competitive stance in global markets.

Small businesses see health insurance costs as the major threat to their survival. When third-party payors are concerned, they want to control spending by enforcing regulatory measures on health care providers. Health care providers come up with countermeasures to offset ever-increasing regulation. Although it is politically unacceptable to talk about cost shifting or rationing of care, these measures are well established in practice as providers try to survive.

Quality of Care

Health care and the medical profession have always been identified with a concern for quality. Even in times of empiricism, practitioners were held accountable and severely punished when they caused harm to the patient. After the medical scientific base was established, society limited the practice of medical sciences to trained professionals and institutions that met certain standards. The medical profession defines "quality of care" and accepts the responsibility of "assuring" quality. Traditional *quality assurance* (QA) activities are based on establishing standards, setting thresholds, and evaluating care when thresholds are reached. QA function has become the focus of external regulation on medical professionals and health care institutions. By default, QA activities have been directed to satisfying the regulators' mandate.

Why does the public have concerns about the quality of care despite established QA programs and watchful eyes of the regulators who aim to assure quality? How can people expect higher quality and at the same time complain about current health care costs? Doesn't higher quality beget increased cost? Does the general public have enough knowledge to judge the quality of care?

It is becoming increasingly apparent that competent medical professionals, high technology, advanced medical research, and sophisticated academic health centers are not synonymous with quality and do not necessarily please the individuals or institutions who purchase health care services. Consumers of health care are asking for *value*. As Reinhardt[16] puts it, the real question the nation must address is not " can we *afford* to spend?" but "is it *worth* spending" X percent of the GNP on academic medicine and health care? The challenge becomes one of *managing* the system of health care so that it consistently produces valuable products or services the public needs and expects for its well-being. Patients' and payors' needs and expectations have to be integrated into the professional definition of *quality care*.

A NEW PARADIGM: QUALITY MANAGEMENT

Academic health centers, as centers of education, research, and health care delivery, can become natural settings to explore and implement the new quality management model which worked so well for the manufacturing and service industries. There are several reasons for the necessity of this exploration:

- AHCs are critical institutions for the development and growth of research, education, and patient care. If these centers do not lead the way to change and improve the U.S. health care system, they will be led by political and regulatory forces.

- Quality management is based on scientific logic and methods that can be easily understood and accepted by academicians. Continued learning and experimentation are essential for both medical and new managerial science.
- Hospitals are experiencing an increasing urgency to implement the new management model, because it provides a fundamentally different view of the relationship between quality and cost. Implementation in the manufacturing sector has proved that high-quality processes and outcomes can result in lower costs, and, conversely, that low quality begets high costs. Therefore, academic medical departments will experience increasing pressures from hospitals for more involvement in the quality process. Finally, as producers of highly specialized and skilled medical professionals, the academic departments will have to find ways to integrate the teachings of the sciences of quality management and medicine. Young professionals need to understand the dynamics of complex systems in which they will work. Even if they choose to have a solo practice, they will remain accountable to the public while dealing with reimbursement issues, regulatory agencies, and liability litigation.

Quality management offers to academic medical centers a systems perspective. Peter Senge in his delightful work, *The Fifth Discipline: The Art and Practice of the Learning Organization,*[18] explains how today's problems were created by yesterday's short-sighted solutions that lacked "systems thinking." The theory of quality management is based on systems thinking, and according to Deming the duty of top leadership is to manage the system for optimization.[20] Academic departments need to see their particular role and relative importance within the larger systems, such as the AHC and the national health care system. Without this perspective, individual departments aim toward optimizing themselves at the expense of the whole.

Although the term used to describe the new paradigm in other industries is *total quality management* (TQM), AHCs and other health care organizations have internalized the new paradigm by calling it *continuous quality improvement* (CQI). Whichever expression is preferred, the basic principles of quality management are the same for all kinds of industries or organizations. The balance of this section, through p. 298, discusses these principles.

Any given system must be recognized and analyzed as a series of processes.

In academic health centers there may be hundreds of processes such as patient care, teaching, information flow, research, grant application, scientific publication, and technological and managerial processes. Focusing on processes rather than exclusively on outcomes provides many advantages. As members of the organization focus on processes, each person can identify his or her relative role in a given process and understand how their work affects and is affected by others. Recognition of the tremendous interdependencies among people leads to an understanding and appreciation of each other's work.

In addition to each person identifying his or her role in any process, each academic medical department and departments of the teaching hospital can also realize their relative importance and interdependence for each interdepartmental process. As illustrated in Figure 16-4, the traditional organizational structure of an academic medical setting is based on multiple departments. However, the functional reality is based on multiple processes that cut across departmental lines. Solutions to most problems, when developed within a single department, usually fall short of improving the whole process. The process focus on the other hand, pulls all the departments which affect the process together, creating the partnership necessary for improvement. For example, the emergency, medicine, radiology, and surgery departments may have to adjust their intradepartmental routines for the evaluation process of a patient with chest pain to make the entire process more effective and efficient.

Utilizing CQI, process analysis tools and techniques provide accurate diagnosis of process problems that are the main source of quality defects. The analytical tools of quality management are more powerful than traditional outcome monitoring because they point out the root causes of process flaws and enable their prevention. Traditional QA focuses on the outliers that do not meet a certain threshold and tries to correct them. It has minimal impact, if any, on average outcome. Quality management, on the other hand, emphasizes best practices and tries to improve the overall performance. Improvement in average outcomes can be substantial (Figure 16-5).

Traditional QA in health care or the grading system in education are similar in the sense that each system measures and monitors individual performance at the end of a process, just like an end-of-the-line inspection in a manufacturing plant. These measures may catch "lack of quality" but do not answer the question "why" and do not prevent the waste. It is also too simplistic to draw a causal relationship between the quality of an outcome and any individual's performance without considering the multiple variables in complex systems. For example, to prevent medication errors the whole process of prescribing, transcription, preparation, transport, and administration needs to be studied and causes of variation need to be analyzed. As another example, the problem of long admission waits at UNC medical center required analysis of the processes of discharge, room cleaning, and admission. Multiple barriers to more timely discharges and admissions were detected and removed. The mere existence of an institutional policy stating that the discharge hour was 11:30 AM couldn't guarantee the desired outcome unless processes were realigned to achieve it.

The organization has to become "customer focused" to achieve quality and competitiveness.

The new paradigm challenges individuals and organizations to identify their "customers" and to design work processes around customers' needs and expectations. The medical profession and academic centers are not accustomed to viewing patients, families, and students as customers. Teaching institutions, by mission, exist to educate students in the way they deem appropriate and not necessarily to please them. But are the needs of the organizations who employ the graduates or the needs of the constituencies whom the graduates serve being fulfilled by the education process? Is there an established feedback process?

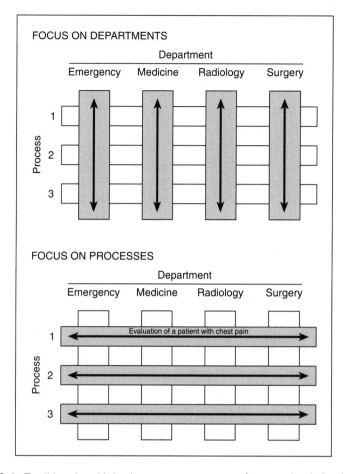

Figure 16-4. Traditional multiple-department structure of an academic health center.

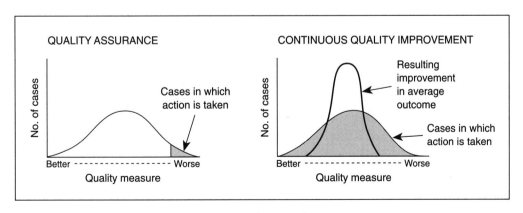

Figure 16-5. Distinctions between quality assurance and quality management utilizing continuous quality improvement (CQI). (From James BC. [1992]. Good enough? Standards and measurement in continuous quality improvement. Bridging the gap between theory and practice. *Hospital Research and Education Trust* [American Hospital Assoc], pp 1-24. As cited in Larkin H. [1992, October, 26]. Redefining quality. Your changing practice. *American Medical News,* pp 13-18.)

Let us analyze the scenario from a different perspective—after all, quality management is called a *new paradigm*. Let us define the *customer* as any person or organization receiving a product, service, or information, and the *supplier* as the person or organization giving that product, service or information.[14] An exchange of money may or may not be relevant within this transaction. This definition makes *customer* an all-inclusive term. We can list the customers of an academic health center as patients, family members, referring physicians, payors of health care, students, physicians in training, grantors of research funds, institutions for whom the research is provided, institutions who employ the graduates, and the public itself.

The customer concept somewhat demystifies the traditional physician-patient relationship, but the realities of the last decade of the twentieth century require sound customer-supplier relationships, not mysticism. Malpractice litigation has already reached a new level of suspicion and has created a new distance between patients and their physicians. Integrating quality, as defined by patients and payors, into the design and delivery of health care can reverse that trend.

Assessment of customers' needs and expectations has to be an ongoing process. Ironically, it may be surprisingly easy for a company to lose touch with customers' needs and expectations or to make corporate decisions based on incorrect interpretation of customers' needs. American car manufacturers found themselves in this ironic situation while the Japanese car makers, under quality management, were systematically assessing the needs and expectations of car buyers around the world. The Japanese efforts have paid off.

Academic medicine and health care in general used to define quality from the professional's perspective. Standards of care, thresholds, professional certification, licensure, and accreditation of institutions and educational programs are the measures used to define and assure quality in patient care and in medical education. None of these measures, however, incorporates the needs and expectations of the users of the system.

Although the patients may not be able to judge the quality of a medical intervention, they form a solid perception of the quality of care they receive based on the way the procedure, intervention, or therapy was explained to them, the extent to which they were involved in the decision making, and the overall friendliness of health care providers and settings.

Referring physicians, on the other hand, expect timely feedback and meaningful communication with the academic center in addition to quality medical interventions for their patients. Payors of health care expect to buy the same high-quality medical care at the lowest price possible. They should not be blamed for their reluctance to pay for the inefficiencies of complex health care organizations. Designing services around customers' needs and expectations will achieve "quality," as defined by the customer, and assure customer loyalty in an increasingly competitive health care environment.

Another important aspect of the new customer concept is the idea of the internal customer. Each step of a work process creates a supplier and a customer role among faculty, administration, departments, and employees. The quality of supplier-customer interactions often determines the quality of the services provided. This point is best illustrated when a patient is referred to an AHC for an evaluation or treatment that involves several departments. The patient's judgment of quality will be shaped by the coordination of his or her overall care among the involved departments. "Best efforts" alone do not necessarily satisfy the expectations of patients and referring physicians. It requires solid understanding and nurturing of internal customer-supplier relationships.

Costs decrease as the reliability of processes increase.

Poor quality has proved costly in the manufacturing industry.[8] Defective products, added inspection and surveillance, wasteful processes, rework, and complaining customers are costly. Cost is incurred to produce a defective part; additional cost is incurred to detect it through inspection. Then the defective part needs to be fixed or discarded and a new, nondefective part has to be produced, adding to the cost figure in either way. Producing it right the first time would have cost much less, and producing it right would have meant quality.

The quality pioneers showed a significant negative correlation between quality and process variation in the manufacturing industry. They found a major opportunity for quality improvement by eliminating variation—unnecessary complexity, redundancy, rework, and waste—in work processes. They showed that quality can be controlled or "assured" only when processes are managed and made more predictable. If a product or service can be produced consistently to satisfy the needs and expectations of the customers, the combined goal of high quality and low cost can be achieved. The product will be of high quality because it will meet the needs and expectations of its customers, and it will be of low cost because the desired outcome will be achieved at the first attempt without rework and waste.

Is this argument applicable to academic health centers? Is there rework and waste? The answer is "yes" for both questions. Lost radiology films, misplaced medical records, illegible orders, medication errors, unsuitable laboratory specimens, unnecessary tests and procedures, and delays and waiting times are a few examples of rework and waste in patient care environments. Health care providers increasingly are being challenged to reduce cost and enhance the quality of patient care by eliminating these types of waste. Similar to the variation in utilization of health services, variation in practice patterns may exist among an academic health center's staff. Variation may result in the inappropriate use of costly resources. The application of CQI methods in daily practice can reduce the variation in resource use, improve patient care, and provide a better educational process for physicians in training. Although the most important single determinant of health care quality may be the knowledge and skills of individual physicians, all variables in the system play an augmentative role. These variables are parts or products of complex processes that can be managed and streamlined to add value while reducing costs.

Quality requires a scientific approach to process analysis and improvement.

Quality improvement requires knowledge of systems, processes, variation, and psychology. While this is different than the professional knowledge of medical disciplines, the scientific approach to process problems has a striking resemblance to the physician's systematic management of a patient's problems. Diagnostic tests need to be performed to formulate specific hypotheses of cause, i.e., causes of disease or causes of process flaws. After testing the hypotheses, a course of treatment needs to be designed and applied, i.e., postsurgical follow-up or monitoring the process improvement.

Systems and processes are composed of people, equipment, supplies, policies, procedures, routines, knowledge, cultural considerations, and communication patterns. All these elements function with a high level of interdependency, just like the organs of the human body. The dynamics of a system or a process cannot be studied with anecdotes, sentinel events, incident reports, or case reviews. Aggregate data and certain analytical tools and techniques are required to analyze and improve processes and systems.

The National Demonstration Project on Quality Improvement in Health Care (1987-1989) served as an experimental trial of the applicability of analytical methods in health care processes.[4] Funded by the John A. Hartford Foundation, the project matched 21 health care organizations with an equal number of industrial quality management experts. Teams used process analysis tools (flow charts, cause and effect diagrams, pareto charts, scattered diagrams, trend charts, control charts, and histograms) to detect root causes of flaws in the processes under study. The trial was a success; the tools were applicable to health care processes.

There is one important difference between the diagnosis and treatment of a patient's problem and that of a process problem: The process problem requires more time. Flow-charting a process cannot be done as quickly as taking an x-ray film, and data collection may take several weeks or months. The scientific approach to quality improvement demands an investment of time at the outset to accurately diagnose the root causes of quality problems. This approach is in fact more time efficient in the long run than interfering with processes on the basis of "gut feelings" in a reactive mode.

Modern quality theory assumes that individuals in a system want to do a good job, but best intentions and creativity are usually hindered by process problems in the system. Quality management requires the diffusion of analytical knowledge to everyone in the organization so that each can be empowered to improve their work processes. Outcome and process measurements are meant to be used as feedback for further analysis and improvement and never as punitive measures. Any clinical outcome, for example, depends on multiple factors in the system. Figure 16-6 demonstrates some of the systems' factors that may effect a patient's outcome in a cause-and-effect diagram. Similar process analysis tools and data will be instrumental in pointing out the root causes of outcome variation. Whether the causes are physician practice differences, inconsistency of support services, or incompatibility of existing policies, they can be eliminated to improve patient outcomes.

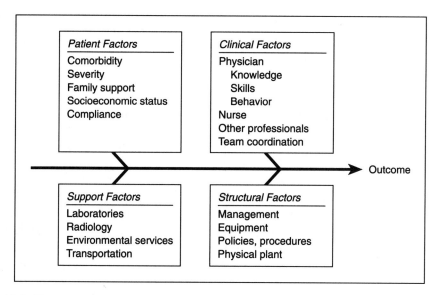

Figure 16-6. There are multiple system factors that will affect a patient's clinical outcome. The same type of cause-and-effect diagram can be used when analyzing other areas of investigation in variations in outcome.

Teamwork is essential to deal with the complexities of organizational systems.

Most organizations, academic medical settings in particular, are too complex for any one individual to have all the answers. Processes cut across departments and involve many people from different levels of the organizational hierarchy. Each individual knows his part of the process but may have an inadequate understanding of the other parts. Process analysis and improvement on the other hand require accurate understanding of the whole process.

Multidisciplinary teams need to be formed by those who work in the same process to do the analytical work and intervention. Teamwork facilitates the realization of being part of the problem and necessitates becoming part of the solution. Quality improvement teams differ sharply by their structure and function from the committees, councils and task forces which are abundant in academic medical centers. Teams are not formed to advise but to analyze and implement changes.

The admission/discharge quality improvement team at the UNC medical center prioritized laboratory and radiology orders for discharge patients, realigned work schedules in support services, redesigned work flow in ancillary services, and improved communication patterns among the involved departments. The team designed and implemented these changes with the full cooperation of involved departments.

Academic centers offer fertile ground for the widespread use of quality improvement teams; and quality teams are beneficial to the organization because (1) teamwork will help the transition from individual to joint responsibility over processes and outcomes; (2) professional autonomy will be complemented by accountability for both outcome and process performance; and (3) professional and administrative authority will transform into leadership which supports participation and customer mindedness.

LEADERSHIP FOR CONTINUING IMPROVEMENT

Leadership has paramount importance in managing and continuously improving quality. As Deming states, "Quality of the output of a company cannot exceed the quality created in the minds of its leaders."[9] Although the leaders establish and communicate their vision for quality, they need to encourage and enable others in the department or hospital to promote team decision-making at the lowest level possible. Participatory management and empowerment may be easier to practice for some department chairmen than for others because of the differences in organizational cultures. Varying departmental and hospital cultures should be adjusted in the long run to optimize the "system" of the academic health center. The center's accountability to the users of its research, education and clinical services requires this optimization. Responsibility for optimization rests with the department chairs, medical and other health professional school leaders and the senior managers in the teaching hospital.

Leaders and organizations have to identify their customers and assess customers' needs and expectations. Although academic medical centers usually have complicated power structures, the leaders can unite around a shared vision and a dynamic planning activity to achieve customer satisfaction. Organizational mission should be revisited to clarify the underlying social need for the organization's existence. Departmental missions must be realigned with the organization's mission. For systems optimization, the interaction and cooperation among academic departments will play a crucial role.

An example of an optimized system is a good symphony orchestra, according to Dr. Deming: "The players are not there to play solos to catch the ear of the listener. They are there to support each other. They need not be the best players in the country."[9] The degree of interdependency inside an academic health center may even exceed the one that exists among the musicians in an orchestra. The challenge for the leaders is to create the desired and expected harmony. Leaders of academic health centers can overcome challenges by not being limited by departmental focus, and instead, pursuing a relentless commitment to meeting the needs and expectations of society.

BIBLIOGRAPHY

1. Barnes BA et al. (1985). Report on variation in rates of utilization of surgical services in the Commonwealth of Massachusetts. *Journal of the American Medical Association, 254,* 371-375.

*2. Berwick DM. (1989). Continuous improvement as an ideal in health care. *New England Journal of Medicine, 320*(1), 53-56.

3. Berwick DM. (1991). The double edge of knowledge. *Journal of the American Medical Association, 266*(6), 841-842.

*4. Berwick DM, Godfrey AB & Roessner J. (1990). *Curing health care.* San Francisco: Jossey-Bass.

5. Blendon RJ, Letiman R, Morrison I & Donelan K. (1990). Satisfaction with health systems in ten nations. *Health Affairs, 9,* 185-192.

6. Bogue EG & Sanders RL. (1992). *The evidence for quality.* San Francisco: Jossey-Bass.

7. Bryce GR. (1991, January). Quality management theories and their application. *Quality,* pp 15-18.

8. Crosby PB. (1979). *Quality is free.* New York: New American Library.

9. Deming WE. (1986). *Out of the crisis.* Cambridge, Mass: MIT Press.

10. Fried RA. (1991). TQM in the medical school: A report from the field. Milwaukee: ASQC Quality Congress Transactions.

11. Guaspari J. (1985). *I know it when I see it.* New York: AMACOM.

12. Juran JM. (1989). *Juran on leadership for quality.* New York: The Free Press.

*13. Kritchevsky SB & Simmons BP. (1991). Continuous quality improvement concepts and applications for physician care. *Journal of the American Medical Association, 226*(13), 1817-1823.

14. Marszalek-Gaucher E & Coffey RJ (1990). *Transforming healthcare organizations.* San Francisco: Jossey-Bass.

*15. McLaughlin CP & Kaluzny AD. (1990). Total quality management in health: Making it work. *Health Care Management Review, 15*(3), 7-14.

16. Reinhardt UE. (1991). The importance of quality in the debate on national health policy. In JB Couch, ed. *Health care quality management for the 21st century.* Tampa: Hillsboro Printing Co.

17. Scholtes PR et al. (1988). *The team handbook.* Madison, Wisc: Joiner Associates.

18. Senge PM. (1990). *The fifth discipline: The art and practice of the learning organization.* New York: Doubleday/Currency.

19. Spechler JW. (1988). *When America does it right: Case studies in service quality.* Norcross, Ga: Industrial Engineering and Management Press.

*20. Walton M. (1986). *The Deming management method.* New York: Putnam Publishing Group.

21. Wennberg J & Gittelsohn A. (1982). Variations in medical care among small areas. *Scientific American, 246,* 120-134.

22. Wennberg JE. (1987). Publication illness rates do not explain population hospitalization rates. *Medical Care, 25,* 354-359.

*Asterisk indicates an article or book that is particularly informative and helpful.

CHAPTER 17

Developing Private Support

James L. Copeland

&.

The ultimate test of a man's conscience may be his willingness to sacrifice something today for future generations whose words of thanks will not be heard.

GAYLORD NELSON

In a time of tight budgets and declining regular sources of revenue, an academic manager's thoughts often turn to establishing a program to develop private gift support. Establishing a broadly based fund-raising program is highly recommended; however, it is not a "quick fix" management decision that will yield immediate unrestricted dollars and budget relief. AHCs best positioned to deal with revenue shortfalls are those which have established an ongoing program of strengthening a constituency and soliciting funds during good budget and revenue support years.

Despite existing economic conditions, you can establish an ongoing fund development program. The important things to consider are a reasonable set of expectations and goals for private gift support. With such goals, as well as an investment in staff, travel, publications, and other related items, you can set your program on a course of long-term growth.

If your program is part of a larger school, university, hospital, or other structure, initial conversations regarding the need for fund-raising assistance must be coordinated with existing public affairs or development offices. There may be staff members who could be committed to work with your department or division. It may also be possible to employ a fund-raising staff member with a shared responsibility for your program and one or two others within the institution. In this way you will benefit from a smaller budget commitment in the beginning, and as the program grows, you can consider expanding the position to full-time.

In thinking about establishing a new fund-raising effort, you will want to understand the following:

- Fund raising is a process that takes time. A minimum commitment to staff of 2 or 3 years is necessary.
- Initial gifts from a new fund-raising effort will probably be earmarked for specific ongoing programs and not left undesignated for your discretionary use.

Yes, we did specify a macro-economist, but we were hoping to find a candidate with a concentration in fund raising.

V.S. Hixson

SOURCE: The Chronicle of Higher Education

- You should insist that your initial fund-raising staff member be experienced, with a successful track record in fund development, preferably for an institution and program similar to yours.
- Employing such a fund-raising staff member will not relieve you from active participation in cultivating and soliciting gifts. Contributors will want to know the highest level administration and will want the assurance of your vision and plan for your program. When you make a commitment to fund raising, you must make an added commitment of your time to this effort; it is a serious mistake to expect otherwise.
- List program strengths and weaknesses along with objectives and goals for fund raising and make them a part of the job description used to recruit a fund-raising staff.
- Those most likely to support your program are individuals who are presently involved or who have benefited from or are interested in the work of your organization. This constituency is critical to your fund-raising success and may include former students, fellows, trainees, house staff, and faculty; present faculty and staff; and satisfied patients, families, and others. A first step in any fund development program is to identify this group of prospective supporters.
- A strong public affairs and public awareness program is essential to creating the best climate for private fund raising. Be sure that there is a coordination of these efforts as you structure a program. Fund development should be considered a principal purpose within these activities.

PHILANTHROPY TODAY

Philanthropy is a tradition in America. In the most recent year reported (1991), private giving totaled more than $124 billion. Nearly 55% of this amount went to religious organizations. Education received 10%, human services 8.5%, health 7.8%, and arts, culture, and humanities groups received 7.1%. Remaining contributions were spread among public service, environment, international affairs, and others (Figure 17-1).

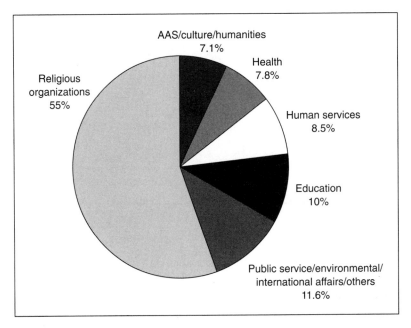

Figure 17-1. In 1991, private donations totaled more than $124 billion, distributed as shown. (From American Association of Fund Raising Counsel [AAFRC]. [1991]. *Giving USA: The annual report on philanthropy.* New York: Author.)

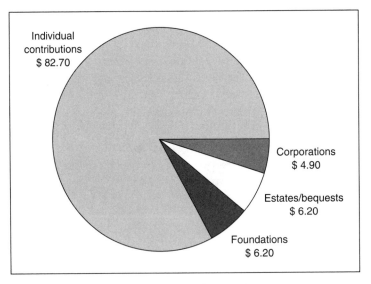

Figure 17-2. Note from this graph that more than 80% of private support comes from individual contributions. (From American Association of Fund Raising Counsel [AAFRC]. [1991]. *Giving USA: The annual report on philanthropy.* New York: Author.)

It is clear that private support makes a difference in the opportunities we have for improving society. What is also instructive to note is that *individuals* contributed $82.70 of every $100 given. Foundations gave $6.20, corporations provided $4.90, and estate gifts and bequests (also individuals) amounted to $6.20 (Figure 17-2).

We know that *people give to people*—people whom they know and respect, people who ask them for support, people who are involved with institutions that have plans and will receive benefit from their gifts. Those people who will support our programs are the individuals who are interested, involved, or who have benefitted from our work. Our goals, therefore, should include ways to interest, involve, and benefit individuals with wealth so that they may become future supporters. To ask individuals for a gift simply because we know they have accumulated resources will usually not succeed. It has been said that "to ask someone for a gift simply because they have money is like asking a beautiful woman to marry you simply because she is single."

We will do better by investing our time in ways to inform capable prospects through meetings, publications, seminars, and visits. We can interest them through task force groups, committees, or by seeking their individual expertise or opinions, then involve them with service or advisory groups, friends, and advocacy committees or boards of directors and trustees. This "cultivation" is central to the fundraising process, and a strategy for continued constituency building must always be in place (Figure 17-3).

In many academic settings, faculty are accustomed to peer review and having support flow as a result of the quality of their work. This is not always the case with private gift support. If a gift is made to support specific research at a neighboring institution, and it is clear the quality of this research is better in your department, this

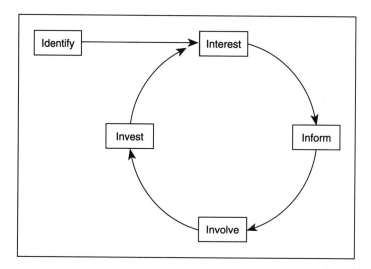

Figure 17-3. The cultivation process for developing support through individuals.

does *not* mean a similar gift to fund *your* department's research will be forthcoming. As noted above, the decision to give was most likely made on the basis of interest, involvement, and direct contact with people at the recipient institution, and the contribution does not reflect a serious evaluation of comparative quality. A decision to give is more often made by the heart; a decision as to how to fulfill the commitment is made by the head.

As you consider private sources of support and build a constituent group, be deliberate and set high standards in recruiting the interest of community leaders. With the help of your trustees, faculty, and others, develop a list of those you wish to involve. Be sure you consider each community "center of influence" and seek the highest-level representation from each. These include business, banking, law, accounting, and publishing, among others. When business competitors with equal strengths are present in your community, seek involvement from both groups (such as rival law firms, local newspapers, corporations) so that you do not become known solely as one of the "competitor's" interests.

Research the individuals identified and set priorities for cultivation and recruitment. Use caution in establishing "boards." Consider friends' groups, a committee of visitors, and the like with specific responsibilities. Include fund raising as a purpose for such groups, along with advocacy and awareness. Recruit those you wish to have lead—face-to-face and personally. Establish clear responsibilities for membership, a regular meeting schedule, and terms of service. Be careful in accepting those who volunteer without being asked. Persist in recruiting from your prioritized list to ensure the result desired in influence, respect, and effectiveness.

COMMON TYPES OF FUNDS

Within the development of private support, there are three commonly used types of funds:
- Annual funds
- Capital campaigns
- Ad hoc campaigns

An *annual fund* is established to identify donors, solicit their first gifts, foster a system of stewardship and reporting, encourage a habit of giving each year, and create an incentive for donors to repeat gifts and increase the level of their gifts. Traditionally, annual funds have been "unrestricted" for current operation of programs or discretionary for use "where needed most" this year. Over time, some have dedicated annual funds to specific programs that require "hard-dollar" budgets. Donor support of these can thereby free budgeted dollars for other current needs: if institutional or departmental funds are budgeted for scholarships or fellowships, making these the focus of annual gifts can free these funds from an annual budget commitment, which then can be used to support new operational items.

The purpose of annual funds is to get the gift, have the gift repeated, and accelerate the amount of the gift.

Capital campaigns are helpful to more mature and established fund-raising programs. Generally these campaigns focus on building programs, major endowments, and other special needs that do not repeat each year. The campaign appeals to larger "gifts from capital" from your donors. Typically, a capital campaign is conducted, asking for 3- to 5-year pledge commitments from established annual donors, while the "annual fund" is also continued.

In advance of your first capital campaign, it is advisable to consider contracting with outside fund-raising counsel for a feasibility study. This study is a series of private, confidential interviews with those most likely to support you, and it can affirm your ability to succeed. Such a study can also identify faults in the perception donors have about your program, weakness in the "case" for support, or other matters critical to your campaign success. Consider investing in a study and following the recommendations before making a commitment to capital campaigning.

History shows that in most capital campaigns the top ten gifts create 33% of the goal, the next 100 gifts create 33%, and all other gifts will compose the remainder. This "rule of thirds" has changed some over the years, and today many find that 90% of the goal is accounted for in the top 100 commitments. Other rules of thumb note that a lead gift of 15% to 20% of the goal is desirable, and "family giving" from faculty, trustees, and alumni should total 20% to 25%.

The decision to embark on a capital campaign should be made carefully and with the understanding of the considerable personal time necessary from the highest level of administration, trustees, and volunteers. Staffing and budget to carry out a highly personalized, volunteer-intensive "peer-to-peer" major gift solicitation must also be a commitment. An example of a capital campaign is the University of Michigan's announcement of a 5-year, $1 billion capital campaign. This is the largest campaign ever for a public university. Yale University, a private institution, also recently announced a $1.5 billion capital campaign. In many institutions today, shrinking state support has forced institutions to seek more private funds to sustain and improve programs. "Private support is absolutely critical," says James J. Duderstadt, President of the University of Michigan, "and we cannot significantly ratchet up our private giving without campaign-level momentum."

Ad hoc campaigns frequently are held to meet a single purpose that is of interest to a part of your constituency, for example, an endowment honoring a revered faculty member—asking students who attended during the faculty member's tenure to provide support. Another example is a campaign for new scientific equipment accomplished by contacting just faculty, former students, and other supporters of that department.

In summary, you can see that the annual fund is the foundation and backbone of other fund-raising programs. The annual fund first identifies the donors who are called upon later for more substantial commitments to the capital campaign or special ad hoc efforts. It is these individuals who will become the volunteer leaders necessary for fund development and other important leadership roles. Before embarking on any of these fund-raising approaches:

- Define specific objectives and the dollar goals required.
- List all those who are prospects for leading the effort.
- Determine the necessary "advance gift" level and list all those, who you believe because of past involvement, will give.

- Recruit leadership and ask for their support and willingness to contact other advance gift prospects. Assign and contact other leadership prospects, asking for a specific dollar amount. Re-evaluate the goal considering the leadership response received.
- List and evaluate the potential gifts of all others to be contacted. Ask those, who have already contributed, to personally visit these prospects.
- Contact those you are unable to call or visit, personally, by mail or phone.
- Celebrate success, acknowledge leadership, report on use and importance of gifts to all involved.

Departments in academic settings should consider the following seven essentials for successful private fund development:

1. The department or program should be legitimate, considered worthy, and fulfilling a perceived public need whose performance merits private support.
2. The department or program needs to establish a dedicated committee of board members composed of representative and influential persons who will personally commit to the campaign and provide it with universal and enthusiastic support.
3. The chair, division chief, or program director must recognize and commit to the importance of public relations and fund raising as a management function and be willing to devote energies to this task.
4. The board or chair should establish a dedicated group of volunteers headed by a capable and influential chair (preferably from the board or another respected committee) who will work for the organization and contribute in an exemplary way.
5. The department or program needs to work closely with the public relations and development staff capable of planning and supporting the campaign and volunteer leaders.
6. The school, department, or program must commit an adequate and reasonable budget for conducting the effort.
7. The chair or director must approach the development of private support with a sense of urgency and understanding of the compelling need to meet the campaign purposes.

TYPES OF FUND-RAISING TECHNIQUES

Once your academic department focuses on the type of development fund you will use, you next need to consider the type of fund-raising technique to employ, for instance:

- Direct mail
- Telemarketing
- Special events
- Foundation grant–making
- Corporate giving

A technique used by many institutions is *direct mail*. Direct mail is frequently used but often misunderstood. The purpose of direct mail is donor acquisition and identifying new supporters for your program. It can be effectively used in contacting large numbers of distant prospects or as a part of your annual fund. It is not appropriate for capital gifts, major gifts, or as a substitute any time that a personal visit is required. Once a donor is identified through direct mail, that donor should be treated more personally and encouraged to repeat and increase his or her level of support. Direct mail is expensive, and a response of 1% to 2% from an unqualified mailing list is considered exceptional.

Telemarketing is also an effective approach for donor acquisition. This technology has developed a sophistication that permits receiving new information about donor interests, and it can be effective as a follow-up to direct mail for upgrading gifts. Some organizations and schools report success in raising pledge commitments of $10,000 to $20,000 by phone. The costs associated with phone-a-thons can also be high in volunteer and staff time if you conduct your own, and in fees if you contract with one of the large reputable firms.

Both direct mail and telemarketing can be justified on a "cost of funds raised" basis *if* you move donors acquired to new fund-raising approaches for cultivation and resolicitation. Remember, donor acquisition is the purpose—do not rely on these techniques alone.

Special events are often effective in expanding your base of donors through cultivation, education, awareness building, and involvement. These events range from tribute and award banquets to sporting events—golf or tennis tournaments, basketball games—to road rallies, flea markets, 5-mile runs, swim-a-thons, rubber duck races, frog hopping, galas, and campaign kick-offs. Such events create opportunities to bring in individuals not already familiar with your program and create a better awareness of your mission and its importance to the community.

Chairs or directors of academic programs must realize that events are costly in volunteer and staff time, and expenses must be closely monitored for the event to be successful. An event should be selected that is complementary to your objectives, and clear goals should be established at the outset. Volunteers are critical to success, since they will recruit others, buy tickets, purchase tables, contact sponsors, and create enthusiasm.

Be cautious of commercialization and approaches from outside groups who wish to have your institution benefit from their event. These can be successful, but they can also exploit your volunteers, prospects, donors, staff, and institutional name in promoting an outside purpose or product. Persons who are your prospects for a $10,000 contribution may feel they have contributed enough by attending the $1000 dinner benefit or working as a volunteer. Special event fund raising is not a good substitute for those positioned to conduct ad hoc or capital campaign efforts. In that case, a well-planned kick-off dinner, hosting friends and donors so that you can clearly explain your plans will better serve your objectives.

Foundation grant-making represents a substantial pool of potential support. Foundations contribute about 6% of the total given in the United States, and by law they must give away some of their earnings each year. Gifts from foundations are often larger than individual or corporate gifts, and some will consider multiyear commitments. A critical first step is to conduct research to identify foundations who support:

- Organizations in your geographic area
- Programs and projects like yours
- Grants in the range you are seeking
- Institutions like yours

There are many directories available that profile foundations, list their directors, state their guidelines, and list their most recent grants by amount and purpose. Many foundations do not have staffed offices, and some have no telephone where you can reach a representative. Where there is staff, telephone or write to seek current guidelines and meeting dates and to describe your planned proposal. Often in these initial calls, program staff are helpful in directing you in ways that can save effort and lead to better reception, consideration, and funding.

Corporate foundation and company giving programs also call for special evaluation to determine interests. Frequently corporate support is based on self-interest and being able to establish a tie between the program's goals and the objectives of the company. Certainly, firms with operations in your geographic region will have greater interest and potential. Firms with whom you do sizable business, or for whom you provide graduates for their employment, and where you have key volunteers working are also stronger prospects.

Other firms, both close to home and away from your region, may also have "matching gift" programs. For example, some major corporations will match donated dollars 3-to-1 or even 4-to-1. This means that if a $100 donation is received from Dr. Smith, and he is employed by a corporation with a 3:1 matching gift policy, your program will receive an additional check for $300. This is a very important way of not only increasing your fund-raising base, but also increasing your corporate contacts. A survey of your donors to identify their employers may lead to increased support. Some large national corporations have established broad program interests that may match your project objectives. Realize, however, that corporate funding cycles may be a year or more, limiting the possibility of an immediate or short-term gift response.

Just as we have noted that the chair or director must be committed and a competent fund-raising staff recruited, an informed faculty must also be committed to make the fund development a success. They must recognize the importance of private support, be willing to subscribe, share the names and interests of those they know who may be prospects, and participate in asking for their support. Although fund raising may be a shocking idea when first presented, repeated mention at staff and faculty meetings, with examples of success, will often lead to wider acceptance and participation. Fund raising is not arm twisting or brow beating but is a means to presenting opportunities for the advancement of your work to individuals capable of assisting. To your satisfaction, many, if not all, will be pleased to have been asked.

Although fund raising is not the panacea to budget difficulties, giving thought now to how private support can create new opportunities for your programs deserves a high priority.

BIBLIOGRAPHY

*1. American Association of Fund Raising Counsel (AAFRC). (1991). *Giving USA: The annual report on philanthropy.* New York: Author.

2. Dove KE. (1988). *Conducting a successful capital campaign: A comprehensive fund-raising guide for non-profit organizations.* San Francisco: Jossey-Bass.

3. Gee AD. (1990). *Annual giving strategies: A comprehensive guide for better results.* Washington, DC: Council for Advancement and Support of Education (CASE).

4. Gurin MG. (1982). *What volunteers should know for successful fund raising.* New York: Stein & Day.

5. Harris AL. (1991). *Raising money and cultivating donors through special events.* Washington, DC: Council for Advancement and Support of Education (CASE).

6. Lord JG. (1984). *The raising of money, thirty-five essentials every trustee should know.* Cleveland: Third Sector Press.

*7. Panus J. (1986). *Mega gifts: Who gives them, who gets them.* Chicago: Pluribus Press.

*8. Pray FC. (1981). *Handbook for educational fund raising.* San Francisco: Jossey-Bass.

*9. Rosso HA. (1991). *Achieving excellence in fund raising.* San Francisco: Jossey-Bass.

*10. Seymour HJ. (1966). *Designs for fund raising.* New York: McGraw-Hill.

FUND-RAISING ASSOCIATIONS

Association for Healthcare Philanthropy (AHP)
313 Park Avenue, Suite 400
Falls Church, VA 22046
(703) 532-6243

Council for Advancement and Support of Education (CASE)
11 Dupont Circle, Suite 400
Washington, DC 20036
(212) 328-5900

National Society of Fund Raising Executives (NSFRE)
1101 King Street, Suite 700
Alexandria, VA 22314
(703) 684-0410

RESOURCES

The Chronicle of Philanthropy (biweekly newspaper)
1155 Twenty-third Street, NW
Washington, DC 20037

The Foundation Directory (annual directory)
The Foundation Center
79 Fifth Avenue
New York, New York 10003

*Asterisk indicates an article or book that is particularly informative and helpful.

CHAPTER 18

Grants and Guidance:
The Role of Fostering Research

Mary Sue Coleman • Robert P. Lowman • Mary A. Belskis

---

*I was asked what I would do with the department of pathology if I were selected
to head it. . . . I replied that I would try to build it up . . . with research people
skilled in experimental pathology . . . and I would hope that the department's
teaching would include a fair amount of exposure of medical students to the major
areas of ignorance in medicine. I said I thought the pathology department, poised
as it was midway between the basic sciences and the clinical disciplines, was in
a good position to pay special attention to ignorance.*

LEWIS THOMAS, *The Youngest Science*

Academic medical centers are exciting institutions that are attractive to faculty
who want to pursue a broad spectrum of activities in addition to clinical medicine. A
crucial part of the academic environment is the intellectual mingling of basic and
clinical research and the opportunity to tackle problems in multidisciplinary teams.
However, attracting good researchers and sustaining the conduct of excellent research require constant administrative attention. It is not sufficient to recruit a few
faculty members who want to conduct research and provide them with some laboratory space. In today's competitive environment, excellent clinical and basic scientists
are in short supply, so developing a successful recruitment strategy and ensuring an
infrastructure that permits leading-edge research are essential.

Most institutions must grapple with tight fiscal resources in all hiring decisions.
Attracting faculty who will be competitive in garnering research funds is expensive.
One cost-effective strategy to recruitment involves the use of a concept called
programmatic clusters. Institutions are unlikely to be able to effectively cover broad
areas of medical research. A planning process might identify institutional strengths
across all departments. The concept of programmatic clusters prompts chairs and
directors to get researchers working with each other. Programmatic clusters add
interest to the research environment as researchers approach a topic from various
perspectives, uniting different areas of expertise. During this exercise individual de-

partment chairs might discover opportunities to link their new hires to existing research areas in other units. For example, a basic science department may have a group of scientists investigating carbohydrate metabolism and synthesis of complex carbohydrates. By taking advantage of this expertise, a clinical department might hire clinician scientists who are interested in studying inborn errors of carbohydrate metabolism. This interest may ultimately lead to gene therapy approaches with another link to a department of medicine where virologists are developing new vector systems.

A second strategy is to identify areas of interest to the department and then hire several new faculty who share complementary research programs. This programmatic cluster approach provides a good intellectual support for the faculty, and it also presents an opportunity to consolidate major equipment and services into shared-use core facilities.

When the recruitment strategy is in place, the next goal will be to make the institution attractive to potential faculty. Hiring decisions are among the most important that department chairs must make. It is an expensive process and requires a continuing investment of time and energy. In today's market, new faculty can command "start-up" packages that include generous support for laboratory equipment and supplies as well as initial funding for technical assistance. It is reasonable to expect that new assistant professors will require some initial concentrated time organizing their laboratories, generating preliminary data, and writing grant applications.

During this development time, new faculty will need financial assistance, released time from clinical and teaching duties, and only limited committee work. This latter protection is particularly important for underrepresented minority faculty members and women. Since these groups are still underrepresented in all of academia, there is a tendency to tap them excessively for committee participation to ensure diverse representation. You will be doing them a far greater favor to delay such assignments until research productivity is apparent and their careers are well on track.

The department should consider all the possible options to facilitate research and development. These options should include support mechanisms and motivational efforts. Some departments have found the role of an internal grants manager to be beneficial. In this role, the internal grants manager provides support to researchers by identifying and informing researchers of funding opportunities, providing up-to-date information on the processing of grants to make the process as easy as possible for researchers, assisting with budget and grant development and maintaining files on awarded grants. Some grant management positions are instrumental in assembling a grants handbook, which can include examples of completed and funded NIH grants, along with samples of completed internal institutional forms. The goal of this and all similar efforts by a departmental grants manager is to simplify and clarify the grants process for your faculty, making research time more productive. A service-oriented staff can be of tremendous value to a department seeking research growth.

If feasible, the department may be organized to provide centralized services or equipment to all faculty, such as media preparation, glassware cleaning, tissue culture, and macromolecular structure analysis. Funding for pilot projects is also useful within a department or at the level of the school. These types of funds can be awarded competitively with the clear understanding that the purpose is to stimulate proposals for external funding instead of to fund faculty who never submit external applications. It is also essential in these stringent budgetary times to have available "safety net" funding to assist faculty who just miss funding and who must resubmit revised applications. It is usually far better to nurture faculty and to keep them going rather than to lose a productive person simply because the competitive environment dictates resubmission of fundable grant proposals.

The department chair and the senior faculty researchers can have a dramatic and positive effect in assisting young faculty in developing their research careers. As new faculty write their first proposals, a department chair should make clear a desire to assist in the process. Senior faculty can be assigned to work with new faculty to discuss research ideas and to critique grant applications. The department chair has the paramount role in setting the tone of a unit, so that young faculty or faculty who need revitalization can seek assistance without embarrassment.

For a departmental chair, one of the first goals in developing a research base will be to help young faculty members flesh out ideas as full-fledged proposals and to submit applications for funding. But there are many pitfalls along the way for new (as well as experienced) faculty members. Garnering funds for research is an ever-

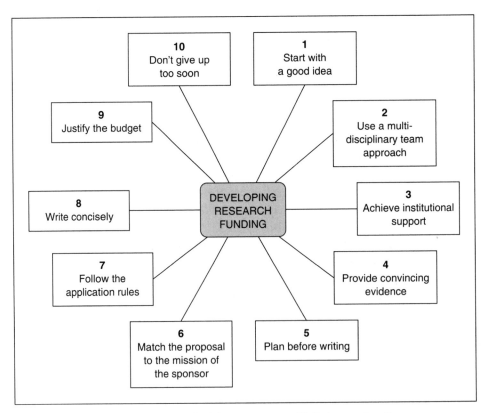

Figure 18-1. How to avoid ten common pitfalls in grant writing.

competitive process. The chair will need to help faculty arm themselves with information about potential successes and failures. To assist in this process, we discuss in the remainder of this chapter ten common pitfalls (Figure 18-1) encountered in grant writing and suggest ways you can help your faculty avoid each.*

Pitfall 1: *The uncritical pursuit of a second-rate research idea*

The single most important criterion for success in the "grants game" is a good idea. While good ideas do not by themselves ensure praise by review groups and a check by return mail, bad ideas almost never are funded. So the first decision for the grant writer is, "Which idea do I pursue?" When the idea is first formulated, an exhaustive search of the existing literature is essential. Questions to keep in mind are: What gap in the literature does the idea address? How will the approach solve an existing problem? Is this problem significant and important to advance knowledge in the area? Does the principal investigator (PI) have the preparation and background to work in the area? Does the institution have the necessary facilities to pursue this idea?

If affirmative answers flow from the questions, the next step is ruthlessly subjecting these ideas to criticism by colleagues in the department or school. This is often a very painful process for any faculty member, because exposing one's ideas is a little like baring one's soul; it is not pleasant to be judged by others. But it is far better to be evaluated in the company of friends before an assistant professor has spent time and effort on an idea that is simply not salable or that may contain a fatal intellectual flaw. And rejection from a sponsor for a bad idea is an experience no one wishes to endure. So, remember rule number 1—make sure your faculty members start with superb ideas!

Pitfall 2: *Failing to consider that research ideas may best be approached with a multidisciplinary team*

Many good research ideas stretch the boundaries of traditional disciplines. The PI may have identified a problem that will require her own expertise but that also spills over into the areas of immunology or biochemistry or physics. If the grant writer's research reaches into diverse areas, you can be virtually assured that it will be reviewed by experts in those disciplines. Those friendly reviewers will home in immediately on any gaps in background, experience, or knowledge. They will be conversant with all of the recent literature in those fields and will be quick to point out the shortcomings of the proposal. You can help faculty avoid this potential problem by urging them to seek out collaborators. Sometimes only a single collaborator is required; however, some problems require a larger team, and your faculty member may not even be best suited to lead the team. This can be especially true for first-time proposal writers or inexperienced investigators. Collaborations with senior

*We wish to acknowledge the contribution of Dr. Bert R. Biles (Kansas State University) in formulating important factors in writing successful grant proposals.

That's *it*? That's peer review?

SOURCE: S. Harris, *American Scientist*

colleagues who offer expertise in areas required for the work and divergent from their background will lend credibility to the proposal. These individuals can also critique the ideas and review the proposal for appropriate language and references for that subdiscipline. If your faculty elect to be part of a team, the leading investigators will play a large role in organizing the grant writing. If your faculty are putting together the collaboration, you need to warn them to be careful that all involved approve the experimental plan and understand their roles in the project. Review groups normally require that the PI document all collaborations. Therefore, you will want to be sure that letters have been included from each individual that spell out specific details of the collaborations. In addition, many funding agencies will require that the PI provide a biographical sketch for all such individuals. A final note: It is *never* a good idea to refer in a proposal to a collaboration that does not yet exist. It might be just your faculty member's luck that the intended collaborator sees the proposal and is surprised and offended by this bit of news.

Pitfall 3: *Attempting a project for which there is insufficient institutional support or a lack of essential resources*

Not every project makes sense at every institution. This can be particularly true for proposals with a clinical or disease mechanism focus. Let's say that one of your young faculty members has discovered a new syndrome related to inherited male-pattern baldness in which the hair turns bright red just before it falls out, and leaves painful skin sores. She discovered this new disease in an indigenous family group while she was on sabbatical in Australia. She was fortunate to have brought clinical materials back to the institution. But now she has a problem—she no longer has continued access to these patients for hair, skin, or blood samples. She can find no similar disease in her own patient populations. It will be almost impossible to pursue this project. The example may sound far-fetched, but similar mistakes abound in grant proposals. Investigators seek to carry out a patient study when they cannot identify an appropriate patient population. Or they may have access to a patient population or propose to use an animal model, but they do not have access to a biostatistician to help decide how many patients or animals should be studied to acquire statistically significant data. It is essential that you encourage your faculty to consider your institutional milieu before writing their proposals. They should consider facilities, equipment (including access to computers), availability of laboratory animals or human subjects, library holdings, natural resources, and the expertise of potential collaborators.

Pitfall 4: *Failing to provide convincing evidence of the feasibility of the project*

The feasibility of any project is best illustrated with preliminary data. Such data are absolutely critical to good proposal writing. Most important is that these data will demonstrate to reviewers that the PI has mastered some of the techniques he is proposing and that he has the ability to carry out part of the research plan. These days, when only 10% to 25% of proposals are funded at most agencies, high-risk ideas for which initial results are not available have a tough time in the competitions. When the PI has demonstrated that some of his ideas are correct by way of data,

I think you should be more explicit here in step two.

SOURCE: S. Harris, *American Scientist*

then he is providing assurances to the reviewers that he knows what he is doing and that they can anticipate useful information from the project.

Departments, and particularly those which expect faculty to obtain extramural funding, should provide money for pilot projects, specifically designed to generate preliminary results. Another fund source may be internal funds that are competitively awarded university-wide. When applying for such internal awards, the PI should tailor the project so that it is clear that he intends to use the funds to generate feasibility data. This is not the occasion to propose a 3- to 5-year project!

Pitfall 5: *Failing to plan before writing, or writing into a dead end*

Proposal planning and writing take enormous amounts of time. Ironically, those who have several years of experience in writing grant applications realize that the actual writing of the research plan should take about 3 or 4 days—but the planning stage will take much longer. For a first grant, a new professor should probably plan to devote several months of his life to this effort. When he sits down with pen in hand and grant forms in front of him, if he is agonizing over the aims and goals of the proposal, he may not have spent the appropriate time in planning the proposal and in gathering background materials. So encourage your faculty to give themselves time and put their ideas out for criticism several months before the grant deadline. Ask your faculty member this basic question: Does the whole proposal depend on a certain outcome of an initial experiment for which he does not have convincing preliminary data? If the answer is yes, then do not allow the proposal to be sent in. This approach is writing oneself into a potential dead end. If this crucial experiment does not work in the way expected and if there are no alternate plans, the entire project collapses. No review group will approve such a proposal, but it is a fairly common mistake that new investigators make.

Pitfall 6: *Failing to match a proposal to the mission of the sponsor*

There are many sources of grant funds for biomedical scientists. The largest of these is the National Institutes of Health. However, many other agencies may have a specific interest in the type of work your faculty do, so it is beneficial to undertake a thorough search for potential funding sources. Most research universities have electronic data bases (many of which have entries for thousands of funding sources) or library resources that list foundations and governmental agencies and describe the sorts of research supported. While the National Institutes of Health and the National Science Foundation do fund the majority of scientific research at universities in the United States, there are more than 7500 foundations listed in the Foundation Directory, and these combined fund a significant amount of the research in U.S. universities. Each entry in this directory has a mission statement and limitations. Other data bases list specific interest areas of government research agencies. As a start, contact the research office in your university and find out what resources are available to your faculty.

Once faculty members have a list of potential sponsors, urge them not to stop! Now they may need to telephone the program officer or the contact person listed for that agency/foundation to discuss the relevancy of the proposal. These individuals expect such calls. They are eager to discuss research plans with faculty members, because they have a goal to fund the best and most relevant projects available to their agency. And they may be able to advise a faculty member that the project is not suitable to their interests. If true, the PI will want to know this before he or she wastes time preparing and sending in a proposal that may be sent back by return mail because the foundation or agency is not interested in such work.

When the grant search is complete, the faculty member must evaluate how the proposal can match the mission of each sponsor selected. By changing the focus slightly, the PI may be able to emphasize the basic science aspects of the project to one agency and the clinical aspects to another agency. Time spent going through this process is often extremely productive. The more the PI can match the work to that which the sponsor wishes to see accomplished, the better the chances for funding.

Pitfall 7: *Failing to follow the application rules set by the sponsor*

Faculty can often obtain application materials for agencies and foundations from the university research office. These offices will check to ensure that the department has the most recent edition of application packets. It is a good idea to contact your research office, even if you have old application forms in your department, because the rules change periodically, even within agencies. Read the program guidelines, the instructions in the application packet, then *reread them*. There is no standard format for proposals, and it is virtually impossible to create a generic grant application that can be sent to multiple agencies. Therefore, the PI must develop each application in accordance with the specific program guidelines. If there is a page limitation, observe it. If a type size and font are specified, use them. If there is a format for biographical sketches, follow it. Make sure also that faculty understand all of the approvals they must obtain from your institution before the proposal is submitted. If they are to do any work involving human subjects, the project must be approved by an Institutional Review Board (IRB). If animals are to be used, they must gain approval from the Institutional Animal Care and Use Committee (IACUC). All of these procedures will be clearly outlined by your institutional research office. Since so many assurances must be gained, it is a good idea to find out about all of these procedures well in advance of the due date of proposals. Institutional committees usually meet only at monthly intervals, which means that faculty need to allow plenty of time for these internal reviews. The PI will be required to submit the final application through institutional channels for official signatures before submission to the funding agency, and it is a good idea to allow several days for this final step. Finally, if there is an established due date for the proposal, note whether it is a receipt deadline or postal mark deadline and meet it.

Many of these rules pertaining to the format of the proposal may seem ridiculous or bureaucratic and not to have anything to do with science. While we may partially agree, that will not prevent your application being returned unreviewed. Don't allow your faculty to fool themselves into thinking the science or content of the proposal will supersede or override any rule that they may consider silly. The odds are that a nonscience reviewer will scrutinize and screen the proposals before anyone ever reads the text. And if a nonconforming proposal does slip through, some scientific reviewers will throw up their hands in disgust if they have to squint to read a tiny type size in a proposal that has too many words crammed on the pages. Remember, the reviewers are just like your faculty: They are overworked, they face deadlines too, and if a proposal is hard to read, they won't even try.

Pitfall 8: *Writing a verbose, jargon-laden, and rambling proposal*

It is very likely that your faculty's proposals will be reviewed by scientists who are experts in some aspect of their fields. However, it is unlikely that they will be conversant with every nuance of any particular proposal. Therefore, faculty must not assume that they can jump into the science without a clear statement of the problem, its history, and how they propose to make an important contribution. Read this critique from a recent proposal:

> The description of the nature of the research and of its significance leaves the proposal broadly stated and without a clear research aim. It is nebulous, diffuse and lacks in clarity. The plans for this study are unevenly developed. The literature review is deficient and does not demonstrate a strong knowledge in the area of concern. The most glaring flaw in this proposal is the lack of specificity in the plans for all important areas of the study described. No adequate description is given of data collection, reduction analysis or evaluation.

To avoid receiving such a critique, encourage your faculty to start with the title of their project and think about what image it conveys. The PI may want to use it to pique the curiosity of the reviewers and set the tone for the proposal, but a word of caution: Some members of congress have actually attempted to remove funding from the NIH and NSF budgets for individual projects because they thought the grant titles sounded frivolous. The abstract should summarize the key features of the work and define the problem in specific and realistic terms. Since this is often made available to the general public, the U.S. Congress or foundation boards of directors to justify more funding for the agency, the PI should write this in language that is understandable to the "educated layperson."

The next section of most proposals is the specific aims or goals statement. The PI will want to make sure that these are precise statements of the hypotheses coupled with the expected outcomes. Alternate strategies should be briefly mentioned. From this section the reviewer should be able to grasp the scope of the problem, the experimental approaches, and why the PI is the person to undertake the research. Although it may seem a tall order to place all this information in such a short section (usually one page or less), outstanding proposal writers do just that.

Now for a cautionary note. As you go through the application packet, it seems that at almost every step the grant writer is asked to restate the significance or rationale. It is very important that the PI resist the temptation simply to repeat an earlier statement from the abstract or from some other section of the proposal! There is nothing reviewers hate more than rereading the same statements over and over again. Alter the wording, paraphrase, do whatever it takes to make these statements novel and fresh. It will not require much additional effort from the grant writer, and it will help at the review stage.

Most agencies will require the PI to include a background section in which he or she must reiterate the significance of the project and the rationale for the approach chosen. Here the PI will want to include a thorough but not exhaustive review of the literature. It is important to include landmark references instead of review articles. Citation of reviews can be useful, but the PI does not want the readers of this proposal to think that he or she has no knowledge of the primary literature in that field. This also runs the risk of irritating some reviewers who may have done critical work in the field if it appears that the PI is not aware of their contributions. So judicious selection of references is important and well worth the time. Some seasoned proposal writers even look up membership on recent review panels to make sure they cite the work of these individuals in their proposals, if that is appropriate. Access to names of those on review panels is usually available from the agency or foundation, and it is perfectly acceptable for the grant writer to request this information. This does not mean that the PI will be given the names of those who might actually review the application, but it will offer a clue about pitfalls to avoid.

Preliminary data and the experimental plan are normally the longest sections of the proposal. Here is the area where the PI's expertise should really shine. Be sure that your faculty have actual data to display and encourage them to spend some time thinking about presentation of those data. Including well-prepared graphs or photos that are well integrated into the text will help the case. The way in which data are presented in a grant proposal is fully as important (if not more so) than presentation of data in a prestigious journal. The charts and graphs should be clear and make the important points that support the plan. This is not the time to include poor-quality photocopies of data prepared for another purpose. Think about a harried reviewer reading too many proposals. Your faculty members want their proposals to stand out and they want the reviewer to be grateful that they have spent so much effort making the science easy to read and the data and its significance easy to grasp. In the experimental plan, the PI needs to continue with clear plans and alternate approaches. Encourage faculty to keep asking themselves, "If the first method does not work, then what will I do?" Your faculty must tell the reviewer what they will do next! The PI needs to generate in the reviewer the feeling that he will be able to overcome any obstacle that might confront him. He also needs to avoid making this section sound like he has copied procedures out of laboratory manuals or protocols. Encourage him to spend time putting the plan into his own words. Be absolutely sure that the techniques he proposes are generally recognized as sound by his colleagues. Young faculty members can usually get help here by asking a senior faculty member to read this section and tell them if they have used the correct experimental strategies.

Finally, when the entire proposal is done, ask your faculty member again: Has he clearly stated the contribution of his project? And why should others care about the knowledge generated from its completion? The more these questions can be answered in the affirmative, the better his chances for success. Now he is ready to give the proposal to colleagues to tear apart before he puts the application into final form.

Pitfall 9: *Failing to justify (really defend) every item in grant budgets*

Probably the most important part of the proposal, outside the research plan, is the budget and its justification. Faculty are sending in proposals because they need funds to carry out projects. What they do not want to assume is that the grant narrative will serve as a good justification for the funds they have requested. Reviewers, after all, will be gauging these budget requests against their own experiences and situations.

Therefore, encourage faculty to plan this section carefully. Advise them to look up the actual prices for supplies, animals, and equipment items. You can be sure that the reviewers will know these, and it is their responsibility to confirm that the budget request is reasonable. The reviewers have the power to cut budgets, and they will most assuredly do that if the PI has not justified every single category of expenditure. They will also be irritated if the PI seems to be always requesting the deluxe model for each piece of equipment. Since most scientists work on tight grant budgets, frugality on the grant writer's part will be seen as a plus. Encourage new faculty members to ask advice from senior scientists in your department. They can help new grant writers decide how much is appropriate for personnel expenditures and how much in supplies each full time worker will require. These figures are relatively constant across disciplines, and PIs should make sure that they are not too far from the norm. The PI must also be sure that she limits her budget to items allowed. Some fund sources do not pay for equipment, and others will not support graduate students or travel. The PI simply needs to be sure that she understands the requirements. Your departmental office staff or your university research office can also often give new faculty members advice on constructing a grant budget or can actually construct it for them. First-time proposal writers should not hesitate to seek this type of advice and help.

A final caution: The federal funding agencies are ever-vigilant about how grant funds are used. If the application reviewers remove funds for an equipment purchase that they judge is not needed, it is probably not a good idea to use grant funds for the purchase anyway. In that event, it would be better to request permission from the agency with a clear justification for the need in the hopes that the PI will be allowed to make the purchase. Good planning and budget justifications should avoid many problems after the project receives the funding required.

Pitfall 10: *Giving up too soon on a potentially fundable idea when it is possible to revise and resubmit your proposal*

When your faculty receive that first letter with the news that a proposal will not be funded, tell them to remember that the file drawers of some of the best scientists in the country are filled with grant applications that did not quite make the funding cut. Consider a few statistics: the Comprehensive Program of the Fund for the Improvement of Post-Secondary Education (FIPSE) funds about 3% of proposals submitted each year; almost 80% of all first-time proposals to the biomedical federal agencies are not funded. As dreary as these statistics sound, revised proposals have a much higher chance of success. At both NSF and NIH, resubmissions have a 50% to 60% rate for funding. So persistence clearly pays off. What you need to convince your faculty is that failure to fund a proposal is not personal and it is not meant to devalue them or their ideas. There are simply a lot of good proposals, and this one is being judged against others that have been rated more highly. However, unless your faculty are told specifically that their ideas or project have no chance for success, the comparative rating tells them that with improvement, their project can be funded.

If a faculty member should receive a critique or funding score (NIH) that indicates she will not make the funding cut, encourage her to contact the project officer immediately by telephone. She should discuss with that person the critique and how she might improve the project. Many agencies send a representative to the review meetings. Those persons take notes and can help faculty interpret the critique. If the faculty member believes that there is a gross error in the review or a serious conflict of interest on the part of the reviewers, she may ask to send a formal rebuttal to the agency. As a consequence, her proposal may be rereviewed by an-other group. Although such errors are rare, they do happen and it is your faculty member's right to consider sending a rebuttal. More often, however, investigators realize that they need to work on the proposal to improve it. After the PI has received assurance that the project should be pursued, encourage her to show the critique to you or some of her colleagues and to ask for suggestions and help. One especially successful strategy is the formation of self-help groups within departments.

Faculty agree to help with each other's proposal rewrites. Often someone slightly outside the field can see flaws and help the PI explain the work more clearly. Or perhaps the PI needs to generate more preliminary data to be convincing. Whatever the comments, now is the time that your faculty member needs support and help from others. Let your faculty member know she is not the only person who has ever had to resubmit an application. In fact, almost all of her colleagues will have had the same experience and will be understanding.

If the faculty member does receive indication that her project has been rejected out of hand with the comment that the ideas have no redeeming qualities, then she needs to start over with a new project. This is sometimes very difficult to accept. However, wasting time on a proposal whose merits are not apparent to others is simply not a good use of time. To help save your faculty from this truly awful fate, we have included the top 10 comments on disapproved or "not recommended for further review" (no hope for salvation) NIH grant applications (see the box below).

With guidance and understanding, a department chair can forge an exciting atmosphere for faculty research. New faculty may very likely have grants that are not funded on that first submission. But it is also important to know that everyone goes through a learning process. We all know that science is a collaborative activity and so is the writing of successful grant proposals and the development of departmental research funding.

TOP TEN COMMENTS ON DISAPPROVED NIH APPLICATIONS

1. The problem is of insufficient importance or is unlikely to produce any new or useful information.
2. The proposed research is based on a hypothesis that rests on insufficent evidence, is doubtful or is unsound.
3. The proposal's tests, or methods, or scientific procedures are unsuited to the stated objectives.
4. The description of the approach is too nebulous, diffuse and lacking in clarity to permit adequate evaluation.
5. The overall design of the study has not been carefully thought out.
6. The investigator does not have adequate experience or training, or both, for this research.
7. The investigator appears to be unfamiliar with pertinent literature or methods, or both.
8. The investigator's previously published work in the field does not inspire confidence.
9. The requirements for equipment or personnel or both are unrealistic.
10. It appears that other responsibilities of the PI would prevent devotion of sufficient time and attention to the research.

These comments are based on actual reviews collected by Linda K. Meadows and Regina H. White. The collected information was presented at the November 1991 NCURA Workshop: Research Administration for the Newcomer, Emphasis on Pre-Award Administration.

BIBLIOGRAPHY

1. *Directory of research grants 1993*. (1993). Phoenix: The Oryx Press.
2. *1992 Catalog of federal domestic assistance*. (27th ed). (1993). Washington, DC: U.S. Government Printing Office.
*3. *Directory of biomedical and health care grants 1993*. (7th ed). (1993). Phoenix: The Oryx Press.
4. *Directory of building and equipment grants*. (1988). (Richard M. Eckstein, researcher). Margate, Fla: Research Grant Guides.
5. Schlacthter GA. (1991). *Directory of financial aids for minorities, 1992-1993*. San Carlos, Calif: Reference Service Press.
6. *Preparing a research grant application to the National Institutes of Health*. (Selected articles). (1989). Bethesda, Md: Department of Health and Human Services.
7. Hillman H. (1977). *The art of winning government grants*. New York: Vanguard Press, Inc.
*8. *How to prepare a research proposal: Guidelines for funding and dissertations in the social and behavioral sciences*. (3rd ed). (1988). Syracuse, NY: Syracuse University Press.
9. Bauer DG. (1984). *The "how to" grants manual*. New York: Macmillan.
10. Steiner R. (1988). *Total proposal building*. Albany, NY: Trestletree Publications.
11. Willner W & Hendricks PB Jr. (1972). *Grants administration*. Washington, DC: National Graduate University.
12. Behling JH. (1984). *Guideline for preparing the research proposal*. (Revised ed). (1984). New York: University Press of America.
*13. *Helpful hints on preparing a research grant application to the National Institutes of Health*. (1991). Bethesda, Md: Office of Grants Inquiries, Division of Research Grants, National Institutes of Health.
*14. Schwartz SM & Friedman ME. (1992). *A guide to NIH programs*. New York: Oxford University Press.

*Asterisk indicates an article or book that is particularly informative and helpful.

❧ Part Four ❧

FUTURE

We don't inherit the future, we achieve it.

ANONYMOUS

CHAPTER 19

Changing Managerial Paradigms

Richard S. Blackburn • Jill Ridky

All progress depends on the unreasonable man.

BERNARD SHAW

"These days the future just isn't what it used to be," reads the caption to a cartoon in a recent business publication, reflecting a belief by managers in most academic health centers that their future is changing far more rapidly and unpredictably than the future their predecessors faced. In this book we have provided information and insights that should make managing in this more tumultuous future somewhat less hectic. But what kinds of demands will this "new" future make on AHCs and their administrators?

Consider one possible answer to this question from the dean of management writers, Peter Drucker. In a recent article in *Harvard Business Review,* Drucker summarized the major stages through which organizations have evolved since the advent of organized enterprises after the Civil War.[1] The first arose from Max Weber's writing about bureaucracy and Frederick Taylor's efforts at describing scientific management. The division of labor inherent in the scientifically managed bureaucracy fostered the creation of a new class of employees. These new employees, separate from the ownership of the enterprise, were needed to ensure the successful integration of the many different tasks now present in organizations. These employees were called managers and their work—management—was distinct from the tasks performed by those they managed. Managers developed policies about how work should be done. Workers did the work with no input into work policies.

The second stage in the evolutionary process of the organized enterprise was the development by duPont and Sloan of what might be called the modern corporation at General Motors. The hierarchical structures espoused by these chief executives in the 1920s emphasized decentralized operational units, centralized staff units, and budgetary and other control systems to maintain both command and control. Drucker believes that most of the world's business organizations currently operate within this stage of development. It can also be safely assumed that such a model reflects life in most AHCs.

In previous chapters we presented information to assist the academic manager in the complex task of managing AHC units within this traditional *command-and-control* culture. In what follows, we assert that the implementation of this information will probably have to occur in a culture unlike that with which academic medical managers have become familiar. To effect this, academic managers will be asked to make fundamental changes in the way they manage and lead their departments or programs. These changes will require leaders to be knowledgeable of several changing management paradigms.

Consider the following comments. Tom Peters notes in *Thriving on Chaos* that "American management will spend the 90s totally reconceptualizing the business organization."[2] If Peters is right, and his statement is applicable to AHCs, then these centers are also entering an era of unprecedented change. Managers of AHCs must stay current with new models of management, and they must use new models that stress employee commitment, cooperation, and communication.

John Millet suggests that "Management should be achieved, not through a structure of subordination of persons and groups, but through a group dynamic work consensus."[3] Organizational culture and managerial philosophy must reflect a set of shared values stressing flexibility, information sharing, and creativity. Or consider the insights of John W. Gardner in *Recovery of Confidence.*[4] Gardner asserts, "The whole system of hierarchical organization erodes the sense of responsibility. It tells the individual in a thousand ways, 'You are not important; what you do will not make a difference.' It exalts form over spirit and stifles individual creativity."[4] Maintaining any employee's sense of value or worth as a human being must be considered when leading and managing organizations.

Each of these comments reflects the underlying characteristics of what Drucker sees as the third evolutionary stage of organized enterprises—the information- or knowledge-based organization. The following discussion compares the characteristics of a knowledge-based organization with its more traditional counterpart.

MOVING FROM A RESOURCE-BASED TO A KNOWLEDGE-BASED ORGANIZATION

Peter Senge of MIT, author of *The Fifth Discipline,*[6] distinguishes a *knowledge-based* organization from what he calls a *resource-based* organization by noting that the former

> . . . also utilizes resources, but its defining characteristic has to do with the knowledge it creates. The knowledge-creating process is fundamental to the [organization's] relationship with all its stake holders. It is embodied in the products and services provided to the customers. It drives the continuous reduction in material resources utilized and harmful by-products, of primary concern for the communities in which the [organization] operates. And it links the [organization's] fortunes intrinsically to the imagination, commitment, and efforts of all its members—rather than being mere "human resources," they are the source and carriers of the [organization's] knowledge.

Figure 19-1 identifies some of the differences between resource-based and knowledge-based organizations on five important managerial tasks. Each of these tasks and how each is performed in the two different organizations is considered.

In the traditional resource-based organization it is the responsibility of the top manager or administrator to establish and communicate the organization's vision. Such an approach may still be appropriate in smaller, entrepreneurial organizations. However, in larger organizations moving from a command-and-control culture to a commitment-and-communication culture, top management must ensure that the corporate vision is shared by professionals and staff members throughout the organization. The best way to ensure that this occurs is to allow a vision or a consensus about organizational direction to emerge from multiple levels in the organization. In the knowledge-based organization it is not management's role to develop the vision unilaterally, but rather to ensure that such a vision exists and that the shared vision is communicated throughout the organization in every possible fashion.

As noted earlier in this chapter, the scientific management approach to designing tasks and organizations separated the responsibilities of thinking about how a job should be done from actually doing the job. In the resource-based organization, members of management think about how tasks should be done, and the remainder of the staff do the tasks as assigned by management. Such a model for organizations might have been appropriate, even effective, when tasks were simple and employees

TASK	TRADITIONAL RESOURCE-BASED ORGANIZATION	CONTEMPORARY KNOWLEDGE-BASED ORGANIZATION
1. Direction setting	Vision from the top	Shared vision (can emerge from many places; top responsible that vision exists)
2. Thinking and executing	Top thinks; local acts	Thinking and acting merged at all levels
3. Nature of thinking	Atomistic thinking	Systemic thinking
4. Conflict resolution	Political resolution	Integrative resolution
5. Role of leadership	Set vision Motivate via rewards and recognition Make key decisions Create structures to control local actions	Build shared vision Motivate via empowerment and inspiring commitment Enable good decisions throughout organization Design learning processes

Figure 19-1. Distinctions between resource-based and knowledge-based organizations in the approach to five important managerial roles. (From Senge PM. [1991, November 14]. *Transforming the practice of management.* Paper presented at the Systems Thinking in Action Conference, Cambridge, Mass.)

were not so well educated. Today's tasks in AHCs are complex, professionals are highly educated, and the environment is unstable and in a constant state of flux. In Senge's knowledge-based organization,[6] thinking and acting is encouraged and rewarded at all levels, from the very top to the very bottom of the organization. Academic health administrators must be willing to share their power and authority throughout their organization. While *empowerment* has been widely publicized, few health care managers actually appreciate what the term means for their employees and how relationships must change between the top managers and the remainder of the organization.

The historical isolation of "thinking skills" at the top of the organization and the bounded cognitive capacities of most managers meant that managerial thinking was frequently atomistic in nature. By *atomistic thinking* we mean the tendency for individuals to make the (usually incorrect) assumption that complex problems have single, identifiable causes. If a cause could be identified and removed, then the problem would be solved. Unfortunately, as many readers can no doubt testify, in most academic health centers problems are far too complex to allow for the discovery and treatment of a single cause. In those cases treating the alleged single cause may lead to additional problems for some other unit in the AHC or may create succeeding problems for the manager making the decision. These succeeding problems reflect second, third, or fourth order effects of a solution designed to "solve" the original problem. Atomistic thinking reduces complex problems to understandable, but simplistic, cause-and-effect relationships. Such thinking prevents the manager from appreciating the "connectedness" of all organizational decisions, actions, and outcomes.

To resolve the incredibly complex problems that confront the administrator, atomistic thinking must give way to thinking from a more systemic perspective. In the knowledge-based organization, employees understand that no single individual can solve all the organization's problems. Similarly, employees appreciate that these problems are not normally the result of some single identifiable cause. *Systemic thinking* helps employees understand the interrelationships between and among their decisions and the impact of these decisions on other individuals and departments at the AHC. Developing the skills necessary to think systematically is made easier by the presence of the shared vision that guides thinking and acting at all levels.

Systemic actions, because they affect other employees and other departments, may lead to conflict within the organization. In resource-based organizations, the "winners" of these conflicts are the parties with the greatest political power. Losers are expected to accept their "defeats" graciously, while maintaining their commitment to both the decision and the organization. But too much of this win-lose, power-based conflict resolution style frequently yields a cadre of "sore losers." Their participation in the decisions resulting from the conflicts that they lose might only be assured by constant surveillance, and their innovation and creativity in service of the conflict decision seems unlikely.

While the knowledge-based organization will also have its share of conflicts, resolution styles will favor dialog and integration of diverse views over the imposition of political will. While initially more time consuming and not necessarily appropriate in emergency situations, integrative conflict resolution, or "win-win" conflict management, typically yields creative and innovative solutions of organizational conflicts. It also yields greater levels of commitment to and cooperation with the ultimate conflict resolution. In the complex environments of today, no single manager can have all of the answers to the problems confronting his or her department or program. The successful administrator in a knowledge-based organization must have the understanding and skills to move beyond advocacy to inquiry and dialog as the bases for conflict management.

In sum, the role of the leader in the knowledge-based organization moves beyond command and control. Visions are not set by top management but are built from the shared input of all employees. Motivation systems move beyond the typical extrinsic rewards and punishments to include the intrinsic motivators of empowerment and commitment. Key decision making is no longer centralized at the top of the organization with structures and control systems designed to ensure obedience. The role of the leader in the knowledge-based setting is to enable or empower appropriate, timely decisions to be made throughout the organization. Structures and control systems function to enable and empower all employees to make systemic decisions that best serve the entire organization.

The move from a resource-based to a knowledge-based management philosophy will be neither easy nor quick. Most managers and organizational members in AHCs received their training in the typical resource-based organization. They have been rewarded and reinforced for managing and working in this way and have been doing so quite successfully in many cases. But the environment in academic health centers is changing too rapidly to maintain this relatively outmoded approach to work. When AHC managers understand and appreciate the chaotic environments in which they must now function, the knowledge-based approach to management will become eminently attractive.

DEVELOPING THE LEARNING ORGANIZATION

Given this discussion, what might such a knowledge-based organization look like, and how would the manager know an effective knowledge-based department or program when he or she saw or developed one? According to Senge, such an organization would be one that is capable of *learning*. In an academic setting, "learning" refers to the ability of faculty, residents, students and staff to "consistently expand their capacity to create the results they truly desire, where new and expansive patterns of thinking are nurtured, where collective aspiration is set free, and where people are continually learning how to learn together."[6] As *Fortune* magazine recently noted, the successful organizations of the 1990s and beyond will be those best able to learn. These organizations will be able to engender employee commitment and capacity to learn at all levels.

Senge suggests that there are five components necessary to generate a learning organization. Each component provides a vital dimension in building organizations that can truly learn. The five components, shown in Figure 19-2, are similar to those characteristic of the knowledge-based organization. Each of these five components

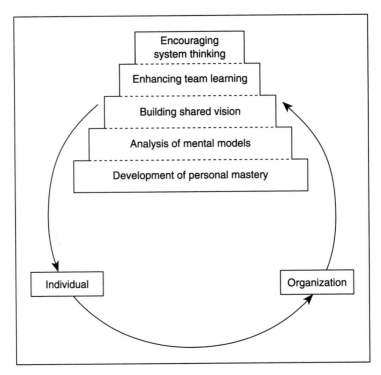

Figure 19-2. The essential five components of a learning organization. (From Senge PM. [1991, November 14]. Transforming the practice management. Paper presented at the Systems Thinking in Action Conference, Cambridge, Mass.)

is briefly discussed next. For a thorough discussion, as well as myriad suggestions for developing each component in your organization, read Senge's book, *The Fifth Discipline.*

Personal mastery. The development of personal mastery requires organization-wide encouragement and support of individual employees in their efforts to clarify their personal visions, focus their energies, and develop the requisite skills and abilities to accomplish these personal visions. According to Senge, personal mastery is the foundation or the cornerstone of the learning organization: "The organization's commitment to and capacity for learning can be no greater than that of its members."[6] To become learning organizations, academic units must encourage the continuous growth of their employees.

Individuals entering academic medicine are intelligent, well-educated, high-energy people, willing to perform on the "cutting edge" and to make a difference. Unfortunately, in many academic health organizations, organizational policies and procedures soon transform active, committed participants into so many worker bees, simply putting in their time. Employees lose their sense of commitment, sense of mission, and the enthusiasm they had when they started their appointment. Encouraging and rewarding employees for continually developing levels of personal mastery in both their current and anticipated job positions is a first requirement for a learning organization.

Mental models. Mental models are the assumptions, generalizations, frameworks, or images employees hold that influence how they understand the world and why they take the actions they do. Mental models affect behavior, and their influence can be pervasive. In learning organizations, employees feel free to disclose, examine, and analyze their own mental models as well as challenge the various mental models held by others. Such a process requires a willingness on the part of top management to act as role models in sharing their mental frameworks and belief structures with others in the department or program.

Shared vision. The importance of building a shared vision has been discussed extensively in the leadership literature as well as earlier in this chapter. Academic organizations cannot achieve or sustain greatness without shared goals, values, and missions. Department chairs or program directors must work to develop a common identity and sense of destiny for all faculty, staff, students, alumni, and other supporters.

Team learning. Effective team learning can produce high levels of synergistic outcomes, so that team accomplishments greatly exceed any single individual accomplishment. When teams function effectively, not only do they produce superb results, but team members also develop more rapidly than if they were functioning by themselves. Team learning begins with *team dialog* as opposed to team discussion. In this context, discussion usually represents the exchange of preconceived ideas in a winner-take-all competition for the adoption of a particular position. Positions are advocated and defended for purposes of arriving at decisions. Dialogue, on the other hand, is the free-flow of information among team members that allows the team to discover insights about its members and itself. "Team learning is vital because teams, not individuals, are the fundamental learning unit in modern organizations."[7] A more complete discussion of work teams and team learning appeared in Chapter 5 of this book.

System thinking. Senge believes that systems thinking is the most important component of the learning organization. He also recognizes that it is the most difficult for individuals and organizations to develop. Consider that all academic organizations and programs are systems. As discussed in Chapter 2, academic organizations consist of both visible and invisible components of interrelated actions. Thus it is difficult for any one manager or organizational member to see and understand the total pattern of these components and how they interrelate and change.

Most managers are able to focus on only one or a few of the components. Managers frequently take actions to solve problems based on developing a rather simple cause-effect link between the actions they take (the cause) and the problem they believe they are solving (the effect). As indicated earlier, these same managers often fail to consider that (1) the problem they are attempting to solve likely has multiple potential causes, only a few of which a single manager can influence, and (2) any action taken or decision made will likely have far-reaching effects that will ripple throughout the organization. These are systemic effects whose impact can only be vaguely determined. As a stone thrown into a pond causes ripples throughout the pond, managerial decisions also create consequences far beyond the intended target. An appreciation of how these multiple consequences may influence the organization is at the heart of systems thinking and is a key prerequisite for the development of a learning organization.

KNOWLEDGE CREATION IN THE LEARNING ORGANIZATION

One outcome of the learning organization is the ability to create knowledge. What is creating new knowledge? Does this mean promoting and developing creativity and the innovative spirit in organizations? Creating new knowledge spans and reaches farther than the customary concepts of creativity and innovation. To create knowledge, organizations must develop the subjective insights, intuitions, and hunches of all organizational members.

Academic health center managers must realize that AHCs function, perform, and achieve with people. As Ikujiro Nonaka says, "An organization is a living organism."[7] In this regard all organizational members must have a shared understanding of what the AHC stands for, its future objectives, the reality of the health care environment today, and how accomplishments and successes can be assured.

Today many AHCs fund and support innovative project programs. Although these programs have produced many productive results, the true knowledge-creating organization is not only about ideas but also ideals, and this in turn feeds into the process of innovation. Developing new knowledge in an organization is not a specialized activity like public affairs or research. "It is a way of behaving, a way of being, in which everyone is a knowledgeable worker, that is to say, an entrepreneur."[8]

For organizations to begin developing new knowledge, the organization must look toward the faculty or organizational member. A brilliant researcher has an insight that leads to a contractual agreement with a private company or produces a patent. A manager's intuitive sense of trends changes the course for a clinical program. A staff member develops a new design for the program's residency operative experience data base, producing greater efficiency and effectiveness. In each of the above examples, the individual knowledge of each member is transferred into valuable and beneficial organizational knowledge. This type of process is ongoing and is a central theme for the knowledge-creating organization. How does this individual knowledge get transformed into knowledge that other organizational members can use? That is, how can organizational knowledge be created?

Nonaka[8] identifies two types of knowledge available in all organizations. The first is *tacit* knowledge. Tacit knowledge is understood and/or developed by the individual but is difficult to articulate. Many of us have experienced knowing more than we could tell. This is sometimes referred to as an organizational member's "know-how." This is seen in the research laboratory, where beyond research funding and research protocols, researchers possess a certain know-how in achieving exciting results in the laboratory. This tacit knowledge or know-how is typically taken for granted by the employee and cannot be well articulated. One reason for this problem of knowledge articulation is the assumption that such information is already known by others in the organization. Not until the organizational member is able to fully explain the tacit knowledge will others exclaim, "That's how you do it!" or "You do it that way?" On the other hand, *explicit* knowledge is formal and systematic knowledge that is already known or is easily communicated and shared with others.

Within a knowledge-creating organization, one finds four basic learning patterns in which the two types of knowledge can be profitably exchanged. The first pattern involves *tacit-to-tacit* knowledge exchange. This is a level of knowledge development in which one individual shares tacit knowledge directly with another. In academic health centers, a clinical faculty member may share tacit knowledge with a resident regarding an innovative procedure in the day-op unit, or a researcher shares skills and insights with a research technician. In both cases the knowledge is learned by observation and practice. Tacit-to-tacit knowledge exchange represents a limited form of knowledge creation. Although a skill is learned by the observer/apprentice, the knowledge is never made explicit and cannot easily be adopted by the organization as a whole.

The second pattern of knowledge exchange is *explicit-to-explicit*. This pattern of exchange occurs when an organizational member combines discrete pieces of existing explicit knowledge into a new form a explicit knowledge. For example, a clinical researcher may collect clinical patient-study reports throughout a program and arrange the study results into a report that identifies a potentially new treatment protocol. Although the results provide new insights about existing knowledge, it doesn't necessarily provide new knowledge about the program.

New knowledge occurs most frequently when the third pattern of knowledge exchange occurs between tacit and explicit knowledge. This pattern occurs when tacit knowledge is made explicit and allows the sharing of this individual know-how with a program or department. The clinical researcher, for example, instead of simply compiling the patient-study report data in a unique way may develop an innovative insight to these findings based upon the researcher's own tacit knowledge developed over the years. The report serves as one artifact for formalizing and communicating this tacit knowledge so that others may adapt and benefit from this explicit description.

The fourth and final pattern of knowledge creation requires explicit-to-tacit knowledge exchange. As more explicit knowledge is communicated and shared throughout the organization, other organizational members will begin to utilize it, understand it and assimilate it with time. A clinical researcher's report shared at a program research conference broadens and expands the organization's knowledge. Other researchers utilize the protocol of the report and eventually the protocol becomes an accepted approach for the program and a part of the researchers' tacit knowledge.

In a knowledge-creating organization, the above four patterns exist in what Ikujiro Nonaka calls a spiral of knowledge[7] (Figure 19-3). These are the stages that an academic health center would encounter as a knowledge-creating program or department is developed. First, the existence of tacit knowledge in the minds of all organizational members needs to be recognized, appreciated, and rewarded. Second, conditions and support must exist to translate the tacit knowledge into explicit knowledge. Third, the department or program integrates the new explicit knowledge through the program or department. Sometimes this means developing a manual or workbook, like a researcher's grant guide. Finally, the acceptance and

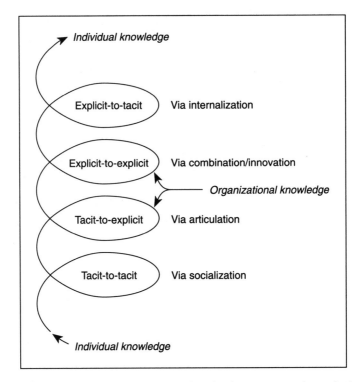

Figure 19-3. The "spiral of knowledge," incorporating the four patterns that exist in a knowledge-creating organization as described by Nonaka. (From Nonaka I. [1991]. The knowledge-creating company. *Harvard Business Review, 69,* 97.)

ongoing integration of the explicit knowledge in the department or program eventually result in the knowledge being shared by all organizational members, which provides the foundation for individual development of new tacit knowledge. If this cycle can be nurtured, an organization's knowledge base will continue to grow.

The key to developing a knowledge-creating company is personal commitment and active involvement of managers and organizational members. Every organizational member must develop a sense of identity with the organization's mission and objectives. The characteristics of Drucker's knowledge organization and Senge's learning organization will nurture the creation of the critical knowledge in the organization of the future.

CONCLUSION

Whenever AHCs decide to employ new management methods, moving from a resource-based to a knowledge-based organization, for example, management must recognize some important considerations. The first is the human reaction to change. Changes and transitions of any sort are difficult for many organizational members to accept. The more substantive the change, the more difficult the process. To facilitate such transformations, organizations must consider the quality of both their communication and their planning. Frequent meetings and ongoing dialog about potential changes are useful and can increase the likelihood of successful change. Discussions of the purpose of the changes are beneficial. It is imperative that members of the unit see the changes as necessary and as solving crucial organizational problems. These discussions will reveal concerns and potential problems in the proposed change process. Developing strategies for the changes and periodic updates on the implementation process will ease the transition. Employees at all levels usually appreciate opportunities to participate in the planning for such changes. True participation should increase employee commitment to the actions taken.

Tomorrow's problems will be vastly different from today's; thus tomorrow's managerial paradigms must also be vastly different. Knowledge-based structures will enable the professional organization to cope with an ever-changing environment while providing organizational members with the sense of learning, accomplishment, and reward.

How an organization is managed is largely determined by what its managers hope to accomplish. The extent to which objectives are accomplished could be one measure of the effectiveness of that organization. One of these objectives could be the continuous pursuit of knowledge or of becoming a learning organization. Successful managerial paradigms will be those that deemphasize traditional command-and-control structures and cultures and emphasize commitment, coordination, cooperation, and communication. The new paradigms will likewise deemphasize hierarchy and individual position and emphasize relationships and team learning. Guided by a shared vision and managed from a systems perspective, these learning- and knowledge-based organizations will learn and prosper to the extent that they assist individual employees to learn and prosper.

BIBLIOGRAPHY

1. Drucker P. (1988). The coming of the new organization. *Harvard Business Review, 66*, 45-53.
2. Peters T. (1987). *Thriving on chaos*. New York: Harper & Row.
*3. Wilson MP & McLaughlin C. (1984). *Leadership and management in academic medicine*. San Francisco: Jossey-Bass.
4. Gardner JW. (1970). *The recovery of confidence*. New York: WW Norton.
5. Senge PM. (1991, November 14). *Transforming the practice of management*. Paper presented at the Systems Thinking in Action Conference,
*6. Senge PM. (1990). *The fifth discipline*. New York: Doubleday Currency.
7. Nonaka I. (1991). The knowledge-creating company. *Harvard Business Review, 69*, 97.

*Asterisk indicates an article or book that is particularly informative and helpful.

CHAPTER 20

The Future:
The Challenge, the People,
the Expectation

D. Kay Clawson

Why are we more successful? Because we are better at change.

SAM WALTON, Founder, Wal-Mart Stores, Inc.

Don't let what you cannot do interfere with what you can do.

JOHN WOODEN, legendary UCLA basketball coach

This book has supplied information necessary for managing an academic health center. The question remains: How can this knowledge best be used to meet the challenges of the future? Regardless of the field of endeavor, only one thing is certain: Change is essential and inevitable, and the rapidity of that change is accelerating at a faster rate than ever before. Institutions *organized* and *managed* so as to change rapidly will be the institutions to prosper in the coming decades. Michael Hammer, president of Hammer and Company, an information technology consulting firm in Cambridge, Massachusetts, notes, "The watchwords of the new decade are innovation, speed, service and quality. Organize around outcomes, not tasks."[1] Success in the future depends on two things—human resources and fiscal resources. How these are managed in a rapidly changing environment are the critical issues and the challenge for administrators at all levels.

THE ENVIRONMENT

To bring about change, in politics, in business and industry, or in any social unit, there must be stresses on the organization to motivate behavioral change before one can bring about institutional change. Although academic health centers are stressed in a variety of directions, they can and should take pride in their past accomplishments and their special role in society. While businesses are failing all around us and many, if not most, are decreasing their number of employees, we note that over the past half century there has been a 50% increase in the number of medical schools, and only one has closed. The ranks of our faculty have increased, and although faculty incomes have not kept pace with expectations, they have risen much faster than the Consumer Price Index. Although research funding never has been sufficient to satisfy the legitimate needs of faculty, it too has grown much faster than other areas of the economy. There had been some decrease in the number of students desiring entry into the health professions, but we are again approaching an all-time high and are able to enroll the best and brightest from high schools and colleges. While we are stressed by increasing demands in patient care and are overburdened by the paperwork (now termed the *hassle factor*), academic teaching hospitals remain the sites of excellence in the delivery of high-tech medical care.

Therefore, why change? We have known success, and while there are ominous signs of discontent and problems on the horizon, what are the forces to bring about change? Those forces are all around us but are felt most critically by the academic administration. Let us briefly examine these forces in the areas of research, education, and patient care.

While *research* dollars continue to grow, a smaller percentage of those dollars is available to the many individual investigators wishing to pursue an idea in the area of their choosing. Society, through its institutions, is saying, "We are willing to pay, but we want to direct the areas of research." Hence we see more rapid growth in research areas such as AIDS, cancer, and aging. In addition, industry is contributing more to university research, but primarily as it benefits their product. Within our institutions we now see some researchers who are unfunded or underfunded (the "have nots"), yet holding on to scarce resources and demanding more support from institutional funds, while other faculty have had huge increases in their funding (the "haves") and are demanding institutional responses of more space, more facilities, and more time to pursue their research efforts. Thus the ability to respond rapidly to new opportunities for the haves while redirecting the efforts of the have nots becomes critical to the expansion and well-being of the research enterprise.

In our *educational* mission, we are faced with an even more difficult task. Schools of nursing and allied health, which once had a single mission with a single degree, are now faced with continuing those programs while adding masters-level programs in a wide variety of subspecialties and, for many, a doctoral program. For the medical school faculty, it is no longer sufficient to produce an undifferentiated M.D. and then to provide opportunities for specialization as selected by the student in the specialties prominent in the departmental organization. Some 50-plus superspecialty certificates or fellowships now exist, at a time when society demands that a larger portion of students enter primary care and preventive medicine. Society no longer is willing to allow a student total freedom in selecting a career, nor the faculty total freedom in influencing students toward the direction of their specialties or subspecialties. There is a clear expectation that curricula will be changed drastically in favor of primary care, preventive, and behavioral medicine and away from a rapid exposure to the wide variety of superspecialties that medical curricula have accommodated in an effort to lure the best students into specialty residency. Superimposed on this is the demand from accrediting agencies and the public for a more decentralized educational experience, moving students from the high-tech specialty university hospital to community settings. All this is taking place with no new resources being provided to carry out this function and with the diminution of the traditional subsidy of medical education from research and patient care funds.

The *patient care* environment is equally stressed. Society demands cost-effective practice (a term that has yet to be clearly defined, except as it relates to decreasing costs). As employers turn to managed health care programs, academic health centers face serious challenges in competing in the market. Academic health centers have continually stressed excellence in patient care, regardless of cost, and have given significant freedom to individual faculty members and residents in deciding what tests to order and how a patient will be treated. As freedom of choice for patient and referring doctor becomes limited, it will be increasingly difficult for academic health centers to compete unless they change the ways in which they educate and provide patient care. Further, the teaching methodology in the clinical setting is heavily labor-intensive, with small class sizes and one-on-one instruction that significantly affects the ability to practice cost-effective medicine. In addition, faculty are primarily selected for their expertise in narrow, highly specialized areas and may not be the best people to serve as primary care role models and to teach primary care or to serve as the first-contact physician/gatekeeper in a managed care system. The problem is further compounded by the relative autonomy of multiple departments organized along specialties, with their faculties frequently having more allegiance to their national specialty organizations than to the institutions for which they work.

Facing all these problems, one would think that an organization, stressed sufficiently, would want and accept change, yet at present most energies are directed at maintaining an archaic health care system in an attempt to bring back the good old days, in lobbying legislatures to secure more funds for a particular unit, whether it be for research dollars, education subsidies, or advancing the technology of individual specialties or increasing their market share of patients. Michael Hammer comments about U.S. companies, "Heavy investments in information technology have delivered disappointing results—largely because companies tend to use technology to mechanize old ways of doing business."[1] Universities and AHCs have fallen into this trap. Rarely are the tremendous talents and energies of our human resources directed at changing the way we do business to respond to a changing environment or to satisfy patients, students, or the people paying the bills. In fact, many an administrator who has attempted to move in that direction has lost the confidence of the faculty and in frustration has left for a simpler life in other areas. Yes, and a few have been fired for failure to lead in the direction desired by the faculty, or for failure to be sufficiently responsive to a board of regents, a legislature, or other political groups.

How does the modern administrator mobilize the wealth of human resources to bring about the changes necessary to meet the challenges of the future? Our major resource, the people who do the work, must function in an environment in which they find satisfaction working toward *societal* and *institutional goals,* as opposed to *individual* and *specialty goals.* That is not an easy undertaking, given human nature.

First, let's look at the words of wisdom offered by Alvin Toffler in *Future Shock,* first published in 1970. Toffler predicted the rapidity of change. He divided people into three categories: past, present, and future people. His astute observation was that there are those people who live in the past, dwell on the past, and hope for the return of the good old days. He notes that these people will be lost in the new era. Second, he points out that the present people, who live in the present, are basically satisfied, although with multiple complaints; they tend to resist change but are capable of making change if approached properly. Finally, there are the future people, who look to the future with great expectation and excitement and expend their physical and emotional energies to bring about change. He predicted that these people are the ones who will prosper in the decades to come. Therefore, our role as administrators in managing the wealth of human resources must be to recognize the difference in people and (1) provide encouragement and reward for the futurists to lead change; (2) spend significant time and energy with the present people who, while not happy with their present circumstances, are frightened to take the bold steps necessary to move into the future; these people need understanding, education, and support in helping them adjust to the rapid changes that our society brings; and (3) cease spending so much of our energies and financial resources on those individuals whose only goal is to attempt to bring back what was good to them in the past. We must give them senior citizen status, a place of honor, but not allow them to pull down the institution by preventing change. This represents a major task for an administrator at any level, because these individuals have earned their place of respect in the academic community through past performance and are sincere in their belief that society and the institution are moving in the wrong direction. They want to hold on to past values and old teaching methods and can be very persuasive in articulating academic freedoms as their arguments against change. But they can immobilize the institution while we lose the very opportunities that are so abundant for academic health centers today.

LESSONS FROM INDUSTRY

Academic health centers can learn from industry. AHCs have also moved from a "cottage industry" environment to colossal conglomerates but are now forced to reorganize, to downsize while still expanding in the market. Issues facing large industries with multiple product lines and diverse services are not that different from those facing the modern academic health center. Our products and services include basic research in the broadest elements of human biology, applied research in each of the multiple systems of the human body, education of the many health professionals at the entry level into their profession, and advanced degrees in the masters and doctoral programs to produce the researchers and teachers of the future. In medicine, there is education leading to the doctoral degree, then advanced education in the various specialties and subspecialties represented by our faculty. We also have "product lines" in the care of patients. Those lines vary from providing total primary health care to providing the most complex tertiary care specialties. They focus on whole population groups as well as individual patients. While caring for patients, we also assume a major responsibility for the continuing education of health professionals throughout the country and the world. Unlike industry, however, where their professionals and staff may be responsible for a single product line, the AHC faculty and staff are engaged simultaneously in a wide variety of diverse activities in multiple product lines, many with conflicting expectations. This causes constant confusion and indeed frustration and occasional hostility in the workforce. As we stress research and competition for grant dollars, we still expect those who can be most competitive to be effective and innovative teachers. In the clinical departments, we expect everyone to provide responsive and quality patient care while carrying out their responsibilities as educators and researchers. Faculty are further stressed when the relative priorities are not the same across departments, and frequently departmental expectations are not aligned with institutional or societal expectations. The undifferentiated baccalaureate student for most disciplines, the M.D. for medicine, is not viewed with the same importance by some faculty members as are masters, doctoral, residency, and fellowship students. This is particularly true in medicine, where medical students are too often seen as potential residents in a given specialty rather than as individuals who should be receiving experience that will encourage them to look at opportunities in primary care and preventive medicine, where there is much societal need. All medical educators have long lamented the "audition year" of medical school—that is, the fourth year—in which students spend much of their time in repetitive rotations in their chosen discipline in order to be competitive for the residency of their choice rather than receiving a broad educational experience. Even when students are assigned to departments in which there should be a broad exposure, they usually are subjected to a series of lectures or rotations with superspecialists. The excitement of high-tech medicine today stimulates students to look at careers in one of these areas. Even for the graduate student or the resident, we narrow the education by focusing on superspecialties without reference to what other disciplines could provide and the knowledge base that would improve the education of the individual.

Another product line is continuing education, which consumes faculty effort and significant time and is frequently more to the benefit of a specialty society and the individual faculty member than to the institution.

The patient care environment in university hospitals is also undergoing great change. Once the mecca for highly specialized tertiary care, it now finds itself having to compete with the numerous physicians who have been produced by this faculty. High-quality tertiary care can be delivered in community hospitals. The situation is further complicated by the fact that most faculty are superspecialized individuals who are neither comfortable with nor trained to teach or provide primary care. With the advent of the managed care system, increasingly the primary care providers are acting as gatekeepers and the university hospitals, with their multiple departments, divisions, specialties, and subspecialties, are not organized to be responsive to the demands of a new system. While all of this is happening in the medical arena, nurses and allied health professionals are requesting independent practices within the academic health center.

In short, we have an industry that has multiple product lines, in which the multiple products are produced by individuals working in all product lines. As industry has long learned, this type of organization is disastrous and hence most businesses have organized their human resources by specific product lines, each with responsibilities and authority for outcomes. Even the most successful companies, such as Hallmark Cards, have had to organize their seasonal (holiday) card line as distinct from their regular (get well, birthday) card line in the design and production of their products. Retail stores, restaurants, and manufacturing firms have learned the painful way that they must reorganize to produce what the customer wants in this changing economy. As Wal-Mart founder Sam Walton said, "Why are we more successful? Because we are better at change." Likewise, AHCs must be able to organize, to meet the expectation of the varying groups they serve, and be able to change direction when needed in a timely manner.

ORGANIZING FOR CHANGE

There is no one way or right way for an academic health center or school of medicine to organize for change. It is essential, however, that the administrative organization be structured so that the individuals working within the organization have clear goals, objectives, and expectations of what will come from their work. The present organizational structure may suffice, *if* all of the administrators operate in a consistent fashion designed to meet the multiple objectives—that is, to satisfy the various needs of the multiple product lines. Academic organizations do exist in which some individuals are given *responsibility* and *authority* in research, others in undergraduate education, and still others in graduate education and increasingly in medical schools, others in meeting patient care expectations and needs. This does not mean that individuals cannot perform in several areas, but it is very difficult, if not impossible, to have the same individual assuming responsibility for the management of the multiple areas that frequently exist and that, in reality, represent conflicts of interest. More commonly, a *matrix organization* is emerging, in which functional and divisional lines are combined to take best advantage of each. Unless carefully managed, however, these too can become divisive and confusing, not only to the internal organization, but also to the external environment. Institutes or centers, such as aging, molecular medicine, and cancer, frequently stimulate research and become a focus for patient care or education. However, they also frequently provide conflicting messages as to where an individual should place his efforts and loyalty. Faculty members usually identify with areas that provide their rewards in terms of space or finance. Some institutions have had a long history of assigning specific functions to individuals, deans, associate deans, or institute directors who assume responsibility to work with faculty, students, and support systems to bring about the desired result in a specific area (research, student education, clinical affairs, and so on). Within these units, there are subunits with distinct responsibilities. Other institutions have organized teaching by systems—that is, cardiac, gastrointestinal, musculoskeletal, and so on—rather than by specialty departments, an approach that has long served to bring faculty together for coordinated research and patient care. However, the splintering of the medical specialties into independent divisions and departments has had a disastrous effect on medical student education and on developing multidiscipline research.

A Contractual Commitment to Productivity

Regardless of the organizational structure used, it is essential to assign *responsibility* and *authority* to manage the activity of each product line to ensure that institutional goals are met. The most effective way in our present environment is to require a contractual relationship with each faculty member on a yearly basis (not to be confused with tenure commitments). The institution, by whatever its governance requires, sets the parameters as to how much will be done in the many areas outlined earlier as "product lines," then each faculty member agrees to spend a certain percentage of efforts in one or more of the areas identified. For example, a faculty member may agree, in discussion with the chair and dean, to spend a major effort in the predoctoral educational program, say 60%, 30% effort in research, and 10% in administrative functions. Another faculty member in the same unit may agree to expend 90% of effort in research, 10% in education, and 0% in administrative functions. In the clinical departments, a percentage of effort in patient care is likewise negotiated. At year's end, each individual's performance will be evaluated in each area. The faculty member spending 30% effort in research would be expected to accomplish a third as much as the individual spending 90% effort in research. Predetermined parameters are used to evaluate productivity in the multiple areas. To avoid bias, it is essential that one individual not make assessments for all areas. Usually the coordinator of a given function will have the most input into evaluating performance in that area; for example, the person assigned to manage the predoctoral program will assess the effectiveness of the individuals teaching in that program. The person assigned to develop the research capability of the unit will conduct the research assessment. The chair's or dean's role is in selecting those individuals and evaluating their performance rather than each faculty member's performance.

While the mechanism just described may seem complicated, it can be accomplished without major changes in governance structure and does allow individual faculty members significant input into the area in which they prefer to function. Over time, a self-selection process occurs in which individuals assume more responsibility in areas where they are most effective, giving up scarce resources and moving away from areas where they are less effective. This improves research, education, and patient care within the institution and allows faculty to participate in the various roles that have been traditional for them. The percentage of effort in each area is controlled by the dean to ensure that the multiple *institutional goals* can be met with the faculty effort assignments. Faculty are then rewarded both financially and by distribution of space and equipment on the basis of how well they perform in the areas assigned as a percentage of the total performance evaluation. This model can function whether the department has a curriculum designed along the systems approach or the more traditional departmental approach, provided it is clear that the evaluations for each component are *not* done by the same individual who can clearly bias the evaluation in favor of a direction he or she perceives to be most important. This structure is facilitated by having specialists within the dean's office who have responsibility for oversight of each of the areas, as well as responsibility for oversight of the physical and financial part of the organization, to ensure that the reward system functions.

The Cross-Functional Matrix Structure

Another option, the matrix organization, which is more in line with the industrial model, represents a reorganization of the institution, deemphasizing departmental organization along disciplines and specialties in favor of units designed to accomplish one or more specific institutional missions. Responsibility for undergraduate programs, graduate programs, basic research, primary care, preventive medicine activities, and tertiary care activities can each be designated to selected individuals. Organization of this kind does not preclude individuals' working in more than one area but assigns primary responsibility in a specific area for which goals and objectives are clearly defined. While this option is more difficult to bring about in the traditional academic setting, some schools have already moved in this direction, particularly in bringing basic scientists of like interests who were dispersed into multiple departments into a single functional unit.

However one chooses to organize, clear lines of authority must exist to meet specific outcomes predetermined by the institution's mission.

MANAGING FINANCIAL RESOURCES

The financial aspect of management runs a close second to the management of human resources. Without sufficient financial flexibility, it is impossible to effectively influence human resources. Thus, to be successful, managers must understand the finances of their organization. John Hogness, former Dean of Medicine and then President of the University of Washington and the Association of Academic Health Centers, has said on many occasions that it took little to be a successful dean (or other administrator) during the era of plenty, when new resources were abundant and, even if they were wasted, always provided enough to satisfy the needs of programs and faculty. The true test of an administrator is how he or she manages in times of plateauing or decreasing resources. During these times, administrators must have knowledge of where inefficiencies exist, where cuts can be made, and where and how to go after new resources. Successful administrators must consciously balance their efforts in improving efficiencies within the organization and seeking new funding for the programs of the organization. It is most difficult to look at one's own operation and see inefficiencies; it is much easier to find them in someone else's operation. All too often this is done within academic health centers, yet it is destructive to morale and works against effective change.

You do not have to be an efficiency expert or a systems engineer to see the many ways time and energy are wasted in the traditional medical school environment. Ambulatory clinics are notorious for wasting people's time, most specifically the patient's time, because they are not organized for a smooth and effective flow of activities but are organized around faculty or student's schedules. Some institutions further complicate their operation by having individuals who are *task* oriented rather than *outcome* oriented. One person does registration and secures the record, another puts the patient in a room, another may assist the doctor, another is responsible for cleaning up, and still another for obtaining billing instructions and delivering the bill. Cross-training is the simplest mechanism to decrease waste in the present system. In some organizations, it has been referred to as the *case manager approach,* where a single person is charged with getting the patient through the system in an appropriate and timely manner, doing all of the functions required except for the highly technical procedures and the specific physician consultation.

Traditional ward rounds are another tremendous waste of energies, with low educational yield for many of the participants. When rounds are directed at the students, house staff and others become bored. When rounds are directed at the residents, much of the students' time is lost and they must seek answers after rounds are completed from residents or attending physicians. Dedicated rounding for specific groups is frequently thought to be too time-consuming for the faculty but, in fact, increases efficiencies of the educational process as well as use of the professional's time. On the educational side, it is all too common to see faculty members carrying out repeated talks on the same subject before each rotating group of students because they do not have time to put their content material into another educational medium. This perpetuates inefficiencies and, while the individual may be deemed to be a charismatic teacher, over time the enthusiasm dwindles, as does the student's learning curve.

Research by its nature is not an efficient enterprise, yet much can be done by management to facilitate the writing of grants and manuscripts and to make sure that faculty members do not spend needless time in procuring supplies, getting instruments repaired, or doing daily housekeeping chores. Successful managers must know how business is conducted and be prepared to orchestrate the operational changes necessary to ultimately save institutional dollars, which can then be rerouted for expansion.

In securing new funding, an administrator must be critical, because it is a truism that those who have the gold rule, and new funding is essential to keeping pace. This means following the research dollars and encouraging faculty to do the same. It means knowing best how to practice medicine to at least cut the losses from what has become a major funding source for medical education, and that means redistribution of resources from areas in which there is little demand or financing to areas where there is great demand. It also means that a creative administrator must take responsibility for institutional well-being and destiny and recognize that it is highly unlikely that additional resources can be gained from expanding student enrollments, from increasing tuition, or from expecting significant new dollars from states or the federal government, except for specific programs.

Successful managers of the future must also critically examine how faculty time is spent. Clinical faculty have long enjoyed the luxury of being able to attend scientific meetings worldwide, presenting papers and conducting continuing education in their area of expertise with little regard for how this activity affects the well-being of the parent institution. Academic institutions may operate continuing education programs at a deficit, yet our faculty may be high-caliber speakers who attract attendance at programs sponsored by specialty societies in which the profit accrues to the society rather than to the faculty or the parent institution. Although it is unpopular to suggest any change in this status quo, this area must be looked at as we strive to become more competitive in managed care markets or compete with such specialty groups as the Mayo Clinic, which has a long tradition of managing the extra activities of its physicians.

We must establish greater institutional loyalty in the pursuit of institutional goals if we are to be successful. Whether in a natural society, a free economy, or a socialist state, individuals and institutions that can adjust rapidly to change will not only survive but will prosper. As institutional administrators at the divisional, departmental, school, or academic health center levels we must act as one of Toffler's futurists and be the role models for others. We must initiate critical internal studies to determine how the departments in our charge can achieve a broader institutional mission.

SELECTING THE LEADER/MANAGER

Much has been written about leadership in universities and health centers, comparing leadership to administration and its inherent bureaucracies. Less has been written about management, largely because faculty professionals do not wish to consider themselves as managers of others, let alone allow themselves to be managed. During the 1960s and 1970s, when money was readily available for higher education or for programs for the public good, leaders were numerous. Anyone with charisma and an idea could find himself or herself moving an institution forward in a direction of achieving some public good without giving much thought to the management of people or resources. As resources began to tighten, the question was raised: Where have all the leaders gone? Unfortunately, the individuals who were so effective in inspiring the faculty were not managers and soon found themselves out of step with a business and political climate that now demands increased accountability, cost-effective performance measures, and doing more with less.

During the years of plenty, growth took place at an unprecedented rate. Health centers expanded facilities and added faculty and support personnel. Little thought was given to systems and to the training of people necessary to manage such complex enterprises. Administrative structures grew as divisions became departments, centers and institutes developed around each popular cause. Associate deans, executive deans, vice-presidents, and directors proliferated. Few had the authority commensurate with the responsibility. At best, the resultant structure could be described as a complex bureaucracy—at worst, a wasteful disaster, using scarce resources and professional time for inappropriate activities. In state-sponsored institutions, the problem was further compounded by a political bureaucracy that placed process ahead of outcome and grew its own bureaucracy as a mechanism for assuring the public that the increasing expenditures were appropriate and necessary. Today we continue to utilize human and fiscal resources to perpetuate—yet work through or around—a bureaucracy that is wasteful and frequently places the academic health center in a noncompetitive posture vis-à-vis streamlined private competition.

To meet the challenge of the future, we must adopt the philosophy expressed by Michael Kami: "Don't try to forecast future external changes in the world. . . . Instead, develop an internal organizational ability to adjust and cope with unpredictability. You must greatly increase your operational flexibility, your speed of reaction, and your ability for fast reversal of prior decisions and policies." [10] To accomplish this goal and prosper, the leaders of our academic health centers must also be skilled managers who can provide a vision and a direction that will maintain academic values in a society too concerned about the here and now, while at the same time managing the institution within the resources available and being responsive to societal needs. *Thus the selection of managers at all levels becomes a critical issue.*

Traditionally the academic selection process is accomplished by a faculty committee. This committee is appointed to represent the diverse interests *within* the institution, and occasionally at the most senior levels, outsiders are appointed to provide input to the process, but rarely are outsiders skilled in the intricacies of academic committeemanship. Individuals on the committee with research interests are determined to find an individual who has established himself or herself as an outstanding researcher, regardless of how narrow the field of interest might be. A few on the committee may want to see proof of each individual's teaching skills, but, more often than not, it is assumed the candidates have such if they have achieved professorial rank. Committee members from the clinical departments come with expectations that the individual will be held in great esteem in his or her specialty society and be able to at least generate self-support through patient care activities. All too often, to achieve consensus on the committee each group compromises on what is felt to be the best candidate, and someone with mediocre credentials is moved forward with little thought of personal characteristics and management skills. After months and occasionally even years of massaging the search process, an individual finally arrives to accept this prestigious management position but lasts only a short time, having been unprepared for the harrowing responsibilities of managing large groups of people in a complex bureaucracy in which it is frequently necessary to give up personal goals and aspirations, or even those of one's discipline, to meet the overall mission of the larger unit. Most such individuals resign in frustration before they are fired but depart the position unhappily and leave their harmful mark by convincing younger colleagues that indeed, there is no hope—that administration is for the inept who cannot do anything else and that life has a better meaning, or that the individuals above them were just plain incompetent.

What are the traits of a leader for the future that a selection committee should seek out and that senior administrators should use judging the appointment of more junior administrators?

A track record of success over a significant period of time in an area germane to the institutional mission. If the individual has not enjoyed true success, whether in research, teaching, or patient care, it is unlikely he or she will have the vision, energy, and ability to be a successful administrator. Watch out for the individual who has enjoyed some success as a researcher and is considered to be a satisfactory teacher and clinician, but has not achieved national credentials for excellence in any area.

An individual who is a futurist by Toffler's definition. Change, the one constant, means it is essential to have individuals in leadership roles who embrace change, are comfortable with it, and can work forward for rapid change under the conditions we now find ourselves in this world economy.

These traits are easily identified. Did the researcher continue to work along lines of the mentor or did he or she pioneer in new directions? Is the educator happy with being a brilliant lecturer, a concerned person for student values, or has he or she pioneered new technologies of education and evaluation? Is the clinician a stable practitioner, utilizing the standards of the day, or has he or she pioneered new and exciting advances in the field?

A people person. This is probably one of the most important attributes and the most difficult to quantify. Because of the highly interpersonal nature of managerial work, people skills are essential for effective leadership. This trait engenders trust, enthusiasm, and involvement by the staff in the leader's goals for the unit. The brilliant researcher may be most comfortable and have a warm relationship with immediate colleagues in the laboratory or the discipline, yet be uncomfortable with others of different persuasions and ideas. The educator may amass great ideas in new technology and assessment tools simply because he or she is uncomfortable dealing with whole classes of students and the vagaries inherent in the current evaluation system. The clinician may tremendously enjoy the one-on-one relationship with both immediate staff and with patients but be uncomfortable in dealing with large numbers of people with diverse ideas.

Comfort with dealing in ambiguities. Is this an individual who requires a yes/no, right/wrong solution? Or can he or she deal comfortably in the gray zones, not finding the lack of concrete answers such a distraction that immobilization results.

An institutional person. Even among junior faculty members, you can spot the individuals who see the broader goal of the institution and place it above their own problems in their area of special interest. They become involved and they are able to pursue individual goals while accepting and working for the broader institutional goals.

Balanced personal life. Many committees have made statements that what an individual does in his or her "off time" is not of anyone's concern. Unfortunately for those in leadership roles, however, it must be the concern of everyone. An institution cannot have its leaders immobilized and ineffective because of alcoholism, family strife, or problems with their personal finances that can occupy much of their time or involve the institution in a scandal. The personal behavior of a leader must be above reproach if he or she expects to have a following among faculty and staff that is necessary to bring about change.

• • •

Hence the university and academic health centers must change the selection process to identify individuals with the above characteristics and give them opportunities to succeed in jobs of ever-increasing responsibility, getting rewards as they work their way up the academic hierarchy. It is absolutely critical that the revolving door of academic administrators be brought to a stop. There must be an orderly mechanism for selecting individuals to pursue careers in academic health center management that can be satisfying and fulfilling and not merely an ego trip, an effort to acquire a larger power base. We must spend as much time in nurturing the qualities that make for quality administrators and future institutional leaders as we do nurturing funded research and attracting increasing numbers of patients. Opportunities have never been greater, and with greater opportunities there are always greater rewards. Our society desperately needs new and more efficient ways to educate tomorrow's health care professionals, conduct research, and care for the increasing population of the United States and the world. That is our challenge.

BIBLIOGRAPHY

1. Hammer M. (1990). Reengineering work: Don't automate, obliterate. *Harvard Business Review,* July-August, pp 104-112.
2. Toffler A. (1970). *Future shock.* New York: Random House.
3. Association of Academic Health Centers. (1991). *From pragmatism to vision, leadership and values in academic health centers.* Washington, DC: Author.
4. The Role of the Academic Health Center in the 21st Century. (1985). Symposium published by Rush-Presbyterian-St. Luke's Medical Center, Chicago,
*5. Bulger RJ. (1992, November). The role of America's academic health centers in a reformed health system. *Journal of American Health Policy.*
6. Lewis IJ. (1984). A view of academic medical centers. *Bulletin of the New York Academy of Medicine, Second Series, 60,* 494-503.
7. Vanselow NA. (1986, Summer). Academic health centers: Can they survive? *Issues in Science and Technology,* 55-64.
8. Schroeder SA, Zones JS & Showstack JA. (1989). Academic medicine as a public trust. *Journal of the American Medical Association, 262*(6), 803-811.
9. Wilson MP & McLaughlin CP. (1984). *Leadership and management in academic medicine.* San Francisco: American Medical Colleges/Jossey-Bass.
10. Kami MJ. (1992). *Trigger points: The nine critical factors for growth and profit.* New York: Berkley Publishing Group.

*Asterisk indicates an article or book that is particularly informative and helpful.

Index